Cracking
the Code

Cracking the Code

Leveraging Consumer Psychology to Drive Profitability

STEVEN S. POSAVAC, EDITOR

M.E.Sharpe
Armonk, New York
London, England

Library of Congress Cataloging-in-Publication Data

Cracking the code : leveraging consumer psychology to drive profitability /
edited by Steven S. Posavac; sponsored by Society for Consumer Psychology.
    p. cm.
Includes bibliographical references and index.
ISBN 978–0–7656–2964–7 (cloth : alk. paper)—ISBN 978–0–7656–2965–4 (pbk. : alk. paper)
1. Consumer behavior. 2. Marketing—Management. I. Posavac, Steven S., 1969–
II. Society for Consumer Psychology.

HF5415.32.C73 2011
658.8′342—dc22   2011003612

Contents

Introduction

Cracking the Code

Steven S. Posavac

The mind of the consumer is complex. Numerous contextual influences interact to drive individuals' deliberations about products and services, and the processes that govern how and when individuals decide to pull the trigger on purchases are both varied and fluid over time and across consumption situations. Moreover, as if the contextual influences on consumerism were not extraordinarily unwieldy in their own respects, consumers are neither blank slates nor carbon copies of each other. Instead, each individual has a host of unique attributes and experiences that influence his or her consumption-related judgments and decisions.

The complex nature of consumer behavior, of course, is why successfully managing a business is so difficult. To win in the marketplace one's strategy must be predicated on accurate predictions of how consumers will react cognitively, emotionally, and ultimately behaviorally, both to products and to product-related communications. Unfortunately, all too often managers fail at the tasks of predicting and influencing consumer behavior. Marketing research, if conducted at all, often misreads potential consumers. New product introductions critical to firms' futures fall flat up to 90 percent of the time, according to some estimates. Predicting and influencing consumers' behavior is made all the more difficult because consumers often are not consciously aware of the factors influencing their thoughts and actions.

Although understanding, predicting, and influencing consumers' behavior is a difficult trifecta to be sure, managers have access to a potentially extraordinarily powerful tool that currently is underleveraged: consumer psychology. Consumer psychologists have produced a wealth of insights that explain how consumers form judgments and make decisions. Such study is intrinsically important because of the key role that consumerism plays in the human experience. If, however, the study of consumer psychology extends only to the level of basic science, researchers take the risk that their science will be impotent and without impact. For consumer psychology research to add tangible value, it is essential that we consider how consumer psychology can be leveraged to help managers be more successful in their jobs and thereby facilitate organizational outcomes.

Unfortunately, there is currently a deep disconnect between the outlets in which consumer researchers publish their insights and the organizations in which marketing is practiced. The result is that the science of consumer psychology is currently being underutilized. Given what would appear to be an enormous potential for consumer psychology knowledge to enhance managerial effectiveness, why does this disconnect between science and practice persist? One key contributor is the fundamental difference between consumer psychologists' and managers' production goals. For consumer psychologists, both intrinsic thrill and professional reward result from advancing knowledge regarding the science of thought and behavior. The relevant product is research published in top journals such as the *Journal of Consumer Psychology,* the *Journal of Consumer Research,* and the *Journal of Marketing Research.* Marketing journals do a great job of ensuring that the research results that appear in the literature are novel and internally valid. That is, when reading a paper in a top journal, one can be confident that the effects or tendencies reported are current and real, and can be replicated by other researchers. Moreover, for a paper to be accepted for publication in a top journal, it is necessary for the authors to provide empirical evidence of a new phenomenon, as well as to document the psychological processes that drive the phenomenon.

The problem is that uncovering a novel finding about consumer behavior is not in and of itself helpful to a manager trying to move a product. Indeed, the way our journals operate is not conducive to the production of research that can be easily and confidently applied. Top journals require such precision in the nailing down of new findings that the paper ultimately must be extremely narrow to meet a journal's requirements. On a related note, the contexts investigated in most consumer psychology journal articles are limited, the range of consumer behaviors studied tends to be small, and the effects of numerous variables that may affect behavior but that are not the focus of the research are held constant in the interest of maximizing scientific integrity. In the real world, of course, there is not much that is held constant; there are many influences on consumers' behavior that simultaneously affect their choices. Moreover, managers have myriad tasks that demand attention, and multiple dials that can be turned and levers that can be pulled. It is the rule rather than the exception that all of these variables interact in complex ways that are typically beyond the scope of any one piece of consumer psychology research.

The purpose of this book is to bridge the gap between academic research in consumer psychology and managerial practice. The authors each started with a bird's-eye perspective on given themes in the consumer psychology literature and distilled a set of implications for action that can immediately facilitate managerial decision making. When we broaden our focus from a single finding or a closely related set of experiments, general implications for the practice of management may emerge. Each of the chapters in this book thus provides an overview of a research stream, which in most cases covers several decades of inquiry. When one takes this approach, the limitations that would constrain any single article are lessened. Although the consumer contexts considered in a given article are limited, the contexts studied in fifty articles are varied. The number of variables explored in any one study is small, but many variables are studied across a large literature.

From this broader view, the authors in this book have been able to glean pearls of wisdom for marketing practitioners. The chapters identify the key findings that have emerged in a variety of crucially important research streams and summarize what these insights into the mind of the consumer mean for managerial action. Bernd Schmitt's incredibly insightful chapter is targeted to academics. Schmitt argues for the importance of relevant consumer psychology research, and offers a framework for crafting research with organizational value.

The subsequent chapters are written for managers who aspire to leverage consumer psychology to improve the effectiveness of their organizations and academics interested in the real-world applications of our science. Hoeffler and Herzenstein discuss the body of knowledge regarding best practices in the management of really new products. Posavac, Sanbonmatsu, and Jain review the growing body of knowledge documenting consumers' tendency toward tunnel vision in thinking about products and services, and offer a series of tactical suggestions for managing the marketing mix.

Several chapters cover issues in marketing communications and advertising. Brumbaugh discusses how to best craft advertising appeals to diverse consumers, as well as how to coordinate ethnocentrically targeted and mainstream marketing efforts. Xie and Boush provide a comprehensive review of what is and what is not deceptive advertising from legal and empirical perspectives, and offer managerial guidance for crafting advertisements that persuade without crossing the line to deception. Bao, Zhang, and Simpson summarize how to coordinate verbal and visual information in print ads, especially for communications regarding imported products. Hsieh, Blower, Li, Jain, and Posavac provide a comprehensive review of what is known about comparative advertising, allowing managers to assess whether a given communication situation is appropriate for a comparative advertising strategy, and if so, how best to design the advertisement or campaign.

Researchers investigating the experiences consumers have with brands and how they create and interpret stories regarding their brand experiences are quickly generating knowledge that is immediately applicable to brand management. Brakus, Schmitt, and Zarantonello discuss a truly paradigm-changing way to conceive of branding and marketing communications in their chapter on experiential marketing. Escalas summarizes how consumers make sense of their brand experiences by constructing brand stories, as well as how managers can leverage consumers' tendency to think about brands in terms of narrative to maximize brand performance. Kwon and Sung delve into the rapidly evolving realm of social media and consider how consumer-generated product reviews affect other consumers and the implications for marketing management.

Two chapters focus on how to better generate consumer insights to drive organizational performance. Cronley, Kardes, Mantel, and Deval discuss the difference between attitudes that are measured in research versus those naturally occurring in consumers' minds, and how to conduct research that is more accurate and more valuable to the organization. Powers presents data showing that consumer negativity is not simply the absence of satisfaction, but instead is a toxic condition that must be avoided if possible and well managed if present.

To maximize one's effectiveness as a manager, it is essential to understand the forces that drive individuals' consumption behaviors. Many of these forces are ethereal and not readily observed. In some cases, consumers themselves may not have a clear appreciation of the determinants of their perceptions, judgments, and choices. Martinez, Cataño, Quintanilla, and Reimann discuss nonconscious processes in consumer behavior and what their implications are for management. Fennell presents a model of consumer action that considers how individuals seek to improve their condition through consumption behaviors.

It is clear that consumer psychologists have a lot to share. Researchers are studying the phenomena that drive business success and failure, and are doing it very well. The knowledge consumer psychologists generate can be of enormous value to managers and, hence, organizations. It is incumbent on researchers to disseminate what we know about the hearts and minds of consumers in formats that can be readily put into action by those on the front lines of business. It is my hope that this book will be an important step toward that goal.

I thank the authors for their efforts, the Owen Graduate School of Management at Vanderbilt University for sponsoring and hosting the conference at which earlier versions of these chapters were presented; Alice Horton for her excellent assistance in planning and running the conference; Kim McClung who is Nashville's premier caterer and event organizer; Sybil L'Heureux and Maureen Writesman for their logistical support; Sean Rhea and James Robbins for their excellent graphic design and website work; Harry Briggs, Elizabeth Parker, and Stacey Victor from M.E. Sharpe, Inc., for their efforts supporting this project; and Austin Graham, Brett Alexander, and Caleigh Rae for their comments during the editorial process.

Cracking the Code

1

Bridging Theory and Practice

A Conceptual Model of Relevant Research

Bernd Schmitt

Merriam-Webster.com defines the word "relevant" as "having significant and demonstrable bearing on the matter at hand." The word "applicable" is listed as a synonym, noting that "applicable suggests the fitness of bringing a general rule or principle to bear upon a particular case." The word "relevant," however, is distinguished from "applicable" in that "relevant implies a traceable, significant, logical connection."

Assessing research in the field of consumer psychology as applicable and/or relevant to business, I would say that most consumer psychology and consumer behavior research is, at best, applicable to some narrowly defined area of business. However, I feel that very little research has had a significant and demonstrable impact on business and thus proven its relevance.

As Harter (1992) noted, relevance is more complex than applicability (or topicality): "a phenomenon that is relevant changes the matter in some way; it adds information, or decreases information, offers a new perspective, or causes other kinds of cognitive change" (pp. 602–3). Change is also at the core of Sperber and Wilson's (1995) discourse-based relevance theory. Relevance is accomplished if the exchange of ideas between parties results in changes in the assumptions of both parties and large contextual effects (Sperber and Wilson 1997; Wilson and Sperber 2005). Whereas applicable research may vaguely relate a theoretical topic to a topic in business practice, relevant research offers more significant opportunities for both researchers and business leaders—opportunities to drive change, add valuable insight, provide new frameworks, and offer new ways of thinking and deciding. To secure such

3

benefits, however, we need to build a bridge between theory and practice and engage in relevant research.

In this chapter, I present a conceptual model of relevant research geared toward the interests of consumer psychologists and consumer behavior researchers affiliated with business schools. I explore specifically the bridge between consumer psychology and behavioral theory to business practice. The relevance issue of consumer psychology research is of course broader, and concerns additional constituents besides businesses (such as consumer groups, nonprofit organizations, and government agencies).

Before presenting the model, I review various perspectives and debates on relevance, ranging from views on relevance in the field of marketing to Kurt Lewin's action theory and the external validity debate.

Relevance in Marketing

Over the last few decades, the issue of relevance has arisen every few years in the field of consumer behavior and in the broader field of marketing. Interestingly, some consumer researchers and marketers would not share my view of our discipline's lack of relevance. For example, Varadarajan (2003) presented a passionate argument for the relevance of marketing research, writing that "from A to Z, practically every topic that is the focus of scholarly research in marketing (e.g., advertising, branding, channels, distribution, e-commerce, franchising, global marketing, innovation, marketing ethics, new product development, pricing, quality, retailing, sales promotion, and strategy) is either integral to the practice of marketing, has public policy implications, or affects society at large" (p. 369). However, are the topics listed by Varadarajan really the focus of scholarly research in marketing, or, for that matter, of concern to consumer psychologists and behavioral researchers? Do articles in consumer psychology and consumer behavior journals really contribute to such topics and provide solutions to practitioners' decision issues?

A quick perusal of the titles of articles published in one of the leading consumer research journals, the *Journal of Consumer Psychology,* suggests that this is not the case. Here are the titles of the top 10 cited articles published in the previous five years. (The journal extracted this information from Scopus on July 25, 2010.)

- "Construal levels and psychological distance: Effects on representation, prediction, evaluation, and behavior"
- "A theory of regret regulation 1.0"
- "The unconscious consumer: Effects of environment on consumer behavior"

- "The ties that bind: Measuring the strength of consumers' emotional attachments to brands"
- "Feelings and consumer decision making: The appraisal-tendency framework"
- "Reflective and impulsive determinants of consumer behavior"
- "The role of conscious awareness in consumer behavior"
- "Free will in consumer behavior: Self-control, ego depletion, and choice"
- "A meditation on mediation: Evidence that structural equations models perform better than regressions"
- "Taboo trade-offs, relational framing, and the acceptability of exchanges"

Note that only one article—the one focused on the emotional attachment to brands—refers to a pertinent marketing topic identified by Varadarajan (2003). All the other articles seem to follow strictly and narrowly the aims and scope of the *Journal of Consumer Psychology* as stated on its website, which in fact shield consumer psychologists from conducting business-relevant research:

> The *Journal of Consumer Psychology* is devoted to psychological perspectives on the study of the consumer. It publishes articles that contribute both theoretically and empirically to an understanding of psychological processes underlying consumers' thoughts, feelings, decisions, and behaviors. Areas of emphasis include, but are not limited to, consumer judgment and decision processes, attitude formation and change, reactions to persuasive communications, affective experiences, consumer information processing, consumer-brand relationships, affective, cognitive, and motivational determinants of consumer behavior, family and group decision processes, and cultural and individual differences in consumer behavior. Most accepted articles contribute to or extend theory in psychology and consumer research by empirical research (often from lab or field experiments, though survey and other methodological paradigms are welcomed as well). Theoretical and/or review articles that integrate existing bodies of research and that provide new insights into the underpinnings of consumer behavior and decision processes are also encouraged.

To be sure, it is valuable that articles in a consumer psychology journal should "contribute to or extend theory in psychology and consumer research." It is surprising, however, that there is no concern whatsoever about business impact, nor about applicability of concepts to any practical area. I would like to note that the *Journal of Consumer Psychology* is not alone in this. Other academic journals show at best a concern for potential applicability of concepts rather than true relevance.

Yet even if these articles are not directly relevant, they may still, as Varadarajan (2003) argued further, affect marketing practice "indirectly," "latently," "serendipitously," or "ex-post," as he put it. Moreover, research may follow some sort of variation of the familiar argument that Mendel's bean counting led to genetics. (Gregor Mendel [1822–1884], an Augustinian priest, studied inheritance in pea plants and unexpectedly became the figurehead of the new science of genetics.) Indeed, as Lehmann (2003) observed, it may be "hard to predict when a piece of research will prove useful. For example, when a highly mathematical paper on the axioms of choice appeared in the *Journal of Mathematical Psychology,* few would have known that it foretold the development of conjoint analysis. . . . Today, conjoint analysis is one of the most widely accepted research tools for understanding consumer choice" (p. 4). However, how many such examples exist? How often does research coming out of the interests of the lonely dedicated scientist produce business impact? Should business schools support any kind of "bean counting" activities by marketing and consumer psychologists because of the slim likelihood of some potential impact in the future, no matter how small?

Or is there a way to increase the probability of impact and thus decide which research may be, more or less, relevant to business? Most important, can we develop a model of relevance that would enhance the probability of such success? The latter concern is the goal of this chapter.

Irrespective of academicians' view of how relevant their research is or potentially might be, there is, unfortunately, increasing evidence that business managers care little about what marketing academics do. In an empirical study of experienced marketing practitioners in a business-to-business context, Ankers and Brennan (2002) found that the marketers knew little about academic research and felt that academicians did not understand the realities of business life and could not communicate effectively with managers. Brennan and Turnbull (2002) identified barriers to collaborations, including different attitudes toward research, dissimilar aspirations and goals, and incompatibilities in the reward and promotion systems.

Also, McAlister (2005) argued that "emerging consumer behavior researchers," that is, doctoral students and junior faculty, believe they cannot publish their work in top-level journals when their work is managerially relevant. Moreover, she argued that some influential scholars are outright disdainful of managerially relevant consumer behavior research. McAlister seems to point to a self-sustaining culture of pure research that does not approve of conducting relevant research and erects barriers to get relevant work published in academic journals.

Lewin's Action Theory

Interestingly, managerially relevant research had not always been viewed with such disdain. Kurt Lewin, the founder of modern social psychology—the very discipline from which many theories and concepts of consumer psychology are drawn—felt that conducting relevant research was of utmost importance. Lewin noted the gap between social theory and social action and the lack of collaboration between practitioners and researchers. He felt that without a bridge between theory and practice, theorists would develop theory that would have no application and practitioners would engage in action uninformed by theory (Cunningham 1993).

Lewin became known for his "field theory" (Lewin 1943); his approach was cognitive in nature. He defined a "psychological field" as the totality of coexisting facts that exist at the time a behavior occurs. The Lewinian field includes, specifically, a person's thoughts about the broader social and work environments.

Lewin also believed in experimentation. However, in line with his gestaltist orientation, he felt research should not reduce human behavior into simple variables that can be manipulated, but should describe what happens holistically in naturally occurring settings (Dickens and Watkins 1999).

Moreover, he felt that to truly understand something one must try to change it. He sought not only to describe or explain a phenomenon, but also to change it. Toward that end, Lewin developed "action theory" in the mid-1940s, using his theories of group dynamics to solve organizational and societal problems (Lewin 1946).

Action theory consists of collaborations between researchers and practitioners. It proceeds "in a spiral of steps, each of which is composed of a circle of planning, action, and fact-finding about the result of the action" (Lewin 1946, p. 38). In the late 1930s, as an alternative to Frederick Winslow Taylor's "scientific management," Kurt Lewin and his students started conducting quasi-experiments in factories to demonstrate the greater gains in productivity possible through democratic participation (Lewin 1920). Adelman (1993) discusses Lewin's early experiments at the Harwood factory where Lewin was hired as a consultant. Dickins and Watkins (1999) provide two examples of Lewin's theory in action, involving cross-functional teams who address deeply rooted organizational issues through recurring cycles of action and reflection: an action research project for Southwest Technologies, a multinational high-tech company, and a case of conflicts experienced by a manufacturing manager.

After Lewin's death in 1947, others developed action theory further. Cunningham views action theory as "a continuous process of research and learning in the researcher's long-term relationship with a problem" (Cunningham 1993, 4). Argyris and Schon emphasize the action component in the practitioner's field: "Action research takes its cues—its questions, puzzles, and problems—from the perceptions of practitioners, local practice contexts. It builds descriptions and theories within the practice context itself, and tests them through *intervention experiments*—that is through experiments that bear the double burden of testing hypotheses and effecting some (putatively) desirable change in the situation" (1991, 86).

Lewin is known for stating that "there is nothing so practical as a good theory" (Lewin 1951, 169). The message was twofold: theorists should develop ideas and theories for conceptualizing practical situations, and practitioners should make use of applied theories and provide data and key information so that theorists can further develop theories to address problems.

Lewin's concept of a theory (such as "field theory" or "action theory") was more a "method" (Lewin 1943) or a conceptual framework than a propositional network of interrelated constructs linked to specific variables. Moreover, the level of analysis was more general than the level of analysis used in most of today's consumer psychology research.

His statement that "there's nothing so practical as a good theory" must be viewed in this context: Field theory and action theory were relevant precisely because they provided a flexible framework and conceptualized practical issues at the right level of analysis. Thus, there was a correspondence between theory and the issues that interested management (leadership style, groups, and work environments) and the decision level they were concerned with.

Current theories and approaches stand in stark contrast to Lewin's, in that they are concerned with narrowly focused, highly specific phenomena. The constructs, processes, and terminologies that are employed to address these issues may be rigorous and well defined, but they do not correspond to the concepts and language that management uses to make decisions. Also, there is an obsessive concern about contaminating concepts, confounding adjacent variables, and sacrificing internal validity. As a result, compared to Lewin, the relevance issue and the term "relevance" are examined in a much more narrow context. The external validity controversy offers a case in point.

The External Validity Controversy

A number of articles published by the *Journal of Consumer Research* in the early 1980s and others found in marketing journals in the late 1990s contributed to what Winer (1999) has referred to as "the external validity controversy."

The term "external validity" (together with "internal validity") was introduced by the statistician Donald Campbell to describe threats to the validity of experimental and quasi-experimental research in psychology (Campbell 1957). It should be noted that the terms have been generalized by some to encompass internal and external validity issues (also referred to as transferability) across the social sciences, including qualitative research and ethnography (Denzin 1978; Lincoln and Guba 1986). In consumer psychology and consumer behavior, however, the debate was focused mostly on experimental studies.

For experiments, external validity has been defined both in terms of certain properties possessing validity (populations, settings, variables, persons, or times) and in terms of relationships between constructs or variables. In his 1957 article, Campbell described external validity as "representativeness or generalisability, to what populations, settings and variables can this effect be generalized?" (p. 297). Cook and Campbell (1979), however, define external validity as "the approximate validity with which we can infer that the presumed causal relationships can be generalized to alternate measurements of the cause and effect and across different types of persons, settings and times" (p. 37).

Adopting Cook and Campbell's (1979) relationship-focused definition of external validity, Bobby Calder, Lynn Phillips, and Alice Tybout examined the concept of external validity in theoretical research in three *Journal of Consumer Research* articles (1981, 1982, 1983). Calder, Phillips, and Tybout (1982) argued for "deemphasizing external validity in theory testing." They contended "that external validity is most appropriately addressed through theory development rather than testing, and that it increases as knowledge accumulates and theories become more complex" (p. 241). Responding to this view, Lynch (1982) argued that "tests of external validity should be routinely incorporated into theoretical experiments" because "if data 'supporting' one's theory lack external validity, the theory lacks construct validity" (p. 238). That is, because a theoretical term is part of a nomological network of constructs, "it is not possible to claim support for construct validity in the nomological sense in the face of a demonstrated failure of external validity of theoretically predicted relationships" (Lynch 1983, 110).

This early debate resulted in useful terminological and conceptual distinctions (theory testing vs. intervention testing, nomological network, construct validity, and others). Yet, these distinctions were focused entirely on methodological and statistical aspects of experimental studies—that is how to construct, conduct and analyze experimental studies. They illustrate that the field was at best concerned with applicability but not with relevance.

In the late 1990s, Winer (1999) revived the debate with an article titled "Experimentation in the 21st Century: The Importance of External Validity" in the *Journal of the Academy of Marketing Science*. Winer (1999) explicitly introduced the term "relevance" into the debate, and provided a broader sociocultural perspective. He argued that "as we move into the twenty-first century, the current state of business schools in which marketing academics reside will require more and more that our research is not only of high quality but relevant. By relevant, I do not mean that research has to directly inform practicing managers. However, I believe it is incumbent on us to be concerned about generalizability of research results beyond the lab into other contexts. This gives practitioners who are interested in applying our work . . . to their problems confidence that empirical results apply to more than 18-to-22-year-olds at large Midwestern universities" (pp. 349–50). Winer recommended that consumer behavior articles be required to have a section indicating how additional studies can increase external validity and proposed "joint ventures" between consumer researchers and marketing science researchers and analyses of real-life datasets (such as scanner panel data).

Calder and Tybout (1999), responding to Winer, laid out the "Calder-Tybout vision," in which researchers pursue either theoretical explanations (research that tests theories and uses theories to explain effects obtained in studies) or effects applications (research that determines whether a theory-based intervention is strong enough to have its intended effects when nontheoretical factors vary). They repeated their principled position: "in our view, the path to greater relevance lies in the appreciation of the power of theory" (p. 364). Lynch (1999), also responding to Winer, indicated his skepticism regarding joint ventures and the use of scanner data, because the scanner analysis of a single packaged good like yogurt may lack generalizability as much as a single experiment. Moreover, Lynch stressed again the intricate link between external validity and construct, or nomological, validity, and concluded, "If Winer's proposals are adopted with a focus of 'external validity through theory' in mind, the science of marketing will prosper. We will be doing our jobs as scientists and business school professors" (p. 375).

A point that has not received sufficient emphasis in the controversy is that it is not easy to distinguish internal from external validity. Indeed, Cook and Campbell (1979), as well as Lynch, view external validity and construct validity as highly related. Furthermore, it may be hard to separate internal and external validity. As Hammersley (1991) pointed out, "findings are either true or false (or approximately true to some degree), they cannot be true in one sense but false in another. The idea that a hypothesis could be internally valid but externally invalid is therefore incoherent. This distinction is based on the false assumption that we can separate the discovery of causal relationships from the question of whether they apply to other cases" (p. 385).

The "external validity" debate and the point of view it reveals illustrate, in my opinion, how poorly and narrowly relevance has been conceived of thus far in our field. First, the term relevance is used without being properly conceptualized. I believe that relevance is more than just a need to consider the issues of generalizability or external validity, and must consider applicability as well. Moreover, relevance is seen as a one-way street: the focus is on *our* theories, *our* methods, *our* findings; with a view that these theories need to be developed, tested and generalized, without making contact and interacting with the outside world. Only after these theories are tested and results are on the table, should they be translated for business audiences to reveal what may be an inherent applicability and relevance. Moreover, there is no consideration of the level of analysis and for whom—and for what—our theories, methods and findings should be relevant. In sum, there is no detailed model and process that lays out how the world of theory may be mapped onto the world of practice, and vice versa.

To improve on the current state of affairs, I present here a model of relevant research. The aim of the model is to build a bridge between the worlds of theory and practice, which is essential to relevant research. The three core parts of the model are as follows:

1. *Dimensions of relevance:* describes criteria that are required to connect the world of theory with the world of practice
2. *Context of relevance:* anchors relevant research in the broader contexts of theory and practice
3. *Process of relevance:* outlines the key steps from discovery to use of relevant research

A Model of Relevant Research

Relevance refers to a connection between two domains (or, philosophically speaking, "worlds")—the world of the researcher and the world of the practitioner. (Henceforth, I will refer to the two worlds as "theory" and "practice.") Each world has certain characteristics. For example, the "theory" world of the consumer psychology researcher includes the goal of testing and advancing psychological theory regarding *consumer* behavior. One of the means for doing so includes conducting experiments. The world of "practice" has its own characteristics: managers, for example, may focus on decision making that increases market share or profitability through repositioning a brand or launching a new product.

Each world also includes a certain language (terminology and jargon). Experimental researchers talk about constructs and variables, covariates and confounding variables, internal and external validity. Practitioners use terms and acronyms like mission critical initiatives, bottom line, and key performance indicators (KPIs). Occasionally, the same term (e.g., "methodology" or "process") may have different meanings in different worlds.

Each world also has certain action components. For example, in the world of theory, the researcher has professional contacts, engages in collaborations with academic researchers, is being promoted or tenured, and receives certain incentives and rewards for conducting his or her research. In the world of practice, managers have a network of professional contacts within an industry, typically work in project teams, and are promoted or fired based on the meeting of business goals.

Relevant research is about creating a bridge between these two worlds and connecting them in terms of goals, language, and desired actions. As discussed earlier, this bridge seems to be missing or broken because of different aspirations, goals, and other incompatibilities (Brennan and Turnbull 2002). Through relevant research we can create a "possible world" that provides mutual benefits, new insight, and a change in perspective and worldviews in the respective worlds.

Dimensions of Relevance

To connect the worlds of theory and practice requires that three criteria be fulfilled. As Figure 1.1 shows, these criteria may be viewed as three dimensions of relevance. The three dimensions are arranged in a hierarchy: dimension 1, applicability, is the most elementary (and thus the weakest) form of relevance. It is a prerequisite for dimension 2, communicability. Dimensions 1 and 2 are prerequisites for dimension 3, which is impact.

Applicability

To be relevant, various aspects of the world of theory must be conceptually related to the world of practice, and vice versa. That is, there must be, in principle, some connection points between theory and practice. Applicability is the weakest criterion and dimension of relevance. Following information science, applicability is about topicality (the matching of topics).

In the academic circles in the world of theory, researchers often try to accomplish applicability by using throw-in sentences in a section labeled "managerial implications" in the "general discussion" of an article. However, without a check on whether practitioners in fact agree that this constitutes a connection to their world, such applications may be misleading and fail to qualify as actual applications.

Figure 1.1 **Dimensions of Relevance**

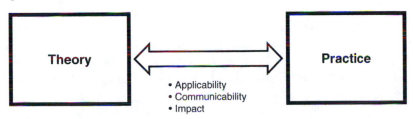

How could we do better? Consider once again the ten most-cited articles listed in the *Journal of Consumer Psychology*. As noted earlier, initially they do not seem to be relevant for business. However, relevance along the applicability dimension could be created if the research issues addressed in these papers were reframed in terms of practical decision issues. That is, what do "construal levels," "regrets," "unconscious processes," "appraisal tendencies" and the like mean in the context of managerial decision making? Manager input may be sought, and the research as a whole conducted not only with an eye toward testing theoretical models but also toward providing business applications. Conversely, a managerial decision issue may be described and analyzed in all its complexity, at the beginning of a research project for example, and then mapped on a consumer psychology theory that preserves the very essence of the issue, rather than being connected to a theory in an arbitrary way.

Trying to achieve applicability requires not only conceptual mapping but also awareness of divergent levels of analysis and assumptions guiding each domain. For example, while the researcher may be interested in transfer processes between working memory and long-term memory that may affect a decision or choice, the managers may be concerned at a much higher level of analysis with how to decide whether to enter a particular target market. The aforementioned transfer process, no doubt, may play a role in the manager's targeted choice; however, without a clear understanding of how it does, or might, the researcher's findings may be seen by the manager as irrelevant.

Communicability

To be relevant along this dimension, a link between the two worlds must be more than a concept; it must be communicated. Communicability is a criterion of relevance because, as we saw, the world of theory and practice differ not only in terms of concepts and frameworks and their corresponding goals, but also in the language that is used to connect these concepts.

Communicability requires either a common terminology that researchers and practitioners share or some translation or interpretation. At best, when relevant collaborations are sought, communicability should be a joint undertaking. To translate retrospectively (e.g., by publishing in business jargon a short version of a piece of research originally communicated in research jargon) is less desirable because a chance for mutual learning of concepts and language has been missed.

Impact

The third dimension of relevance is based on applicability and communicability but goes beyond them. In fact, following Sperber and Wilson's (1997) relevance theory, as well as our definitional understanding of relevance, impact is what moves relevance from a communicated connection between theory and practice to an actual one.

Following this dimension, theories must be used in practice and change something in practice to be relevant; and practice must have an impact on the design and conduct of research. The impact dimension thus requires documented change—a change in mind-set, a change in how decisions are made, a change in actions—both in business practice and "in the lab," because the two worlds are truly relevant to each other and no longer based on separate and perhaps incompatible objectives.

The Context of Relevance

So far, I have discussed the three dimensions of relevance (applicability, communicability, and impact) in the abstract. I have provided some examples and illustrations but I have not looked at relevant research issues in the context of an actual "theory-and-practice" bridge. This section contextualizes relevant research by pointing to four aspects of that context: issue, level, target, and outcome (see Figure 1.2).

Issue

When discussing relevant research and deciding on the current and/or potential degree of relevant research, it is important to ask the question, "What about the research is or could be relevant for business, or, conversely, what about a business issue could be relevant for a researcher?" First, a theory or framework may be relevant to business, or a closely examined business issue may lead to a new theory. Second, rather than an entire theory or framework a new concept may be relevant to business or may emerge from business practice.

Figure 1.2 **The Context of Relevance**

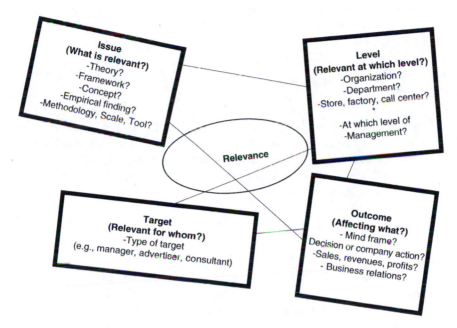

Third, relevance may also be achieved through an empirical finding. Finally, it may be achieved through a methodology, scale, or a tool or device.

Level

After that simple question, the next question to ask is: "At which level will the research be relevant to business, or at which level will a business issue have impact on academic research?" Could the theory, concept, finding, or methodology impact an entire organization, a department, or customer touch point (e.g., store, factory, call center)? At which level of management will the impact occur (senior, middle, line management)? These are all questions of relevance level. Conversely, could a development in business revamp an entire research paradigm (as recent drastic changes in the advertising industry may do); will it result in a new research stream (as usage of the Internet has), or will it trigger new methodological development (e.g., measurement of social media)?

Target

Another question to ask is, "Who is the target of relevant research?" This question broadly concerns the specific profession or industry. Is the theory, concept, finding, or methodology—at whatever level—supposed to be relevant for a manager, an advertiser, a consultant? Conversely, for which research target will a business issue be relevant? Will it be a researcher at an academic institution (psychology department, business school, or communications program) or a researcher in industry?

Outcome

The final question to ask is, "What exactly will be the relevant outcome?" If research is relevant in the sense of having impact, then what will that impact be? Will the research result in a change of mind? Will it affect decision making? Will it impact consumers through company actions? Will it result in higher sales, revenues, profits? Will it build new business relations?

Additional Considerations

Admittedly, the various aspects listed as part of the context of relevance may read like a laundry list of issues rather than a theoretically derived list. Moreover, the examples given and questions asked are certainly not comprehensive. The key point here is to provide a structure for considering context issues—that is, what kind of research needs to be conducted in order to be relevant to various issues, at various levels, for various targets, and to result in various outcomes.

In general, relevant research can claim more significant impact when the issue is broader (e.g., framework rather than finding); when the level of analysis is higher (e.g., corporate senior management rather than individual touch point); when the target is broader (business as a whole rather than one type of business or profession); and when the outcome refers to widespread action taken as a result of the research. I agree with the editor of this book, Steven Posavac, that research streams rather than individual articles are more likely to be relevant to business, especially if they focus on broader issues and at a higher level of analysis. (The brand experience framework discussed in a later chapter in this book provides an example from my own work.)

Most current consumer psychology research unfortunately seems to focus on narrow issues at an extremely detailed and low level of analysis. Moreover, the issues investigated (e.g., the vast literature on advertising) have relevance at best for a very targeted profession (e.g., the creative departments in ad agencies, which incidentally often reject guidance through research). Finally, the outcomes (say, the dependent variables of most experimental consumer psychology research) are far removed from outcome variables that managers value. Clearly, enhancing research relevance would require that consumer psychology researchers become more aware of the context of relevance when deciding what kind of research to conduct and designing their research projects.

The Process of Relevance

The conceptual model of relevant research also addresses the discovery and usage processes. Figure 1.3 shows the steps of this process, accompanied by examples of academic and business factors that are critical at each step to guarantee relevance. (Academic factors are shown in vertical type and business factors are shown in horizontal type.)

The process begins with the identification of a relevant topic—that is, a topic that is applicable, can be communicated, and has potential impact in both worlds. Often, a key academic factor in topic identification is an unsolved aspect of an existing theory. An example of a business factor is an unresolved, practical challenge. Thus, a researcher concerned about conducting relevant research should behave like a Lewinian action researcher and develop his or her topic based on an unresolved practical issue rather than basing it on his or her knowledge of prior research. As Figure 1.3 shows, both academic and industry factors should also be considered at each of the following steps: background research and theory development; empirical design; measurement and results; and, finally, in dissemination and usage. In the latter two steps in particular, a researcher concerned about relevance will not only communicate with academics but disseminate the research in industry outlets, with the ultimate goal of affecting both academic and industry circles.

Broadly speaking, the process model suggests revised roles for consumer psychology and behavioral researchers. Researchers who are truly concerned about the relevance of their work may view themselves as more than researchers. They may also be engaged in case writing, public speaking at industry conferences, executive teaching in companies, and consulting with companies. These activities are learning and sharing opportunities that increase the relevance of their research. Such activities are currently viewed as separate from research, and even as "a waste of time," but in my model they are an integral part of the relevant research process and should be encouraged. Additional contact points and activities between academics and practitioners can enrich research and make it more relevant by contributing new, pertinent ideas at the front end and increase the chance of industry distribution of results at the back end.

Summary

In principle, consumer psychology has a lot to contribute to business. The degree of relevant contribution, however, depends on how consumer psychology

Figure 1.3 **The Process of Relevance**

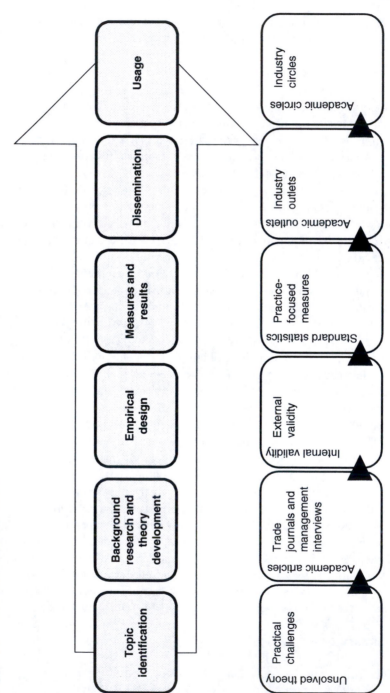

and consumer behavior research is organized and conducted. Given current expectations and views in the field, our research aims, at best, to be generally applicable to business; yet, it seems to have only very limited impact on business practice. This can change if conducting business-relevant research is not seen as contaminating the pure nature of academic research but viewed as a mandate for any consumer psychologist residing in a business school. That is, only truly relevant research is business scholarship.

Toward that end, I have described a model of relevant research that helps to bridge the worlds of theory and practice. The model provides three criteria (or dimensions) of relevance; explores the context of relevance (i.e., which issue is relevant at which level, for what target, and with what outcome); and describes the process of relevance (from the initial topic identification and theory development phases to the dissemination of results and usage).

I hope that my model is not only useful for individual researchers to assess how relevant their research projects are or how they may increase the relevance of their research. In the spirit of Winer (1999), the model may also be used prescriptively, for example, by academic decision makers (such as editors, presidents of associations, deans, and department heads). For example, relevance may be viewed as one aspect of research and manuscript quality. Moreover, the three dimensions of relevance I described and the context-of-relevance part of the model may be used to assess whether a submitted manuscript is likely to be of high relevance. Toward that end, an index of relevance may be developed (similar to reliability and validity). More than that, awards may be created and grants awarded for relevant research. Finally, promotional decisions may be based not only on academic rigor but also on whether or not the academician's research is relevant. In sum, incentives and rewards may be provided to ensure that future consumer psychology research is more relevant than most research today.

References

Adelman, C. 1993. "Kurt Lewin and the Origins of Action Research." *Educational Action Research* 1: 7–24.

Ankers, P., and R. Brennan. 2002. "Managerial Relevance in Academic Research: An Exploratory Study." *Marketing Intelligence and Planning* 20: 15–21.

Argyris, C., and D. Schon. 1991. "Participatory Action Research and Action Science Compared." In *Participatory Action Research,* ed. by W.F. Whyte. Newbury Park: Sage.

Brennan, R., and P. Turnbull. 2002. "Sophistry, Relevance, and Technology Transfer in Management Research: An IMP Perspective." *Journal of Business Research* 55: 595–602.

Calder, B., L. Phillips, and A.M. Tybout. 1981. "Designing Research for Applications." *Journal of Consumer Research* 8: 197–207.

———. 1982. "The Concept of External Validity." *Journal of Consumer Research* 9: 240–44.

———. 1983. "Beyond External Validity." *Journal of Consumer Research* 10: 112–14.

Calder, B., and A.M. Tybout. 1999. "A Vision of Theory, Research, and the Future of Business Schools." *Journal of the Academy of Marketing Science* 27: 359–66.

Campbell, D. 1957. "Factors Relevant to the Validity of Experiments in Social Settings." *Psychological Bulletin* 54: 297–312.

Cook, T., and D. Campbell. 1979. *Quasi-Experimentation.* Chicago: Rand McNally.

Cunningham, J.B. 1993. *Action Research and Organizational Development.* Westport, CT: Praeger.

Denzin, N. 1978. *The Research Act.* New York: McGraw-Hill.

Dickens, L., and K. Watkins. 1999. "Action Research: Rethinking Lewin." *Management Learning* 30: 127–40.

Hammersley, M. 1991. "A Note on Campbell's Distinction Between Internal and External Validity." *Quality and Quantity* 25: 381–87.

Harter, S.P. 1992. "Psychological Relevance and Information Science." *Journal of the American Society for Information Science* 43: 602–15.

Lehmann, D. R. 2003. "The Relevance of Rigor." MSI Reports: Working Paper Series 1 (03–001), 83–91, Marketing Science Institute, Cambridge, MA.

Lewin, K. 1920. *"Die Sozialisierung des Taylorsystems."* ("Social Aspects of the Taylor System"). *Praktischer Sozialismus,* 4.

———. 1943. "Defining the 'Field at a Given Time.'" *Psychological Review* 50: 292–310.

———. 1946. "Action Research and Minority Problems." *Journal of Social Issues* 2: 34–46.

———. 1951. *Field Theory in Social Science; Selected Theoretical Papers.* Ed. D. Cartwright. New York: Harper & Row.

Lincoln, Y.S., and E. Guba. 1986. "But Is It Rigorous? Trustworthiness and Authenticity in Naturalistic Evaluation." *New Directions for Program Evaluation* 30: 73–84.

Lynch, J. 1982. "On the External Validity of Experiments in Consumer Research." *Journal of Consumer Research* 9: 225–39.

———. 1983. "The Role of External Validity in Theoretical Research." *Journal of Consumer Research* 10: 109–11.

———. 1999. "Theory and External Validity." *Journal of the Academy of Marketing Science* 27: 367–76.

McAlister, L. 2005. "Toward Insight and Relevance." *Journal of Public Policy and Marketing* 21: 143–45.

Sperber, D., and D. Wilson. 1995. *Relevance: Communication and Cognition,* 2d ed. Oxford: Blackwell.

———. 1997. "Remarks on Relevance Theory and the Social Sciences." *Multilingua* 16: 145–51.

Varadarajan, P.R. 2003. "Musings on Relevance and Rigor of Scholarly Research in Marketing." *Journal of the Academy of Marketing Science* 31: 368–76.

Wilson, D., and D. Sperber. 2005. "Relevance Theory." In *Handbook of Pragmatics,* ed. L. Horn and G. Ward, 607–32. Oxford: Blackwell.

Winer, R.S. 1999. "Experimentation in the 21st Century: The Importance of External Validity." *Journal of the Academy of Marketing Science* 27, 349–58.

2

Optimal Marketing for Really New Products

Using a Consumer Perspective to Improve Communications

Steve Hoeffler and Michal Herzenstein

Twenty years ago two inventors set out to improve upon one of the most ubiquitous of all inventions "the wheel." Franco Sbarro and Dominique Mottas separately patented two new designs that eliminated the central hub. The appearance of the hubless (or centerless) wheel is striking and with the development of prototype cars, motorcycles, and bikes, developers were excited about the prospects for their really new products (RNPs). In fact, the website for the Osmos orbital wheel touts such positive keys to success as: "level of innovativeness, use improvement, market stability, broad target market, and competitive prices and quality" such that "the success of the product will be guaranteed." Of course, these products have yet to make a dent in the approximate 4 million wheels that are produced daily around the world, highlighting the challenges that even something as straightforward as "reinventing the wheel" does not guarantee success in the marketplace. In fact, we would like to assert that, with respect to RNPs, the decisions managers face about marketing strategies play an important role in the success (or failure) of an RNP.

With incrementally new products, many of the implementation decisions are not really decisions at all. For example, when introducing a new laptop into the market, managers' main decision is the choice of outlets to use for distribution (from web-based sources to company-owned stores and other traditional retailers). Yet, there are fewer decisions to make regarding how to position the product, which particular features and benefits to highlight when promoting the product, or how to price it (since the range is pretty much predetermined by the market). Such decisions, positioning, and pricing are crucial for RNPs, as they help to define the industry for prospective consumers. For example, when the first digital cameras hit the market, they were actually categorized (or labeled) not as digital cameras, but instead as "filmless cameras." Furthermore, consumers were unsure about where to find the new digital cameras in stores: in the computer aisle or the camera aisle? To many people this question was not trivial. The confusion arose from the unclear positioning of the first digital cameras; that is, were they cameras or computers? Interestingly, professional photographers were more likely to look for digital cameras in the computer aisle. They reasoned that if there is no film it cannot be a camera (Moreau, Markman, and Lehmann 2001). When introducing an RNP, managers must learn about the potential target audiences. In the case of digital cameras, novices (or amateur photographers) adopted digital cameras faster than professional photographers. If managers had exclusively targeted more experienced photographers, adoption and ultimate acceptance in the market would have been delayed.

In this chapter we examine decisions that managers have to make when introducing RNPs, and evaluate these decisions through the eyes of consumers. By reviewing both the academic literature and recent introductions of RNPs we aim to provide managers with concrete and easy-to-follow advice on communicating such products to the market. We first present definitions of RNPs and discuss how they are different from incrementally new products. Next we present the Kano model for classifying consumer requirements and satisfaction. Using the Kano model as a lens, we then examine several issues in communicating the innovative features of RNPs to consumers (such as how consumers learn about RNPs, the role of consumers' prior knowledge, and the cost associated with learning and uncertainty about the product). Finally, we offer prescriptive advice on communication strategies for the issues presented in the chapter.

What Makes a New Product Really New?

What makes a new product really new and how does this distinction affect managers' decisions? Past research on incrementally new products (INPs) and RNPs identifies several differences, which are important in understanding how to market RNPs. Zhao, Hoeffler, and Dahl (2009) define RNPs as products that enable consumers to do things they were not able to do with products that already exist in the market. For example, TiVo enabled viewers to pause live TV, digital cameras enabled consumers to easily edit and share pictures and videos, and Segway enabled pedestrians to move faster with no effort. These capabilities and benefits may be difficult to communicate to consumers because they are so new that consumers may not understand how they work or why they should want them (i.e., the benefits provided). Thus, activities and benefits that consumers have never experienced may prove difficult to explain.

Even when consumers understand and look favorably upon an RNP, they often find that the new benefits of an RNP come at a cost; that is, they will have to learn how to purchase and use the RNP correctly in order to enjoy its benefits (Urban, Weinberg, and Hauser 1996). This is one of the main differences between INPs and RNPs—all of us know what to look for when purchasing a new laptop, but we need to learn how to purchase (and use) a Segway or a TiVo. This issue brings several challenges to marketers regarding the positioning of an RNP. A related definition of RNPs is that they change consumers' daily behavior (Gourville 2006; Urban et al. 1996). One challenge for marketers is encouraging consumers to change their behavior and to realize that the benefits they are gaining from the RNP surpass the benefits they are losing (familiarity, comfort, ease). This may lead consumers to perceive risk and to be uncertain about a product, because there is a possibility that they will not be able to master the RNP or because the RNP is so new that it may not be technologically mature (Herzenstein, Posavac, and Brakus 2007). For example, the first generation of airbags in cars injured passengers when they inflated in even minor fender benders and the first generation of Segways fell down when the battery was near the end of its charge, causing injuries to riders. Financial risk may also be an issue. For example, in the recent competition between Sony and Toshiba regarding the format for high-definition DVDs, Sony and its Blu-ray player won out. Consumers who bought Toshiba's HD-DVD players will probably need to eventually purchase a Blu-ray player since the formats are incompatible. These examples demonstrate that it may be difficult to convince consumers to adopt RNPs early, so marketers and engineers face the difficult task of convincing consumers that the RNP is safe and easy to use.

Another challenge associated with RNPs is that the product category may be unclear because the item can be placed in more than one existing product class (Moreau, Markman, and Lehmann 2001). Is the TiVo a computer or a VCR? Is a digital camera a computer or a camera? This confusion may actually benefit marketers as they have more flexibility when choosing a positioning (i.e., a product category) that will enable them to optimize consumer performance expectations from the product and, in turn, preferences, satisfaction, and word-of-mouth, as well as in-store placement and sales. Another advantage of the ability to choose the product's category is that it also defines the competition for the product and allows managers to choose positioning that reduces competitors or demonstrates the benefits of the product in the best light.

Because RNPs provide new (and sometimes unclear) benefits to consumers, often requiring considerable consumer learning and behavior change, and may involve financial or even physical risk, consumer response to such products is often difficult to predict and can vary widely depending on how a product is positioned (Hoeffler 2003). One reason it is hard to predict consumer response is that consumers experience uncertainty when estimating the usefulness of RNPs and thus marketers are unable to accurately predict their response. Consumer expertise in the product category plays a major role in their response to an RNP. Some consumers who consider themselves expert in a category are often more resistant to adoption (or less likely to realize the new benefits of the RNP) because the RNP poses a threat to their existing expertise. Managers can bypass many of these issues by allowing a more flexible positioning for the RNP. Research has shown that consumers' preferences are malleable to RNPs positioning (categorization). Back to the digital camera example, consumers who looked for the digital cameras in the camera aisle reported higher performance expectations than those who looked for it in the computer aisle. This in turn affected their preference for the camera (Moreau, Markman, and Lehmann 2001).

The Kano Approach to Customer Satisfaction and Requirements Classification

In the early 1980s Professor Noriaki Kano of Rika University in Tokyo and his colleagues developed a model that helps understand customer-defined quality and customer satisfaction (Kano et al. 1984). Their basic premise relies on the idea that an asymmetry exists between factors that result in satisfaction and those that lead to dissatisfaction. Analogously, job satisfaction as described by Herzberg and colleagues (Herzberg 1968; Herzberg, Mausner, and Snyderman 1959) is often a function of motivating factors such as achievement, recognition, and responsibilities, while job dissatisfaction is often a function of factors such as company policy, relationship with the supervisor, and salary. In the 1970s, when Kano was working with Konica, the camera company, he began to see that consumers may not always be able to articulate their needs and requirements, but they may still expect products to fulfill these needs. As described by Scholtes (1997), Konica's sales and research group asked Kano to help them develop a highly differentiated new camera. Konica's past market research showed that, when asked directly, consumers requested very minor improvements to existing cameras. However, Kano believed that consumers often do not know how to articulate their real needs, and that really new innovations can only be designed after the development team has a deep understanding of these difficult-to-articulate needs. Kano sent a team to commercial photo processing labs to investigate pictures taken by consumers.

They found that many pictures came out blurry, under- or overexposed, and even blank. The result of this investigation was the development of a set of features to address these problems (or needs): auto focus, built-in automatic flash, and automatic film rewinding. These features, which were innovative at the time, became common.

Taking his insights from Konica's market research together with the adaptation of Herzberg's ideas, Noriaki Kano and others from Rika University developed a framework for understanding customer satisfaction. The framework suggests that customers' ideas about quality and needs are often unclear but can become clear if we ask the right questions. Once we understand customers' concerns, many requirements emerge and they fall into the following categories (Figure 2.1).

1. Requirements to Which Customers Are Indifferent

Quality elements (requirements) do not always affect customer satisfaction. (These are plotted along the x-axis in Figure 2.1.) An example is ambient lights in the interior of a car. Consumers may be satisfied even if the car does not have ambient light and, conversely, they may be unsatisfied if the car does have it. Thus, these types of requirements are not helpful in differentiating between brands.

2. "Must Have" (Basic) Customer Requirements

These are requirements that consumers believe the product must have. They will be less satisfied if the product has less of them (less functional) but will not be more satisfied than "neutral" if the product has more of them (more functional). (Satisfaction from these requirements is represented by the curve in Figure 2.1 plotted in the lower half of the graph [dissatisfaction]). An example of such a requirement is brakes in a car. Having poor brakes will result in dissatisfaction but having excellent brakes will not raise the level of satisfaction because good brakes are expected in cars and are a basic criterion for this product. Customers regard the "must have" requirements as prerequisites—taking them for granted—and therefore do not explicitly request them. Such requirements rarely lead to competitive advantage because customers will only be interested in brands that fulfill these requirements and thus most competitive offerings will include them.

3. Performance Customer Requirements

For these requirements, customer satisfaction from the product is proportional to the degree of the benefit that is included (where more is always perceived as better).

Figure 2.1   **Kano's Model of Customer Satisfaction**

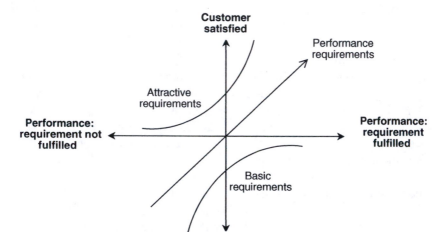

These requirements relate to the straight line in Figure 2.1. The 45-degree line that runs through the origin suggests that when the performance requirements are low (or a product is less functional) then customers are less satisfied, and when the performance requirements are high (product is more functional) then customers are more satisfied. An example is miles-per-gallon (MPG) in cars: customers are generally more satisfied when the MPG is high and less satisfied when it is low. These requirements are usually explicitly demanded by customers and are proven to be useful in differentiating between brands (in comparison ads for example).

4. Attractive (Exciting) Customer Requirements

These are requirements that lead to greater customer satisfaction if the product has more of them (more functional) but customers remain neutral if the product has fewer (less functional). Consumers are generally not aware of the potential availability of these features. (These requirements are plotted in the "satisfaction" half of Figure 2.1.) One example is a heated steering wheel. Consumers may not be unsatisfied if the car does not have a heated steering wheel but may be more satisfied if this feature is available. These requirements are often provided by new and innovative features and therefore are neither explicitly expressed nor expected by the customer. However, they are crucial in creating competitive advantage.

The Kano model further suggests that this classification is dynamic in the sense that requirements or needs that were exciting in the past may become performance or even basic needs in the future (Bayus 2008; Carpenter and Nakamoto 1989). For example, air-conditioning was considered a luxury in cars in the 1950s but it is a basic requirement today, along with airbags, antilock braking systems, and multiple cup holders. Marketers have an opportunity to shape customer expectations by changing the "image" of features that could alter their typical move from exciting to performance and, finally, basic. Similarly, marketers have an opportunity to define new features as exciting, creating a competitive advantage over other products in the category. A cup holder in a car may seem trivial but consumers consistently rated the cup holder's usefulness as high (making the cup holder a performance need), which has led to an increase in the number of cup holders included in a vehicle (as many as eleven cup holders in one minivan). Currently, multiple cup holders have become a basic feature in virtually all new cars.

There are several advantages to the classification of customer requirements following Kano's framework. First, product requirements and needs are better understood and the focus of marketers and engineers should be on the features that are directly related to satisfaction. A related advantage is that this classification sets clear priorities in product development. For example, it is not very useful to improve must-have requirements if they are already at a satisfactory level. It is more efficient to allocate R&D resources to improve performance and attractive (exciting) features, as they are more likely to impact customer satisfaction. Additionally, understanding which requirements are must-haves and which are attractive helps in situations where there is a trade-off between them (i.e., both requirements cannot be fulfilled together). In such cases, clearly the must-have requirements should be fulfilled. The second advantage of such a classification is that it allows companies to differentiate their products by discovering new attractive and exciting features and incorporating them. A product that fulfills only the basic requirements may be perceived as average and not differentiated from the competition, leading to lower satisfaction and loyalty (because consumers will find it interchangeable). Finally, by classifying a product's features into these categories marketers can better forecast consumers' satisfaction level with the product (Huiskonen and Pirtillä 1998).

As a result of these advantages, the Kano approach has been widely used by engineers who have integrated it into an approach called quality function deployment (QFD). This customer-oriented approach to product development provides structure for design teams as they develop new products. QFD helps a company to make key trade-offs between what the customers want and what the company can afford to build (Govers 1994). The first steps in QFD are identifying consumers' needs; prioritizing them; understanding consumers' perceptions regarding quality, satisfaction, and competitive advantage; and translating these needs into product attributes (Hauser and Clausing 1988). Adding Kano's approach to the process helps engineers to classify consumer needs into basic, performance, and exciting, which helps in achieving higher customer satisfaction (Matzler and Hinterhuber 1998). Similarly, service providers use the Kano approach to classify consumer needs to ensure consistent high-quality service, which can be translated into greater profits for companies (Zeithaml, Berry, and Parasuraman 1996). We adapt the Kano model to elucidate the challenges associated with communicating the benefits found in RNPs in a manner that is acceptable to consumers.

Communicating Basic, Performance, and Exciting Needs

When introducing an RNP marketers must first create awareness of the product among prospective customers (Montaguti, Kuester, and Robertson 2002). Marketers should communicate the products' benefits in a way that addresses consumers' needs. Following Kano's classification of requirements and needs we begin by examining the communication of basic needs. These needs are trivial, expected, and assumed as given, so focusing on them may takeaway from marketers' ability to differentiate their brand or establish it as an RNP (Moreau, Hoeffler, and Kubowicz-Malhotra 2010). Take for example the Chevrolet Volt (the company's new electric car), which is considered an RNP because consumers have to learn how to use it, and using it will require a change in consumer behavior, (i.e., plug it into an outlet to charge it). The Volt can seat four adults comfortably and reach a maximum speed of 100 miles per hour. But why would marketers emphasize these basic features in their communication to customers? One reason may be that it helps in cueing the appropriate product category for the product (Moreau, Markman, and Lehmann 2001). Consumers will understand that the Volt is similar to any other sedan (and is not a tiny car that cannot be driven on the highway). We discussed categorization and its importance earlier and suggested that through advertising, marketers can influence the product class to which the RNP will belong according to consumers' perceptions. Cueing the appropriate category can be accomplished visually, by using a picture of the category member exemplar, or conceptually, by labeling the category in an ad (Florian 1994). Often, and perhaps especially when consumer involvement is low, pictures can convey basic needs faster and easier (Feiereisen, Wong, and Broderick 2008) and leave more processing resources for the more difficult-to-understand needs, such as the exciting needs.

Performance needs are directly related to consumer satisfaction from the product. These needs are translated into product requirements that are often requested by consumers. Consumers want to know how well the product will fulfill the need and therefore marketers often communicate this. One advantage of such communication is that it helps consumers evaluate the RNP on familiar criteria (Moreau, Lehmann, and Markman 2001). For example, in the introduction of the Volt, initially General Motors (GM) announced that it achieved 230 MPG, which many found misleading (including competitors and the U.S. Environmental Protection Agency), because it is partially powered by an electric engine. Later, GM explained that the correct terminology is "miles per charge," which indicates the range (40 miles per charge) and cost ($1.50 a day), so that potential consumers can evaluate this requirement using their existing criteria for the product category. However, using existing criteria makes it difficult to differentiate an RNP from currently available products. Thus when marketers communicate the features that address a performance need, they may limit the perception of newness (Hoeffler 2003). Therefore, along with the miles per charge, GM began communicating the Volt's new technology, addressing consumers' concerns about ease of use in an effort to relate new benefits to consumers' existing perceptions.

Exciting needs translate into attractive product requirements that can exponentially increase consumer satisfaction. Using these requirements, marketers have an opportunity to significantly differentiate a product. However, this comes at a price, because consumers may not understand the new benefits or their importance. For example, when the iPad was introduced, industry critics commented that they did not really understand what need the product satisfied. It is less than a laptop, not a phone, and much heavier and cumbersome than the iPod Touch.

Summarizing the confusion, David Pogue, a *New York Times* blogger, wrote, "It may change an industry or two, or it may not. It may introduce a new category—something between phone and laptop—or it may not. And anyone who claims to know what will happen will wind up looking like a fool." Clearly, one of the difficulties in introducing an RNP is communicating how it fulfills exciting needs. Furthermore, it has been shown that creating inaccurate and overconfident expectations about the product's usability may elicit negative emotions among consumers that have a powerful influence on product evaluations and satisfaction (Wood and Moreau 2006). Indeed, many critics commented on Apple Inc. CEO Steve Jobs's excessive use of words such as "phenomenal," "amazing," and "incredible" when he introduced the iPad as perhaps creating unrealistic expectations (Stone 2010).

After becoming aware of the exciting benefits, consumers must then process and understand how these benefits benefit them. These activities are not trivial, especially when they refer to RNPs that are completely novel. How then do consumers learn about RNPs and become able to answer these questions? Generally there are two ways in which learning can occur: internally, by transferring knowledge from the familiar to the novel domain, or externally, by acquiring knowledge from advertisements, word of mouth, product demonstrations, or by direct experience with the product (Gregan-Paxton and John 1997). In the next sections we discuss the advantages of each method and suggest ways to harness them to expedite learning.

Learning is also a function of expertise in the product class. Expertise can affect consumers' perceptions and preferences of an RNP. Another related issue is the costs consumers' may attach to the learning process. If costs are too high (product is too difficult to use or time-consuming to understand), preferences are negatively impacted. There are several ways to reduce these perceived learning costs. Finally, uncertainty regarding the nature of the exciting features can also occur. Uncertainty can slow adoption, so it is important for companies to find ways to address potential uncertainty.

Consumer Learning

While consumers become exposed to RNPs from advertising and product demonstrations (external learning), it is very likely that they come to understand the product and its potential benefits through a process of internal knowledge transfer from familiar to new domains (Gregan-Paxton and John 1997). Generally there are two types of internal knowledge transfer: one is category based and refers to transferring knowledge from one or multiple product categories to another; the second is analogical and refers to the use of something familiar in understanding something unfamiliar.

Internal Learning: Category-Based

Categorization plays a central role in new-product learning (Sujan 1985) Consumers often base inferences and preferences on categories cued in advertising (Moreau, Markman, and Lehmann 2001). However, an RNP often does not belong to any clear product category (by definition it creates a new category; Lehmann 1994). How then do consumers learn about the exciting features of an RNP using category-based internal learning? Clearly the traditional definition of this type of learning cannot be applied to RNPs (Gregan-Paxton et al. 2002) because the conceptual distance between the RNP and previously encountered categories makes it difficult for consumers to access and apply existing knowledge; that is, the mere encounter with the RNP may not activate the relevant knowledge structure from consumers' memory.

Consumers are affected by category cues marketers use in advertising an RNP, so we begin by examining how categories are cued, that is, visually or conceptually. When showing people a picture of a cell phone but calling it a

PDA, most people believe it is a cell phone (Matan and Carey 2001), this is because, in the artifact category (manmade items such as PDAs), the category label tells people what the product does rather than what it is (Barton and Komatsu 1989). In artifact categories, perceptually cued categories (those using pictures) are considered more diagnostic than those that are conceptually cued (using words), the former category type (perceptual) was found to exert more influence on consumer inferences and preferences (Gregan-Paxton, Hoeffler, and Zhao 2005) than the latter (conceptual).

Ample research shows that consumers often find it difficult to draw inferences from multiple categories and end up using a single one because it is the most salient and also because of the processes of selective attention (Macrae, Bodenhausen, and Milne 1995). Marketers must develop an understanding of which category may become more salient and use this knowledge to direct consumers in their acquisition products in the appropriate category. For example, Moreau, Markman, and Lehmann (2001) show that when an advertisement for an RNP labels it as belonging to several product categories, the first category mentioned in the ad has the most influence on how consumers categorize the product and on their expectations and preferences. Gregan-Paxton and colleagues (2005) show that consumers tend to use the category that is perceptually rather than conceptually cued if the former is more familiar. Put differently, consumers who see a familiar picture tend to rely on it for categorization, regardless of how the product in the picture is labeled.

Internal Learning: Analogical

When Steve Jobs revealed the iPad and its e-book reading capabilities he compared it to reading real books in the sense that the iPad has a "bookshelf" full of books, people can "turn pages" as they read, and the pictures are in color. Mr. Jobs wanted prospective customers to understand how the iPad works as an e-book reader by relating the experience to one with which everyone is familiar. Similarly, when the first PDAs were introduced and people were not sure what they were or what they did, the related familiar knowledge would have been a secretary's job description (Gregan-Paxton et al. 2002).

When an RNP is truly novel, consumers may not be able to learn its exciting features by associating them with an existing product category because the RNP does not readily fit into any particular category. When this happens marketers often find that teaching by analogy is more effective (El Houssi, Morel, and Hultink 2005; Feiereisen et al. 2008; Gregan-Paxton and John 1997). Learning by analogy is the process of applying information about a familiar domain to a novel domain (Gregan-Paxton et al. 2002). The two domains do not have to be even remotely related. Gregan-Paxton and John

(1997) describe an advertisement for Sybase's RemoteWare, which is software that allows companies to move critical sales data between their retail or hospitality sites and corporate headquarters. A Sybase advertisement for software, which at first was an RNP and had abstract benefits that consumers found difficult to understand, compared it to a frog. This is clearly a strange comparison, but the text in the ad made the similarities between frogs and the benefits of RemoteWare clear (e.g., both frogs and the software userbase multiply by the hundreds).

The process of learning by analogy includes three stages (Falkenhainer, Forbus, and Gentner 1989): Consumers first access the familiar domain by retrieving it from their long-term memories, map the familiar and new domains by identifying structural similarities between them and highlighting the commonalities, and generate inferences about the unfamiliar domain. While the last two stages are the core of analogical reasoning, the first stage (access) is a critical prerequisite to useful knowledge transfer (Clement and Gentner 1991) and can be potentially influenced by marketers (as the ad for RemoteWare demonstrates).

Learning about RNPs using analogies is effective for several reasons. First, analogies are not constrained by product categories or closely related information and therefore can be more effective than comparisons that are more literal, called "literal similarity comparisons" (El Houssi et al. 2005). Going back to the PDA example, a literal similarity comparison would probably be a mobile phone, which shares several attributes with the target object, but is less able to convey the new and exciting features of the PDA (namely managing office-related tasks). The second reason is that the nature of RNPs, and especially for products based on new technologies, is somewhat abstract, and to learn about it consumers must make it more concrete. Using an analogy or comparing an RNP to something familiar serves to make it more concrete so consumers understand what the new technology is and what it can provide (Gregan-Paxton and John 1997). The third reason analogical learning is effective is that it often requires significant elaboration, as the connection between the familiar and new domains may not be straightforward (i.e., how can a PDA function like a secretary?). The result of this process is that the commonalities of the two domains become salient (Markman and Medin 1995). Finally, and very important, research shows that analogical learning can produce positive affect (Gregan-Paxton et al. 2002). Analogies provide a meaningful link between familiar and novel domains, thus facilitating the process of resolving the incongruity between the RNP and existing knowledge and greatly reducing the degree of cognitive change required to create the initial understanding and representation of the novelty of the RNP in consumer memory. Since analogical learning makes it possible for consumers to represent the RNP as an extension of familiar knowledge (even remotely), this process elicits positive emotions in consumers.

While analogical learning can be more effective than categorical learning, especially when an RNP is completely novel, research shows (El Houssi et al. 2005) that this learning does not increase consumer preference toward an RNP compared with the use of literal similarities (a learning process that draws on conceptually nearer domains). Analogical learning does increase comprehension as compared to other methods, but comprehension itself, while required, is not sufficient to increase consumer appreciation of an RNP. Therefore, El Houssi and colleagues (2005) suggest that marketers do not use analogies solely to explain key benefits of an RNP to consumers, but to dramatize or sell the benefits to them as well.

Although analogical learning has substantial benefits, without sufficient knowledge in the familiar domain and processing resources to be allocated to the task, learning cannot occur (Roehm and Sternthal 2001). That is, consumers must have the ability to learn (i.e., both knowledge and processing resources). If they *can* learn, then persuasion is higher in ads containing analogies than in those containing literal similarity comparisons. This is because the former leads to more intensive mapping between the new and familiar domains than the latter.

The prescriptive advice to marketers that arises from research on both categorical and analogical learning is that to increase comprehension of the exciting benefits and thus positive emotions toward an RNP (and perhaps preferences), marketers should closely guide consumers not only to the familiar domain (or product category) but also to the knowledge consumers should draw from that domain. Research clearly documents the difficulties in the success of analogical learning. Both knowledge and processing resources must be available, which means that even experts in the base (familiar) domain may not be able to learn by analogy if they lack processing resources (Roehm and Sternthal 2001). Similarly, category-based learning may also prove difficult, especially if the RNP is so novel that consumers must draw inferences from multiple product categories (because the product does not fit into any single category). Therefore, Moreau, Markman, and Lehmann (2001) suggest that consumers learn faster from multiple product categories if the appropriate information transferred from each category is clearly delineated for them. Further, we suggest that, when using analogies, marketers should practice what we call guided analogies. We define these as analogies presented to consumers where the outcome (or what is to be learned) from the transfer from one domain to another is explicitly stated. Guided analogies may be more effective than traditional analogies because, if correctly executed, comprehension should occur faster, which in turn can enhance the intensity of the experienced positive emotions toward the process and, perhaps, the product.

External Learning

Consumers often learn about RNPs and their innovative features directly from the manufacturer (in the form of advertising, company websites, demonstrations, etc.); from other consumers (word of mouth); from experts (articles in newspapers for example); and from direct experience with the product. The latter can be both real and virtual by, for example, using the product or watching a video about it. All these methods are considered external learning because consumers learn from sources other than their own knowledge.

One method that has proven very useful for consumer learning about RNPs is mental simulation (Hoeffler 2003). This is similar to role taking, or imaginatively putting oneself in another situation or place. It is often used in advertising, as consumers are encouraged to think about using the product. Such mental simulations (or visualizations) can be considered a form of surrogate experience with the new product; however, they may not be easy to accomplish with RNPs because consumers may not understand how to use them and thus may not be able to visualize themselves using them (Dahl and Hoeffler 2004). When used correctly, though, visualization tools can be very useful as they facilitate information processing without overloading the decision maker, because he or she will understand the novel information faster (Feiereisen et al. 2008).

One clear implication from prior research on visualization is that consumers cannot easily visualize themselves using an RNP, finding it easier to visualize others using it (Dahl and Hoeffler 2004). When visualizing others using the RNP, consumers are less likely to think about how the RNP may fit within their existing personal usage patterns and thus constraints driven by their own usage patterns are less likely to surface. Instead, consumers' attention is directed to the reasons why other consumers may value the RNP and its benefits. Another reason to encourage consumers to use visualizations with a more general approach (i.e., the use by others, not oneself) is because consumers do not have autobiographical memories related to an RNP and thus will find it difficult to accomplish the visualization task (which may in turn lead to negative emotions or frustration; Zhao et al. 2009). Consumers have a tendency to rely on the most readily available experience (i.e., what is salient in their memory) when asked to visualize a situation (because it is the easiest approach), and this tendency might prove difficult when consumers lack such experiences (Zhao et al. 2009). Thus, marketers should try to push consumers to either visualize other people using the product or push the limits of their own experiences. Similarly, Moreau and Dahl (2005) suggest that when working on a creative task, people often use the easy approach and implement either the first solution that comes to mind or a solution based on a category exemplar. People will stray away from the easy approach and expend more cognitive resources on the task only if constraints are operating such that they limit the use of more trivial solutions. While this may prove to be good advice for marketers, it comes at a price. Research on ease of imagining versus difficulty of imagining (Sherman et al. 1985) shows that consumers will find a hypothetical outcome to be more plausible if they can easily imagine it. Because the exciting features of RNPs are often difficult to imagine, consumers may infer that they are unlikely to work properly, thereby increasing the uncertainty surrounding the performance of the RNP (Ziamou 2002).

It is important, though clearly difficult, for marketers to try to get consumers to relate an advertisement for an RNP to themselves in some way because this leads to better memory of the ad and the RNP and more positive attitudes toward both (Dahl and Hoeffler 2004). If this process is easy for consumers, even when autobiographical memories are lacking, then consumers may find the RNP more relevant and more persuasion may take place. One way to get consumers to easily relate an RNP to themselves is to ask them to relate it more generally to a broad audience. Once they do that and find that the RNP is not threatening, then applying it to themselves may prove easier because they have avoided the phase of shortsighted, biased, internal evaluations. Clearly, as introduction of the RNP to the market nears (many RNPs are introduced weeks and even months before they actually enter the market, for example the iPad), marketers should encourage consumers to concretely visualize themselves using the product rather than abstractly visualizing others using it. Along these lines, Castaño and colleagues (2008) suggest that communication on the RNP will be most effective if consumers first engage in the more abstract "why-thinking" (visualizing why they would use the product) before engaging in the more concrete "how-thinking" (visualizing how they use the product). This two-step process has been shown to lower consumer uncertainty and increase adoption and satisfaction. Embarking on both why-thinking and how-thinking simultaneously, however, increases decision difficulty for consumers because they may perceive that they are faced with a trade-off between desirability (the new benefits of an RNP) and feasibility (adoption of RNPs often requires new learning and a change in consumers' daily routines; Thompson, Hamilton, and Petrova 2009). The result of this heightened decision difficulty is often negative and includes postponing the decision or lowering commitment to the chosen option if a decision does occur. Therefore, advertisers should not use both types of visualization simultaneously.

Finally, visualizations should be promoted by framing the positive outcomes (benefits) of the product. This may sound like trivial advice, but many existing communications for RNPs mention that the product is very new and imply that it has not been used by many consumers (along the lines of "be the first to try . . ."). This statement may appeal to a very small group of innovators but may scare away many potential customers who might associate such an announcement with the product being unproven (Herzenstein et al. 2007). Similarly, directing consumers' attention to the "old way of doing business" that will be replaced by the RNP may increase the appeal of the "old way," because it is familiar and easy, and decrease the appeal of the RNP, because of the costs that are associated with it (Gourville 2006). Ample research in behavioral decision theory supports this premise by showing that for most people, losses loom larger than gains (Kahneman and Tversky 1979).

Role of Expertise

Both types of internal learning require some knowledge of the base domain, the one from which marketers hope consumers draw knowledge. How does the extent of consumer knowledge in the base domain affect learning and comprehension of the RNP, and, in turn, the evaluation of the RNP? One could imagine that consumers who are experts in the base domain will find it easier to comprehend the innovative features of the RNP because they are able to process more information and understand it more quickly. Research shows that this is not the case (Moreau, Lehmann, and Markman 2001). Indeed, compared with novices, experts in the base domain are less likely to comprehend innovative features and perceive products as less beneficial. As a result, experts had lower preferences for the product as compared to novices. The reason for this outcome is that the experts' knowledge is entrenched in existing domains and therefore is less flexible when being transferred to other domains. When the product at hand is only incrementally new (thus stays within the product category in which consumers have significant prior knowledge) then expertise helps increase comprehension, appreciation, and preference.

When consumers have high prior knowledge in the base domain, they often incorrectly generalize from that knowledge and assume they know how to use the RNP properly (Wood and Lynch 2002). Marketers need to jolt experts by demonstrating that there is a substantial change represented in the new product, one that significantly diverges from current standards. This can be done superficially (although it must be very clear) with a new design or different packaging. The purpose is to communicate to experts that their knowledge may be obsolete when it comes to an RNP.

Expertise in the new domain (post purchase) is very important to loyalty, as it may increase cognitive switching costs. This is because experts' knowledge structures are entrenched and may be difficult to change, so marketers may attempt to capitalize on these switching costs by increasing the depth of consumer knowledge after purchase, thereby turning novices into experts in the new domain (Moreau, Lehmann, and Markman 2001).

Learning Costs

Learning about the exciting innovative features of an RNP may come at a cost to consumers because they may need to expend time and effort (mainly cognitive but sometimes physical) in order to understand how to use the product. Marketers should realize that the perceived learning costs (rather than the actual ones) play a significant role in shaping preferences for RNPs. When an RNP is especially innovative and complex, its exciting features my actually reduce product evaluation and preference because consumers may infer that higher learning costs are required. Moreover, the negative effect of the novel features on evaluation can persist even after consumers are given explicit information about the benefits of these features (Mukherjee and Hoyer 2001). Thus, a clear challenge to marketers is to reduce perceived learning costs

Demonstrations of a product, both live (a chef uses a new appliance at Williams-Sonoma) and virtual (watching a video that shows how the product works) can reduce the perceived learning costs because consumers can easily see how the product is being used and better understand its benefits (Wood and Moreau 2006). Clearly, when the demonstration is live consumers are able to ask questions and receive more tailored information. Consumers can also try the product themselves. When the Segway was introduced, many consumers did not understand how exactly this vehicle makes turns and goes forward or backward. Yet these issues were easily understood once people tried the product. Demonstrations, however, may not increase preference if customers do not find the novel features easy to use or desirable.

Research shows that while consumers often claim they want more features and capabilities before they purchase a product (i.e., consumers focus on the desirable aspects of the product), they often do not use many of the innovative features. This may be because the new features are more difficult to use than consumers thought (Thompson, Hamilton, and Rust 2005). Put differently, consumers generally give less weight to usability when they are about to purchase the product, and instead focus on why the product is good (thinking about the product more abstractly). Postpurchase, usability becomes increasingly more important component.

Another significant cost for consumers is the loss of benefits related to adopting a new product (Gourville 2006). Even for highly innovative RNPs that define new product categories, competition from existing products might still be significant. One reason that consumers may feel that their losses from not using the old products are greater and more significant than their gains from using the new product. These losses are often related to convenience (no need to change behavior); familiarity; comfort; and perhaps even safety (consumers know the old technology works well but may not be sure about the new one).

When promoting an RNP it is important that marketers emphasize ease of use while not withholding benefit information (Mukherjee and Hoyer 2001). Further, it is useful to provide compelling evidence that the product is easy to use. This could be accomplished by testimonials by real people who have used the product and found it easy to master. However, and especially when products are complex, benefit information is very important because it can reverse the negative effect of the perceived learning costs on evaluation and preference. One way to reduce these "complexity expectations" (defined by Wood and Moreau [2006] as ease of use, learning time, and learning difficulty) is with demonstrations in high-involvement sales channels such as online forums or stores frequented by the target market.

Role of Uncertainty

Consumers experience greater uncertainty when estimating the benefits of an RNP compared with those of an INP (Hoeffler 2003). This uncertainty is a key issue in the acceptance of an RNP (Herzenstein et al. 2007; Ziamou 2002). Uncertainty can be associated with a variety of aspects: the product itself, customer needs and behavior, and market reaction (i.e., the development of complementary products).

Product-related uncertainty is often derived from unclear benefits (can the electric car really drive forty miles on one gallon of gas without recharging?). Companies that can alleviate product-related uncertainties in their communication should be able to increase adoption (Ziamou 2002). If the product is introduced long before it is available in the market, then communication that encourages consumers to think about the outcome of using the product (benefits) can be effective in reducing performance uncertainty, bolstering positive feelings, and enhancing behavioral intentions to purchase the product (Castaño et al. 2008). Closer to the adoption, however, communication has to change and encourage consumers to think about the process of using the product. This type of communication has been shown to be effective when consumers are closer to purchase, by reducing the perceived switching costs and affective uncertainties, thereby increasing adoption intentions (Castaño et al. 2008).

Sometimes more information about the features and benefits of the RNP may increase consumers' uncertainty because they will be able to imagine more scenarios in which the RNP might fail, especially for an RNP that is based on a new technology (Ziamou and Ratneswar 2002). The advice for managers is that they should be sensitive to the nature of the technology when determining the amount of information they communicate to consumers regarding novel features.

Social issues related to an RNP may also be a source of uncertainty. Will society at large and consumers' close friends and colleagues appreciate their purchase of an RNP and bolster the users' social status? If the answer is unclear, consumers may be reluctant to adopt the RNP (especially the most innovative ones). For example, the wearable computer, when introduced, received rave reviews for solving problems of pedestrians who wish to use handheld devices while walking. The wearable computer has a headphone with a small screen that is placed directly in front of one eye, leaving the other eye available to watch where one is going. However because this device seemed so unique and different from existing products, it did not catch on and smartphones and other, less novel, handheld devices continue to lead that market. One possible solution to this issue is to get celebrities to endorse RNPs. This can potentially help with contagion processes and enhance social approval.

The second source of uncertainty relates to consumers' perceptions of their own ability to learn. Consumers may not be certain of their ability to master the new innovation (Herzenstein et al. 2007) and may associate high learning costs with the RNP or associate adverse consequences to the outcome of their inability to master it. For example, if consumers have some uncertainty regarding their ability to use an electric car, they may attach severe consequences to it, such as getting into an accident or buying an expensive car that does not really satisfy their needs. These uncertainties can be alleviated with product demonstrations or by communications that encourage product visualization.

The third source of uncertainty relates to the market and the technology's ability to catch on. For example, when the first DVD player was introduced, consumers had to repurchase their entire movie libraries because VHS tapes could not be played on DVD players. Similarly, when the iPod and iTunes were introduced, people had to recreate their music library to fit that format. In both cases, consumers experienced some uncertainty regarding whether indeed all movies will be available on DVD and songs available on iTunes. Because RNPs may require the use of complementary hardware (DVDs) or software (applications for the iPhone that take advantage of its gyroscopes) that is often supplied by an independent third party, then some customers will probably decide to delay their adoption of the RNP until complementary technologies become available and even abundant (Min, Kalwani, Robinson 2006).

In February 2002 Sony developed Blu-ray disc technology in association with nine partners (companies that produce the players). In August 2002 Toshiba announced a competing standard, HD-DVD, and founded its own association. The DVD "war" lasted almost five years with Toshiba formally "losing" in March 2008 when it announced it would close its HD-DVD unit. At that time, the Blu-ray Disc Association had twenty partners, including all the major Hollywood movie studios. During the five years in which both standards were available, many consumers adopted the HD-DVD player, but these consumers will probably need to purchase the Blu-ray player if they wish to continue watching movies in high definition at home. Consumers who decided to wait until one technology emerged as the clear "winner" of this competition are those who experience high market uncertainty, which validated their decision to delay adoption. Research on RNPs supports the outcome of this example and suggests that a dominant product design for an RNP can take years to emerge (Min et al. 2006).

While consumer uncertainty regarding an RNP can be substantial, firms introducing them also experience uncertainties regarding adoption. However, firms are better able to reduce uncertainties related to making adoption decisions because, compared with consumers, firms have access to much more information, such as prelaunch market research and R&D data about the product and its test results (Montaguti et al. 2002).

Conclusion

The first and perhaps most important role of marketing with respect to RNPs is to build awareness for the product. It has been consistently shown that awareness is essential for the success of an RNP (Sorescu, Chandy, and Prabhu 2003; Montaguti et al. 2002). As a general rule, adoption will occur when a perceived relative advantage of an innovation is seen to outweigh any adoption hurdles (Montaguti et al. 2002). The hurdle is expressed in terms of the perceived utility of the new benefits versus the variety of costs consumers are required to expend—actual costs (e.g., related to switching technologies and price of the RNP) and cognitive costs (learning). The advantages of the innovation become clearer to consumers as more information about the RNP becomes available. After adoption, the role of marketing is to help in building brand equity for the RNP and differentiating the product from competitors (Sorescu et al. 2003).

When marketers make decisions regarding the copy of an ad and what type of learning (internal vs. external) to encourage, they must realize that the type of RNP plays an important role. Research on a variety of RNPs suggests that images may be more appropriate in conveying information for hedonic products as consumers can easily visualize themselves using the product, while words can better communicate the advantages of utilitarian products and encourage consumers to engage in mental simulation regarding the use of such products (Feiereisen et al. 2008).

In terms of positioning and the aspects of RNPs that should be promoted, there is no clear advice. Two schools of thoughts exist: Some researchers find that firms should only emphasize product innovativeness when it relates to the relevant concepts of product advantage, and existing technologies should be used to enhance customer understanding (Catalone, Chan, and Cui 2006). Put differently, RNPs should be positioned as a leap forward in existing product categories. Other researchers, however, suggest that the positioning of an RNP should be based on the radicalness of the technology and thus encourage the creation of new product categories (Friar and Balachandra 1999). To appeal to current customers who are familiar with the basic applications of the new technologies, companies should employ expansion strategies and provide new applications. These strategies suggest that RNPs should be positioned as creators of new product categories.

In conclusion, in employing a consumer perspective to evaluate communication decisions for RNPs, it is clear that such decisions should be based on the type of RNP, the features that marketers communicate, and the consumers' learning strategies marketers wish to foster.

References

Barton, M.E., and L. Komatsu. 1989. "Defining Features of Natural Kinds and Artifacts." *Journal of Psycholinguistic Research* 18: 433–447.

Bayus, B. 2008. "Understanding Customer Needs." In *Handbook of Technology and Innovation Management,* ed. S. Shane, 115–41. West Sussex, UK: Wiley.

Calantone, R.J., K. Chan, and A.S. Cui. 2006. "Decomposing Product Innovativeness and Its Effects on New Product Success." *Journal of Product Innovation Management* 23: 408–21.

Carpenter, G.S., and K. Nakamoto. 1989. "Consumer Preference Formation and Pioneering Advantage." *Journal of Marketing Research* 26: 285–98.

Castaño, R., M. Sujan, M. Kacker, and H. Sujan. 2008. "Managing Consumer Uncertainty in the Adoption of New Products: Temporal Distance and Mental Simulation." *Journal of Marketing Research* 45: 320–36.

Clement, C.A., and D. Gentner. 1991. "Systematicity as a Selection Constraint in Analogical Mapping." *Cognitive Science* 15: 89–132.

Dahl, D.W., and S. Hoeffler. 2004. "Visualizing the Self: Exploring the Potential Benefits and Drawbacks for New Product Evaluation." *Journal of Product Innovation Management* 21: 259–67.

El Houssi, A.A., K.P.N. Morel, and E.J. Hultink. 2005. "Effectively Communicating New Product Benefits to Consumers: The Use of Analogy Versus Literal Similarity." *Advances in Consumer Research* 32: 554–59.

Falkenhainer, B., K.D. Forbus, and D. Gentner. 1989. "The Structure-Mapping Engine: Algorithm and Examples." *Artificial Intelligence* 41: 1–63.

Feiereisen, S., V. Wong, and A.J. Broderick. 2008. "Analogies and Mental Simulations in Learning for Really New Products: The Role of Visual Attention." *Journal of Product Innovation Management* 25: 593–607.

Florian, J.E. 1994. "Stripes Do Not a Zebra Make, or Do They? Conceptual and Perceptual Information in Inductive Inferences." *Developmental Psychology* 30: 88–101.

Friar, J., and Balachandra R. 1999. "Spotting the Customer for Emerging Technologies." *Research-Technology Management* 42: 37–43.

Gourville, J.T. 2006. "Eager Sellers and Stony Buyers: Understanding the Psychology of New-Product Adoption." *Harvard Business Review* 84: 98–106.

Govers, C.M.P. 1994. "What and How of Quality Function Deployment (QFD)." *Proceedings of the Eighth International Working Seminar on Production Economics*, Innsbruck, Austria.

Gregan-Paxton, J., J.D. Hibbard, F.F. Brunel, and P. Azar. 2002. "'So That's What That Is': Examining the Impact of Analogy on Consumers' Knowledge Development for Really New Products." *Psychology and Marketing* 19: 533–50.

Gregan-Paxton, J., S. Hoeffler, and M. Zhao. 2005. "When Categorization is Ambiguous: Factors That Facilitate the Use of a Multiple Category Inference Strategy." *Journal of Consumer Psychology* 15: 127–40.

Gregan-Paxton, J., and D.R. John. 1997. "Consumer Learning by Analogy: A Model of Internal Knowledge Transfer. *Journal of Consumer Research* 24: 266–84.

Hauser, J.R., and D. Clausing. 1988. "The House of Quality." *Harvard Business Review* 63–73. Available at http://www.csuchico.edu/~jtrailer/HOQ.pdf, accessed February 26, 2011.

Herzberg, F. 1968. "One More Time: How Do You Motivate Employees?" *Harvard Business Review* 46: 53–62.

Herzberg, F., B. Mausner, and B. Snyderman. 1959. *The Motivation to Work.* New York: Wiley.

Herzenstein, M., S.S. Posavac, and J.J. Brakus. 2007. "Adoption of New and Really New Products: The Effects of Self-regulation Systems and Risk Salience." *Journal of Marketing Research* 44: 251–60.

Hoeffler, S. 2003. "Measuring Preferences for Really New Products." *Journal of Marketing Research* 40: 406–20.

Huiskonen J., and T. Pirtillä. 1998. "Sharpening Logistics Customer Service Strategy Planning by Applying Kano's Quality Element Classification." *International Journal of Product Economics* 56: 253–60.

Kahneman, D., and A. Tversky. 1979. "Prospect Theory: An Analysis of Decision Making Under Risk." *Econometrica* 47: 18–36.

Kano, N., S. Tsuji, N. Seraku, and F. Takahashi. 1984. "Attractive Quality and Must-Be Quality." *Hinshitsu: The Journal of Japanese Society for Quality Control* 14: 39–48.

Lehmann, D.R. 1994. "Characteristics of 'Really' New Products." Paper presented at the Marketing Science Institute Conference, Boston, September 29–30.

Macrae, C.N., G.V. Bodenhausen, and A.B. Milne. 1995. "The Dissection of Selection in Person Perception: Inhibitory Processes in Social Stereotyping." *Journal of Personality and Social Psychology* 69: 397–407.

Markman, A.B., and D.L. Medin. 1995. "Similarity and Alignment in Choice." *Organizational Behavior and Human Decision Processes* 63: 117–30.

Matan, A., and S. Carey. 2001. "Developmental Changes within the Core of Artifact Concepts." *Cognition* 78: 1–26.

Matzler, K., and H.H. Hinterhuber. 1998. "How to Make Product Development Projects More Successful by Integrating Kano's Model of Customer Satisfaction into Quality Function Deployment." *Technovation* 18: 25–38.

Min, S., M.U. Kalwani, and W.T. Robinson. 2006. "Market Pioneer and Early Follower Survival Risks: A Contingency Analysis of Really New Versus Incrementally New Product Markets." *Journal of Marketing* 70: 15–33.

Montaguti, E., S. Kuester, and T.S. Robertson. 2002. "Entry Strategy for Radical Product Innovations: A Conceptual Model and Propositional Inventory." *International Journal of Research in Marketing* 19: 21–42.

Moreau, C.P., and W.D. Dahl. 2005. "Designing the Solution: The Impact of Constraints on Consumers' Creativity." *Journal of Consumer Research* 32: 13–22.

Moreau, C.P., S. Hoeffler, and C. Kubowicz-Malhotra. 2010. "Building Evolutionary Bridges for Revolutionary Products." Working paper, Owen Graduate School of Management, Vanderbilt University.

Moreau, C.P., D.R. Lehmann, and A.B. Markman. 2001. "Entrenched Knowledge Structures and Consumer Response to New Products." *Journal of Marketing Research* 38: 14–29.

Moreau, C.P., A.B. Markman, and D.R. Lehmann. 2001. "'What Is It?' Categorization Flexibility and Consumers' Responses to Really New Products." *Journal of Consumer Research* 27: 489–98.

Mukherjee, A., and W.D. Hoyer. 2001. "The Effect of Novel Attributes on Product Evaluation." *Journal of Consumer Research* 28: 462–72.

Roehm, M.L., and B. Sternthal. 2001. "The Moderating Effect of Knowledge and Resources on the Persuasive Impact of Analogies." *Journal of Consumer Research* 28: 257–72.

Scholtes, P. 1997. *The Leaders' Handbook.* New York: McGraw-Hill.

Sherman, S.J., R.B. Cialdini, D.F. Schwartzman, and K.D. Reynolds. 1985. "Imagining Can Heighten or Lower the Perceived Likelihood of Contracting a Disease: The Mediating Effect of Ease of Imagery." *Personality and Social Psychology Bulletin,* 11: 118–27.

Sorescu, A.B., R.K. Chandy, and J.C. Prabhu. 2003. "Sources and Financial Consequences of Radical Innovation: Insights from Pharmaceuticals." *Journal of Marketing* 67: 82–102.

Stone, B. 2010. "Live Blogging the iPad Product Announcement." *New York Times,* January 27. Available at http://bits.blogs.nytimes.com/2010/01/27/live-blogging-the-apple-product-announcement/, accessed February 26, 2011.

Sujan, M. 1985. "Consumer Knowledge: Effects on Evaluation Strategies Mediating Consumer Judgments." *Journal of Consumer Research* 12: 31–46.

Thompson, D.V., R.W. Hamilton, and P.K. Petrova. 2009. "When Mental Simulation Hinders Behavior: The Effects of Process-Oriented Thinking on Decision Difficulty and Performance." *Journal of Consumer Research* 36: 562–74.

Thompson, D.V., R.W. Hamilton, and R.T. Rust. 2005. "Feature Fatigue: When Product Capabilities Become Too Much of a Good Thing." *Journal of Marketing Research* 42: 431–42.

Urban, G.L., B.D. Weinberg, and J.R. Hauser. 1996. "Premarket Forecasting of Really New Products." *Journal of Marketing* 60: 47–60.

Wood, S.L., and J.G. Lynch, Jr. 2002. "Prior Knowledge and Complacency in New Product Learning." *Journal of Consumer Research* 29: 416–26.

Wood, S.L., and P.C. Moreau. 2006. "From Fear to Loathing? How Emotion Influences the Evaluation and Early Use of Innovations." *Journal of Marketing* 70: 44–57.

Zeithaml, V.A., L.L. Berry, and A. Parasuraman. 1996. "The Behavioral Consequences of Service Quality." *Journal of Marketing* 60: 31–46.

Zhao, M., S. Hoeffler, and D.W. Dahl. 2009. "The Role of Imagination-Focused Visualization on New Product Evaluation." *Journal of Marketing Research* 46: 46–55.

Ziamou, P. 2002. "Commercializing New Technologies: Consumers' Response to a New Interface." *Journal of Product Innovation Management* 19: 365–74.

Ziamou, P., and S. Ratneswar. 2002. "Promoting Consumer Adoption of High-Technology Products: Is More Information Always Better?" *Journal of Consumer Psychology* 12: 341–51.

3

Consumer Tunnel Vision and Implications for Managing the Marketing Mix

Steven S. Posavac, David M. Sanbonmatsu, and Shailendra Pratap Jain

Although managers and academic consumer psychologists often have differing priorities, one common interest is learning how to better predict and influence consumers' choices. In recent years consumer psychologists have made great strides in understanding how people make judgments and decisions in increasingly complex and data-rich environments. Each consumer need can be met with an array of products and services that compete for share of consumers' wallets. A vast amount of information is available about consumer options, and the total pool of information is increasing as social media augment an already cluttered media space in offering product and brand information.

Consumer psychologists have shown that a key strategy people use to manage their information-rich worlds is to base judgments and decisions on only a small subset of the available information. By efficiently forming evaluations and making choices based on a limited amount of information, while ignoring or not processing other information, consumers can successfully complete a host of tasks that compete for limited mental resources. This selective use of information by consumers is akin to tunnel vision, with consumers often selectively considering and using information, which affects their judgments and decisions.

Our understanding of consumers as selective processors of information has developed exponentially in recent years. Indeed, researchers have been making a great deal of progress understanding how consumers' tendency to use limited information in their judgments affects product evaluations and choice (e.g., Larrick 2009; Sanbonmatsu et al. 1998; Tanner and Carlson 2009; Tversky and Koehler 1994; Windschitl et al. 2008). Unfortunately, this increase in theoretical knowledge has not yet been translated into comprehensive prescriptive advice for marketing managers.

The purpose of this chapter is to summarize what we know about the consumer as a selective information processor, and what this tendency toward tunnel vision means for those who are on the front lines of applied consumer behavior. We first review the growing literature on selective processing and discuss how and why consumers tend to think in this way. We then cover a host of important consumer behaviors that are driven by selective processing, and move on to suggest specific tactics whereby marketers can apply tools to drive selective consideration of their brands, and accordingly capture additional sales. The general rule that guides all of our specific tactical suggestions is that consumers are typically happy to consider a very small subset of available information when making consumption-related judgments and choices. If marketers can influence what information consumers consider when making product judgments, they can accordingly also have a powerful impact on the choices that are made.

Selective Processing: Why Consumers Consider a Fraction of the Available Information and What the Consequences Are

Navigating everyday life requires making many judgments that guide subsequent behavioral decisions. For example, if the room one is in feels too warm, one must figure out why the temperature is elevated to take some action to remedy the problem. For most of us, our first guess for why a room is too warm would be that the thermostat is turned up. With this hypothesis in mind, it is straightforward to check the thermostat to see if our hypothesis is correct. If the evidence is consistent with the hypothesis, that is, if the thermostat is indeed turned up, the action to turn the thermostat down is obvious. If the thermostat is not turned up, another hypothesis regarding the cause of the high temperature needs to be generated and investigated.

This simple example of trying to discern why a room feels too hot demonstrates a common process by which people navigate their everyday lives, including their consumption-related decision making. People often have to figure out whether a given possibility is a good one, whether the possibility is an answer to a problem such as figuring out why the room is too warm, or how to address a consumer need. When confronted with a judgment problem (Why is the room too hot? Which detergent should I purchase? Will I enjoy driving this car?), a focal hypothesis often emerges. When considering running shoes, for example, a single brand often becomes the focus of consideration because of an advertisement that is seen, or a display at the store, or one's memory of prior consumption. Once a given brand has become focal, consumers typically then test the hypothesis that the brand will suit their needs. If consumers conclude that the hypothesis is true, a choice is often made.

Generally, researchers have shown that selective hypothesis testing often governs consumer judgment and choice (Posavac, Kardes, and Brakus 2010; Sanbonmatsu et al. 1998). Usually consumers start with the assumption that an option under consideration is a good one. Indeed, most products available are decent at least at performing the core function for which they were designed. For example, all brands of laundry detergents clean clothes, and all cheddar cheese brands alleviate hunger. Once a given hypothesis is identified (e.g., "Tide would be a great choice"), consumers typically search for evidence that would support that a given hypothesis is correct. Evidence may come from memory, including recollections of prior consumption experiences (including those of family and friends), as well as information from marketing communications, and contextual information such as brand name, packaging, and signage. If evidence supporting the focal hypothesis is found, either with regard to specific information or more general positive feelings, often the consumer concludes that it is correct. A consumer considering Tide might recall that it has worked in the past and that the brand is trusted, and thus will choose to purchase the brand.

Once a focal hypothesis has been identified, several potential biases enter into the process by which consumers determine if the hypothesis is true. Consumers typically search for evidence that would be present if the hypothesis were true. In addition, biases in the interpretation of information (Carlson, Meloy, and Lieb 2009; Meyvis and Janiszewski 2002), as well as in the aggregation of the evidence, tends to lead consumers to perceive focal hypotheses to be correct (Ehrich and Irwin 2005; Schulz-Hardt et al. 2000). Thus, when a given possibility is identified as a focal hypothesis, that hypothesis is at a tremendous advantage of being perceived as the best hypothesis (Fox and Levav 2000). For example, Sanbonmatsu, Posavac, and Stasny (1997) demonstrated that simply being considered first greatly increased the favorability with which a focal job candidate was perceived, as well as increasing the perceived likelihood that he or she would be hired.

Why do consumers think about their options selectively? Consumers must address myriad needs, which typically may be met with several alternatives, each of which have multiple attributes. For a consumer to make the best decision in line with his or her preferences, all of the options should be carefully compared, and the option that offers the best combination of attributes should be chosen. For example, to be confident in making the best choice, a runner buying shoes might consider brand reputation, durability, cushioning, fit, weight, and so on, for all of the possible shoe options. If our runner considers all of her options along the range of attributes, she is quite likely to be happy with her choice because the shoes will serve her well. Thinking carefully about all options in this matter is likely to lead to better choices than is a selective strategy of focusing on one possibility at a time (e.g., deciding if an initially considered shoe is above threshold, then rendering choice). Unfortunately, although comparative processing is very likely to yield a choice that matches preferences, thinking in this way is very mentally demanding. Being more selective allows individuals to conserve energy, and to efficiently navigate their daily tasks.

Although selective processing is quite efficient, thinking in this way can sometimes pose the risk that a suboptimal option will be accepted because the range of available evidence has not been sufficiently considered. The problem is that individuals tend to assume that an initial hypothesis is true, and search for evidence that would verify the hypothesis. Thus, an initially considered hypothesis, whether regarding the temperature of a room or the worthiness of a brand, is at a competitive advantage because if evidence supportive of the hypothesis can be found, the hypothesis is likely to be perceived as correct or best.

Of course, not all hypotheses that emerge as focal are chosen. Even though an initially considered hypothesis is likely to be confirmed given the availability of at least some supportive evidence, individuals typically conclude that a focal hypothesis is false if evidence is hard to come by. In this case, individuals are likely to reject that hypothesis and consider another. One of the coauthors once attempted to find a restaurant in a new city based on the virtual recommendation of a GPS unit, and formed the hypothesis that the suggested restaurant would be a good dinner choice. However, upon discovering the poor neighborhood in which the restaurant was located, as well as its filthy exterior, the hypothesis was soundly rejected and another dinner option was generated.

Overall, selective information processing is an efficient strategy that often leads to good behavioral decisions. Accordingly, individuals often base myriad judgments and choices, including consumer choices, on selective processing. If we understand these basic mechanisms and tendencies in human thought, we can predict how consumers will behave in given contexts and develop strategies for influencing them more effectively. This chapter reviews a variety of consumer behaviors that have been shown to be driven by tunnel vision induced by selective processing, then discusses how tools available to marketers may be used to leverage consumers' selective processing tendencies to improve firm performance.

Selective Processing and Consumers' Product Judgments

Consumers' tendency to think selectively affects their judgments and choices when they consider a single brand. Often consumers' focus is directed to one brand, for example by an advertisement, a sales promotion offer, the brand being highlighted at the point of purchase (e.g., if the brand is placed on an end-cap), or offered at a single-brand store. Judgments of single brands are often governed by a brand positivity effect, in which overly favorable evaluations of a focal brand result when consumers consider the merits of the brand in isolation, without comparison to alternatives (Posavac et al. 2004). When consumers think selectively in this fashion about a brand that has become the focus of attention, bias in information gathering and interpretation often causes judgments of the focal brand to be more favorable than the evidence justifies. That is, consumers often misperceive a focal brand as being of particularly high utility because they fail to consider how the focal brand compares against other options.

As an example of this process, consider a consumer in need of Spanish olives. A consumer walking down a grocery isle is likely to first notice a brand that stands out, either due to optimal shelf placement (e.g., at eye level), or because the brand has been assigned a large area on the shelf. Suppose the consumer fixates on Casillas brand olives because they are salient. The consumer's consideration is likely to focus on Casillas as the consumer evaluates the hypothesis that Casillas would be a good choice. Available evidence in this case would consist of cues that the consumer expects would be related to brand quality, such as visual cues (e.g., if the olives are green with bright pimento, they must be good), a legitimate-sounding brand name, and attractive packaging. If the focal brand is perceived to meet some threshold for utility, the consumer is likely to choose the brand. Note that selective processing often precludes other brands from being considered, even though they may be fine choices that would meet the consumer's needs. Often, as long as there is some favorable evidence regarding the focal brand, it will appear to be particularly good in a way that the evidence does not really justify. Brand positivity effects have been demonstrated in a variety of categories; from hotels, to televisions, to shoes, and laundry detergents.

When Is Selective Processing Particularly Likely to Affect Consumer Choice?

Although the process by which selective consideration can lend competitive advantage to a brand is common, consumer research has discovered a set of factors that determine when this effect will be more or less powerful. One of these factors is consumers' *initial attitude* toward an option that comes to be the focus of attention (Posavac, Sanbonmatsu, and Ho 2002). When consumers are considering the merits of a given option, important input comes from experiences they have had with the product and information they have gathered about the product from sources such as their own experiences with the product, advertisements, comments of friends, and so on. If consumers have an existing favorable attitude toward an option, selective focus on that option is likely to lead to that option being perceived as even more favorable, often well beyond the scope of reality. In contrast, a disliked option is very unlikely to benefit from selective consideration. In fact, when consumers consider disliked products, their dislike is likely to become stronger. This is an important tendency, because it shows that facilitating selective consideration is a strategy to augment product development and marketing communications, not a replacement.

Although selective processing may often steer choice in favor of an initially considered option, consumers with *expertise* in a given domain are typically much less likely to be affected in this way (Posavac et al. 2005). Consumers gain expertise by making a decision in a given category multiple times, and thus are likely to come to know the options well and be well calibrated regarding the importance of the various attributes of each alternative. Accordingly, experts are much more likely than nonexperts to be able to generate multiple alternatives, and make trade-offs between alternatives that are immune from context effects. Thus, expert consumers (e.g., those who make frequent repeat purchases within a category, i.e., industrial buyers) are much less likely to be susceptible to selective processing manipulations. Posavac et al. (2005), for example, reported that the hotel preferences and choices of consumers with high expertise regarding travel were much less affected by selective processing than were those of nonexperts.

Research in a variety of contexts has shown that selective processing is consumers' default tendency when assessing options (Wang and Wyer 2002). However, the judgmental context can induce comparative processing. When consumers are either explicitly instructed to compare alternatives, or they write down their opinions regarding several alternatives prior to making a decision, they are much more likely to make the necessary comparisons between options that lead to bias-free choice (Posavac et al. 2004; Posavac et al. 2009).

Predecisional Distortion

One way that selective processing can lead an initially considered option to come to be perceived more favorably than warranted occurs when one choice option emerges as an early leader in the choice process (Russo, Meloy, and Medvec 1998; Carlson, Meloy, and Russo 2006). Often the early leader enjoys a substantial advantage because consumers interpret product information in a biased fashion that supports the leader. Specifically, consumers' evaluation of the evidence is distorted in favor of an option that comes, for whatever reason, to the forefront when consumers are weighing choice options. With the early leader benefiting from being the focus of selective consideration, consumers are often likely to ultimately conclude that the early leader is the best choice. This is one reason why a pioneering brand, or the first brand to enter a new market, is at a tremendous advantage (Kardes et al. 1993).

Many men shopping with women for engagement rings find that a ring considered early in the search process ends up becoming the selection, no matter how many additional rings are considered or jewelry stores are visited. This tendency is quite ubiquitous because of predecisional distortion—one ring from one store quickly emerges as the leader, and subsequent processing of information proceeds in such a way as to make the focal ring appear particularly striking. The implication of research in predecisional distortion for managers, of course, is that marketing dollars spent in the service of one's brand being identified as a leader early in the choice process are likely to pay significant dividends.

Omission Neglect

Consumers rarely have complete information about a product when making a purchase. For example, marketing communications often present attributes that favor the promoted brand, while leaving other attributes unmentioned. Consumers typically base their product judgments on the basis of the information that is presented (e.g., in an advertisement or by a salesperson), while neglecting to consider information that has been omitted. Often judgments are formed that are far too extreme when consumers fail to account for information that is unknown. Indeed, limitations in the evidence regarding a product are all too often not recognized (Kardes et al. 2006; Muthukrishnan and Ramaswami 1999; Sanbonmatsu et al. 2003).

The omission neglect tendency is great news for the marketing manager responsible for a product that is less than perfect. Given that consumers tend to selectively consider information that is presented while neglecting missing information, marketers can often drive product evaluations by presenting the subset of information about their products that is most favorable. In general, consumers do not recognize what they do not know and will happily form product judgments and make choices based on the information that marketers give them. For example, marketers can often successfully differentiate on a feature or features on which their product has a competitive advantage. Most consumers will judge the product based on the information that they are given and not account for what is unknown. Thus it is often relatively easy for marketers to compensate for a product's weakness on one dimension by highlighting a strength on another.

There are some important limitations to the omission neglect tendency. When consumers are either expert with regard to a product or its category, or missing information becomes more obvious (e.g., if consumers consider their criteria before receiving a marketing communication), their awareness of missing information increases and they form more moderate judgments (Kardes et al. 2006). Thus, marketers should pay close attention to the communications of their rivals. If a key competitor is presenting advertisements that selectively discuss attributes that are favorable to the competitor, the competitor can be undercut with a strategy of making the previously missing information conspicuous. By educating consumers in this way, they are much less likely to be influenced by the competitor's marketing efforts.

Consumers' tendency to fail to recognize missing information is not limited to product attributes. Indeed, consumers often do not realize when consideration sets from which they are making choices are missing options that may well be preferred (Kardes et al. 2002). The implication for marketers is that consumers' consideration sets are quite fluid, and that the potential exists to substantially modify which options consumers consider by strengthening the association between a given brand and the category to which it belongs (Posavac et al. 2001), and by framing specific consideration sets for consumers in marketing communications.

Perceptions of Relationships Between Attributes

It is important to note that in addition to affecting consumers' judgments of products and product attributes, selective processing can also influence consumers' perceptions of the relationship between attributes. For example, consumers often perceive that there is a stronger relationship between a product's price and quality than is objectively true. When deciding how much to spend on a product, consumers often guess how well price predicts a product's quality because consumers want a good product, but not to overspend. Thus, when consumers perceive that there is a strong relationship between price and quality in a given category, they typically are much more willing to pay (Cronley et al. 2005).

Selective processing affects these inferences because consumers usually focus on examples of products that conform to their preexisting beliefs when inferring how good a predictor of quality price is in a given consumption context. Selective consideration of poor products that are inexpensive and strong products with a high price tag then leads consumers to have further exaggerated beliefs about the strength of the price-quality correlation (Kardes et al. 2004). Thus, overall, consumers typically dramatically overestimate how strongly related products' prices and quality are.

Marketers can leverage this process in two ways. First, given the typical belief that a high price signals quality, in some contexts marketers can spur demand simply by using higher prices on products. Second, managers may sometimes benefit by manipulating consumers' perceptions of the strength of the price-quality relationship in a given category (Cronley et al. 2005; Kardes et al. 2004). A retailer, for example, may want to encourage purchases of higher-end products due to their higher margins. In this case, managers should create a buying context that facilitates consumers' selective consideration of brands that is consistent with the expectation that prices and quality are strongly related. Specifically, brands should be rank ordered as a function of price (e.g., so that it is easy for consumers to find examples of low price/low quality products as well as high price/high quality products) in a cognitively busy environment that contributes to high need for closure (e.g., instill time pressure or create a distracting physical environment). In other circumstances marketers may wish to foster a perception of more independence between price and quality, for example when trying to move overstock of low-end items. In this case, products should be displayed randomly with regard to price, and consumers should be given ample time to shop in a distraction-free environment.

General Managerial Take-Aways

Research in selective processing has produced the clear conclusion that consumers' tunnel vision tendencies contribute to a "first-come-first-confirmed" process in consumer decision making. That is, consumers do not always give equal consideration to all alternatives, and those alternatives that come to receive early consideration in the judgment and choice process are much more likely to be chosen compared to other alternatives that do not emerge as focal options. This tendency is not limited to choice alternatives such as specific brands, but also to theories about relationships between consumer-relevant variables (e.g., price and quality).

The advantage brands get by being considered early in the judgment process is particularly likely to affect consumer behavior when alternatives are not salient or known. When there is not a crystallized consideration set before the judgment process begins, an alternative that has become focal will guide consumers' choice processes such that the focal brand is likely to be misperceived as being more favorable than objectively justified (i.e., versus other options within the category, which the consumer never considered); and is more likely to be purchased. Thus, when alternatives are not salient in the decision context and the consumer is less than expert, selective processing is very likely to determine consumers' perceptions and choices.

Five Points of Brand Strategy

When selective processing is likely to direct consumers' choices, marketers should be aware of five consequences relevant to their strategic planning. First, *it is critically important to be considered early in the decision process.* To the extent that one's brand is the focus of consumers' attention, it is at an advantage with regard to being chosen because consumers' judgments of the brand are likely to be quite favorable. Moreover, as long as consumers are happy with the first brand that is considered, competitors may never cross consumers' minds.

Second, *it is important to measure brand accessibility compared to other brands in the category throughout the product life cycle.* Because the accessibility of a brand, and accordingly its likelihood of being the focus of consumers' tunnel vision, is so impactful in driving consumer choice, it is essential for marketers to monitor how their brand stacks up against competitors on this key dimension. The best measure of brand awareness is likely to be unaided recall (versus recognition), because those brands that are most strongly linked to the product category are most likely to be considered first.

Third, *a general shift in communications emphasis from building knowledge regarding features and benefits toward building brand accessibility may be warranted, especially when alternatives aren't salient or well-known.* Although experts do a good job of considering a wide range of options, consumers are generally nonexperts with regard to most categories. Thus, money spent building awareness is likely to pay back with bountiful interest due to the brand positivity effect.

Fourth, *when a brand is underperforming, a strategy of facilitating selective consideration, as opposed to extensively revising the brand, should be considered.* Such a strategy is much cheaper, and can be accomplished much more quickly, than rebranding. Moreover, an awareness-building strategy poses a much lower risk of alienating core customers who typically resent when favorite brands change their meaning.

Finally, a fifth implication is that *the benefits of pursuing comparative advertising should be weighed against the risks that such advertising increases the accessibility of one's competitor.* If a competitor is sure to be considered because it is established and well-known, is a category share leader, and/or possesses a high share of voice in the media space, this risk of comparative ads is not a problem because awareness of the competitor is likely to be high in any event. If, however, consumers are likely to think of a given brand first, using comparative advertisements carries the risk of making competitors focal and actually lowering purchase likelihood of the target brand, no matter what is said in the advertisement.

What Makes a Brand Focal?

Given that consumers tend to process information selectively, and that brands that receive early consideration in the choice process are at tremendous advantage to ultimately be chosen, it is of clear importance for managers to understand what leads a brand to receive selective consideration. If we have a solid grasp on what the determinants are of whether a brand will become the focus of consumers' tunnel vision, it is possible to make decisions regarding management of the marketing mix that can leverage consumers' selective processing tendencies.

One key factor that can lead to a brand becoming focal at the time of decision making is its *salience*. The salience of alternatives is a property of the decision context, and a brand is salient to the extent that it is prominent in the decision-making environment. Brands that are salient jump out of the background and demand the attention of the consumer. For example, simply being placed on an end-cap increases the salience of a brand and increases its sales. Packaging can contribute to brand salience if it is unique, or bright, or new (e.g., themed holiday packaging). Point-of-purchase materials such as displays and signage also increase salience. Aspects of communications elements can draw consumers' attention as well increasing brand salience (e.g., using a black-and-white television advertisement when other advertisements are in color, novel promotions).

The *accessibility* of a brand refers to how strongly the brand is represented in a consumer's memory. Accessibility is important because accessible brands are likely to be generated from memory when a consumer considers a product category. For example, if Diet Coke is accessible for a given consumer, when she is thirsty the possibility of a Diet Coke will come to mind very quickly. Accessibility is a property of the consumer and is facilitated by both the recency and frequency of activation of the brand. That is, brands that have been recently considered (e.g., due to a recently seen advertisement or recent consumption) or are frequently activated (e.g., are often chosen or are supported by heavy advertising) are accessible. Both recency of consideration and frequent consideration contribute to a strong association between the brand and category in the mind of the consumer.

Managing the Marketing Mix: Tactical Considerations

At one level, the implications for marketing tactics are clear. Managers should strive to increase the *salience* of their brands and brand communications, and increase the strength of association between their brands and the relevant superordinate category to maximize the *accessibility* of their brand. How should managers attempt this? What are the best tactics? The next sections review options in the marketers' toolbox that are effective in leveraging consumer tunnel vision to drive organizational performance.

Advertising Tactics

Both the salience and accessibility of brands can be increased through advertising. With regard to salience, the potential upside of being considered early in the decision process may justify spending to maintain scheduling continuity versus buying pulses several times a year. With a continuous schedule, consumers are likely to receive brand messages close to the time when they are making purchase decisions, and are accordingly likely to consider the target brand when they find that they need to make a purchase from a given category because of the brand's salience (Ephron 1998).

Brand accessibility can be increased by enhancing the depth of processing of the link between a brand and a category (Fazio, Herr, and Powell 1992). That is, when consumers are devoting attention to the brand-category link, and thinking in deep ways about it, the link becomes very strong very quickly. Consumers can be led to deeply process brand-category links through the use of mystery advertisements in which the brand being advertised as well as the relevant category are not clear for the majority of the advertisement. Only at the end of the advertisement, when viewers' attention is spurred by the ambiguity of the advertisement, are the brand and category revealed. To the extent that the advertisement is well done with regard to creative, consumers develop strong brand-category associations from mystery advertisements because their processing of the brand and category is at a very deep level. An example of a mystery advertisement that was very successful was Monster. com's "When I Grow Up" Super Bowl advertisement, which put the company on the map. In this black-and-white ad, children say a series of increasingly preposterous career-related statements such, as, "When I grow up I want to file all day. I want to claw my way all the way up to middle management. I want to be replaced on a whim. I want to have a brown nose." At the end of the ad, the text, "What did you want to be?" appears, followed by, "There's a better job out there—Monster.com." This advertisement was very successful because it introduced Monster.com as a job search firm. Although very little was achieved for the brand besides establishing awareness, the ad was a great success because at the inception of a brand the most important goal of marketing is to develop awareness.

A second way that advertisements can drive brand accessibility is by leading consumers to repeatedly link the brand to its category (Posavac et al. 2001). For example, one of the most valuable brand symbols to emerge in recent years is the Aflac duck. Aflac advertisements use a variety of creative executions with the primary goal of prompting consumers to rehearse the notion that Aflac offers supplementary insurance, and that supplementary insurance pays bills that regular insurance does not pay if one gets injured. The advertisements feature the Aflac duck repeating the company name while engaging in a series of slapstick misadventures. As a result of this campaign, the Aflac brand has the highest awareness among firms that offer supplemental insurance.

Social Media and Brand Relationship Tactics

Social media is a very attractive platform for encouraging selective consideration of brands, because increasing the brand's touch points with consumers serves to increase the frequency and recency of activation of the brand, as well as processing depth. For example, Starbucks has emerged as a social media leader, much to the benefit of their brand (Quenqua 2010). The key elements of Starbucks' social media strategy include developing the most popular Facebook page for a brand, a Twitter feed for customer service, and a YouTube channel. This multifaceted approach to brand building goes well beyond reinforcing a positioning; it is an enduring commitment to maintaining strong brand accessibility among the firm's most profitable customers. It comes as little surprise that Starbucks was able to raise its prices, which are already famously above commodity levels, in a poor economy in the fall of 2010.

Although social media provides an excellent vehicle to drive selective brand consideration, if a firm can build relationships between its customers and its brand, the likelihood that the brand will be the first considered when a purchase occasion arises will be dramatically increased. A great example of an offline tactic is Harley-Davidson's rallies. These rallies involve Harley riders getting together for a ride on a prescribed route, and bonding with each other and the brand. Of course this is tremendous for developing brand meaning, but also keeps the brand strongly accessible in consumers' minds. The possibilities for brand managers to develop similar strategies for their brands are seemingly limitless, bounded only by the creativity of the manager.

Sponsorship Tactics

Sponsorships may be a particularly cost-effective means of driving brand consideration. In a typical sponsorship relationship, a firm provides payment for the right to place its name in a salient way at events such as sporting contests, entertainment, artistic venues, and so on. Linking a corporate name to an entity provides consumers with multiple activations of the brand name, thus increasing the likelihood that the brand will be activated when the consumer later considers the category to which the brand belongs.

One consideration for managers considering using sponsorships to facilitate tunnel vision focused on their brand is that enduring sponsorships, as opposed to one-offs, will be vastly more effective because frequency of brand activation over time is essential to build strong brand awareness. For example, mixed martial arts clothing manufacturer TapouT made heavy use of sponsorships to grow from a $30,000 brand in 1999 to a $200 million brand in 2009. The backbone of TapouT's marketing strategy was the sponsorship of fighters and events, such as the now iconic Ultimate Fighting Championship. When a mixed martial arts fan watches a fight, the TapouT brand name is repeatedly processed because of its presence on fighters' clothing and its appearance on the fight venue itself (padding on seams in the cage, the mat, and on signage). Frequent pairings of the brand and mixed martial arts has led to tremendous success for the TapouT brand and the purchase of TapouT by Authentic Brands Group.

In addition to prompting frequent activation of a brand name, sponsorships can be very effective at facilitating the activation of the brand at the right time, that is, in close proximity to when consumers are looking to make a purchase. Bridgestone tires sponsors the National Hockey League's Winter Classic, a very popular outdoor hockey game played each year on January 1st. This sponsorship features the Bridgestone name at center ice, along the dasher boards, and in various media presentations. Given that this game is played in January, Bridgestone ensures that its name is likely to have been recently activated prior to consumers' need to purchase tires, which often emerges in the winter. As is often the case with sponsorships, Bridgestone's NHL sponsorship is very well targeted to the majority of hockey fans who live in the northern United States and Canada.

It should be noted that for sponsorships to be valuable for a brand by prompting frequent brand activations when consumers want to buy, it is essential that what is sponsored is consistent with brand meaning. Frequency and recency of activation are purely cognitive phenomena, but consumers' inferences of brand meaning will be affected by the brand associations that sponsorships develop between the sponsored entity and the brand. Thus, it is important to carefully choose sponsorship entities that have associations consistent with a manager's aims for his or her brand.

Licensing Tactics

Once a strong brand name is established, firms may be able to increase sales of a new product by associating the brand name with the new product. For example, the Nickelodeon channel's heroine Dora the Explorer, whose fame was gained in a children's animated television series, appears on items as diverse as sleeping bags, lunch boxes, backpacks, and clothing. The brand owner can either decide to manufacture the new product or receive a fee from another company in exchange for the right to use the brand name and related elements in the marketing of the product. For many young girls, a sleeping bag that features Dora is worth far more than a plain sleeping bag, and parents are correspondingly willing to pay more for the licensed product than a nonlicensed equivalent.

Research on selective processing suggests that licensing may often offer much more value to the brand than simply added revenue. Consider the Veggie Tales children's entertainment brand, a brand featuring a cast of talking vegetables that appears in Christian-themed movies, DVDs, CDs, and books. Although the target market has very favorable attitudes toward the brand, one way to increase sales will be for the brand to maintain strong top-of-mind awareness among children. Veggie Tales recently entered a licensing agreement in the manufacturing of Veggie Tales branded fruit snacks, available at grocery stores. The snack product does not add significantly to the brand in the ways we usually think about brand meaning. Indeed, consumers do not learn anything about either the content or entertainment value of the DVDs, and whether the snacks are tasty or not does not seem to increase the likelihood of a child asking for a Veggie Tales DVD for her birthday. However, the snacks do provide a revenue stream while providing an enduring brand reminder in an additional place in the home (e.g., the pantry), and accordingly contribute to ongoing brand awareness. Thus, done well, licensing can drive both the frequency of brand activation and the likelihood that the brand will be considered in close proximity to a relevant purchase situation.

The traditional branding view of licensing is that at best the licensed product should help build brand associations, but at worst not harm the brand by invoking contradictory associations (e.g., high-end fashion brands are often tempted to affix their name to cheap accessory items, but doing so can undermine the stature of the brand). In addition to revenue, the utility of licensing as a tool to drive selective consideration of the brand may be underappreciated. This upside may alleviate concerns about whether a given licensing opportunity is brand building as it has been traditionally conceived. That is, a licensed product may well contribute to brand success even if it does not deepen brand meaning, as long as it increases awareness. Of course, it is very possible for licensed products to be inconsistent with brand meaning, in which case any benefit with regard to brand awareness may be counteracted.

Trade Sales Promotion Tactics

In addition to the obvious upsides of facilitating distribution by providing incentives to elements of the distribution channel, brand salience can be increased when manufactures buy favorable treatment for their brand from the trade. For example, manufacturers can secure optimal retail placement (e.g., end-caps, eye-level shelves), and leverage "billboard effects" in which a large area of shelf space is occupied by a given brand. By being considered first when a consumer is looking for a brand from a given category, a brand is at a substantial competitive advantage. The benefits conveyed by selective processing account for the high rates manufacturers are willing to pay for prime placement.

In addition to retail placement, firms can use incentives to guide the behavior of sales staff such that particular options are suggested to consumers. For purchases in which consumers are less than expert, "push money" can have a significant impact on brands' market share. Push money is allocated by manufacturers to be paid to retail salespeople if certain brands are purchased. During his youth, one of the authors worked for a sporting goods retailer that was flooded with opportunities to earn push money. Despite knowing very little about the relevant trade-offs in categories such as tennis racquets, fishing poles, and running shoes, confident recommendations were made to consumers as a function of the push money available for given brands.

Another way that tunnel vision focusing on a brand can be facilitated through trade promotion is the use of cooperative merchandizing efforts in which manufacturers work with retailers in the creation and placement of point-of-purchase materials, store ads, and so on. To the extent that manufacturers are willing to invest in retailers' marketing efforts on behalf of their brands, target brands can be highlighted and thus become the first considered within a category, and, as detailed earlier, accordingly gain market advantage.

Consumer Sales Promotion Tactics

Marketers often find themselves in the position of being responsible for a good product that is nevertheless unlikely to sell well because consumers are likely to consider competing brands earlier in the choice process. For example, new brands, or smaller share brands, are much less likely to receive consideration compared to larger-share, better-established brands. Thus, the marketing task is to increase the likelihood of the target brand becoming focal for consumers who are ready to buy. Marketers have long recognized the power of sales promotions targeted to consumers to increase brand awareness. Indeed, a well-executed sales promotion can increase both the salience and accessibility of a target brand.

Although more expensive than other options in the marketers' toolbox, the gold standard for inducing trial, and thereby building brand awareness, is sampling. Sampling is a flexible tool, and many products and services can be adapted to allow consumers to receive or experience a sample. Two reasons why sampling may be so effective at prompting selective consideration of a brand is that consumers are generally very favorable to samples (up to 70 percent of consumers who receive a consumer packaged goods sample will use it), and actual experience results in deep brand processing, which boosts accessibility.

In addition to increasing brand accessibility by stimulating trial, consumer-oriented sales promotions can be used to increase brand salience. A number of tactics that add immediate value for consumers such as premiums, rebate/refund offers, on-pack or in-store coupons, and special packs offering product bonuses (e.g., 15 percent more free) are extremely effective to direct consumers' attention to a given brand. Once the consumer's attention is focused on a brand, the value added by the promotion becomes an important input into the consumer's consideration of the hypothesis that the focal brand will successfully meet a need.

Other sales promotion tools that add less immediate value for consumers, but that nevertheless can be very effective at increasing brand salience, include contests and sweepstakes. For example, Guitar Center has held "King of the Blues" contests in which guitar players compete for prizes based on their musical skills. The first level of the competition is in Guitar Center stores, and contestants who do well move on to competitions at regional and national levels. This contest is very effective at communicating specific brand aims as well as increasing the salience of Guitar Center during the contest and contributing to lasting increased brand accessibility, which is potentially much more important.

One underutilized benefit of consumer sales promotions is the potential to increase advertising salience. For example, Kellogg's embarked on an awareness-building advertising campaign when it recognized that although consumers generally held positive attitudes toward Corn Flakes, the advanced age of the brand led to it being overlooked in favor of newer brands. The inspired campaign encouraged consumers to, "Taste them again for the first time." Had Kellogg's engaged in a sampling campaign at the same time the advertisements were being run, and thereby gave consumers the chance to taste Corn Flakes, advertising would have likely been much more effective because its salience would have been enhanced (Schultz, Robinson, and Petrison, 1998).

A final way that consumer-oriented sales promotions can drive the salience and accessibility of brands is by serving as an enduring reminder of the brand. For example, coupons are often saved for a period before redemption, and branded premiums may remain in consumers' homes indefinitely (e.g., one of the authors received a Pinnacle golf hat several years ago with purchase of a pack of balls that still has a place in his closet). The bottom line for managers is that marketing dollars spent to increase either the salience of a brand or the likelihood that consumers will quickly recall the brand are likely to pay back attractively.

Other Integrated Marketing Communications Tools That Can Be Leveraged to Drive Selective Brand Consideration

The importance of having chronically high brand awareness is a contributor to the growth of public relations and publicity in the marketing mix. One oft-cited concern with traditional advertising is that although advertising allows for broad dissemination of brand-relevant information and can drive awareness, consumers are becoming increasingly jaded toward marketing and are likely to counter-argue messages to which they are exposed. By engaging in activities that are not as directly tied to a selling proposition, firms can increase brand awareness with less potential for consumers to discount the message. Thus, although it is harder to deliver brand-specific information when marketing dollars are spent on public relations and trying to obtain publicity, when a brand is highlighted in this way it may lead to significantly increased awareness. For example, when a firm participates in a Habitat for Humanity project and receives news coverage for their charitable behavior, the activation of the brand in the mind of viewers will lead to higher brand awareness, yet there are no specific brand claims for viewers to counter-argue.

Direct communications of a selling proposition from the manufacturer to the consumer, such as direct mail or e-mail, may be particularly effective when consumers are unlikely to engage in comparison shopping. When consumers are not expert and are under time pressure, and the decision is low-involvement, direct mail may be a good strategy because consumers may be willing to make a purchase if a salient option is perceived to be above some threshold. That is, consumers may be disposed to evaluate the merits of the product or service without consideration of how the focal brand stacks up against competitors, and the purchase decision will be a sole function of the attractiveness of the offer (i.e., versus the attractiveness of other options within the same category). One notable potential upside of direct mail is the possibility of pre-empting consideration of competitors by presenting consumers with a solution when they are ready to buy. Due to consumers' tendency to engage in selective processing, evaluations of a direct mail offer are likely to be better than they should be because consumers are unlikely to think carefully about how the product or service highlighted in the offer compares to other alternatives. For example, a consumer considering adding a deck in the backyard is quite likely to carefully consider information sent by a contractor if the information is received early in the decision process.

On the Breadth of the Implications of Consumer Tunnel Vision: The Case of Brand Extensions

Hopefully this chapter has been successful at summarizing consumers' tendency for tunnel vision, the consequences for choice, and implications for managers. It is our belief that in coming years more implications of tunnel vision driven by selective processing will be uncovered, specifically with regard to more effectively managing brands. For example, researchers have applied selective processing concepts to understand how to best manage brand extension decision making (Kapoor, and Heslop 2009; Milberg, Sinn, and Goodstein 2010; Oakley et al. 2008). Branding researchers have typically focused on the fit between a parent brand and a proposed extension in evaluating the attractiveness of the extension. However, as Kapoor and Heslop (2009) note, the ultimate success of a brand extension relies not only on the fit with the parent, but also how well the extension stacks up against the competition. When researchers evaluate consumer reactions to a proposed extension in the absence of competition, biased findings are likely to result due to consumers' selective processing of the proposed extension, and firms may overestimate the likelihood that a given extension will be successful. Indeed managers, like consumers, are susceptible to misjudging the value of options due to selective processing (this may account for the high failure rate of new product introductions, up to 90 percent by some estimates). Only when proposed extensions are evaluated in the context of competitors (i.e., only when comparative processing is induced) will consumer evaluations approximate what is likely to happen in real consumption contexts. By understanding how selective processing may lead to erroneous exuberance regarding proposed extensions, firms can become better calibrated regarding market potential, and accordingly can make better strategic decisions.

Conclusion

As we learn more about how consumers make decisions it is becoming increasingly clear that when a choice option receives selective consideration it gains a tremendous advantage. Even if consumers do not learn anything new about a given option, if it becomes focal early in the decision process consumers are much more likely to overestimate the utility offered by the option and, ultimately, to choose it. This tunnel vision process is often so powerful that it can overwhelm attitudes in driving choice (Posavac et al. 2002). Thus, marketers should strive to enhance the likelihood that their brands will receive such privileged consideration using the tools discussed in this chapter. Indeed, investments in making a given brand the focus of consumers' consideration are likely to pay attractive dividends in choice share, even if consumers' brand knowledge and attitudes are not appreciably changed. Such investments may be particularly attractive because the economics of buying consideration are often much more favorable compared to comprehensive brand enhancements.

References

Carlson, K.A., M.G. Meloy, and D. Lieb. 2009. "Benefits Leader Reversion: How a Once-Preferred Product Recaptures Its Standing." *Journal of Consumer Research* 46: 788–97.

Carlson, K.A., M.G. Meloy, and J.E. Russo. 2006. "Leader-Driven Primacy: Using Attribute Order to Affect Consumer Choice." *Journal of Consumer Research* 32: 513–18.

Cronley, M.L., S.S. Posavac, T. Meyer, F.R. Kardes, and J.J. Kellaris. 2005. "A Selective Hypothesis Testing Perspective on Price-Quality Inference and Inference-Based Choice." *Journal of Consumer Psychology* 15: 159–69.

Ehrich, K.R., and J.R. Irwin. 2005. "Willful Ignorance in the Request for Product Attribute Information." *Journal of Marketing Research* 42: 266–77.

Ephron, E. 1998. "The New Recency Planning." *Mediaweek* 8: 14–15.

Fazio, R.H., P.M. Herr, and M.C. Powell. 1992. "On the Development and Strength of Category-Brand Associations in Memory: The Case of Mystery Ads." *Journal of Consumer Psychology* 1: 1–13.

Fox, C.R., and J. Levav. 2000. "Familiarity Bias and Belief Reversal in Relative Likelihood Judgment." *Organizational Behavior and Human Decision Processes* 82: 268–92.

Kapoor, H., and L.A. Heslop. 2009. "Brand Positivity and Competitive Effects on the Evaluation of Brand Extensions." *International Journal of Research in Marketing* 26: 228–37.

Kardes, F.R., M.L. Cronley, J.J. Kellaris, and S.S. Posavac. 2004. "The Role of Selective Information Processing in Price-Quality Inference." *Journal of Consumer Research* 31: 368–74.

Kardes, F.R., G. Kalyanaram, M. Chandrashekaran, and R.J. Dornoff. 1993. "Brand Retrieval, Consideration Set Composition, Consumer Choice, and the Pioneering Advantage." *Journal of Consumer Research* 20: 62–75.

Kardes, F.R., S.S. Posavac, D. Silvera, M.L. Cronley, D.M. Sanbonmatsu, S. Schertzer, F. Miller, P.M. Herr, and M. Chandrashekaran. 2006. "Debiasing Omission Neglect." *Journal of Business Research* 59: 786–92.

Kardes, F.R., D.M. Sanbonmatsu, M.L. Cronley, and D.C. Houghton. 2002. "Consideration Set Overvaluation: When Impossibly Favorable Ratings of a Set of Brands Are Observed." *Journal of Consumer Psychology* 12: 353–61.

Larrick, R.P. 2009. "Broaden the Decision Frame to Make Effective Decisions." In *Handbook of Principles of Organizational Behavior,* 2d ed., ed. E.A. Locke, 461–80. West Sussex, UK: Wiley.

Meyvis, T., and C. Janiszewski. 2002. "Consumers' Beliefs About Product Benefits: The Effect of Obviously Irrelevant Product Information." *Journal of Consumer Research* 28: 618–35.

Milberg, S.J., F. Sinn, and R.C. Goodstein. 2010. "Consumer Reactions to Brand Extensions in a Competitive Context: Does Fit Still Matter?" *Journal of Consumer Research* 37: 543–53.

Muthukrishnan, A.V., and S. Ramaswami. 1999. "Contextual Effects on the Revision of Evaluative Judgments: An Extension of the Omission-Detection Framework." *Journal of Consumer Research* 26: 70–84.

Oakley, J.L., A. Duhachek, S. Balachander, and S. Sriram. 2008. "Order of Entry and the Moderating Role of Comparison Brands in Brand Extension Evaluation." *Journal of Consumer Research* 34: 706–12.

Posavac, S.S., J.J. Brakus, M.L. Cronley, and S.P. Jain. 2009. "On Assuaging Positive Bias in Environmental Value Elicitation." *Journal of Economic Psychology* 30: 482–89.

Posavac, S.S., F.R. Kardes, and J.J. Brakus. 2010. "Focus-Induced Tunnel Vision in Managerial Judgment and Decision Making: The Peril and the Antidote." *Organizational Behavior and Human Decision Processes* 113: 102–11.

Posavac, S.S., F.R. Kardes, D.M. Sanbonmatsu, and G.J. Fitzsimons. 2005. "Blissful Insularity: When Brands Are Judged in Isolation from Competitors." *Marketing Letters* 16: 87–97.

Posavac, S.S., D.M. Sanbonmatsu, M.L. Cronley, and F.R. Kardes. 2001. "The Effects of Strengthening Category-Brand Associations on Consideration Set Composition and Purchase Intent in Memory-Based Choice." In *Advances in Consumer Research,* vol. 28, ed. M.C. Gilly and J. Meyers-Levy, 186–89. Provo, UT: Association for Consumer Research.

Posavac, S.S., D.M. Sanbonmatsu, and E.A. Ho. 2002. "The Effects of the Selective Consideration of Alternatives on Consumer Choice and Attitude-Decision Consistency." *Journal of Consumer Psychology* 12: 203–13.

Posavac, S.S., D.M. Sanbonmatsu, F.R. Kardes, and G.J. Fitzsimons. 2004. "The Brand Positivity Effect: When Evaluation Confers Preference." *Journal of Consumer Research* 31: 643–51.

Quenqua, D. 2010. "Starbucks' Own Good Idea." *Marketing News,* February 25: 23–25.

Russo, J.E., M.G. Meloy, and V. Medvec. 1998. "Predecisional Distortion of Product Information." *Journal of Marketing Research* 35: 438–52.

Sanbonmatsu, D.M., F.R. Kardes, D.C. Houghton, E.A. Ho, and S.S. Posavac. 2003. "Overestimating the Importance of the Given Information in Multiattribute Consumer Judgment." *Journal of Consumer Psychology* 13: 289–300.

Sanbonmatsu, D.M., Posavac, S.S., Kardes, F.R., and Mantel, S.P. 1998. "Selective Hypothesis Testing." *Psychonomic Bulletin and Review,* 5, 197–220.

Sanbonmatsu, D.M., S.S. Posavac, and R. Stasny. 1997. "The Subjective Beliefs Underlying Probability Overestimation." *Journal of Experimental Social Psychology* 33: 276–95.

Schultz, D.E., W.A. Robinson, and L.A. Petrison. 1998. *Sales Promotion Essentials.* New York: McGraw-Hill.

Schulz-Hardt, S., D. Frey, C. Luthgens, and S. Moscovici. 2000. "Biased Information Search in Group Decision Making." *Journal of Personality and Social Psychology* 78: 655–69.

Tanner, R.J., and K.A. Carlson. 2009. "Unrealistically Optimistic Consumers: A Selective Hypothesis-Testing Account for Optimism in Predictions of Future Behavior." *Journal of Consumer Research* 35: 810–21.

Tversky, A., and D.J. Koehler. 1994. "Support Theory: A Nonextensional Representation of Subjective Probability." *Psychological Review* 101: 547–67.

Wang, J., and R.S. Wyer. 2002. "Comparative Judgment Processes: The Effects of Task Objectives and Time Delay on Product Evaluations." *Journal of Consumer Psychology* 12: 327–40.

Windschitl, P.D., J.P. Rose, M.T. Stalkfleet, and A.R. Smith. 2008. "Are People Excessive or Judicious in their Egocentrism? A Modeling Approach to Understanding Bias and Accuracy in People's Optimism." *Journal of Personality and Social Psychology* 95: 253–73.

4

How to Target Diverse Customers

An Advertising Typology and
Prescriptions from Social Psychology

Anne M. Brumbaugh

Increasing diversity and decreasing advertising budgets present an unprecedented challenge for marketers who need to create ads that resonate with more and more different types of people using less and less money. One way to do this cost effectively is to create a single campaign that attempts to target everyone without excluding (or offending) anyone. The problem with this solution is that by creating ads that don't really tap into a particular segment's unique ethos, they don't really speak to anyone in a meaningful way. Yes, they may be clever and capture many consumers' attention (which is, after all, a major goal of advertising). However, they will not resonate deeply with anyone, failing to link the ad, product, and brand with each consumer's identity. Though cost-effective, this strategy may not be message-effective.

When marketers do have the luxury of budget resources and segment expertise, they may create highly targeted subcampaigns for one or few particular ethnoracial minority target market segments. These efforts frequently draw on the expertise of specialized ad agencies that focus on a particular ethnoracial segment and do, indeed, create highly effective, narrowly targeted ads for that segment. These ads use almost exclusively actors and themes unique to the targeted group and are placed in media narrowly associated with readership among that group. Such subcampaigns are frequently "ghetto-ed" away from the mainstream marketing program under units with relatively fewer personnel, financial resources, and clout compared to the main marketing organization. There may be little integration or coordination with mainstream efforts, and when resources tighten these subcampaigns (and indeed, the units responsible for them) may even disappear (Cunningham 1999).

Research from the esoteric academic world of social psychology and consumer behavior has quite a bit to say about a highly effective (yet relatively rare) middle ground that combines the universal themes common to mainstream campaigns with symbols and cues that resonate with minority target audiences to court a wide range of diverse consumers. In this chapter, I introduce the three main target-marketing processes that research has shown to drive consumer processing of and affinity for targeted advertising. These processes—identification, targetedness, and internalization—imply different types of consumer engagement with marketing messages that are induced by using different types of cues in targeted advertisements. By carefully selecting the types of cues used in advertisements, marketers may strategically leverage these processes to their advantage. Different combinations of cues yield different types of ads that induce different types of processing among different audiences on which I base my typology of targeted advertising. By understanding this typology and using it to design advertising campaigns, marketers may gain advertising efficiencies between mainstream and targeted campaigns.

The bulk of this chapter details how these different types of ads are constructed, provides examples of each type, discusses the targeting processes that are evoked among diverse viewers by each ad type, and offers prescriptive advice for how to combine different types of ads into an effective targeted advertising campaign. This chapter offers academics interested in managerial implications of the principles of consumer psychology a succinct review of targeting processes as applied to advertising design, integrating social psychology, consumer behavior, and advertising research into a simple framework for understanding cognitive processes that underlie target marketing. For managers interested in learning how to use social psychology to improve their advertising outcomes, this chapter provides clear and detailed direction for how to create advertising to leverage these different targeting processes to enhance the effectiveness of their ad executions and avoid backlash among nontarget markets.

Targeting Processes

Consumer behavior and social psychology research is replete with studies that investigate how target marketing works among majority and minority populations. This research shows clearly that three main processes drive favorable target-marketing effects, yielding different types of positive outcomes for advertisers: identification, targetedness, and internalization.

Identification

The first work on target-marketing processes and effects found that identification was a key process by which individuals connect with targeted advertisements (cf. Whittler 1989; Whittler and DiMeo 1991). Also called homophily

(Simpson et al. 2000), identification occurs when a target viewer perceives himself to be similar to a character shown in an ad mainly due to shared physical appearance or membership in a minority ethnoracial group (Swartz 1984). Such similarity causes the viewer to adopt the message conveyed in the ad (for example, that the product is appropriate for him) via a process called identification whereby the viewer, in the absence of other information, infers that the similar source is like himself and is therefore persuaded by the message the source espouses (Kelman 1958, 1961). Because the association between the viewer and the source is relatively superficial, persuasion and attitude change caused by identification processes are less enduring and more easily altered than persuasion and attitude change caused by more effortful or meaningful processes.

To induce identification, advertisers include characters in ads that are members of the same ethnoracial group as their target customers. Within a dominant white society, membership in a numerically rare ethnoracial group makes one's ethnoracial identity chronically salient—brought to the cognitive fore—and is therefore a key facet of one's identity (McGuire et al. 1978). This distinctiveness causes identification effects to be robust among members of ethnoracial minorities for whom membership in an ethnoracial group makes them both socially and numerically distinctive within a broader society (Grier and Desphande 2001; McGuire and McGuire 1981; McGuire et al. 1978). Because the consumer and character shown in the ad share a relatively rare, important self-defining trait that makes them distinctive vis-à-vis the dominant majority culture, the consumer notices, experiences identification, and has a more favorable disposition toward the ad (Grier and Brumbaugh 2004; Grier and Desphande 2001; Wooten 1995). In contrast, research shows that this does not occur as frequently for dominant majority culture consumers (i.e., whites in the United States) because being a member of the dominant culture is neither numerically rare nor particularly meaningful as compared to distinctive ethnoracial minority group membership (McGuire et al. 1978; Perry 2001). Therefore, identification is not a prominent driver of target-market effects for dominant-majority whites.

Targetedness

Targetedness occurs when a targeted viewer perceives herself to be within the desired target market of an ad (Aaker, Brumbaugh, and Grier 2000; Grier and Brumbaugh 1999). Feeling targeted—and indeed, wooed—by an advertiser causes the viewer to have a favorable disposition toward the ad, its message, and the product it promotes (Brumbaugh and Grier 2006). People in consumer cultures have significant persuasion knowledge that not only makes them skeptical toward disingenuous or manipulative targeting attempts (Friestad and Wright 1994, 1998; Sims 1997), but also makes them appreciate the fact that they are important enough to a firm to be the focus of marketing (Grier and Brumbaugh 2007). Perceiving that their attention and consumption dollars are desired, in an authentic or value-creating way makes people like the ad, product, and brand (Grier and Brumbaugh 1999; Sims 1997). Source cues that tend to induce identification among distinctive minorities (but less so nondistinctive majorities) work to induce targetedness among nondistinctive majorities (but less so distinctive minorities; Grier and Brumbaugh 1999). As a consequence, targetedness is a more common driver of favorable target market effects among members of the white mainstream than is identification (Aaker et al. 2000). To create targetedness among mainstream white consumers, advertisers need to include mainstream characters that are similar to these consumers in ways other than ethnoracial group membership, including life stage, age, gender, role (i.e., parent, employee), or product user (Grier and Brumbaugh 1999).

Internalization

Internalization occurs when a targeted viewer feels an affiliation with a character in an ad that transcends mere physical similarity, and perceives that he shares the values and beliefs that the character is thought to possess. By feeling a deeper association with the character, the viewer comes to believe (versus merely adopt or share) the favorable message the character espouses: the character's belief becomes the viewer's own belief (Kelman 1961). When this happens, persuasion and attitude change are more stable and enduring than when brought about by other, more superficial processes (Johnson and Eagly 1989; Kelman 1958).

To create internalization, advertisers need to complement similar ad sources with additional nonsource cues that reinforce why the ad character believes in the product and why that character should be believed. Such cues may include elements that reinforce shared values related to the choice or use of the product (i.e., signs that both the character and consumer are good parents, effective workers, or kinder people because they choose and use the product). In addition, for ethnoracial minority consumers, such cues may also include subcultural elements that reinforce the meaning of shared ethnoracial group membership, that is, symbols associated with their subculture that distinguish the ad character and viewer as members of the subculture as distinct from the dominant culture (Aaker et al. 2000; Grier and Brumbaugh 2004). Not only do such cues enable viewers to assess similarity between themselves and the ad sources, they also convey shared subcultural content and meaning, which become the basis for internalization of the ad message (Brumbaugh 2002; Grier and Brumbaugh 1999).

Targeting Cues

Source Versus Nonsource Cues

By combining different types of cues associated with different ethnoracial target groups in a single ad, advertisers may induce specific targeting processes and influence the nature and depth of affiliation that diverse viewers feel toward their products. One way of categorizing ad cues is whether they have to do with the people shown in the ad (source cues) or not (nonsource cues; Brumbaugh 2002). Different combinations of source and nonsource cues lead to different interpretations of the intended target and induce different target-market processes.

Source cues include information related directly to the characters shown in an ad. These are the most influential cues used to indicate an ad's intended target (Brumbaugh 2002; Grier and Brumbaugh 1999). Research shows that the visually salient traits of the characters depicted in an ad (skin color, hairstyle, facial structure, stature, etc.) are processed quickly and automatically, allowing the viewer to make a rapid initial categorization of the characters as similar or dissimilar to himself based on physical markers of race and gender (Ito and Urland 2003). Other source-related cues, such as the clothes the characters wear, the situations in which they appear, the roles they play, and so on, likewise add information that may further signal the viewer's similarity to the sources (Aboud and Skerry 1983; Andrews and Shimp 1990; Jaffe and Berger 1994; Platow, Mills, and Morrison 2000).

Nonsource cues are everything else in the ad unrelated to the source and are processed less quickly than sources cues (Chaiken 1980; Ito and Urland 2003). The background setting, ad copy, depiction of the product, the medium in which the ad is placed, and so on, all tell the viewer something about his relationship with the product and brand, including whether he is in the marketer's intended target market or not, whether the product category is appropriate for him, and whether he can afford the product. These cues help the viewer further refine his judgment of the ad vis-à-vis himself. Thus, an initial (dis)similarity judgment based on physical markers of race or gender may be further reinforced or attenuated by other cues that signal (dis)similar ethnoracial group membership, socioeconomic status, lifestyle, interests, or product needs (cf. Brumbaugh 2002).

Exclusive Versus Inclusive Nonsource Cues

Another way of categorizing cues is based on whether they signal viewer inclusion in a target market or their exclusion from it. For example, consider an ad that shows a character who appears to be of Asian descent. If this ad further features Mandarin language, shows Chinese cultural symbols, and promotes a product used mainly by first-generation Chinese Americans, then members of the presumed intended target market (first-generation Chinese Americans) might interpret the source and other cues together using deeper cultural knowledge that others outside the subculture do not possess. These target-market viewers decode the meaning of the ad source using their sub-cultural knowledge in ways others outside the subculture cannot. In contrast, viewers not in the target market would likely interpret those cues as indicating that they are unambiguously not in the intended market and are effectively excluded from it. The language and cultural symbols not interpretable by those outside Chinese culture are interpreted only as indicating that these others are not being sought by this advertiser.

In this example, it was the nonsource cues that gave further meaning to both the presumed intended target ("this ad is for me based on my Chinese heritage") and nontarget markets ("this ad is not for me and I am excluded from the target market because I am not of Chinese heritage"). Thus, I categorize such cues as "exclusive"—cues that signal that an ad is intended exclusively for members of a distinctive target segment and exclude others outside that segment (Brumbaugh 1995). Exclusive cues are frequently subculture-bound—uniquely and unequivocally associated with a subculture within a broader dominant culture, and thus uninterpretable to those outside the subculture. Only members of the intended segment have the knowledge and motivation to interpret the subcultural cues shown in the ad, and those outside the intended segment use those cues to infer that the ad is not for them.

In contrast, if instead that the ad showed an Asian-looking character shuttling his family consisting of a wife, son, and daughter away from a middle-class home in a moderately priced sport utility vehicle for which the ad was created—a situation and symbols of a "normal" American family—the fact that he is Asian may become irrelevant for non-Asians viewing the ad. Indeed, the apparent ethnoracial group membership of the source may be rendered moot because of the preponderance of cues that signal that this ad and vehicle are for middle-class families with children—a much more inclusive target market than the previous ad example implied. Thus, I categorize such cues as "inclusive." They signal that the ad is intended for a broader, more diverse audience than the ethnoracial group membership of the source would suggest. Such cues frequently reference parts of the dominant culture that are widely shared by both majority and minority group members. In the United States, for example, such cues might include middle-class lifestyles, larger nuclear families, patriotic themes, depictions of social gatherings, athletic or sports-related images, and scenes related to national holidays.

Though their origins may derive from aspects of the dominant majority ethnoracial culture (that is, white European in the U.S.), inclusive cues are, by this definition, not associated with a single (sub)cultural group and are known to, understood by, and shared among all members of the society with which they are associated (Devos and Banaji 2005). Therefore, although the ads may include sources with physical characteristics associated with a particular demographic segment subscribed by race, ethnicity, or gender, the addition of other nonsource cues that broaden the appeal based on other nonpeople meanings conveyed by the ad (the basic need satisfied by the product category, the universality of the scene depicted, the universal values shared by the sources) enables members of other ethnoracial groups to relate to the ad message based on their membership and participation in the broader dominant cultural society.

Target Ad Typology, Examples, and Processes

It is this combination of source and nonsource cues that determines whether a viewer infers that an ad is or is not for her (consciously or unconsciously, automatically or through more effortful processing) and that drives how she processes the ad. Although the number of combinations of source and exclusive or inclusive nonsource cues may seem infinite, a simple typology of five types of ads that combine different cue types provides a straightforward and relevant framework for advertisers seeking to court diverse consumers (see Figures 4.1 and 4.2). In this section, I explain this typology and provide examples of each type of ad using African American executions.

Minority Target Exclusive Ads

When one refers to "targeted ads," one usually thinks of minority target exclusive ads. These highly targeted ads combine sources from a specific minority group (frequently an ethnoracial minority group, though not necessarily) with exclusive nonsource cues associated uniquely with that group and signal clearly the intended targets' inclusion in the ad as well as nontargets' exclusion from it. Figure 4.3 shows two minority target exclusive executions. When taken together, black sources and exclusive nonsource cues convey subcultural information related exclusively to African American culture that lie in contrast to dominant white Anglo-American culture.[1]

In the Kodak ad, the presence of the grandfather signals extended family that is culturally relevant for the target (Taylor, Jackson, and Chatters 1997). His attire and the curtain in the background use fabrics that support an Afro-

Figure 4.1   **A Typology of Targeted Advertising**

		Source Cues	
		Minority target only	White and minority target	White only
Nonsource Cues	Minority exclusive	Minority target exclusive ads		
	Inclusive	Minority target exclusive ads	Mainstream inclusive ads	White inclusive ads
	White exclusive			White exclusive ads

centric theme and create affiliation among target viewers and are likely to be interpreted by some nontarget viewers as exclusionary—the intended target is specifically African American. The situation in which the family elder is telling a story to younger family members pays homage to subcultural and family traditions (Horton and Horton 1997). Taken alone, any one of these nonsource cues may not convey unambiguously an African American subcultural message. However when taken together in combination with the black sources, the message communicates a uniquely African American message that may only be accurately decoded by African American target market members using their knowledge of the subculture, and may signal exclusion to nontarget market members (Brumbaugh 1995, 2002).

Compared to the nonsource cues depicted in the Kodak ad, the nonsource cues in the McDonald's ad may initially seem less noticeable. However, they, too, support an exclusively African American message. Neither girl shown in the ad has "good hair" more associated with mainstream expectations and norms (Samuels 2009) and one has markedly darker skin than is typical for a more inclusive execution (Mayo, Mayo, and Mahdi 2005). The reference to entrepreneurship is likely to resonate with an African American target due to African Americans' historical exclusion from conventional economic institutions (Boyd 2008). Most important, however, is the explicit textual reference to black and African American institutions and McDonald's support of the African American community (Berta 2008). Such overt references to the minority target not only reinforce the targeted message for African Americans, but likewise explicitly exclude others from the ad.

For target African American consumers, these two ads trigger both identification and internalization processes that foster acceptance of the ad message (Aaker et al. 2000; Appiah 2001). The similar sources generate quick "for me" categorizations that lead to identification, and the supporting nonsource cues that reinforce a subculture-based African American message

Figure 4.2 **Predominant Target Processes by Ad Type**

Viewer type	Processes	Ad type				
		Minority target exclusive ads	White inclusive ads	Mainstream inclusive ads	Minority target inclusive ads	White exclusive ads
White	Me/Not me	Not me	Me	Maybe me	Maybe me	Me
	Targetedness		Strong	Moderate	Moderate	Strong
	Identification					High ID only
	Internationalization					High ID only
Minority	Me/Not me	Me	Maybe me	Maybe me	Me	Not me
	Targetedness		Low ID only	Low ID only		
	Identification	Strong, especially high ID	Low ID only	Moderate	Strong, especially high ID	
	Internationalization	Strong, especially high ID			Moderate, especially high ID	

Figure 4.3   **Minority Target Exclusive Ads**

lead to internalization (Aaker et al. 2000; Brumbaugh 2002). That is, not only do the characters in the ads look like the target, but they share a common experience as African Americans and similar beliefs and values that make them unique and special vis-à-vis the dominant majority. Identification with the similar source leads to an immediate but less-pronounced attitude change, and integration of the ad message with one's beliefs via internalization causes this attitude change to be more long-lived (Kelman 1961). Furthermore, these effects are particularly pronounced among distinctive target market viewers who identify strongly with their ethnoracial subculture. For these viewers, ethnoracial identity is more chronically accessible and linked to their self-concepts than for dominant culture viewers, and thus has a greater influence on cognitive processes and reactions to ethnoracially targeted ads (Grier and Brumbaugh 2004; Whittler, Calantone, and Young 1991; Wooten 1995).

In contrast, the very same exclusive nonsource cues that reinforce a subculture-based message for African American viewers are likely to be interpreted by others as excluding them—signaling they are not in the courted target market. Nontarget market viewers will likely stop processing the ad once they have come to the quick realization that the ad is not intended for them. This may occur nearly immediately due to the use of black-only sources or milliseconds later should they engage in greater processing of the nonsource cues that further exclude them (Brumbaugh 2002; Grier and Brumbaugh 1999). Some viewers may actually experience unfavorable attitude change based on their negative perceptions of the target market. Research suggests, for example, that highly prejudiced individuals might experience backlash in response to highly targeted ads intended for audiences for which they have unfavorable attitudes, hurting their attitudes toward the product and brand (Bush, Hair, and Solomon 1979; Oakenfull and Greenlee 2004).

Inclusive Ads

If one were to conduct a content analysis on a broad swath of ads in the United States, it is likely that inclusive ads would constitute a large majority. To signal that all consumers are invited to consider themselves part of the target market, these ads utilize inclusive nonsource cues that are associated with aspects of the dominant culture that are available and accessible to all members of the dominant culture. A hallmark of inclusive ads is that the backgrounds and nonsource cues are ambiguous or universal enough that sources from any ethnoracial group look at home in the ad. Necessarily, however, the individuals shown in these ads are members of particular ethnoracial groups. Therefore, the combination sources from a particular ethnoracial group with inclusive nonsource cues constitute three different types of inclusive ads that give rise to subtle differences in target market process depending on if the viewer is (dis)similar to the ad source: white inclusive ads, minority target inclusive ads, and mainstream inclusive ads.

White Inclusive Ads

Figure 4.4 shows two white inclusive ads that feature white-only sources combined with inclusive nonsource cues. The Oscar Mayer ad shows a white boy biting into a hot dog set against a backdrop of a rained-out backyard cookout. The implied theme of social gathering is combined with a charcoal grill to create an all-American tableau that is accessible to and holds appeal for most Americans (Galosich 2000). The middle-class setting and the absence of details that might imply a particular subsegment allow most viewers to put themselves (or their families) in the situation. Likewise, the Windex ad shows a man in a bathrobe standing in front of his modest home after he has cleaned his windows. Though ethnoracial disparities in home ownership exist, most Americans of all ethnoracial groups own or aspire to own their own home (Bergman 2004; Fannie Mae 2010). The socioeconomically modest setting excludes few on the basis of class, and the chores associated with home ownership are universally despised.

Figure 4.4   **White Inclusive Ads**

Many people who subscribe or aspire to a middle-class American life-style may find the universal themes depicted in these ads attractive and compelling. For white viewers, source similarity based on factors other than shared white race (role, gender, and so on) yields a quick "for me" assessment, and the inclusive nonsource cues reinforce a dominant culture execution. Together, these cues trigger a strong feeling of targetedness that creates favorable attitudes among these consumers (Aaker et al. 2000). For nonwhite viewers, the nonsource cues provide additional information other than ethnoracial group membership on which they might evaluate their similarity to and identification with the characters shown in the ad (i.e., as parent, home owner, or chore doer; Brumbaugh 2009). If nonwhite viewers find such a basis for similar comparison and experience a "for me" reaction, their attitudes are likely to be influenced favorably by identifica-tion with the source (Aaker et al. 2000). For nonwhite viewers who do not identify strongly with their ethnoracial group (i.e., Webster 1992; Whittler et al. 1991), targetedness may also occur and result in favorable ad at-titudes (Brumbaugh and Grier 2010). In all cases, viewers respond to the universality of the message as they decode it based on their knowledge of the dominant culture and their place within it. The boy and man in the ads could be of another ethnoracial group with little change in the meanings derived from the ad.

Minority Target Inclusive Ads

Figure 4.5 shows two minority target inclusive ads that feature only black sources. The first is an Oscar Mayer execution very similar to the white inclusive Oscar Mayer ad and shows a black boy of similar age eating a simple bologna sandwich against a blurred, ambiguous interior background that might be inferred to be lunchtime in anyone's simple, bright kitchen. Again, the middle-class background, commonplace lunch scene, and absence of exclusive nonsource cues associated with a particular ethnoracial group allow most viewers to put themselves or their families into the scene. The Lowes ad is similar and depicts a somewhat more upscale but neutral-toned kitchen with a mom and daughter enjoying a tea party with the ubiquitous toy tea set. The kitchen is suggestive of a higher-than-middle-class lifestyle to which many would aspire, and the absence of cues associated with any particular ethnoracial group facilitates viewers' inclusion in the execution and message.

For black viewers, the black sources in these ads generate a quick "for me" assessment much like minority target exclusive ads would, leading to identification processes that favorably influence ad attitudes. Internalization processes generally do not result from these ads because there are no African American exclusive nonsource cues to trigger subculture-based processing. However, the presence of ethnoracially similar sources may be enough to yield internalization processes among high ethnoracial identifiers for whom membership in the ethnoracial group is particularly salient and meaningful (Aaker et al. 2000; Grier and Brumbaugh 2004). For most white viewers, the universality of the scene makes the ethnoracial group membership of the sources irrelevant, and similarity based on cues unrelated to ethnoracial group membership (i.e., being a parent vis-à-vis these ads) yields favorable target-edness effects that may have a favorable effect on ad attitudes (Brumbaugh 2009; Brumbaugh and Grier 2006). Once again, that the boy, woman, and girl in these ads could be of another ethnoracial group with little change in the meanings derived from the ads is characteristic of an inclusive execution.

Mainstream Inclusive Ads

Finally, Figure 4.6 shows two mainstream inclusive ads that show sources from different ethnoracial groups in the same execution. In the "Real Parents Real Answers" ad, five high school boys representing different ethnoracial groups dominate the field. The antismoking message is likely to resonate with parents of all cultural groups as the incidence of underage smoking and tobacco addiction is problematic across all ethnoracial groups (Ellickson

Figure 4.5 **Minority Target Inclusive Ads**

et al. 2004). The bleachers convey neither a particularly wealthy nor poor high school and thus signal most families' inclusion in the execution, and the "Real Parents, Real Answers" tag ling invites all parents to consider themselves part of the intended target. In the Domino Sugar ad, two white and two light-skinned black children participate in a bake sale (Mayo et al. 2005). The red, white, and blue colors and the "Great American Bake Sale" text convey a patriotic American culture message, and copy that refers to "you" and "our kids" signals inclusion to most (if not all) viewers.

These ads are intended to capture the attention of most (if not all) consumers by depicting characters similar to most (if not all) consumers on the basis of a shared experience in the dominant American culture. The ads reinforce a culture nonspecific message by using cues that transcend subcultural group, that is, higher-order societal norms, use of the product category, brand information, and so on. Though more cynical consumers may view these ads as formulaic and contrived in that they are carefully engineered to include one of each of a number of ethnoracial or other social groups, most consumers respond favorably to the inclusive message the ads are intended to convey. White consumers respond similarly as they would to minority target inclusive ads, experiencing targetedness if they perceive themselves to be in the target market based on similarity with one of the sources on the basis of gender, age, or role (Grier and Brumbaugh 1999). Likewise, members of one of the

Figure 4.6   **Mainstream Inclusive Ads**

distinctive ethnoracial groups depicted may feel affiliated with one or more of the sources, but not on the basis of shared ethnoracial group membership. The presence of one or more sources outside of one's ethnoracial group, particularly a white source, precludes the possibility of ethnoracially-based identification, but signals instead an inclusive message that members of the included distinctive groups may note and appreciate (Brumbaugh and Grier 2006). As a consequence, they too may experience similarity and identification based on gender, age, role, and so forth (Aaker et al. 2000). Low ethnoracial identifiers may acknowledge the advertisers' targeting effort and experience more favorable attitudes via targetedness as well (Brumbaugh 2009; Brumbaugh and Grier 2006).

White Exclusive Ads

Though some people may find the idea difficult to understand and even somewhat controversial, some executions include white source cues in combination with white Anglo culture-specific nonsource cues that together act to exclude others outside that ethnoracial group. Though the dominant culture is white Anglo and other ethnoracial minorities have significant knowledge about it and are, by definition, members of it, some images are so closely allied with white racial group membership that they signal the explicit exclusion of nonwhite others. For example, people of color have a long history of being excluded from full participation in elite country clubs (Mayo 1998), financial institutions (Santiago, Gardener, and Molyneux 2005), and education establishments (Schaefer 1996), and thus images of white sources in such contexts may signal a message of exclusion for people of color. Additionally, different ethnoracial groups' participation in some activities common for white Anglo Americans is far less than their proportion in the population, for example, winter sports (Black Meetings and Tourism 2008), swimming (Associated Press 2008), or recycling (Nixon and Saphores 2009). As a consequence, depictions of such activities also constitute exclusive white cues that nonwhite viewers interpret as "not me" (Brumbaugh 2002). Comedians and writers who comment on the state of race in the United States frequently have uncanny insight into uniquely Anglo white images and norms, for example, Sarah Silverman (Justin 2002), Chris Rock (Houpt 2001), and George Lopez (Anonymous 2007). When these images and norms are combined with white sources in ads, they yield executions that effectively exclude all but white Anglos from the target market (Brumbaugh 1995). Additionally, certain stylistic cues also convey a uniquely white message, including cool pastel colors, particularly blues and greens and an absence of reds and yellows, indicators of elite socioeconomic status, neutral tans, "clean lines," simple backgrounds, sans serif fonts, and others (Brumbaugh 1995). When ads combine white sources with these types of stylistic cues, white exclusive executions may result.

Figure 4.7 shows two examples of white exclusive ads. The ClubMed ad shows a white couple in white clothing, uses cool muted blue and green tones, and depicts a nuclear family frolicking on an otherwise deserted beach. Ample blank space, sans serif fonts, and copy that emphasize higher-end features of a ClubMed vacation combine to convey a message that viewers who are not white Anglos might infer excludes them. In contrast, an execution designed to be more inclusive might use larger serif font, show the family dressed in different, more colorful outfits, include more people on the beach engaging in a variety of activities, contain reds and yellows, and emphasize the benefits (versus existence) of the club's offerings. Likewise, the Moen ad shows only a white male against a stark white background and a white bathroom sink empty of all but a white tube of toothpaste and toothbrush. The absence of color, clean lines of the product promoted, minimal sans serif font, and text suggesting an expensive custom bathroom and individualistic worldview ("My bathroom was designed for my world") support a white exclusive ad message.

Most white viewers respond to such executions in much the same way as they do white inclusive executions, experiencing a rapid "for me" assessment and strong targetedness that favorably influences ad attitudes (Brumbaugh

Figure 4.7   **White Exclusive Ads**

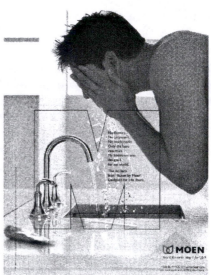

2002). Research suggests that some high white identifiers—those who identify strongly with white Anglo ethnoracial beliefs, values, and behaviors—may also experience identification with the ethnoracially similar source and internalization of the message reinforced by culture-consistent nonsource cues contained in these ads (Brumbaugh and Grier 2010). Most nonwhite non-Anglo viewers, however, respond to these executions with rapid "not me" assessments, and may either fail to process the message at all or may recognize their exclusion from the ad and respond negatively with less favorable ad attitudes (Brumbaugh 2002; Brumbaugh and Grier 2006; Grier and Brumbaugh 1999).

Bottom Line: How to Target Diverse Consumers

The different targeting processes that the five types of ads induce among distinctive minority consumers have important implications for how the different types of ads could be combined in advertising campaigns targeting diverse consumers. Advertisers need to think strategically about creating portfolios of different types of ads to signal who they are courting and how they are courting them. Depending on the long-term targeting goals, combining different types of ads in a targeted effort may yield better outcomes than using one or few.

Distinctive Minority Consumers Only, Ever

The most exclusive effort is one that targets only a single distinctive minority target market and never seeks to target other consumers. For companies that market offerings like hair care products for black consumers, Spanish language media for Hispanic consumers, and other goods and service uniquely tied to a single group, this is an appropriate strategy. Not surprisingly, advertisers in this situation should (and indeed do) use minority target exclusive ads placed in highly targeted media. The exclusive ad type leads to internalization processes among target viewers and links the brand's targeted positioning to their ethnoracial identity.

The use of narrowly targeted media supports this type of ad in two ways. First, it is the most efficient use of media budget in that no funding is wasted on exposing those outside the target market to the ad. Second, consumers who have chosen to consume the ethnoracially targeted medium will be predisposed toward a uniquely ethnoracial subculture message either because of strong ethnoracial identification that led them to choose the medium in the first place or because of the temporary salience of their ethnoracial group membership that reading the targeted medium engenders (cf. Green, 1999). In either case, the medium itself becomes yet another exclusive targeting cue that reinforces the subcultural message, further enhancing enduring, subculture-based attitude change.

In addition, however, marketers following this strategy could consider adding target market inclusive ads placed in mainstream media to their advertising portfolio for several reasons. First, the use of mainstream media broadens the exposure of the message to target members who do not use ethnoracially targeted media, particularly those who are low ethnoracial identifiers. Second, doing so exposes target consumers to two different executions that induce different processes. The minority target exclusive ad in targeted media leads to internalization that creates a link between the viewer's ethnoracial identity and the brand, and the minority target inclusive ad in mainstream media leads to identification that reinforces this link with the viewer's identity as a member of the dominant culture. These two paths are complementary and utilizing both creates stronger, more favorable, more enduring attitude change. Finally, placement of the brand's message in mainstream media adds credibility to the campaign because of the implied budget involved and the firm's willingness to use broader, higher-cost media for a smaller, narrower target segment. Such a tactic can have great return in good will and credibility among the target segment (Cunningham 1999).

Distinctive Minority Consumers Only, For Now

Many firms start with a unique selling proposition designed for a single customer segment but don't necessarily intend to target solely that segment forever. Clearly, such firms need to use target market exclusive ads in targeted media and target market inclusive ads in mainstream media as advocated here to court effectively consumers in their initial intended target market. However, use of target market ads alone (exclusive or inclusive) may lead mainstream and other consumers to infer over time that they are not (and will never be) in the intended market. To combat this, the firm needs to utilize at least some mainstream inclusive ads in mainstream media even before they are ready to extend their targeting efforts in order to preclude the unique association of their brand with a particular target segment. Such a tactic benefits the firm's efforts at targeting the current target market segment by reinforcing the uniquely subcultural message espoused in the targeted ads with executions in mainstream media that talk to their subcultural viewers based on their membership in the dominant culture. Importantly, however, this tactic generates exposure among future mainstream and other consumers with a message that they are (or will be) among the consumers the firm values.

Diverse Consumers via a Mainstream Campaign

For many companies that do not limit their target market based on ethnoracial or cultural group membership, a mainstream campaign that does not focus on a single group to the exclusion of others is appropriate. However, many companies rely far too heavily on white inclusive ads in mainstream media for such a campaign and presume such ads will be welcome by all. While exposure to a single white inclusive ad will not cause nonwhite consumers to infer they are not in the target market, repeated exposure to such ads without exposure to other more inclusive ads may send a more exclusive message over time than the firm intends (cf. Williams, Qualls, and Grier 1995). Therefore, a truly mainstream campaign needs to include white inclusive, mainstream inclusive, and minority target inclusive executions in mainstream media. Such a portfolio of ads seen by diverse consumers will not only enhance ad attitudes via targetedness (among white consumers) or identification (among distinctive minority consumers), but will expose the same consumers to multiple related (but different) executions espousing a similar message, reinforcing favorable attitude change.

The Future: Distinctive Minority Consumers as a Unique Part of a Mainstream Campaign

As consumer populations become more diverse and media become more fragmented, courting different types of consumers via a mainstream campaign as noted here is likely to become less and less effective. Consumers of products that aren't specifically targeted for different subgroups are nonetheless going to come to expect marketing attention that speaks to them on the basis of meaningful traits and needs, including ethnoracial or other distinctive group membership. For ethnoracial minorities who are growing in size and buying power, this means using targeted ads and media within the context of an overall mainstream campaign.

To do this effectively, marketers are going to need to think about what their targeted executions will be even before a single frame is shot or word of copy is written for the mainstream campaign, because the mainstream campaign needs to be constructed to allow minority target executions to relate to it. This relationship may be the use of the same actors as sources, the use of some of the same copy, or the use of the same graphical elements in both the mainstream and targeted executions. As a consequence, the mainstream campaign needs to rely less on exclusive dominant culture cues (i.e., white) and more on those elements that are truly universal among all potential consumers.

Advertisers need to change their starting point for designing their advertising campaigns. Rather than starting with the mainstream campaign and then creating targeted executions for each ethnoracial segment that frequently fails to reference the original campaign, advertisers need to first begin with a consideration of what a series of targeted executions might look like for their different types diverse consumers—including white exclusive ads—and use those images to generate the mainstream inclusive, white inclusive, and minority target inclusive ads that would constitute the mainstream campaign. The mainstream campaign would necessarily relate back to the targeted campaigns and reinforce the exclusive ads in more efficient media, with messages that support a shared brand experience across all consumers, and across various aspects of consumers' identities. Such a strategy requires that advertisers think about the core brand concepts that are universally valued across all their segments while simultaneously considering how to convey those concepts best to each distinct target segment.

Note

1. I use the term "black" to refer to visually salient phenotype markers related to source cues and the term "African American" to refer to psychological and cultural aspects of membership in the social group.

References

Aaker, J.A., A.M. Brumbaugh, and S.A. Grier. 2000. "Non-Target Market Effects and Viewer Distinctiveness: The Impact of Target Marketing on Attitudes." *Journal of Consumer Psychology* 9: 127–40.

Aboud, F.E., and S.A. Skerry. 1983. "Self and Ethnic Concepts in Relation to Ethnic Constancy." *Canadian Journal of Behavioural Science* 15: 14–26.

Andrews, J.C., and T.A. Shimp. 1990. "Effects of Involvement, Argument Strength, and Source Characteristics on Central and Peripheral Processing of Advertising." *Psychology and Marketing* 7: 195–214.

Anonymous. 2007. "How Far Is Too Far? What's Funny and What's Offensive These Days Is Sometimes Hard to Tell." *San Jose Mercury News,* March 3, 2007.

Appiah, O. 2001. "Black, White, Hispanic, and Asian American Adolescents' Responses to Culturally Embedded Ads." *Howard Journal of Communications* 12: 29–48.

Associated Press. 2008. "Nearly 60 Percent of Black Children Can't Swim." May 1. Available at www.msnbc.msn.com/id/24411271/, accessed August 13, 2010.

Bergman, H. 2004. "Nonwhites Getting More Loans, but More Denials, Too." *American Banker* 169: 3.

Berta, D. 2008. "McD's Diversity Efforts Honored at White House." *Nation's Restaurant News* 42: 14.

Black Meetings and Tourism. 2008. "Ski Feature." Available at www.blackmeetings andtourism.com/Articles/Dec-07-Jan-08/Ski_Feature-2.aspx, accessed August 10, 2010.

Boyd, R.L. 2008. "Trends in the Occupations of Eminent Black Entrepreneurs in the United States." *Journal of Socio-Economics* 37: 2390–98.

Brumbaugh, A.M. 1995. "Managing Diversity: A Cultural Knowledge Approach to Communicating to Multiple Market Segments." Ph.d. diss., Duke University, Durham, NC.

———. 2002. "Source and Nonsource Cues in Advertising and Their Effects on the Activation of Cultural and Subcultural Knowledge on the Route to Persuasion." *Journal of Consumer Research* 29: 258–69.

———. 2009. "Why Do I Identify with Thee? Let Me Count Three Ways: How Ad Context Influences Race-Based Character Identification." *Psychology and Marketing* 26: 970–86.

Brumbaugh, A.M., and S.A. Grier. 2006. "Insights from a 'Failed' Experiment: Directions for Pluralistic, Multiethnic Advertising Research." *Journal of Advertising* 35: 35–47.

———. 2010. "The Impact of Chronic Ethnoracial Identification and Transitory Ethnoracial Salience on Source-Related Target Marketing Processes." Working paper, College of Charleston, SC.

Bush, R.F., J.F. Hair Jr., and P.J. Solomon, P.J. 1979. "Consumers' Level of Prejudice and Response to Black Models in Advertisements." *Journal of Marketing Research* 16: 341–45.

Chaiken, S. 1980. "Heuristic Versus Systematic Information Processing and the Use of Source Versus Message Cues in Persuasion." *Journal of Personality and Social Psychology* 39: 752–66.

Cunningham, D. 1999. "One Size Does Not Fit All." *Adweek* 40: 4.

Devos, T., and M.R. Banaji. 2005. "American = White?" *Journal of Personality and Social Psychology* 88: 447–66.

Ellickson, P.L., M. Orlando, J.S. Tucker, and D.J. Klein. 2004. "From Adolescence to Young Adulthood: Racial/Ethnic Disparities in Smoking." *American Journal of Public Health* 94: 293–99.

Fannie Mae. 2010. "New Nationwide Survey Provides Comprehensive Look at Sentiment Toward Housing." Fanniemae.com, April 6. Available at www.fanniemae.com/newsreleases/2010/4989.jhtml, accessed August 4, 2010.

Friestad, M., and P. Wright. 1994. "The Persuasion Knowledge Model: How People Cope with Persuasion Attempts." *Journal of Consumer Research* 21: 1–31.
———. 1998. "Everyday Persuasion Knowledge." *Psychology and Marketing* 16: 185–94.
Galosich, A. 2000. "Industry News." *National Provisioner* 214: 13.
Green, C.L. 1999. "Ethnic Evaluations of Advertising: Interaction Effects of Strength of Ethnic Identification, Media Placement, and Degree of Racial Composition." *Journal of Advertising* 28: 51–64.
Grier, S.A., and A.M. Brumbaugh 1999. "Noticing Cultural Differences: Ad Meanings Created by Target and Non-Target Markets." *Journal of Advertising* 28: 79–93.
———. 2004. "Consumer Distinctiveness and Advertising Persuasion." In *Diversity in Advertising,* ed. J.D. Williams, W. Lee, and C.P. Haugtvedt, 217–35. Hillsdale, NJ: Lawrence Erlbaum.
———. 2007. "Compared to Whom? The Impact of Status on Third Person Effects in Advertising Persuasion in a South African Context." *Journal of Consumer Behaviour* 6: 5–18.
Grier, S.A., and R. Desphande, R. 2001. "Social Dimensions of Consumer Distinctiveness: The Influence of Social Status on Group Identity and Advertising Persuasion." *Journal of Marketing Research* 38: 216–24.
Horton, J.O., and L.E. Horton. 1997. *A History of the African American People: The History, Traditions and Culture of African Americans.* Detroit, MI: Wayne State University Press.
Houpt, S. 2001. "I'm Black. What's Rougher Than That?" *Globe and Mail,* February 24, 6.
Ito, T.A., and G.R. Urland. 2003. "Race and Gender on the Brain: Electrocortical Measures of Attention to the Race and Gender of Multiply Categorizable Individuals." *Journal of Personality and Social Psychology* 85: 616–26.
Jaffe, L.J., and P.D. Berger. 1994. "The Effect of Modern Female Sex Role Portrayals on Advertising Effectiveness." *Journal of Advertising* Research 34: 32–42.
Johnson, B.T., and A.H. Eagly. 1989. "Effects of Involvement on Persuasion: A Meta-Analysis." *Psychological Bulletin* 106: 290–314.
Justin, N. 2002. "Can Race Be a Laughing Matter?" *Star Tribune,* August 23, 23E.
Kelman, H.C. 1958. "Compliance, Identification, and Internalization: Three Processes of Attitude Change." *Journal of Conflict Resolution* 2: 51–60.
———. 1961. "Processes of Opinion Change." *Public Opinion Quarterly* 25: 57–78.
Mayo, D.T., C.M. Mayo, and S. Mahdi. 2005. "Skin Tones in Magazine Advertising: Does Magazine Type Matter?" *Journal of Promotion Management* 11: 49–59.
Mayo, J.M. 1998. *The American Country Club: Its Origins and Development.* Piscataway, NJ: Rutgers University Press.
McGuire, W.J., and C.V. McGuire. 1981. "The Spontaneous Self-Concept as Affected by Personal Distinctiveness." In *Self-Concept: Advances in Theory and Research,* ed. M.D. Lynch and K. Gergen, 147–71. New York: Ballinger.
McGuire, W.J., C.V. McGuire, P. Child, and T. Fujioka. 1978. "Salience of Ethnicity in the Spontaneous Self-Concept as a Function of One's Ethnic Distinctiveness in the Social Environment." *Journal of Personality and Social Psychology* 36: 511–20.
Nixon, H., and J.M. Saphores. 2009. "Information and the Decision to Recycle: Results from a Survey of U.S. Households." *Journal of Environmental Planning and Management* 52: 257–77.

Oakenfull, G., and T. Greenlee. 2004. "The Three Rules of Crossing Over from Gay Media to Mainstream Media Advertising: Lesbians, Lesbians, Lesbians." *Journal of Business Research* 57: 1276–85.

Perry, P. 2001. "White Means Never Having to Say You're Ethnic: White Youth and the Construction of 'Cultureless' Identity." *Journal of Contemporary Ethnography* 30: 56–91.

Platow, M.J., D. Mills, and D. Morrison. 2000. "The Effects of Social Context, Source Fairness, and Perceived Self-Source Similarity on Social Influence: A Self-categorisation Analysis." *European Journal of Social Psychology* 30: 69–81.

Samuels, A. 2009. "Chris Rock." *Newsweek* 154: 69.

Santiago, C., E.P.M. Gardener, and P. Molyneux. 2005. *Financial Exclusion.* New York: Palgrave Macmillan.

Schaefer, R.T. 1996. "Education and Prejudice: Unraveling the Relationship." *Sociological Quarterly* 37: 1–16.

Simpson, E.M., T. Snuggs, T. Christiansen, and K.E. Simples. 2000. "Race, Homophily, and Purchase Intentions and the Black Consumer." *Psychology and Marketing* 17: 877–89.

Sims, R. 1997. "When Does Target Marketing Become Exploitation?" *Marketing News* 31: 10.

Swartz, T.A. 1984. "Relationship Between Source Expertise and Source Similarity in an Advertising Context." *Journal of Advertising* 13: 49–54.

Taylor, R.J., J.S.J. Jackson, and L.M. Chatters. 1997. *Family Life in Black America.* Thousand Oaks, CA: Sage.

Webster, C. 1992. "The Effects of Hispanic Subcultural Identification on Information Search Behavior." *Journal of Advertising Research* 43: 54–92.

Whittler, T.E. 1989. "Viewers' Processing of Actor's Race and Message Claims in Advertising Stimuli." *Psychology and Marketing* 6: 287–309.

Whittler, T.E., R.J. Calantone, and M.R. Young. 1991. "Strength of Ethnic Affiliation: Examining Black Identification with Black Culture." *Journal of Social Psychology* 131: 461–67.

Whittler, T.E., and DiMeo, J. 1991. "Viewers' Reactions to Racial Cues in Advertising Stimuli." *Journal of Advertising Research* 31: 37–46.

Williams, J.D., Qualls, W.J., and Grier, S.A. 1995. "Racially Exclusive Real Estate Advertising: Public Policy Implications for Fair Housing Practices." *Journal of Public Policy and Marketing,* 14, 225–244.

Wooten, D.B. 1995. "One-of-a-Kind in a Full House: Some Consequences of Ethnic and Gender Distinctiveness." *Journal of Consumer Psychology* 4: 205–224.

5

Where to Draw the Line?

Managerial Implications of Behavioral Research on Deceptive Advertising

Guang-Xin Xie and David M. Boush

Advertising practitioners sometimes face an inconvenient problem: a persuasive advertisement is considered deceptive by consumers and regulators. Competitors and consumer advocates may also challenge the ad for creating false impressions or beliefs, and the disputes may end up in court. For example, AT&T filed a lawsuit against Verizon Wireless in November 2009, seeking to stop its rival from using "misleading" wireless coverage maps in national advertising campaigns (Cheng 2009). In May 2010, Washington-based advocacy group Competitive Enterprise Institute (CEI) filed a formal complaint against General Motors (GM), charging GM with deceptive advertising. A GM national TV ad said it had paid back its bailout loan from the government. CEI argued that the repayment actually came from another government bailout account provided by the Troubled Assets Relief Program (TARP) (Thomaselli 2010b).

Deceptive advertising disputes can be costly. In an event study, for example, Tipton, Bharadwaj, and Robertson (2009) demonstrated that incidents of exposed deceptive advertising were associated with a loss of eighty-six million dollars for the median-sized pharmaceutical firms in the research sample. More specifically, many believe that deceptive advertising partially accounts for the irrational buying and investing behaviors in the real estate market, which ultimately led to the subprime mortgage crisis (Perry and Motley 2009). As a result, it is widely anticipated that regulators such as the Federal Trade Commission (FTC) will be more empowered to scrutinize advertising practices with regard to loan modification and foreclosure rescue (Sichelman 2009). Some advertising professionals are particularly concerned about the possibility that advertising agencies could become more liable for clients' deceptive claims (Thomaselli 2010a).

Existing legal and intra-industry self-regulatory systems have prevented many but not all deceptive practices. Advertising agencies often hire legal professionals to screen out controversial advertising claims. The lawyers can study the industry-specific regulations and cases intensively to make recommendations. However, every once a while, big brands make big news for being caught making deceptive advertising claims. The actual number of deceptive ads may far exceed what it appears to be since smaller agencies and marketers may escape public attention. The general distrust of advertisers among the public remains strong. A 2007 Gallup/USA Today poll found that advertising practitioners are ranked third from last among professionals in public perception of honesty and ethics, just ahead of lobbyists and car salesmen (Neff 2010).

The "lawyer-solve-all" approach can be further improved from a perspective that has been largely neglected by practitioners—conducting empirical studies. In fact, behavioral researchers have studied deceptive advertising for more than four decades regarding the following: (a) under what conditions consumers think or feel that an ad is deceptive (e.g., Boush, Friestad, and Rose 1994; Burke et al. 1988; Haefner and Permut 1974; Russo, Metcalf, and Stephens 1981); (b) the psychological and behavioral consequences of deception (e.g., Darke and Ritchie 2007; Urbany, Bearden, and Weilbaker 1988); and (c) what measures to take in correcting a deceptive ad (e.g., Darke, Ashworth, and Ritchie 2008; Shimp and Preston 1981). These streams of research provide different viewpoints and methods that could enhance practitioners' abilities to screen out potentially deceptive ads if they are well-integrated with the existent internal clearance procedures. In other words, getting into the mind of the consumer can help practitioners to draw a line between persuasive and deceptive advertising.

This chapter is organized into four sections. It begins with the legal and behavioral definitions of advertising deception, followed by empirical measurements. The next section discusses extant research that demonstrates the effect of deceptive advertising on consumers and some boundary conditions. The final section extends to remedies for the potentially damaging effects of deceptive advertising: affirmative disclosure and corrective advertising. Managerial implications are discussed at the end of each section.

Definitions

Many behavioral researchers hold a different view from regulators about how to define advertising deception. Some argue that consumers' false beliefs are a sufficient criterion to conclude the deceptiveness of an ad, despite their purchase intention or behaviors (e.g., Armstrong, Gurol, and Russ 1979;

Gaeth and Heath 1987; Gardner 1975, 1976). Legally, however, a deceptive ad must also be material to significantly influence consumer purchases (e.g., Richards 1990; Richards and Preston 1992). In this section, we discuss some fundamental differences between the legal and behavioral definitions of deceptive advertising.

Legal Definition

Advertisers across industries follow specific guidelines provided by federal regulators (e.g., Federal Trade Commission, Food and Drug Administration), intra-industry self-regulatory organizations (e.g., Advertising Standards Authority, Better Business Bureau), and media outlets (e.g., NBC, Google). The legal definition is of ultimate importance for practitioners. The law allows individual companies to file civil suits against competitors for false or deceptively misleading advertising claims under section 43(a) of the Lanham Act, "a plaintiff must demonstrate that the commercial advertisement or promotion is either literally false, or that it is likely to mislead and confuse consumers." In addition to proving that a claim is deceptive and material, the plaintiff also has to show damages. The following five requirements for proving a Lanham Act case serve as a useful basis for discussion: (1) a false statement of fact about its own or another's product; (2) the statement actually deceives or has the tendency to deceive a substantial segment of the audience; (3) the deception is material, in that it is likely to influence the purchasing decision; (4) the defendant causes its false statement to enter interstate commerce; and (5) the plaintiff has been or is likely to be injured as a result of the false statement.

The purpose of federal regulations is generally more preventative than punitive. As one of the most important government regulators, the FTC is responsible for prohibiting unfair or deceptive advertising practices. The FTC (1983) has been updating the definition over time and the most commonly cited refers to, "a representation, omission or practice that is likely to mislead the consumer acting reasonably in the circumstances, to the consumer's detriment." Note that advertisers' intent to deceive is not at issue if a dispute must be solved in court. The court does not care whether the deceptive claim is purposeful. The law considers a claim to be illegally deceptive if it has the tendency to deceive a reasonable consumer in a way that is likely to materially affect his or her decision to buy the advertised product (Ford and Calfee 1986; Jacoby and Small 1975; Richards and Preston 1992). (The discussion on filing lawsuits over advertising deception is beyond the scope of this chapter. For more information, see Brandt and Preston 1977; Richards 1990; Scammon and Semenik 1983.)

Behavioral Definition

In the behavioral research literature, advertising deception usually is defined on the basis of consumer beliefs. Beliefs are descriptive statements about object attributes or consequences (Pollay and Mittal 1993). Deception occurs when consumers believe something untrue as a result of the misleading elements in advertisements (Olson and Dover 1978; Permut and Haefner 1973). Gardner (1975, 41) defined advertising deception as an outcome: "If an advertisement (or advertising campaign) leaves the consumer with an impression(s) and/or belief(s) different from what would normally be expected if the consumer had reasonable knowledge, and the impression(s) and/or belief(s) is factually untrue or potentially misleading, then deception is said to exist." Olson and Dover (1978, 30) proposed a simple version following the same reasoning: "Deception is considered to occur when consumers acquire demonstrably false beliefs as a function of exposure to an advertisement." Advertising deceptiveness, in comparison, refers to the *likelihood* or *capability* that the advertisements can mislead consumers to hold false beliefs and to make purchase decisions that they would not otherwise (Richards 1990). In reality, such negative outcomes are often anticipated rather than the actual consequences. That is, as long as an advertisement is highly *likely* to mislead the consumers to their detriment, it is considered deceptive (Ford and Calfee 1986).

In comparison, legal deceptiveness requires the establishment of "materiality," the notion that a deceptive advertisement must be effective enough to lead to detrimental outcomes (for a review, see Richards and Preston 1992). Advertisers sometimes use "puffery," or claims that a reasonable consumer understands to be obviously exaggerated, dramatized, and nonfactual (Kamins and Marks 1987). If an automobile insurance commercial shows someone rinsing the car bumper and the water automatically fixes all the dents, reasonable consumers would take it as an exaggerated analogy. Therefore, puffery is usually not considered to be material and therefore not deceptive. Even when consumers acquire false beliefs about the product merits, a misleading ad may not be regulated by the FTC if its impact is trivial (Richards 1990, 17–19). A questionable ad can be legally nondeceptive if the large majority of consumers are not likely to make the purchase, and thus no further serious consequences occur. This suggests a well-known controversy, the "n% problem" (Ford and Calfee 1986; Jacoby and Small 1975; Mazis 2001; Scammon and Semenik 1983). The question is: what exact percentage of the targeted consumers must be misled for an ad to be deceptive? Further, when the percentage is small but the sheer number of consumers is large, would the seriousness of harm increase and the ads be more subject to regulation? To our knowledge, there is no consensus yet about the specific procedure or method to set up a particular threshold. For each ad the percentage must be judged against its own standard, not some universally applicable cutoff (Russo et al. 1981).

Common Types of Advertising Deception

Deceptive advertising has been classified by type, which also implies variation in degree. Gardner (1975) argued that deceptive advertising consists of unconscionable lies, claim-fact discrepancies, and claim-belief discrepancies. Russo and colleagues (1981) refined these categories as fraud, falsity, and misleadingness: fraud means advertisers' deliberate intent to create false beliefs; falsity refers to the existence of a claim-fact discrepancy; and misleadingness is the belief-fact discrepancy. For most consumers, it is not easy to technically verify claim-fact discrepancies prior to purchases. Therefore, most researchers focused on the belief-fact discrepancy, that is, the misleading features of deceptiveness (e.g., Andrews, Burton, and Netemeyer 2000; Burke, Milberg, and Moe 1997; Gaeth and Heath 1987; Shimp and Preston 1981). According to Russo and colleagues (1981, 128), an advertisement is misleading, "if it creates, increases, or exploits a false belief about expected product performance."

Deceptive advertising also differs according to the tactics employed. An advertisement can mislead consumers by claims, implications, and misrepresentations. The deceptive claims consist of fabrication, distortion, or omission of factual information. Claims about specific facts (e.g., technical features) are usually verifiable. Implications are not literally stated but can be inferred on a reasonable basis. Preston (1977) summarized ten types of implications from cases between 1970 and 1976, which has been proven rather comprehensive given today's standard. These implications include: expansion, demonstration, inconspicuous qualification, inconspicuous context, uniqueness, reasonable basis, no qualification, significance, social concerns, and third-party implications (for detailed definitions and examples, see Preston 1977; Richards 1990). Misrepresentations refer to nonverbal manipulations to create or exploit false beliefs in favor of the sellers. The literal statements can be true, but consumers are not aware of the manipulative tactics and make purchases that they would not have made otherwise. Examples may include bait and switch, graphical distortion, faked testimonials, and disguised endorsements (for more details, see Boush, Friestad, and Wright 2009).

Managerial Implication

It is important to keep in mind that consumers may be misled not only by the advertising claims, but also by implications and the presentations. In particular, some advertisers believe that the statement of personal opinions is nondeceptive, such as, "We are the best restaurant in _____" and "We have a better service/price than _____." In fact, it depends. If the claims are accompanied by more concrete verifiable details, the advertisers may be in trouble. For instance, Pizza Hut filed complaints against Papa John's for its national advertising campaign "Better ingredients, better pizza" (Kramer 1999). The ad campaign alleged that Papa John's sauce and dough were better than Pizza Hut's because they were made with fresh tomatoes and filtered water. Papa John's may argue that it is a fairly subjective statement of opinion; but Papa John's also claimed that its "vine ripened tomatoes" were superior to the "remanufactured tomato sauce" used by Pizza Hut and its fresh dough and filtered water created a better-tasting pizza. By pointing to specific differences between itself and Pizza Hut and by failing to present at trial any scientific support or the results of independent surveys to substantiate its claims (e.g., taste tests), Papa John's had subjected itself to a claim that its advertising might mislead consumers (Kramer 1999). Although eventually Pizza Hut lost the lawsuit largely due to the lack of evidence to support the "materiality" of the Papa John's ads (Gindy 2001), both companies should have learned a lesson. If Pizza Hut could have demonstrated empirically the ads actually influenced consumers' purchasing decisions, the results of the legal battle could be quite different. On the other side, Papa John's could have considered how to empirically demonstrate the nondeceptiveness of their ads prior to finalizing the campaigns. This leads to the next subject: how to measure advertising deceptiveness and the effects on consumers.

Measurements

This section introduces three behavioral paradigms that empirically demonstrate advertising deceptiveness. In fact, it is difficult to develop accurate and reliable measurements of advertising deceptiveness. The federal regulatory agencies tend to avoid relying on empirical evidence because this procedure consumes enormous amounts of time and resources (Richards 1990). Regulators simply cannot afford to run an empirical study for each complaint, considering the large number of cases they must deal with on a daily basis. To do so will probably also undermine the authority of the regulatory institutions and complicate the jurisprudential process. However, consumer testimonies and surveys have played an increasingly important role as corroboration of evidence (Andrews and Maronick 1995; Armstrong 1983; Barone et al. 1999; Brandt and Preston 1977; Cohen 1972). For practitioners, understanding the measurement issues largely serves a preventative purpose: when needed, could an ad copy survive an empirical test?

Over the past four decades, behavioral researchers have used three major approaches to measure the extent to which a questionable advertisement misleads consumers: normative, salient, and descriptive techniques. These methods largely rely on self-report questionnaires that are administrated during or after exposure to the advertisements. Note that previous research does not focus on advertisers' intentions to deceive consumers (e.g., fraud or unconscionable lie). Rather, issues have largely centered on the fact-claim discrepancy and belief-claim discrepancy. Fact-claim discrepancy is relatively straightforward, since it involves comparing claims with verifiable facts. For example, AT&T's 2009 "the Nation's Fastest 3G Network" campaign claimed their wireless network covered 97 percent of Americans. If challenged, the regulatory institutions may ask AT&T to present objective evidences to substantiate the claim. However, it is usually impractical for consumers to verify all the technical details as they are reading or watching an advertisement. Instead, they often infer from the messages about any potential fact-claim discrepancies, which are essentially based on personal beliefs. Thus, behavioral researchers have primarily examined belief-claim discrepancies with empirical measurements.

Normative Measurement

The goal of normative belief methods is to test whether advertising claims lead to false consumer beliefs about product attributes and/or performance. The presumption is that the advertisers make certain claims that can be verified objectively as true or false. Then consumer product beliefs can be evaluated as true or false as well. A typical approach is to ask research participants fact-based true/false questions about the advertised products after exposure to ads. The percentage/number of falsely held beliefs is compared with that of the control group. The differences between groups indicate the existence of levels of deceptiveness. This approach has been proven quite useful when the ad claims are fact-based (e.g., Barbour and Gardner 1982; Gardner 1975, 1976; Maronick 1991).

Further, consumer false belief is necessary but not sufficient to demonstrate deceptiveness. Advertisements sometimes are not directly responsible for creating false beliefs, but exploit consumers' existing false beliefs. Such deceptiveness can be demonstrated by measuring belief changes: an increased level of false beliefs after exposure to a deceptive advertisement, or the reduced level of false beliefs after exposure to a corrective advertisement (Russo et al. 1981). In terms of the research design, participants should be randomly assigned to the control group (without exposure to an ad), the experiment group (exposure to an ad), and the correction group (exposure to the corrected ad without the questionable claims). The differences across groups indicate the existence of levels of deceptiveness. Ideally, the approach should also be used for a representative group of "reasonable" consumers in a relatively naturalistic setting to maximize external validity.

Salient Belief Measurement

Salient belief methods are based on a notion consistent with the FTC definition of advertising deception. That is, an ad can create false beliefs when not all of these beliefs are pertinent to the purchase decision. To be of any concern, the false beliefs must be relevant to consumers' decisions to purchase a brand in the product category (Armstrong and Russ 1975). In particular, the consequential purchase behaviors must be to their detriment. Operationally, the salient belief approach consists of three steps: (1) identifying claims that relevant consumers perceive the ad is making; (2) determining externally which of the claims are false; and (3) measuring the perceptions, beliefs, and salience of a representative sample of consumers exposed to the ad (Armstrong et al. 1979; Barry 1980).

Note that a deceptive ad does not always change consumers' beliefs, but is still effective by changing the importance of the existing beliefs (Russo et al. 1981). A literally true claim can be deceptive if it misleads reasonable consumers to mentally discount defensive beliefs and the consequences are detrimental. For example, a weight-loss program ad may claim that a new diet plan is effective without exercises. The implication that exercise is unnecessary for all people can be questioned if some actually think exercise is no longer important.

Descriptive Measurement

The descriptive measurement approach relies on the assumption that consumers are able to make their own judgments about the extent to which an advertisement is deceptive. In this approach, consumers are shown the ad copies and asked to indicate what they think about the advertisements. Questions can be either general or specific, including consumer impression (e.g., Gardner 1975), perceptions (e.g., Johar 1995), and judgments (e.g., Darke and Ritchie 2007; Snyder 1989). Free or cued recall, thought-listing, and numeric multiple-item scales are often used. For example, researchers can simply ask how misleading or deceptive respondents think an ad is on a 7-point scale (1 = not at all; 7 = very much). For this method to reflect the perceived deceptiveness only, researchers must use properly designed and controlled procedure. For instance, individuals' general advertising skepticism (Obermiller and Spangenberg 1998) is often statistically controlled by techniques such as Analysis of Covariance (ANCOVA), linear regression, and structural equation modeling.

In the literature, the descriptive approach is usually not used to establish or verify the existence of advertising deception. Instead, researchers are more interested in factors that influence how deceptive an ad is perceived to be. In other words, they often used descriptive methods to measure ad deceptiveness as a dependent variable for theoretical purposes. An important question emerges: when and to whom is the ad more or less deceptive? Chances are that some consumers are more vulnerable to ad deception than others. Children, for example, may lack adequate self-protective abilities to guard against misleading tactics (Barry 1980). This notion leads to the effects of deceptive advertising, which is the focal interest for many behavioral researchers.

Managerial Implication

The essence of empirical measurements is to show the causal relationship between deceptive ads and consumers' acquired or strengthened false beliefs about a product. Some argue that such false beliefs must be important enough to influence purchase decision to consumers' detriment (e.g., Richards and Preston 1992). When the advertising claims are about verifiable facts, the advertisers or the advertising agencies should get ready to provide evidence to substantiate their claims. When the claims have implications that can be interpreted in various ways, they should use extra caution about the statement of opinions. A subjective personal opinion can be seriously challenged. If needed, normative belief methods provide a relatively conservative benchmark about how likely an ad claim is to be deceptive. An internal clearance procedure can be enhanced with the addition of empirical tests. The key is to adapt causal research designs whereby the effect of questionable claims/implications on consumer beliefs can be isolated.

Effects

The literature in the 1970s primarily has focused on defining, identifying, and measuring advertising deception (e.g., Gardner 1975, 1976). During the 1980s, more research has examined the effects of advertising deceptiveness on consumer product beliefs, perceptions, and purchase intentions (e.g., Blair and Landon 1981; Burke et al. 1988; Gaeth and Heath 1987; Kinnear and Root 1988; Liefeld and Heslop 1985; Mobley, Bearden, and Teel 1988; Urbany et al. 1988). Since the 1990s, researchers have become more interested in the boundary conditions of the negative effects of deceptiveness (e.g., Barone and Miniard 1999; Johar 1995; Johar and Simmons 2000; LaTour and LaTour 2009; Shanahan and Hopkins 2007). More recently, more attention has centered on consumers' defensive responses to advertising deception such as persuasion knowledge (e.g., Boush et al. 1994; Friestad and Wright 1994), skepticism (e.g., Obermiller and Spangenberg 1998), and distrust (e.g., Darke and Ritchie 2007; Darke, Ashworth, and Main 2010). In this section, we briefly summarize some of the key findings about: cognitive and emotional effects, boundary conditions, and consumer defensiveness.

Cognitive and Emotional Effects

Blatantly false claims in national advertising campaigns have become less common and most alleged deceptive advertisements now use subtle and implicit tactics (Mazis 2001). As mentioned earlier, the typical manipulative tactics often involve some kind of subjective and evaluative statements that appear to be personal opinions (e.g., superiority implication in incomplete comparative claims). It has been well documented that some of these tactics can be quite effective: consumers do tend to form more false beliefs and more favorable perceptions of the advertised products, compared to the control condition or the corrected ads condition wherein potentially misleading tactics are neutralized or disclosed (e.g., Barone and Miniard 1999; Cunningham and Cunningham 1976; Liefeld and Heslop 1985; Olson and Dover 1978; Shimp 1978; Urbany et al. 1988). For instance, Burke et al. (1988) examined consumer responses to four types of attribute statements of ibuprofen-based brands: no attribute information, truth, expansion implication, and inconspicuous qualification implication. The results show that both claim implications increased consumers' false attribute beliefs on headache pain relief, side effects, and speed of relief, compared with the control conditions. In another study, Barone and Miniard (1999) showed the subjects a partial comparative ad containing a combination of comparative and noncomparative advertising claims. They found a "copy × copy" interaction when consumers acquired beliefs that the advertised brand was better than the competitor, not only along the attributes featured in the comparative claim, but also those in the noncomparative claim. In that sense, consumers can be misled even when the literal claims are true.

When consumers detect the manipulative attempts (although sometimes biased against advertisers), they tend to respond rather negatively in terms of their general impression (e.g., Gardner 1975) and specific brand/product perceptions (e.g., Olson and Dover 1978). Such negative effects can be cognitive, emotional, or both. For example, Mobley, Bearden, and Teel (1988) compared the use of tensile price claims (e.g., save *up to* 50 percent) and specific price reduction. The results suggest that the vague characteristics of tensile claims elicited more negative thoughts about the advertisements than the standard price promotions. In another study on social marketing, Shanahan and Hopkins (2007) found that deception (using actors as the victims in anti–drunk driving print ads) led to less intense emotional responses, less positive attitude toward the ad, and weaker willingness to donate to the nonprofit, compared to the portrayal of real victims.

Most previous research has centered on verbal or written forms of deception. Only a few studies have addressed the graphical, sound, and sensory elements in deceptive advertising (e.g., LaTour and LaTour 2009; Miniard et al. 1991). With today's digital design and computer animation technologies, such practices have become more commonplace. For instance, a fast-food chain commercial could use artful portrayals (e.g., coloring and lighting) to artificially enhance the food's visual appeal. Further, there is a lack of research on misleading ads that are also very entertaining, inspirational, or creative as to distract consumers from defensive reasoning. Despite the tremendous progress over almost forty years, more research is needed to address these voids in the literature.

Boundary Conditions

Boundary conditions refer to the constraints of an observed effect: an established relationship between *X* and *Y* may change, when *Z* is taken into consideration. In a broad sense, any relationship between two variables is bounded by other factors. It can be aggravated, attenuated, mediated, or modified, depending on the other factors included in the system. For example, a cynical person may hold a much stronger negative attitude toward advertising in general than a pragmatic person. A given individual may be more attentive to deceptive claims when he is highly involved in processing the ad information and is less likely to be misled. Or the opposite could happen: one could be highly involved in the subject matter (e.g., the claimed benefits), less attentive to deceptive claims, and thus more likely to be misled.

Boundary conditions can be roughly categorized as situational variations and individual differences. *Situational variation* refers to momentary changes in the context or a person (e.g., attention, mood, suspicion). *Individual difference* refers to relatively stable or dispositional characteristics of a person (e.g., gender, personality). Most previous studies have explored boundary conditions to some extent. Operationally, researchers have investigated what kind of situational or individual differences could interact with certain types of advertising messages (e.g., comparativeness, puffery, extremity). In a stricter sense, the different types of deceptive ads can be part of the context as situational variations. In this section, we consider them separately to highlight some of the interactions. Below we discuss some salient boundary conditions documented in the research literature.

Three main types of situational variables have emerged from previous studies. The first group of variables center on whether consumers have the diagnostic schema to detect deceptive implications and tactics, such as product knowledge (Andrews et al. 2000); awareness of pricing tactics (Blair and Landon 1981; Liefeld and Heslop 1985; Urbany et al. 1988); brand usage experience (Barone, Palan, and Miniard 2004); and advertisers' reputation (Goldberg and Hartwick 1990). Another set of variables deals with how consumers process the advertising claims and make inferences about product attributes, including processing involvement (Johar 1995); inferential strategies (Barone and Miniard 1999); and information relevancy (Lee and Mason 1999). The last type addresses the emotional states that influence consumers' processing abilities and foci (LaTour and LaTour 2009). Overall, these studies suggest that detection of deceptive advertising is a difficult task that demands certain amounts and types of mental resources. If the resources are not available or are insufficient, consumers become more susceptible to deceptive advertising.

Previous research has also documented some individual difference variables that reflect consumers' abilities to guard against deceptive ads. According to John and Cole (1986), age difference is indicative of the severity of memory- and knowledge-based deficits when people process advertising information. More specifically, Gaeth and Heath (1987) found that young adults were less susceptible to misleading techniques than older adults in the research samples, not due to the ease of memory retrieval but rather the tendency to scrutinize advertisements more thoroughly. Interestingly, Barone et al. (2004) found that gender moderates the susceptibility to the "copy × copy" interactions, which were described earlier. Males were more susceptible than females in general, but female nonusers were more susceptible than male nonusers. In addition, consumers' general skepticism toward advertising (Obermiller and Spangenberg 1998) and the specific knowledge about advertising tactics (Boush et al. 1994) have been found to influence negative attitude toward the ads and brands. Such nonbiological individual differences are largely due to socialization processes (John 1999), whereby consumers learn to effectively (sometimes with biases) cope with deceptive persuasion attempts. This concept leads to the next topic on consumer defensiveness against advertising deception.

Consumer Defensiveness

It is well documented that due to suspicion of an ulterior sales motive, consumers tend to be skeptical about marketers' manipulative intention in general (Campbell and Kirmani 2008). One of the well-studied sources of distrust is consumer persuasion knowledge—schema about marketers' motives and persuasion tactics (Friestad and Wright 1994). When accessible and diagnostic, persuasion knowledge alerts consumers to detect, resist, and control a manipulative attempt (Wright, Friestad, and Boush 2005). During the past two decades, researchers have found that persuasion knowledge leads to mixed responses toward marketers, depending upon individual characteristics and the specific persuasion contexts (e.g., Campbell and Kirmani 2000; Kirmani 1990, 1997; Kirmani and Campbell 2004; Kirmani and Zhu 2007).

More recently, Darke and Ritchie (2007) have developed a theory of defensive suspicion: the notion that distrust is a self-protection heuristic. It postulates that once consumers recognize the threat of being influenced in an unfair way, a defensive motivation is activated in a relatively automatic process (Main, Dahl, and Darke 2007). The negative responses serve as a preventive function to reduce the risk of being deceived. These responses are fast and strong enough to outweigh the accuracy motivation to systematically consider the alternative reactions. As a result, the negative judgments apply not only to the deceptive advertisers, but also carry over to the subsequent advertisers, even if they are not deceptive (Darke et al. 2008, 2010).

On the other hand, there is also some evidence that shows the vulnerability of the defensive mechanism. The defense is bounded. First and foremost, consumers in general are not persuasion or product experts who can effectively guard against an undue influence. Product knowledge asymmetry alone, for example, can weaken the effect of suspicion (DeCarlo 2005). Even when consumers are aware of a marketer's sales motive, a number of factors can disrupt the alerting system, such as momentary cognitive busyness (Campbell and Kirmani 2000); agent-consumer relationships (Kirmani and Campbell 2004); and persuasion knowledge confidence (Ahluwalia and Burnkrant 2004). As a result, at a conscious or subconscious level, consumers can easily switch away from the defensive mode. For example, when salespeople are likeable and physically attractive, consumer responses tend to be more positive despite suspicion (Reinhard, Messner, and Sporer 2006). In another study, Sengupta and Dahl (2008) found that male consumers tended to respond more favorably to the ads with sex portrayals than females, even when they were aware that the sex appeals were an advertising tactic. Simply put, consumers can knowingly but also willingly give up the defensiveness.

Managerial Implications

Although individual studies address narrowly defined questions in specific contexts, together they reveal an important pattern. Many consumers are susceptible to the superiority implications of product attributes, especially those combined with technical information. The simple fact that some supportive details exist can be an important heuristic enhancing trustworthiness regardless of the extent to which they logically substantiate the superiority claims or implications. In other words, consumers can be skeptical but do not always think critically. This kind of easygoingness can both work for and against advertisers. When consumers comprehend an ad, they can be less careful and acquire false beliefs easily. They may sometimes misinterpret the claimed benefits and hold unrealistic expectations beyond what the advertisers want them to. When the product performance falls short of expectations, they can ascribe the discrepancies to the advertiser's intention and tactics to deceive consumers. As a result, they may never come back to the advertised brands and even spread negative word-of-mouth. To prevent this from happening, advertisers may consider the use of affirmative disclosure and corrective messages, the subject discussed in the next section.

Remedies

The most common regulatory remedies for potential advertising deception are affirmative disclosure and corrective advertising (Jacoby, Nelson, and Hoyer 1982). Affirmative disclosure refers to *in-ads* statements or qualifications designed to provide additional information to prevent consumers from being making false judgments about the primary claims or messages (Andrews et al. 2000). Corrective advertising refers to a firm's *after-the-fact* statements or qualifications to change consumers' impression, knowledge, and beliefs acquired from the primary advertising claims. It is called "corrective" because firms that have misled consumers would have to rectify its deception with further ads (Wilkie, McNeill, and Mazis 1984). This section introduces some of the basic findings about the effects of affirmative disclosure and corrective advertising.

Affirmative Disclosure

Affirmative disclosure addresses the additional product information that is not included or highlighted in the primary advertising messages. The regulatory requirements for disclosure are based on two main assumptions: (1) consumers have a right to be informed as well as not to be deceived; and

(2) effective information dissemination can be accomplished with more specific communication standards (Frech and Barksdale 1974). The required disclosures are intended to ensure proper presentations of the commodities with respect to a variety of matters such as the ingredients, price, quality, purity, origin, attributes or properties, safety, risk, warnings, and nature of manufacture. The fundamental standard for effective disclosure is that it must be "clear and conspicuous" (Hoy and Stankey 1993). For example, the Food and Drug Administration has implemented stricter guidelines for food packaging and labeling toward full disclosure of product information since 1973. The disclosure includes a number of aspects including nutrition, cholesterol, fat acid, flavor and spice, special diet use, identification of imitation food, and nonstandardized foods (Frech and Barksdale 1974).

However, a large body of existing research has suggested that the inclusion of affirmative disclosures in advertisements often fail to remind consumers about the potential risks (e.g., Andrews et al. 2000; Foxman, Muehling, and Moore 1988; Jacoby et al. 1982; Johar and Simmons 2000; Liebert et al. 1977; Moorman 1990; Muehling and Kolbe 1998; Stern and Harmon 1984). One of the main reasons is that consumers do not pay enough attention to the disclosure (Foxman et al. 1988; Muehling and Kolbe 1998). Further, even when the disclosure was noticed and encoded, the effectiveness was less than satisfactory (Stewart and Martin 1994). To address the underlying mechanisms, Johar and Simmons (2000) investigated a number of potential moderating factors (e.g., cognitive capacity, time, explicitness of disclosure, accuracy incentive) in relation to the use of disclosures to correct invalid brand-quality inferences. They found that highly accessible but invalid inferences were hard to correct with disclosures. Consumers must be motivated, capable, and have sufficient cognitive resources to *encode* and *utilize* the corrective information. The current regulations largely focus on ensuring *encoding,* but do not guarantee consumers *use* the information to make product inferences.

Corrective Advertising

Corrective advertising is comparable to a public confession of having sinned (Wilkie et al. 1984). Its effects are twofold: intended and unintended. The intended effect is to correct false beliefs due to exposure to a previous misleading advertisement. A number of studies have supported the notion that a corrective ad can reduce some false product beliefs if comprehended correctly (e.g., Bernhardt, Kinnear, and Mazis 1986; Mizerski, Allison, and Calvert 1980). Note that the effectiveness is also bounded, depending upon message strength (Dyer and Kuehl 1974); publicity context (Tyebjee 1982); and prior brand evaluation (Johar 1995). The documented unintended effect is often called the "spill-over" bias (Darke and Ritchie 2007; Darke et al. 2008). That is, a corrective ad targets only a limited number of product attributes such as price and performance. It is not surprising that such an ad would hurt the perceptions of other attributes and the deceptive brands. In addition, the implications are much broader: the negative effect applies not only to other products or attributes advertised by the firms, but also to ads from second-party firms. Such a generalized bias or distrust can be hard to neutralize unless credible independent third-party sources are involved (Darke et al. 2010).

Managerial Implications

Practitioners should be aware that the characteristics of the remedies (e.g., language, format, placement, duration) may be equally or more confusing to consumers than the messages they are designed to clarify. The likely impact of remedies must be thoroughly assessed and evaluated before such statements are inserted in advertising. As for affirmative disclosure, it is not enough to simply add disclaimers. Advertisers should create effective communications to increase the chance that reasonable consumers take them more seriously. For example, in some British supermarkets, the "traffic-lighting" food labels are displayed on the package front. The labels use red, yellow, and green circles to indicate how healthy products are in four categories: fat, saturated fat, sugar, and salt (Cendrowicz 2010). Consumers may not only become more attentive, but also be cued to think more. In the case of corrective advertising, the best way is to avoid using it at the first place. This practice does not only elicit negative reactions against product attributes, the brand, and firm reputation, it could also lead to a generalized bias over other product attributes and second-party firms. For those nondeceptive victim firms, it may help to distance their ads from the corrective ones if feasible.

Further, some of the novel practices and specific procedures have not been detailed by the regulators, fearing the precise terms might result in evasion. For example, the FTC's "Guides Concerning the Use of Endorsements and Testimonials in Advertising" (2009) state that "If the advertiser does not have substantiation that the endorser's experience is representative of what consumers will generally achieve, the advertisement should clearly and conspicuously disclose the generally expected performance in the depicted circumstances, and the advertiser must possess and rely on adequate substantiation for that representation." Given this, an advertiser may comply with the FTC regulation as long as the general expectation is disclosed in some way. Whether such disclosure is fully comprehended is not guaranteed. In the era of social media, some marketing techniques without full disclosure have already elicited negative backlash. For example, there is an increasing concern over firms fabricating personal reviews and ratings on websites such as Yelp.com and Amazon.com. More research is needed to address these emerging issues.

Summary

This chapter reviews four areas of research: (1) what elements or tactics in an ad are likely to be considered deceptive; (2) how to measure perceived deceptiveness; (3) the psychological and behavioral consequences of exposure to deceptive advertisements; and (4) measures to correct false beliefs and restore some trust. For practitioners, the most important implication is that avoiding deception is complicated but worthwhile. When a client wants to make a claim and gives the substantiation from their scientists and experts, the agency may have difficulty assessing how a layperson would evaluate the evidence. Well-trained professionals may differentiate a statement of opinion from deception, but it often occurs when the implications appear to be inappropriate but also hard to reject completely. After all, the advertising agencies depend upon clients' money to stay in business. As we mentioned earlier, the line between black and white can be blurred. Common sense and legal experiences help; but preventative caution is also much needed.

Second, as Freer (1949, 360) pointed out more than half a century ago, "Good advertising not only tells the literal truth but also avoids possible deception through subtle implication or omission." As we notice from recent research and legal cases, it can be useful for practitioners to think about a hypothetical marketplace where the burden of proof is on the seller to show that no deceptiveness occurs. If the seller would have to avoid misleading the buyer in any way, and the legal standard truly was no tolerance of deception, what should he do? Given practical constraints, it is unlikely for advertisers to disclose all detailed product information, let alone their sales intentions and persuasion tactics. However, it is plausible for credible third-party sources such as *Consumer Reports* to provide more comprehensive disclosure. A recent *Consumer Reports* article on iPhone 4G's reception problem quickly generated negative word-of-mouth among consumers and industry analysts, which may have hurt Apple's brand image and stock price (Hill 2010). How to work with such information brokers will be an increasingly important issue for advertisers.

Third, from an implementation standpoint, it can help to establish an independent internal clearance procedure whereby potentially deceptive ad copy can be identified at early stages. The key is to effectively differentiate factual from evaluative claims, and actively check the need of substantiation with technical evidence. The proposed empirical test can be used if necessary, and it can serve a preventative purpose. Practitioners do not have to actually run consumer surveys all the time, but they may want to keep in mind that regulators, advocators, and competitors may do so in some cases. To be cautious, practitioners may run small-scaled copy tests when needed.

To sum up, the goal of this chapter was to lobby advertisers to avoid deception and to describe specific ways to accomplish this. Fair practices are closely tied to advertisers' reputation and financial performance. We hope behavioral research can be more relevant for practitioners to get a better sense of the "Dos and Don'ts" in fair advertising practices. More specifically, we have discussed some empirical methods to measure and evaluate advertising deceptiveness. Practitioners can use them to formulate supportive arguments, control the damages, and manage public relations when applicable.

References

Ahluwalia, R., and R. Burnkrant. 2004. "Answering Questions about Questions: A Persuasion Knowledge Perspective for Understanding the Effects of Rhetorical Questions." *Journal of Consumer Research* 31: 26–42.

Andrews, J.C., S. Burton, and R. G. Netemeyer 2000. "Are Some Comparative Nutrition Claims Misleading? The Role of Nutrition Knowledge, Ad Claim Type and Disclosure Conditions." *Journal of Advertising* 29: 29–42.

Andrews, J.C., and T.J. Maronick. 1995. "Advertising Research Issues from FTC Versus Stouffer Foods Corporation." *Journal of Public Policy & Marketing* 14: 301–309.

Armstrong, G.M. 1983. "A Longitudinal Evaluation of the Listerine Corrective Advertising Campaign." *Journal of Public Policy & Marketing* 2: 16–28.

Armstrong, G.M., M.N. Gurol, and F.A. Russ. 1979. "Detecting and Correcting Deceptive Advertising." *Journal of Consumer Research* 6: 237–46.

Armstrong, G. M., and F. A. Russ. 1975. "Detecting Deception in Advertising." *MSU Business Topics,* 23: 21–32.

Barbour II, F.L., and D.M. Gardner. 1982. "Deceptive Advertising: A Practical Approach to Measurement." *Journal of Advertising* 11: 21–30.

Barone, M.J., and P.W. Miniard. 1999. "How and When Factual Ad Claims Mislead Consumers: Examining the Deceptive Consequences of Copy × Copy Interactions for Partial Comparative Advertisements." *Journal of Marketing Research* 36: 58–74.

Barone, M.J., K.M. Palan, and P.W. Miniard. 2004. "Brand Usage and Gender as Moderators of the Potential Deception Associated with Partial Comparative Advertising." *Journal of Advertising* 33: 19–28.

Barone, M.J., R.L. Rose, P.W. Miniard, and K.C. Manning. 1999. "Enhancing the Detection of Misleading Comparative Advertising." *Journal of Advertising Research* 39: 43–50.

Barry, T.E. 1980. "A Framework for Ascertaining Deception in Children's Advertising." *Journal of Advertising* 9: 11–18.

Bernhardt, K.L., T.C. Kinnear, and M.B. Mazis. 1986. "A Field Study of Corrective Advertising Effectiveness." *Journal of Public Policy & Marketing* 5: 146–62.

Blair, E.A., and E.L. Landon, Jr. 1981. "The Effects of Reference Prices in Retail Advertisements." *Journal of Marketing* 45: 61–69.

Boush, D.M., M. Friestad, and G.M. Rose. 1994. "Adolescent Skepticism Toward TV Advertising and Knowledge of Advertiser Tactics." *Journal of Consumer Research* 21: 165–74.

Boush, D.M., M. Friestad, and P. Wright. 2009. *Deception in the Marketplace: The Psychology of Deceptive Persuasion and Consumer Self-Protection.* New York: Taylor and Francis.

Brandt, M.T., and I. Preston. 1977. "The Federal Trade Commission's Use of Evidence to Determine Deception." *Journal of Marketing* 41: 54–62.

Burke, R.R., W.S. DeSarbo, R.L. Oliver, and T.S. Robertson. 1988. "Deception by Implication: An Experimental Investigation." *Journal of Consumer Research* 14: 483–94.

Burke, S.J., S.J. Milberg, and W.W. Moe. 1997. "Displaying Common but Previously Neglected Health Claims on Product Labels: Understanding Competitive Advantages, Deception, and Education." *Journal of Public Policy & Marketing* 16: 242–55.

Campbell, M.C., and A. Kirmani. 2000. "Consumers' Use of Persuasion Knowledge: The Effects of Accessibility and Cognitive Capacity on Perceptions of an Influence Agent." *Journal of Consumer Research* 27: 69–83.

———. 2008. "I Know What You're Doing and Why You're Doing It: The Use of Persuasion Knowledge Model in Consumer Research." In *Handbook of Consumer Psychology,* ed. C.P. Haugtvedt, P.M. Herr, and F.R. Kardes, 549–71. New York: Taylor and Francis.

Cendrowicz, L. 2010. "Will Europe Green-Light New Food Labels?" *Time,* March 18.

Cheng, R. 2009. "AT&T Sues Verizon." *Wall Street Journal,* November 4.

Cohen, D. 1972. "Surrogate Indicators and Deception in Advertising." *Journal of Marketing* 36: 10–15.

Cunningham, W.H., and I.C.M. Cunningham. 1976. "Consumer Protection: More Information or More Regulation?" *Journal of Marketing* 40: 63–68.

Darke, P., L. Ashworth, and K. Main. 2010. "Great Expectations and Broken Promises: Misleading Claims, Product Failure, Expectancy Disconfirmation and Consumer Distrust." *Journal of the Academy of Marketing Science* 38: 347–62.

Darke, P.R., L. Ashworth, and R.J.B. Ritchie. 2008. "Damage from Corrective Advertising: Causes and Cures." *Journal of Marketing* 72: 81–97.

Darke, P.R., and R.J.B. Ritchie. 2007. "The Defensive Consumer: Advertising Deception, Defensive Processing, and Distrust." *Journal of Marketing Research* 44: 114–27.

DeCarlo, T. 2005. "The Effects of Sales Message and Suspicion of Ulterior Motives on Salesperson Evaluation." *Journal of Consumer Psychology* 15: 238–49.

Dyer, R.F., and P.G. Kuehl. 1974. "The 'Corrective Advertising' Remedy of the FTC: An Experimental Evaluation." *Journal of Marketing* 38: 48–54.

Ford, G.T., and J.E. Calfee. 1986. "Recent Developments in FTC Policy on Deception." *Journal of Marketing* 50: 82–103.

Foxman, E.R., D.D. Muehling, and P.A. Moore. 1988. "Disclaimer Footnotes in Ads: Discrepancies Between Purpose and Performance." *Journal of Public Policy & Marketing* 7: 127–37.

Frech, W.A., and H.C. Barksdale. 1974. "Food Labeling Regulations: Efforts Toward Full Disclosure." *Journal of Marketing* 38: 14–19.

Freer, R.E. 1949. "Informative and Non-Deceptive Advertising." *Journal of Market-ing* 13: 358–63.

Federal Trade Commission (FTC). 1983. "FTC Policy Statement on Deception. Letter to the Hon. John D. Dingell, October 14." Available at http://ftc.gov/bcp/policystmt/ad-decept.htm, accessed March 2, 2011.

———. 2009. "Guides Concerning the Use of Endorsements and Testimonials in Advertising." 16 CFR Part 255. Available at http://ftc.gov/os/2009/10/091005 revisedendorsementguides.pdf, accessed March 2, 2011.

Friestad, M., and P. Wright. 1994. "The Persuasion Knowledge Model: How People Cope with Persuasion Attempts." *Journal of Consumer Research* 21: 1–31.

Gaeth, G.J., and T.B. Heath. 1987. "The Cognitive Processing of Misleading Adver-tising in Young and Old Adults: Assessment and Training." *Journal of Consumer Research* 14: 43–54.

Gardner, D.M. 1975. "Deception in Advertising: A Conceptual Approach." *Journal of Marketing* 39: 40–46.

———. 1976. "Deception in Advertising: A Receiver-Oriented Approach to Under-standing." *Journal of Advertising* 5: 5–19.

Gindy, D.M. 2001. "Duel Between Pizza Hut and Papa John's Comes to an End." *Los Angeles Daily Journal,* June 26.

Goldberg, M.E., and J. Hartwick. 1990. "The Effects of Advertiser Reputation and Extremity of Advertising Claim on Advertising Effectiveness." *Journal of Con-sumer Research* 17: 172–79.

Haefner, J.E., and S. Permut. 1974. "An Approach to the Evaluation of Deception in Television Advertising." *Journal of Advertising* 3: 40–44.

Hill, K. 2010. "Consumer Reports iPhone 4s Snub Casts Harsh Light on Apple." *MacNewsWorld,* July 13.

Hoy, M.G., and M.J. Stankey. 1993. "Structural Characteristics of Televised Advertis-ing Disclosures: A Comparison with the FTC Clear and Conspicuous Standard." *Journal of Advertising* 22: 47–58.

Jacoby, J., M.C. Nelson, and W.D. Hoyer. 1982. "Corrective Advertising and Affir-mative Disclosure Statements: Their Potential for Confusing and Misleading the Consumer." *Journal of Marketing* 46: 61–72.

Jacoby, J., and C. Small. 1975. "The FDA Approach to Defining Misleading Advertis-ing." *Journal of Marketing* 39: 65–68.

Johar, G.V. 1995. "Consumer Involvement and Deception from Implied Advertising Claims." *Journal of Marketing Research* 32: 267–79.

Johar, G.V., and C.J. Simmons. 2000. "The Use of Concurrent Disclosures to Correct Invalid Inferences." *Journal of Consumer Research* 26: 307–22.

John, D.R. 1999. "Consumer Socialization of Children: A Retrospective Look at Twenty-Five Years of Research." *Journal of Consumer Research* 26: 183–213.

John, D.R., and C.A. Cole. 1986. "Age Differences in Information Processing: Understanding Deficits in Young and Elderly Consumers." *Journal of Consumer Research* 13: 297–315.

Kamins, M.A., and L.J. Marks. 1987. "Advertising Puffery: The Impact of Using Two-sided Claims on Product Attitude and Purchase Intention." *Journal of Ad-vertising* 16: 6–15.

Kinnear, T.C., and A.R. Root. 1988. "The FTC and Deceptive Advertising in the 1980s: Are Consumers Being Adequately Protected?" *Journal of Public Policy & Marketing* 7: 40–48.

Kirmani, A. 1990. "The Effect of Perceived Advertising Costs on Brand Perceptions." *Journal of Consumer Research* 17: 160–71.

———. 1997. "Advertising Repetition as a Signal of Quality: If It's Advertised So Often, Something Must Be Wrong." *Journal of Advertising* 26: 77–86.

Kirmani, A., and M.C. Campbell. 2004. "Goal Seeker and Persuasion Sentry: How Consumer Targets Respond to Interpersonal Marketing Persuasion." *Journal of Consumer Research* 31: 573–82.

Kirmani, A., and R. Zhu. 2007. "Vigilant Against Manipulation: The Effect of Regulatory Focus on the Use of Persuasion Knowledge." *Journal of Marketing Research* 44: 688–701.

Kramer, L. 1999. "Court Says Papa John's Ad Misled." *Advertising Age,* November 22.

LaTour, K.A., and M.S. LaTour. 2009. "Positive Mood and Susceptibility to False Advertising." *Journal of Advertising* 38: 127–42.

Lee, Y.H., and C. Mason. 1999. "Responses to Information In-Congruency in Advertising: The Role of Expectancy, Relevancy, and Humor." *Journal of Consumer Research* 26: 156–69.

Liebert, D.E., J.N. Sprafkin, R.M. Liebert, and E.A. Rubinstein. 1977. "Effects of Television Commercial Disclaimers on the Product Expectations of Children." *Journal of Communication* 27: 118–24.

Liefeld, J., and L.A. Heslop. 1985. "Reference Prices and Deception in Newspaper Advertising." *Journal of Consumer Research* 11: 868–76.

Main, K.J., D.W. Dahl, and P.R. Darke. 2007. "Deliberative and Automatic Bases of Suspicion: Empirical Evidence of the Sinister Attribution Error." *Journal of Consumer Psychology* 17: 59–69.

Maronick, T.J. 1991. "Copy Tests in FTC Deception Cases: Guidelines for Researchers." *Journal of Advertising Research* 31: 9–17.

Mazis, M.B. 2001. "FTC *v.* Novartis: The Return of Corrective Advertising?" *Journal of Public Policy & Marketing* 20: 114–22.

Miniard, P.W., S. Bhatla, K.R. Lord, P.R. Dickson, and U.H. Rao. 1991. "Picture-Based Persuasion Processes and the Moderating Role of Involvement." *Journal of Consumer Research* 18: 2–107.

Mizerski, R.W., N.K. Allison, and S. Calvert. 1980. "A Controlled Field Study of Corrective Advertising Using Multiple Exposures and a Commercial Medium." *Journal of Marketing Research* 17: 341–48.

Mobley, M.F., W.O. Bearden, and J.E. Teel. 1988. "An Investigation of Individual Responses to Tensile Price Claims." *Journal of Consumer Research* 15: 273–79.

Moorman, C. 1990. "The Effects of Stimulus and Consumer Characteristics on the Utilization of Nutrition Information." *Journal of Consumer Research* 17: 362–74.

Muehling, D.D., and R.H. Kolbe. 1998. "A Comparison of Children's and Prime-Time Fine-Print Advertising Disclosure Practices." *Journal of Advertising* 27: 37–48.

Neff, J. 2010. "Ad Industry Battles Back Against Bad Rep, Forms Ethics Institute." *Advertising Age,* June 7.

Obermiller, C., and E.R. Spangenberg. 1998. "Development of a Scale to Measure Consumer Skepticism Toward Advertising." *Journal of Consumer Psychology* 7: 159–86.

Olson, J.C., and P.A. Dover. 1978. "Cognitive Effects of Deceptive Advertising." *Journal of Marketing Research* 15: 29–38.

Permut, S.E., and J.E. Haefner. 1973. "Exploring Deception and Puffery in Television Advertising." *Journal of the Academy of Marketing Science* 1: 156–67.

Perry, V.G., and C.M. Motley. 2009. "Where's the Fine Print? Advertising and the Mortgage Market Crisis." *California Management Review* 52: 29–44.

Pollay, R.W., and B. Mittal. 1993. "Here's the Beef: Factors, Determinants, and Segments in Consumer Criticism of Advertising." *Journal of Marketing* 57: 99–114.

Preston, I.L. 1977. "The FTC's Handling of Puffery and Other Selling Claims Made "by Implication." *Journal of Business Research* 5: 154–81.

Reinhard, M., M. Messner, and S. Ludwig Sporer. 2006. "Explicit Persuasive Intent and Its Impact on Success at Persuasion: The Determining Roles of Attractiveness and Likeableness." *Journal of Consumer Psychology* 16: 249–59.

Richards, J.I. 1990. *Deceptive Advertising: Behavioral Study of a Legal Concept.* Hillsdale, NJ: Lawrence Erlbaum.

Richards, J.I., and I.L. Preston. 1992. "Proving and Disproving Materiality of Deceptive Advertising Claims." *Journal of Public Policy & Marketing* 11: 45–56.

Russo, J.E., B.L. Metcalf, and D. Stephens. 1981. "Identifying Misleading Advertising." *Journal of Consumer Research* 8: 119–31.

Scammon, D.L., and R.J. Semenik. 1983. "The FTC's 'Reasonable Basis' for Substantiation of Advertising: Expanded Standards and Implications." *Journal of Advertising* 12: 4–11.

Sengupta, J., and D.W. Dahl. 2008. "Gender-Related Reactions to Gratuitous Sex Appeals in Advertising." *Journal of Consumer Psychology* 18: 62–78.

Shanahan, K.J., and C.D. Hopkins. 2007. "Truths, Half-Truths, and Deception." *Journal of Advertising* 36: 33–48.

Shimp, T.A. 1978. "Do Incomplete Comparisons Mislead?" *Journal of Advertising Research* 18: 21–27.

Shimp, T.A., and I.L. Preston. 1981. "Deceptive and Non-Deceptive Consequences of Evaluative Advertising." *Journal of Marketing* 45: 22–32.

Sichelman, L. 2009. "FTC Files Enforcement Actions." *National Mortgage News,* April 13.

Snyder, R. 1989. "Misleading Characteristics of Implied-Superiority Claims." *Journal of Advertising* 18: 54–61.

Stern, B.L., and R.R. Harmon. 1984. "The Incidence and Characteristics of Disclaimers in Children's Television Advertising." *Journal of Advertising* 13: 12–16.

Stewart, D.W., and I.M. Martin. 1994. "Intended and Unintended Consequences of Warning Messages: A Review and Synthesis of Empirical Research." *Journal of Public Policy & Marketing* 13: 1–19.

Thomaselli, R. 2010a. "Ad Groups Warn Finance Bill Puts FTC on Steroids." *Advertising Age,* April 20.

———. 2010b. "Watchdog Slams GM Ad in FTC Complaint." *Advertising Age,* May 4.

Tipton, M.M., S.G. Bharadwaj, and D.C. Robertson. 2009. "Regulatory Exposure of Deceptive Marketing and Its Impact on Firm Value." *Journal of Marketing* 76: 227–43.

Tyebjee, T.T. 1982. "The Role of Publicity in FTC Corrective Advertising Remedies." *Journal of Public Policy & Marketing* 1: 111–21.

Urbany, J.E., W.O. Bearden, and D.C. Weilbaker. 1988. "The Effect of Plausible and Exaggerated Reference Prices on Consumer Perceptions and Price Search." *Journal of Consumer Research* 15: 95–110.

Wilkie, W.L., D.L. McNeill, and M.B. Mazis. 1984. "Marketing's "Scarlet Letter": The Theory and Practice of Corrective Advertising." *Journal of Marketing* 48: 11–31.

Wright, P., M. Friestad, and D.M. Boush. 2005. "The Development of Marketplace Persuasion Knowledge in Children, Adolescents, and Young Adults." *Journal of Public Policy & Marketing* 24: 222–33.

6

Verbal and Visual Information Interaction in Print Advertisements

Yeqing Bao, Shi Zhang, and James T. Simpson

All forms of marketing communications use a combination of verbal and nonverbal elements to deliver the intended message (Houston, Childers, and Heckler, 1987). In the case of print advertisements, the nonverbal elements are often called visual elements. Formally, the verbal elements in print ads refer to the textual portion of the message, and the visual elements refer to the image or pictorial portion. Although some print ads are almost exclusively verbally or visually based, the vast majority are a combination of the two. Therefore, the current chapter focuses on ads composed of both visual and verbal elements.

We begin with a discussion of the associative network theory of person memory, which provides an important foundation for research on consumer information processing. We then review previous research on how consumers respond to print ads containing both visual and verbal information and two dominant approaches are revealed: congruity superiority and incongruity superiority. Results of earlier studies are found to be inconclusive. We offer a broader perspective that considers the moderating effects of consumer motivation, the level of information incongruity, and boundary conditions that involve task complexity and type of incongruity (e.g., verbal and visual). This broader perspective is applied to the case of designing print ads to promote products with unfavorable country of origin (COO); brand name characteristics (i.e., verbal); and a spokesperson (i.e., visual) in the U.S. market. Specific management principles are discussed.

Theory on General Information Processing

Information in Memory

An abundance of research has noted that information is stored as a system of nodes in the memory (Anderson 1984; Anderson and Bower 1973;

Paivio 1986; Srull 1981). Each node represents a concept, such as apple or the color red, and nodes are linked to other nodes through pathways to become a network. The pathway represents the association between nodes, for example, "some apples are red." Thus, the pathways are not only mechanical linkages between nodes in a correlational sense, they also represent meanings or relations between the nodes (Barsalou 1991). The stronger the link between the concepts, the closer the association is between the nodes. Memory networks are expanded when new information produces new nodes that are linked to existing nodes. Retrieval of information results in an activated node spreading randomly through the network, stimulating those nodes that are closely associated with the activated node. The strength of the relationships and the number of associations between the existing nodes will determine the probability that a node is stimulated by the activated nodes (Anderson and Reder 1979). While this framework is well established in the literature, researchers have found that all information is not processed in the same way. Specifically, verbal and visual information are stored and processed differently.

Dual Coding of Verbal Versus Visual Information

It has been suggested that the human brain's left hemisphere plays a dominant role in processing verbal information (e.g., Geschwind 1979). Verbal information is often received, filed, and handled sequentially in a verbal system (Paivio 1986). Hence, verbal information tends to produce few main and interaction feature effects (Holbrook and Moore 1981).

In contrast, researchers suggest that the right hemisphere plays a dominant role in processing visual information (e.g., Geschwind 1979). Further, visual information is perceived, stored, and processed simultaneously in an imagery system (Paivio 1986). Hence, visual information tends to produce many main and interaction feature effects (Holbrook and Moore 1981).

The notion that there are discrete information-processing modes for handling verbal and visual information and that the two modes or processes (a) are fully specialized in the left or right brain hemispheres (b) correspond precisely to sequential versus simultaneous processing, or (c) that verbal or visual task inputs completely determine processing style and response outputs is considered by some researchers to be overly simplistic (Holbrook or Moore 1981). An alternative view supported by an abundance of research is that verbal and visual information processing should be regarded on a continuum, or as a combination of both modes in which certain tendencies or correspondences exist. This approach suggests that differences exist in the imagery value of certain words and in an individual's level of cognitive processing.

First, certain words have a higher "imagery value" than other words; that is, certain words are more likely to evoke images in a person's mind. For example, the word "table" evokes an image more easily than the word "freedom" (Unnava and Burnkrant 1991). Yet rhetoric research indicates that minor changes in an image can result in significant textual interpretations (McQuarrie and Mick 1999). Hence, verbal information may result in both verbal trace and visual trace, although the verbal trace is typically more salient. Similarly, visual information may result in both visual and verbal traces, although the visual trace is more salient (Rossiter and Percy 1980).

Second, even though verbal and visual systems are conceptually distinct, they are closely interconnected (Paivio 1971, 1986). Depending on the level of a person's cognitive processing, both verbal and visual elaboration may occur, and the consequent responses may be stored in and associated with either or both systems. Paivio delineates three distinct levels of cognitive processing. The most basic level of processing is "representational processing." It entails the direct activation of either the verbal or imagery systems depending on whether the stimulus is verbal or visual. The next level of processing is "referential processing." It entails the establishment of connections between the verbal and imagery system. Connections allow for evocation of imagery responses from verbal stimuli or verbal responses from visual stimuli. The highest and most complex processing level is "associative processing." This level occurs when verbal and visual stimuli that are associated with other verbal and visual stimuli become part of the knowledge base. Therefore, all else being equal, higher processing levels result in greater verbal and visual information interconnected with imagery and verbal systems.

The memory network model and the dual processing framework discussed here provide theoretical guidance to most research on consumer response to print advertisements consisting of a combination of verbal and visual information. Accordingly, visual information tends to be simultaneously processed and is more likely to yield both imagery and verbal traces. Thus, visual information tends to result in redundant coding and multiple associations, which makes visual information easier to memorize and recognize. Paivio and Csapo (1973) refer to this phenomenon as the "picture superiority effect." When applied to advertising research, a consensus exists among researchers that the picture superiority effect results in print ads with both verbal and visual images gaining more attention and yielding greater recall than print ads with verbal information only (e.g., Childers, Heckler, and Houston 1986; Childers and Houston 1984; Kim and Lennon 2008; Roman and Maas 2003). A final reason to include pictures in print advertisement is supported by Mitchell's (1986) finding that positively evaluated pictures result in a more positive attitude toward the advertisements, which further boosts attitude toward the focal brand. While these frameworks provide substantial guidance to researchers, scholars continue to seek insights into what combination of visual and verbal information would be most effective in print advertisements.

Verbal and Visual Information Interaction in Print Ads

In an effort to provide additional insights on how the combination of verbal and visual information influences consumers' responses to print ads, research has focused on two broad streams of research. One stream examines the effects of verbal and visual information on consumers' memory of the ad contents (e.g., Heckler and Childers 1992; Schmitt, Tavassoli, and Millard 1993; Unnava and Burnkrant 1991). The second stream examines the effects of verbal and visual information on consumers' attitudinal responses to the print ads (Lee and Mason 1999; Peracchio and Meyers-Levy 1994). Some researchers examine both effects together (e.g., Edell and Staelin 1983), since memory provides an important basis for understanding consumer information processing while attitude has a predicted link to consumer purchase behavior (Houston, Childers, and Heckler 1987; Lynch and Srull 1982). This research has been indecisive and has generated mixed results. The lack of consensus in this research is rooted in the multiple approaches to predicting the impact of both verbal and visual information in print ads. Two dominant approaches are congruity superiority and incongruity superiority. We also offer a broader perspective.

Congruity Superiority

One school of researchers argues that a simple pairing of verbal and visual information will not necessarily increase recall. These advocates of the congruity superiority approach argue that the facilitating effect between verbal and visual information requires a congruent relationship between the two stimuli.

Lutz and Lutz (1977) were among the first to note this effect in the advertising context. They examined the effect of interactive verbal and visual information on learning. They found that visual and verbal information are interactive when an image integrates brand name and product class in a single picture (e.g., a flying rocket-shaped man is used to represent the Rocket Messenger Service). Alternatively, information is noninteractive when the image depicting the brand or product is presented separately from the verbal form of the product. These researchers also found that interactive presentation of the verbal and visual information results in greater brand name recall than noninteractive presentations of information. Hence, the integration of the verbal and visual information into a single image facilitates greater recall of the advertised information.

Similarly, Edell and Staelin (1983) examined consumers' responses to framed versus unframed ads. In framed ads, information is stated both verbally and visually where the visual picture functions as an illustration of the verbal message. In unframed ads, only the visual element *or* the verbal information is presented. Results of this research support superior recall for the framed ads.

Schmitt, Tavassoli, and Millard (1993) further refined and extended the research on interactions between the visual and verbal descriptions. This study divided the verbal information into brand name and copy, and then examined the effect of the relationship between the three ad components (brand name, copy, and picture) and consumers' memory. The study results revealed that ads with congruent components, where conceptual or lexical relations exist among the ad components, generated better recall than ads with incongruent components, where there was no relationship among the ad components. Moreover, ads with congruency among all three ad components generated greater recall than ads with congruency between only two ad components, and congruent ads with pictures generated greater recall than ads with only words. This stream of research generally supports the view held by many advertising professionals that visual and verbal components should convey the same message and that the visual components should be used to reinforce copy or message claims (Arens, Schaefer, and Weigold 2009; Belch and Belch 2009; Schultz 1981).

Incongruity Superiority

A second research stream advocates an alternative view, which is termed the "incongruity superiority effect." The rationale for this approach is based primarily on Hastie's (1980) associative storage-and-retrieval model of person memory, which hypothesizes that information incongruent with a prior expectation is more difficult to comprehend. This increased difficulty resulting from incongruent information stimulates more elaborate processing and creates a larger number of associative pathways linking the incongruent information to existing knowledge. In one of the original incongruity studies, Houston, Childers, and Heckler (1987) tested an expectation-disconfirmation model to examine consumers' responses to the interactive ads. The study found that ads consisting of semantically discrepant visual and verbal components resulted in superior recall versus ads consisting of semantically consistent verbal and visual components, because an interactive visual image establishes an expectation about the content of verbal material. While the use of incongruent verbal and visual information results in more elaborate information processing, more extensive memory networks for the ad, and better memory of the brand name and product class, the researchers found that recall of product attributes is greater for congruent ads than for incongruent ads. This study further revealed that certain exposure conditions or individual factors such as high involvement or individual motivation must be present to allow elaborative processing. The absence of certain conditions leads to a diminished incongruity superiority effect.

A complication of both the congruent and incongruent superiority effects is that most objects have multiple meanings. In other words, two elements may be congruent on one dimension but not on another. In a study of the nature of congruency, Heckler and Childers (1992) proposed that relevancy and expectancy are two salient dimensions of incongruity. Relevancy refers to the degree to which a piece of information pertains to the meaning of the advertising theme and reflects how the information helps to identify the primary theme communicated by the ad. Expectancy refers to the degree to which a piece of information falls into some predetermined pattern or structure evoked by the ad. Thus, information congruency or incongruency can be depicted as four conditions along the two dimensions (relevant-irrelevant vs. expected-unexpected).

Lee and Mason (1999) provided a good illustration of the four conditions listed earlier in an advertising context. Consider a courier service advertisement with copy promoting fast delivery service—an ad with a fast delivery theme. Expected visual information in the ad might be a fleet of delivery trucks cruising at high speeds. Unexpected visual information might be a fleet of delivery trucks with bullet-shaped containers cruising at high speed. Both visual examples are relevant in that they help consumers identify with the ad theme—fast delivery. But they differ in expectancy. The regular delivery trucks fit the existing schema of courier service equipment, while the bullet-shaped trucks do not. In contrast, if the visual depiction of fast trucks is replaced with a group of smiling delivery people, the information becomes irrelevant to the theme of fast delivery even if it may fit the reader's existing image of the delivery personnel. Should the visual depiction be replaced with an elephant hauling a few packages, then the information is neither expected nor relevant to the fast delivery theme. However, if the ad theme was changed to service friendliness rather than fast delivery, the visual of delivery trucks cruising at high speed would be irrelevant while the visual of smiling delivery persons would be relevant. Thus, the nature of congruity or incongruity of the verbal and visual information depends on their relationships to the ad theme.

Multiple experiments in the Heckler and Childers (1992) study show that not all incongruities are equivalent. Overall, incongruity along the expectancy dimension elicits greater recall as does congruity along the relevancy dimension. Lee and Mason (1999) extended Heckler and Childers' expectancy-relevancy classification to include information incongruency through humor. In addition, they examined the effect of incongruency on attitude in both immediate and delayed responses. The pattern in Heckler and Childers' study was replicated, which supports the validity of the expectancy-relevancy conceptualization of the incongruity. Finally, even though the unexpected-irrelevant information is highly memorable, it yields less favorable attitudes than expected-relevant information.

A Broader Perspective

While the studies described here reflect the importance of congruity and incongruity in understanding the complexities of the interaction of visual and verbal information on consumers' response to print ads, the results from these studies are inconclusive. The absence of a coherent relationship between memory and attitude, as well as the impact of different levels of motivation and incongruity and specific boundary conditions on consumer response to print ads, suggest that we consider a broader perspective.

First, both memory and attitude have been shown to be important effects in consumer behavior; yet extant research suggests that there is no simple relationship between these two concepts. One reason is that consumers do not always retrieve and use the original product information in their formation of attitudes, nor do they consistently ignore the specific information (Loken 1984; Wright 1975). The extent to which consumers use the information in the ad depends on the task or situation. For example, Loken and Hoverstad (1985) reported that the relationships between recalled facts and attitudes were nonsignificant in the case of an evaluative task, but often significant in the case of a choice task. The research by Heckler and Childers (1992) and Lee and Mason (1999) shows that when the information in the ad is unexpected-irrelevant, the consumer considers it to be highly memorable. Hence, specific information could be perceived as positive or negative, which likely would result in positive or negative attitude toward the ad. This positive or negative attitude toward the ad could have direct impact on a consumer's attitude toward the brand (Mitchell 1986). A highly activated memory may yield a positive or negative attitude toward the advertised brand. Therefore, the inconsistency between congruity and incongruity superiority effects as related to memory and attitude may be simply inherent in human nature.

Second, the degree of incongruity and consumer motivation makes a difference in a consumer's response to an ad containing both visual and verbal elements. Although not specifically related to the verbal-visual interaction in print ads, research in both psychology and consumer behavior has reported that consumers' evaluation of a product or brand is impacted by the congruity of the information provided to the consumer (e.g., Mandler 1982; Meyers-Levy and Tybout 1989; Peracchio and Meyers-Levy 1997). In general it is expected, ceteris paribus, that information congruity will lead to a favorable response since consumers prefer cues that conform to their expectations and facilitate classification. Yet when incongruity is introduced, a favorable or unfavorable evaluation typically depends on how readily the processor can satisfactorily resolve the incongruity (Mandler 1982). It is argued that the affect resulting from the consumer's reaction to incongruity may itself contribute to an individual's evaluation of a product. Further, a more specific finding was that the actual level of incongruity influences the nature of the information processing and ultimately the product evaluation. Meyers-Levy and Tybout (1989) provide support for Mandler's multilevel proposition that the process of responding to different levels of congruity influences consumer evaluations. Their results suggest that moderate levels of incongruity lead to more favorable evaluations than either schema congruity or extreme schema incongruity. This stream of research promotes the existence of an inverted-U relationship in high-involvement scenarios in which moderate incongruity leads to more favorable product or brand evaluations than either congruence or extreme incongruence. Yet under low-involvement scenarios, the relationship between congruity and evaluation is linear. In other words, congruent scenarios lead to higher evaluations than incongruent scenarios. When confronted with incongruity in a low-involvement scenario, product evaluations are often affected by peripheral information (e.g., Petty, Cacioppo, and Schumann 1983). Moreover, the incongruity is treated as negative input and leads to low evaluations.

Closely related to the domain of verbal-visual interaction in print ads, Miniard and associates (1991) examined the moderating role of involvement in consumers' response toward ads containing a picture that either conveyed product-relevant information or irrelevant information. Although the picture-product relevant ads were generally more persuasive, the researchers did find some evidence of a moderating effect for involvement. Specifically, the picture and involvement manipulation revealed a more substantial impact on consumer attitudes and purchase intentions when involvement was high than when it was low.

Finally, the proposition that boundary conditions affect a consumer's reaction to print ads containing both visual and verbal content supports a broader perspective. Most of the previously reviewed results are main effects. Yet once the researcher introduces complex interaction effects, the results are both less consistent and less clear-cut (e.g., Heckler and Childers 1992;

Lee and Mason 1999). In a meta-analysis of the memory effect for general expectancy-congruent and expectancy-incongruent information, Stangor and McMillan (1992) found several moderator variables that influence the strength of the congruent or incongruent information's effects on memory. These moderating variables include the strength of the expectancy used to guide information processing, the complexity or cognitive demands of the processing task, set size, the type of expectancy, the type of target, respondents' information-processing goals, and the delay between exposure to the stimulus information and the memory test. The verbal-visual information interaction in print ads represents only part of the expectancy congruency in a variety of specific contexts. While very little research is available in this area compared to research on the general expectancy congruency, some consistent insights are beginning to emerge. For instance, Lee and Mason (1999) found that the effect of immediate and delayed responses on the information incongruity has a differential impact on consumers' response to ads.

In summary, while research indicates that ads with a combination of both verbal and visual information tend to be more effective than ads with verbal information only, research on what combinations of verbal and visual information work better is still inconclusive. A broader perspective suggests that this effect should be examined in conjunction with moderating variables such as consumer motivation, the level of information incongruity, and boundary conditions that involve task complexity and type of incongruity. In general, when consumers are low in involvement, congruity is preferred to incongruity between verbal and visual elements. When consumers are high in involvement, moderate incongruity is preferred to either congruity or extreme incongruity between verbal and visual elements.

In the following section, we apply this broader perspective to the case of designing print ads to promote products with unfavorable country of origin (COO) and using brand names that are either foreign-sounding or familiar to Americans.

Application to Market Entry

While there are several different approaches to evaluating the optimal integration of visual and verbal information in print, the results of prior research provide important guidance to advertising professionals. Rather than attempting to validate the general principles of ad design, we apply the results of prior research to the specific topic of a brand entry into the U.S. market. Seven principles are introduced to provide guidance to advertising professionals and researchers concerned with the design of effective print ads to promote products with unfavorable COO in the U.S. market.

Background

As the world's largest consumer market, the United States attracts products from most developed and developing countries. The globalization of the world economy means a substantial increase in the number of firms from developing countries entering the U.S. market, including those from China, India, and Mexico. While the tendency is to focus on competitive prices, these firms also must develop effective promotion strategies for their product offerings. International advertising literature provides little guidance for firms from developing countries that plan to enter the U.S. market; most studies instead focus on how U.S. companies should promote products in other countries. Based on the review of the research on verbal and visual interaction in print ads, we propose a series of principles that managers can apply in promoting products from developing countries in the U.S. market. In an effort to provide specific guidance, our principles pertain primarily to the roles of the brand name (verbal information) and spokesperson (visual information) and their roles in moderating the impact of COO information (verbal information) on product evaluations.

Country-of-Origin Effect

Researchers recognize the influence of a product's COO information on consumer product evaluation (e.g., Bilkey and Nes 1982; Chuang and Yen 2007; Hong and Wyer 1990). At the most basic level, COO refers to the place the product was manufactured. Yet, the COO concept has been extended to encompass the country of design, the country that assembled the product, or the country that houses the brand's headquarters (e.g., Agrawal and Kamakura 1999; Chao 1993). Moreover, the COO literature reports that despite product-specific variations, consumers in developed countries often hold less favorable views of products produced in developing countries. For instance, Johansson and Nebenzahl (1986) show that U.S. consumers consistently rate Germany as the best car-producing country and the Philippines as the worst.

There are instances where a country has nation equity with both performance and emotional components much like a brand name has brand equity (Agrawal and Kamakura 1999; Maheswaran and Chen 2006). Hence, a country's government and companies may elect to promote the image of their country in order to increase nation equity, which should benefit all products from that country. A nation equity–building strategy would suggest that companies may volunteer to include COO information in their advertisements even when target consumers currently have an unfavorable view of the country. For example, American consumers' unfavorable view of China often adversely affects American consumers' evaluation of products from China. Yet the Chinese beer manufacturer Harbin boldly stated its COO with the phrase, "Harbin lager, imported from China," in an ad featured in the July 2007 issue of the Northwest Airlines in-flight magazine. Is this advertising approach a good idea?

A strong brand image, however, has been found to have a shielding effect against low-quality COO in global manufacturing (Jo, Nakamoto, and Nelson 2003; Lee and Ganesh 1999). Hence, firms from developing countries that plan to enter the U.S. market may attempt to mitigate or even change an unfavorable product image through advertising or other means. Both branding and product endorsement research suggest that using an effective brand name and spokesperson might help.

Brand Name

An effective brand name can identify the sources of a product, differentiate the product from its competitors, and serve as a proxy for quality in the absence of other quality indicators (Aaker 1991; Keller 1998). Firms that elect to introduce their products into foreign markets typically consider two brand-naming options. The first option is to enter a foreign market with the firm's existing brand name. Alternatively, the firm may register a completely new name. The first option offers the advantage of possibly leveraging the brand name in the global market. However, there is a risk that the existing brand name may be inappropriate for the new market. Inappropriate names, even for a perceived high-quality product, can be detrimental. For example, General Motors' inability to sell its Chevy Nova in Latin America provides a classic example of inappropriate brand naming since "no va" means "it doesn't go" in Spanish (Zhang and Schmitt 2001).

Alternatively, a firm might choose to promote a completely new and effective brand name. For instance, a British electronics firm attempted to exploit the favorable image of Japanese electronic products by entering foreign markets with the Japanese-sounding brand name, Matsui. Although the British firm assembled its products in countries all over the world, other than Japan, the perceived Japanese brand name helped the firm succeed in various markets (Bergiel and Bergiel 1999).

There are many examples of firms using both brand-naming strategies successfully. For instance, the Korean company Samsung Electronics successfully entered the U.S. market with its original brand name (Samsung) on all its products. But Sunbeam entered the Italian market with several respected brand names obtained when it acquired local companies (e.g., Rowenta and Oster). Since there is evidence that firms have succeeded with both brand-naming strategies, the more important question is how to effectively promote either one.

Spokespersons

Research has shown that the appropriate selection and use of a spokesperson can be an effective strategy for brand promotion. But important strategy decisions must be made, such as whether the firm should use a celebrity or a "common" spokesperson. Ohanian (1991) finds that a celebrity spokesperson often solicits more favorable responses to an advertisement than an anonymous one. On the other hand, a celebrity spokesperson can be expensive, and the results are equivocal. For example, researchers demonstrate that consumers view an advertisement or product unfavorably if incongruity exists between the product characteristics and the physical attractiveness of a celebrity spokesperson (e.g., Kamins 1990).

Hence, an important question for companies promoting products in the U.S. market is whether or not to use a spokesperson in the advertisement. If so, which spokesperson alternative (i.e., common person or celebrity) works best with brand-naming strategy? The literature provides little guidance on this topic to firms in developing countries that wish to promote their products in the United States. This study attempts to fill that void by examining specifically COO information and spokesperson alternatives in association with a product with a foreign-sounding brand name versus one with an American-sounding name.

Advertising Design Principles

Based on the current literature on verbal and visual interactions in print ads, one can conclude that brand name and COO represent verbal information and spokesperson represents visual information.

Spokesperson Effect

Past research has focused primarily on the importance of including visual information in advertising. Specifically, past research suggests that, when an advertisement contains both explicit visual and explicit verbal claims about different product attributes, consumers' inferences about missing attributes will be dominated by the visual claim in the ad (Smith 1991). Thus, we propose that in general a spokesperson should be included.

This principle is also consistent with a long-held tradition in advertising research that advocates the importance of the source in attracting consumers' attention. The "source" often refers to the person communicating a marketing message either directly or indirectly (Belch and Belch 2009). Yet some ads do not involve a person in the message. In those instances, the source is the focal organization. The literature suggests that using an appropriate spokesperson can be an effective mechanism for breaking through the consumer's perceptual screen and attracting his or her attention (Arens, Schaefer, and Weigold 2009). Further, product information provided by spokespeople may be assimilated more effectively by the receiver since individuals tend to identify more readily with people than with organizations. Thus, ads with either celebrity or common spokespeople will generate more favorable responses than ads that lack a spokesperson.

Using a celebrity may cost more than using a common person, but a celebrity spokesperson is also expected to achieve a higher degree of attention than a common spokesperson because of heightened credibility and attractiveness. This celebrity advantage should result in more favorable responses to the ad. The celebrity effect is more evident when there is a match between the celebrity's characteristics and the brand's intended image (Kamins 1990). This stream of research suggests the following two principles, which are widely known:

P1: Ads with spokespeople (celebrity or common) tend to generate more favorable responses than ads with no spokesperson.
P2: Resource-permissive, celebrity spokespeople should be used since they generate more favorable responses than ads with common spokespeople.

Brand Naming Effect

When a new company from a developing country enters the U.S. market, the company may choose either an American- or foreign-sounding brand name. The information congruency perspective posits the use of an American spokesperson because an American-sounding name would result in congruency between the verbal and visual elements while a foreign-sounding brand name would result in incongruency. For the most common low-involvement consumers and low-involvement purchase situations, advertisements with congruent messages generate a more favorable attitude than incongruent messages (Mandler 1982). Hence, the American-sounding brand name is preferred.

This logic also is consistent with research by branding scholars, who argue that the linguistic component of a word may directly affect the function of a brand name (Huang and Chan 1997). The pronunciation of the brand name is one such linguistic dimension. Several researchers have developed guidelines that call for brand names with easy pronunciation and high familiarity (Kohli and LaBahn 1997). An easy-to-pronounce brand is expected to foster a sense of familiarity with the brand and increase the consumer's ability to both process and retrieve information related to the brand. It is expected that Americans will find traditional Western- brand names to be more familiar and easier to pronounce than foreign-sounding brand names.

P3: In the U.S. market, American-sounding brand names are preferred to foreign-sounding names in common low-involvement advertising situations.

Research has also shown that when consumers are either motivated to process information or are in high-involvement situations, moderate information incongruency results in better responses than either congruent or extreme incongruent information (Mandler 1982; Meyers-Levy and Tybout 1989; Peracchio and Meyers-Levy 1997). Thus, in high-involvement situations, the incongruency between a foreign-sounding brand name and an American spokesperson may result in better responses. This reasoning is in accord with brand naming in the pharmaceutical industry, where uncommon names abound. Since most consumers tend to be highly involved in decisions about their medications, they tend to be indifferent to uncommon brand names. Thus, the following principle is recommended:

P4: In the U.S. market, an American spokesperson promoting foreign-sounding brand names would be equally preferred to American-sounding brand names in high-involvement advertising situations, or the foreign-sounding brand names may even be preferred.

COO Effect × Brand Naming Effect

Previous COO research reports that consumers respond more positively to products from countries that the consumers view favorably (Bilkey and Nes 1982; Peterson and Jolibert 1995). More specifically, consumers in developed countries view products from developing countries as having lower quality, while consumers in developing countries tend to view products from developed countries as having higher quality (Wang and Lamb 1983). Consistent with these findings, we expect that U.S. consumers will evaluate a brand less favorably when its advertisement includes a cue that the product comes from a developing country. Therefore, in most cases, brands with unfavorable COO should refrain from revealing COO information in advertising.

However, as discussed earlier, countries or companies may elect to reveal the COO even though the COO may negatively impact the country's effort to build up long-term national equity. Under this condition, research on verbal-visual incongruency is relevant and provides guidance on designing an effective print ad.

Information incongruity will likely exist when an advertisement promoting an American-sounding brand name also includes unfavorable COO information. The perceived contradiction between the unfavorable COO and the American-sounding brand names may further increase the negative effect of the unfavorable COO among consumers, which should lead to an unfavorable product evaluation (Kirmani and Shiv 1998; Mandler 1982). Alternatively, an advertisement promoting a foreign-sounding brand name that also contains an unfavorable COO cue should result in information congruity. This congruent alignment of unfavorable COO and foreign brand name should neutralize the negative affect of either the foreign-sounding brand name or the unfavorable COO information. This logic is in accord with past research that for low-involvement consumers or situations, congruency yields better attitude than incongruency (Mandler 1982; Meyers-Levy and Tybout 1989; Peracchio and Meyers-Levy 1997). Therefore, if included, the unfavorable COO information should be accompanied by a foreign-sounding brand name.

P5: The unfavorable COO information, when used, should be combined with a foreign-sounding brand name in common low-involvement advertising situations.

In high-involvement situations, the incongruency between the unfavorable COO information and the American-sounding brand name may not hurt, since consumers respond better to information incongruity than congruity. Alternatively, the ELM model specifies that consumers in high-involvement situations process advertising information mainly via the central route. They pay less attention to peripheral cues such as brand name and COO than to more essential product attribute information (Petty, Cacioppo, and Schumann 1983). Hence, the incongruity between the two peripheral cues (brand name and COO) has little impact. Therefore, the following principle is suggested:

P6: The unfavorable COO information combined with an American-sounding brand name will not impair consumer response in high-involvement advertising situations.

COO × Spokesperson Effect

Every product must carry some form of brand name in its advertising, so we consider the combined effects of unfavorable COO information and an American spokesperson in American- and foreign-sounding brand name scenarios.

In the case of an American-sounding brand name, the presence of information about an unfavorable COO creates information incongruity. Adding an American spokesperson does not reduce this incongruity and may actually increase information incongruity by introducing a potential discrepancy between the American spokesperson and the unfavorable COO information. Thus, adding an American spokesperson to the advertisement, which has an American-sounding brand name and an unfavorable COO, should cause a consumer's product evaluation to remain the same or possibly deteriorate compared to using no spokesperson in the advertisement. However, in the absence of unfavorable COO information, adding an American spokesperson to the advertisement with an American-sounding brand name should result in information congruity. Hence, compared to no spokesperson, adding an American spokesperson should elevate the consumer's evaluation of the product. This notion suggests an interaction effect of the American spokesperson and unfavorable COO on consumers' product evaluation.

In contrast, in the case of a foreign-sounding brand name, the presence of information about an unfavorable COO would lead to information congruity. However, adding an American spokesperson to the advertisement, which has a foreign-sounding brand name and unfavorable COO information, disrupts this congruity. The resulting incongruity exists between the foreign-sounding brand name and the American spokesperson. It also exists between the unfavorable COO and the American spokesperson. These incongruities should lower consumers' product evaluation. However, in the absence of the unfavorable COO information, adding an American spokesperson to the promotion with a foreign-sounding brand name results in information incongruity. The resulting incongruity should lower product evaluation, though not as much as when the promotion also includes COO information. This again implies an interaction effect between the American spokesperson and unfavorable COO on consumers' product evaluation. Essentially, a spokesperson moderates the effect of COO on consumers' product evaluation such that the unfavorable COO effect of a developing country becomes favorable when no spokesperson is used compared with when an American spokesperson is used, particularly when the brand name is foreign-sounding. This leads to the following principle.

P7: When both COO and a foreign-sounding brand name are included, a nonspokesperson visual is preferred to a spokesperson visual.

Summary

This chapter reviews extant literature on verbal and visual information interactions and the resultant consumer responses to print ads. The literature has focused on the congruity or incongruity of verbal and visual information contained in advertisements. The results of this research suggest that, in general, consumers in low-involvement situations respond more favorably to advertisements with congruent presentations of verbal and image information. However, moderate incongruent arrangement results in more favorable responses than either congruent or extreme incongruent arrangements.

We also apply the findings from existing advertising research to a particular market entry situation. Specifically, we have developed seven principles that should assist advertising managers to design effective print ads to promote products from countries with unfavorable COO perceptions in the U.S. market. These seven principles are derived from existing theoretical inferences. Two of the principles (P1 and P2) proposed in this chapter have been documented in the literature, while the rest are new and have just begun to be subjected to empirical tests (Bao, Simpson, and Zhang 2010). Hence, managers are urged to consider and apply these principles with informed caution. Moreover, our article should be viewed as a call for empirical tests of these principles. Our study focuses primarily on verbal and visual information interaction in the print media. The discussed phenomenon exists in media other than print advertisements, and consumers' response patterns likely differ in nonprint media. For instance, while visual information typically plays a dominant role in print ads, Kim and Lennon (2008) report that detailed verbal information is more important than visual information in Internet shopping. Future research is needed to extend our understanding of how verbal and visual information interact in a variety of media such as broadcast and Web-based.

Evaluating the interaction of visual and verbal information in marketing communications in different languages and cultures is another fertile avenue for future research. While there is a shortage of this research, two important studies provide preliminary insights on the importance of language and culture in advertising research. Tavassoli and Lee (2003) found bilingual consumers respond differentially to advertising copy in different languages. In addition, Six (2005) concluded that Russian consumers often held negative attitudes toward Western advertisements since they respond to ad appeals very differently than typical Western consumers do. The globalization of business necessitates that we extend advertising research into international markets.

References

Aaker, D. 1991. *Managing Brand Equity.* New York: Free Press.
Agrawal, J., and W.A. Kamakura. 1999. "Country of Origin: A Competitive Advantage?" *International Journal of Research in Marketing* 16: 255–67.
Anderson, J.R. 1984. "Spreading Activation." In *Tutorials in Learning and Memory,* ed. J.R. Anderson and S.M. Kosslyn, 61–90. New York: Freeman.
Anderson, J.R., and G.H. Bower. 1973. *Human Associative Memory.* Washington, DC: Winston.

Anderson, J.R., and L.M. Reder. 1979. "An Elaborative Processing Explanation of Depth of Processing." In *Levels of Processing in Human Memory,* ed. L.S. Cermak and F.I.M. Craik, 385–403. Hillsdale, NJ: Lawrence Erlbaum.

Arens, W.F., D.H. Schaefer, and M. Weigold. 2009. *Essentials of Contemporary Advertising,* 2d ed. New York: McGraw-Hill/Irwin.

Bao, Y., J.T. Simpson, and S. Zhang. 2010. "Reducing Unfavorable Country of Origin Impact: Roles of Brand Name and Spokesperson." Working paper, University of Alabama–Huntsville.

Barsalou, L. 1991. "Frames, Concepts, and Conceptual Fields." In *Frames, Fields, and Contrasts: New Essays in Semantic and Lexical Organization,* ed. E. Kittay and A. Lehrer, 21–74. Hillsdale, NJ: Lawrence Erlbaum.

Belch, G.E., and M.A. Belch. 2009. *Advertising and Promotion: An Integrated Marketing Communications Perspective,* 8th ed. New York: McGraw-Hill/Irwin.

Bergiel, B.J., and E.B. Bergiel. 1999. "Country-of-Origin as a Surrogate Indicator: Implications/Strategies." *Journal of Global Competitiveness* 7: 187–95.

Bilkey, W.J., and E. Nes. 1982. "Country-of-Origin Effects on Product Evaluations." *Journal of International Business Studies* 8: 89–99.

Chao, P. 1993. "Partitioning Country of Origin Effects: Consumer Evaluations of a Hybrid Product." *Journal of International Business Studies* 24: 291–306.

Childers, T.L., S.E. Heckler, and M.J. Houston. 1986. "Memory for the Visual and Verbal Components of Print Advertisements." *Psychology & Marketing* 3: 137–50.

Childers, T.L., and M.J. Houston. 1984. "Conditions for a Picture-Superiority Effect on Consumer Memory." *Journal of Consumer Research* 11: 643–54.

Chuang, S., and H.R. Yen. 2007. "The Impact of a Product's Country-of-Origin on Compromise and Attraction Effects." *Marketing Letters* 18: 279–91.

Edell, J.A., and R. Staelin. 1983. "The Information Processing of Pictures in Print Advertisements." *Journal of Consumer Research* 10: 45–61.

Geschwind, N. 1979. "Specialization of the Human Brain." *Scientific American* 241: 180–99.

Hastie, R. 1980. "Memory for Behavioral Information that Confirms or Contradicts a Personality Impression." In *Person Memory: The Cognitive Basis of Social Perception,* ed. R. Hastie, 155–77. Hillsdale, NJ: Lawrence Erlbaum.

Heckler, S.E. and T.L. Childers. 1992. "The Role of Expectancy and Relevancy in Memory for Verbal and Visual Information: What Is Incongruency?" *Journal of Consumer Research* 18: 475–92.

Holbrook, M.B., and W.L. Moore. 1981. "Feature Interactions in Consumer Judgments of Verbal Versus Pictorial Presentations." *Journal of Consumer Research* 8: 103–13.

Hong, S.T., and R.S. Wyer. 1990. "Determinants of Product Evaluation: Effects of the Time Interval Between Knowledge of a Product's Country-of-Origin and Its Specific Attributes." *Journal of Consumer Research* 17: 277–88.

Houston, M.J., T.L. Childers, and S.E. Heckler. 1987. "Picture-Word Consistency and the Elaborative Processing of Advertisements." *Journal of Marketing Research* 24: 359–69.

Huang, Y.Y., and A.K.K. Chan. 1997. "Chinese Brand Naming: From General Principles to Specific Rules." *International Journal of Advertising* 16: 320–35.

Jo, M.S., K. Nakamoto, and J.E. Nelson. 2003. "The Shielding Effects of Brand Image against Lower Quality Countries-of-Origin in Global Manufacturing." *Journal of Business Research* 56: 637–46.

Johansson, J.K., and I.D. Nebenzahl. 1986. "Multinational Expansion: Effects on Brand Evaluations." *Journal of International Business Studies* 17: 101–26.

Kamins, M. 1990. "An Investigation into the 'Match-up' Hypothesis in Celebrity Advertising: When Beauty May Be Only Skin Deep." *Journal of Advertising* 19: 4–13.

Keller, K.L. 1998. *Strategic Brand Management.* Upper Saddle River, NJ: Prentice-Hall.

Kim, M., and S. Lennon. 2008. "The Effects of Visual and Verbal Information on Attitudes and Purchase Intentions in Internet Shopping." *Psychology & Marketing* 25: 146–78.

Kirmani, A., and B. Shiv. 1998. "Effects of Source Congruity on Brand Attitudes and Beliefs: The Moderating Role of Issue-Relevant Elaboration." *Journal of Consumer Psychology* 7: 25–47.

Kohli, C., and D.W. LaBahn. 1997. "Creating Effective Brand Names: A Study of the Naming Process." *Journal of Advertising Research* 37: 67–75.

Lee, D., and G. Ganesh. 1999. "Effects of Partitioned Country Image in the Context of Brand Image and Familiarity." *International Marketing Review* 16: 18–39.

Lee, Y.H., and C. Mason. 1999. "Responses to Information Incongruency in Advertising: The Role of Expectancy, Relevancy, and Humor." *Journal of Consumer Research* 26: 156–69.

Loken, B. 1984. "Attitude Processing Strategies." *Journal of Experimental Social Psychology* 20: 272–96.

Loken, B., and R. Hoverstad. 1985. "Relationships Between Information Recall and Subsequent Attitudes: Some Exploratory Findings." *Journal of Consumer Research* 12: 155–68.

Lutz, K.A., and R.J. Lutz. 1977. "Effects of Interactive Imagery on Learning: Application to Advertising." *Journal of Applied Psychology* 62: 493–98.

Lynch, J.G., and T.K. Srull. 1982. "Memory and Attentional Factors in Consumer Choice: Concepts and Research Methods." *Journal of Consumer Research* 9: 18–37.

Maheswaran, D. 1994. "Country of Origin as a Stereotype: Effects of Consumer Expertise and Attribute Strength on Product Evaluations." *Journal of Consumer Research* 21: 354–65.

Maheswaran, D., and C.Y. Chen. 2006. "Nation Equity: Incidental Emotions in Country-of-Origin Effects." *Journal of Consumer Research* 33, 370–76.

Mandler, G. 1982. "The Structure of Value: Accounting for Taste." In *Affect and Cognition: The Seventeenth Annual Carnegie Symposium on Cognition,* ed. M.S. Clark and S.T. Fisk, 3–36. Hillsdale, NJ: Lawrence Erlbaum.

McQuarrie, E.F., and D.G. Mick. 1999. "Visual Rhetoric in Advertising: Text-Interpretive, Experimental, and Reader-Response Analyses." *Journal of Consumer Research* 26: 37–54.

Meyers-Levy, J., and A.M. Tybout. 1989. "Schema Congruity as a Basis for Product Evaluation." *Journal of Consumer Research* 16: 39–54.

Miniard, P.W., S. Bhatla, K.R. Lord, P.R. Dickson, and H.R. Unnava. 1991. "Picture-Based Persuasion Processes and the Moderating Role of Involvement." *Journal of Consumer Research* 18: 92–107.

Mitchell, A.A. 1986. "The Effect of Verbal and Visual Components of Advertisements on Brand Attitudes and Attitude Toward the Advertisement." *Journal of Consumer Research* 13: 12–24.

Ohanian, R. 1991. "The Impact of Celebrity Spokespersons' Perceived Image on Consumers' Intention to Purchase." *Journal of Advertising Research* 31: 46–54.

Paivio, A. 1971. *Imagery and Cognitive Processes.* New York: Holt, Rinehart, and Winston.

———. 1986. *Mental Representations: Dual Coding Approach.* New York: Oxford University Press.

Paivio, A., and K. Csapo. 1973. "Picture Superiority in Free Recall: Imagery or Dual Coding?" *Cognitive Psychology* 5: 176–206.

Peracchio, L.A., and J. Meyers-Levy. 1994. "How Ambiguous Cropped Objects in Ad Photos Can Affect Product Evaluations." *Journal of Consumer Research* 21: 190–204.

———. 1997. "Evaluating Persuasion-Enhancing Techniques from a Resource-matching Perspective." *Journal of Consumer Research* 24: 178–91.

Peracchio, L.A., and A.M. Tybout. 1996. "The Moderating Role of Prior Knowledge in Schema-based Product Evaluation." *Journal of Consumer Research* 23: 177–92.

Peterson, R.A., and A. Jolibert. 1995. "A Meta-Analysis of Country-of-Origin Effects." *Journal of International Business Studies* 26: 883–96.

Petty, R.E., J.T. Cacioppo, and D. Schumann. 1983. "Central and Peripheral Routes to Advertising Effectiveness: The Moderating Role of Involvement." *Journal of Consumer Research* 10: 135–46.

Roman, K., and J. Mass. 2003. *How to Advertise,* 3d ed. New York: Thomas Dunne Books.

Rossiter, J.R., and L. Percy. 1980. "Attitude Change Through Visual Imagery in Advertisement." *Journal of Advertising* 9: 10–16.

Schmitt, B.H., N.T. Tavassoli, and R.T. Millard. 1993. "Memory for Print Ads: Understanding Relations Among Brand Name, Copy, and Picture." *Journal of Consumer Psychology* 2: 55–81.

Schultz, D.E. 1981. *Essentials of Advertising Strategy.* Chicago: Cram.

Six, I. 2005. "What Language Sells: Western Advertising in Russia." *Journal of Language for International Business* 16: 1–12.

Smith, R.A. 1991. "The Effects of Visual and Verbal Advertising Information on Consumers' Inferences." *Journal of Advertising* 20: 13–23.

Srull, T.K. 1981. "Person Memory: Some Tests of Associative Storage and Retrieval Models." *Journal of Experimental Psychology: Human Learning and Memory* 7: 440–63.

Stangor, C., and D. McMillan. 1992. "Memory for Expectancy-Congruent and Expectancy-Incongruent Information: A Review of the Social and Social Developmental Literatures." *Psychological Bulletin* 111: 42–61.

Tavassoli, N.T., and Y.H. Lee. 2003. "The Differential Interaction of Auditory and Visual Advertising Elements with Chinese and English." *Journal of Marketing Research* 40: 468–80.

Unnava, H.R., and R.E. Burnkrant. 1991. "An Imagery-Processing View of the Role of Pictures in Print Advertisements." *Journal of Marketing Research* 28: 226–31.

Wang, C., and C.W. Lamb. 1983. "The Impact of Selected Environmental Forces upon Consumers' Willingness to Buy Foreign Products." *Journal of Academy of Marketing Science* 11: 71–83.

Wright, P.L. 1975. "Consumer Choice Strategies: Simplifying vs. Optimizing." *Journal of Marketing Research* 12: 60–67.

Zhang, S., and B.H. Schmitt. 2001. "Creating Local Brands in Multilingual International Markets." *Journal of Marketing Research* 38: 313–25.

7

Comparative Advertising Research

A Review and Research Agenda

Meng-Hua Hsieh, Kyra Blower, Xingbo Li,
Shailendra Pratap Jain, and Steven S. Posavac

During the 2010 Super Bowl, Teleflora promised its delivery of flowers in person, as opposed to in a box, in an effort to differentiate itself from some of the competitors. Hyundai Sonata claimed that it had "better paint quality than Mercedes CLS550." In fact, Hyundai's use of comparative advertising featuring Mercedes as the reference point has been consistent in recent times, with its advertisement for Hyundai Genesis (aired during the 2008 Super Bowl) comparing its passenger space to the Mercedes S-class and its price to the Mercedes C-class. In print, Sprint advertises its "most reliable 3G network in comparison to AT&T and Verizon in a 13-city 3G performance test," Domino's states that the taste of its "oven baked sandwiches beat Subway," and Subaru goes on record with the headline, "Well done to Audi and BMW for winning the beauty contest. From the winner of the 2006 International Engine of the Year: Subaru." Finally, the intensity and frequency of comparative claims may make them the norm in political advertising.

Since the Federal Trade Commission's (FTC) endorsement in the 1970s, the use of comparative formats in advertising has increased significantly in the United States. An unpublished content analysis of print ads conducted by one of the authors found that in 2004, approximately 40 percent of all ads were comparative in nature. Of those, close to 30 percent directly named a competitor while the rest made indirect comparisons in which competitors were not explicitly named (e.g., "Better Than the Leading Brand" and "Best in Class").

A question that is yet to be resolved is whether comparative advertising is effective. This question was originally raised by Wilkie and Farris (1975) more than three decades ago in an article in which they encouraged researchers to address this issue. Since that pivotal article, several investigations have focused on this question and findings have been reported in pursuit of answers. The goals of this chapter are (1) to provide a review of comparative advertising research to date; (2) to consolidate these findings into a meaningful framework that enables managers and researchers to understand some of the outcomes of comparative advertising exposure and some of the moderators of its effectiveness; (3) to identify factors that have been underexplored in literature; and (4) to lay out an agenda for future research. In the next section, we review and summarize research in the field and outline the key positive, negative, and mixed outcomes associated with comparative advertising.

Outcomes of Comparative Advertising Exposure: Research Findings

Positive Outcomes

Elaboration

It has been argued that comparative advertisements may be more stimulating and personally relevant because they provide more information than noncomparative advertisements. Indeed, several researchers (Dröge 1989; Muehling, Stoltman, and Grossbart 1990; Pechmann and Esteban 1993; Pechmann and Stewart 1990) have found that comparative ads garner greater attention and evoke more cognitive activity and elaboration relative to noncomparative ads. Dröge (1989) specifically argues that comparative ads may induce greater attention and elaboration because they are likely to be processed more centrally as compared to noncomparative ads, and reports findings congenial with this proposition.

Awareness and Recall

Consistent with the logic that the increased attention to comparative ads should enhance recall (Wilkie and Farris, 1975), comparative advertising studies report superior short-term memory for both message content and the advertised brand name (Jain and Hackleman 1978; Pechmann and Stewart 1990; Prasad 1976). However, Donthu (1992) notes that recall associated with comparative advertising tends to be in direct proportion to the level of intensity. Furthermore, day-after recall measures show that forgetting moderates the memory advantage of comparative ads, leading to the possibility of misidentification of the advertised brand (Pechmann and Stewart 1990).

Brand Positioning

Comparative ads may reduce perceived differences between the advertised brand and the comparison brand. This in turn could lead to the advertised brand gaining a more competitive position in the marketplace. Convergent with this proposition—and particularly for new brands—comparative ads have been found to be successful in anchoring challenger brands closer to the market leader (Dröge and Darmon 1987; Johnson and Horne 1988), associating them with the market leader, and reducing perceived differences between the brands (Dröge 1989; Gorn and Weinberg 1984; Sujan and Dekleva 1987). In addition to increasing perceived similarity between brands, direct comparisons (in which competitors are referred to by name) on typical attributes can simultaneously differentiate the challenger brand from the leader by creating a perception that the leader is inferior on the featured attributes (Pechmann and Ratneshwar 1991). In line with this finding, comparative advertisements emphasizing differences between brands appear to be successful at eliciting more differentiative but fewer associative thoughts (Manning et al. 2001).

Sales and Market Share

Using a structural demand model in the context of analgesic advertising, Liaukonyte (2009) argues that a 10 percent increase in comparative advertising may have the potential to increase market share of the advertised brand from 0.5 percent to 3 percent. Macarthur (2007) further suggests that when "properly executed," comparative advertisements can boost sales performance anywhere from 15 percent to 20 percent. Furthermore, with proxy measures in a field experiment on coupon redemption, Demirdjian (1983) has demonstrated that comparative advertising can have a significant influence on purchase behavior.

Negative Outcomes

Informativeness

One of the key objectives underlying the FTC's original advocacy for comparative advertisements was that comparative advertising may facilitate consumers' decision process by providing a greater amount of information. However, this speculation remains controversial. In fact, several studies have consistently found that comparative ads are no more informative than noncomparative ads (Golden 1979; Levine 1976; McDougall 1978; Pride, Lamb, and Pletcher

1979; Shimp and Dyer 1978). The findings that comparative advertisements do not provide greater information may be driven by the low message believability associated with them.

Believability

Although it was originally proposed that comparative advertisements would be perceived to be more truthful (Wilkie and Farris 1975), research has consistently refuted this claim (Barry and Tremblay 1975; Golden 1979; Prasad 1976; Shimp and Dyer 1978; Swinyard 1981; Wilson and Muderrisoglu 1980). Poor message believability and credibility may be among the most detrimental effects of comparative advertisements, thus being the primary argument against the overall effectiveness of comparative advertising.

Counterargumentation

A consequence of the poor believability of comparative advertisements is an increase in counterargumentation they evoke, potentially hindering attitude change and claim acceptance, thereby lowering message effectiveness (Belch 1981; Stutts 1982; Swinyard 1981; Wilson and Muderrisoglu 1980). Counterargumentation in a comparative advertising context has been found to also mediate the negative effect of perceived manipulative intent on both believability and brand attitudes (Jain, Buchanan, and Maheswaran 2000). Similarly, perceived ad deceptiveness and activated persuasion knowledge (e.g., suspicion about firms' motives and skepticism about the ads) mediate the interaction effect of regulatory focus and salience of manipulative intent of the comparative ads on brand attitude (Kirmani and Zhu 2007). In an interpersonal sales context, Campbell and Kirmani (2000) found that when the salesperson's ulterior motivations were highly accessible, consumers' persuasion knowledge was activated and consumers perceived the salesperson to be less sincere, regardless of consumers' cognitive capacity.

Mixed Outcomes

Attitude Toward Advertisement

Barry (1993) and Rogers and Williams (1989) posit that comparative ads lead to attitudes that may be at least as favorable as noncomparative ads, have the potential to be more liked than noncomparative ads (see also Goodwin and Etgar 1980; Neese and Taylor 1994), and that these positive attitudes toward the advertisement may transfer to the advertised brand (MacKenzie, Lutz, and Belch 1986; Muehling 1987). However, this conclusion is undermined by conflicting evidence that comparative advertisements generate less favorable attitudes (Belch 1981; Gorn and Weinberg 1984; Swinyard 1981) as they are perceived to be less personal, less friendly and pleasant, more aggressive and intense, and less believable and honest (Dröge 1989). Grewal and colleagues' (1997) meta-analysis concurs in its finding that comparative advertisements are perceived as less likable than noncomparative advertisements.

Attitude Toward the Brand

Conclusions about attitudes toward the advertised brand remain similarly conflicted. Contrary to attitudes toward the advertisement itself, results from the meta-analysis cited earlier concludes that attitudes toward the advertised brand are more positive when a comparative format is used (Grewal et al. 1997). However, this superiority of comparative ads has been found to hold only when introducing new brands (Etgar and Goodwin 1982; Iyer 1988) and for current users of the advertised brand (Shimp and Dyer 1978). In addition, Barry (1993) concludes that there is only marginal support for the view that comparative ads generate positive attitudes, as most research has shown no difference based on ad format (Belch 1981; Goodwin and Etgar 1980; Gorn and Weinberg 1984; Hackleman and Jain 1979). Importantly, other researchers find support for the view that comparative ads may actually generate less favorable brand attitudes (Rogers and Williams 1989; Stutts 1982; Swinyard 1981) by resulting in source derogation (Belch 1981) and negative attributions of manipulative intent toward the advertised brand (Jain et al. 2000).

A Contingency Approach

While the above-mentioned outcomes of comparative advertising exposure are not based on an exhaustive literature review, they do indicate that findings pertaining to the effects of comparative advertisements are often at odds with one another. Two potential explanations may be forwarded to account for these contradictory results. One possibility is that a consistent definition of comparative advertising is lacking (Barry 1993). For example, the pivotal article by Wilkie and Farris (1975) defines comparative advertising as advertising that features an advertiser referring to a competitor by name and comparing itself with the competitor on specific attributes. Over time, this format of comparative advertising has come to be referred to as a direct comparison. Jackson, Brown, and Harmon (1979) take a broader approach and focus on comparisons in which direct naming of competition is avoided in favor of indirect references to competitors made by the advertiser (e.g., "Better Than the Leading (or # 1) Brand," "Superior to Ordinary Brands," "Best in Class"). These comparative ads are now termed indirect comparisons. To address this variation in definitions of comparative ads, some researchers have explicitly examined the relative effectiveness of direct and indirect comparisons versus noncomparative ads in the same investigation (e.g., Goodwin and Etgar 1980; Pechmann and Stewart 1990; Pride et al. 1979).

Another possible explanation is that the boundary conditions or moderators of consumer-side responses to comparative advertising have not been examined comprehensively. Indeed, much of comparative research in the past two decades has focused on this latter possibility and has attempted to delineate conditions in which comparative ads may be more or less effective (e.g., Jain, Agrawal, and Maheswaran 2006; Jain and Maheswaran 2000; Jain et al. 2000; Jain and Posavac 2004; Pechmann and Esteban 1993; Thompson and Hamilton 2006).

Based on the two foregoing possibilities, we propose a contingency view of comparative advertising effectiveness. In particular, we outline a moderator model that identifies factors relating to the stimulus, situation, and the message recipient that may influence the strength and/or direction of comparative advertisement effectiveness. In doing so, we accomplish two purposes: (1) we capture past findings at a high level, integrating them into the proposed framework; and (2) we outline an agenda for future research in comparative advertising.

The Moderator Model

We organize our proposed moderators of comparative advertising effectiveness based on Pechmann and Ratneshwar's (1992) framework, which investigates the impact of stimulus, situational, and individual factors on consumers' co-variation judgments. Further, by drawing upon Grewal and colleagues' (1997) Hierarchy of Comparative Advertising Effects Model, we categorize the different dependent variables of effectiveness examined in extant comparative advertising research. Figure 7.1 illustrates this framework. In the next section, we discuss the model in greater detail.

Stimulus Factors

An emerging consensus among comparative advertising researchers is that the effectiveness of comparative advertising may be contingent on many stimulus factors that can be conceptually integrated to define a relevant comparative advertising typology. In support of this view, we propose a typology that

Figure 7.1 **The Moderator Model of Comparative Advertising Effectiveness**

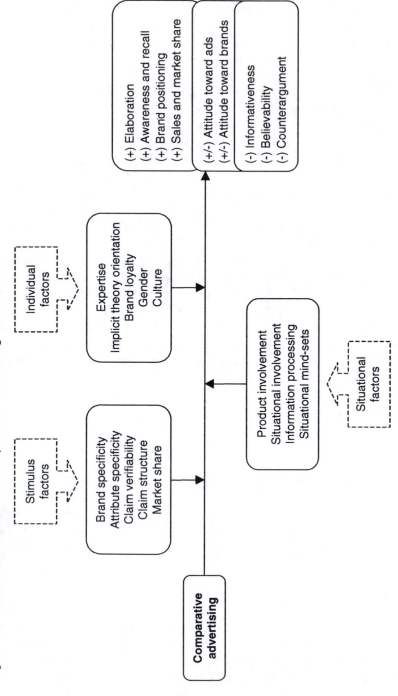

successfully classifies several of the preexisting descriptions and usages of comparative advertising (Barry 1993; Lamb, Pride, and Pletcher 1978; Muehling and Kangun 1985). In particular, we integrate past findings into four stimulus-based dimensions believed to moderate the relationship between comparative advertisements and their outcomes.

Brand Specificity

To date, most comparative advertising research has focused on the *brand specificity* of the advertisements, that is, the extent to which the competing brand is identified and the number of comparison brands mentioned within the advertising. This has led to differentiating comparative advertising as either a direct or indirect comparison. Direct comparisons specifically identify the comparison brand by name, whereas indirect comparisons identify the competition as "the leading brand," "other brands," or use some type of proxy image such as trademark colors or similar-looking symbols. As was true for comparative versus noncomparative advertising, results have been mixed as to whether direct or indirect comparisons are more effective (e.g., Goodwin and Etgar 1980; Pechmann and Stewart 1990; Pride et al. 1979) and appear to depend on other stimulus, situational, and individual factors. For example, Grossbart, Muehling, and Kangun (1986) found that comparative ads with both verbal and visual cues that identified the competitor generated more recall than comparative ads with only one form of identification (verbal or visual references). However, advertisements with only verbal references to the competitor resulted in more favorable attitudes toward the advertised brand and greater acceptance of claims than ads with both verbal and visual identifications. Furthermore, Pechmann and Stewart (1990) found that compared to indirect comparisons, direct comparisons enhanced attention, recall, and purchase intentions, but these findings were moderated by market share of the advertised brand and the comparison brand.

Attribute Specificity

Comparative ads vary in terms of the number of point-by-point attribute comparisons made within the advertisement and the alignability of those attributes. Most comparative advertisements compare brands based on at least one attribute. Research has shown that attribute-by-attribute comparisons facilitate assessment and evaluation of the advertised product's benefits relative to those of competition (Miniard et al. 1993; Rose et al. 1993). Although Goodwin and Etgar (1980) showed that using a greater number of attributes in the comparison may have greater information utility there is also some evidence for the likelihood of information overload under such circumstances. Thus, the intermediate level (five attributes) was superior on promoting higher quality of the advertised brand over other leading brands.

In contrast, some advertisements do not emphasize product attributes, but refer only to market standing or consumer preference for the advertised brand. Although non–product-based comparisons generate similar beliefs regarding product attributes as well as beliefs in positioning the new brand closer to the leading brand, the confidence in beliefs about attributes and the clarity of the brand image appears to be inferior to product-based comparisons (Dröge and Darmon 1987).

A final aspect of attribute specificity refers to the alignability of the attributes or the ease with which brands can be compared along these attributes. As alignability among attributes in comparative advertising decreases, the evaluation of the advertised brand also decreases because of the perceived need for more cognitive resources (Zhang, Kardes, and Cronley 2002). Zhang and Markman (1998) specifically found that attributes that were comparable along some dimension but differed across competing brands enjoyed higher recall than attributes that were common to both brands and attributes that had no correspondence with each other (i.e., were nonalignable). Further, common attributes had higher recall than completely differing attributes.

Claim Verifiability

Comparative advertisements may vary in the degree to which the advertiser's claim or information provided therein is verifiable. Claim verifiability may include whether the claim relies on attributes that are verifiable prior to purchase/consumption, objective measures, or personal judgments and whether the claim has been substantiated. Jain et al. (2000) found that comparative advertisements featuring search attributes (those that can be verified prior to consumption) elicited significantly higher believability than those featuring experience attributes (verifiable only after consumption). Comparative claims based on experience attributes were associated with greater perceived manipulative intent and were subject to greater counter-argumentation. Wilson (1976) similarly found that comparisons based on subjective, nonfactual claims were perceived as less believable and more offensive.

Unsubstantiated claims of implied superiority have been considered a form of puffery and potentially misleading to consumers. Snyder (1989) found that implied superiority claims did not increase believability, perceptions of brand quality, or interest in the brand over noncomparative advertisements even when concrete attributes were featured or the claim was supported by consumers or independent researchers. Even for substantiated claims, while they may be perceived as somewhat more helpful (McDougall 1978), perceptions of test fairness are subject to the independence, subjects, and methodology (Boush and Ross 1986). Substantiated claims that do not provide such information have not been found to significantly influence purchase intentions, believability, or credibility (Golden 1979).

Claim Structure

Claim structure encompasses the relative strength of claimed superiority, the overall valence of the message, and the clarity of the conclusion. Comparative advertisements have been classified in terms of whether they present one-sided arguments that stress only positives about the advertised brand or two-sided arguments in which both positives and negatives about the advertised brand are expressed. In general, disclaiming superiority on at least some attribute increases positive attitudes and purchase intentions toward the advertised brand (Etgar and Goodwin 1982; Swinyard 1981). Specific to valence, Jain and Posavac (2004) found that comparative advertisements that featured positive aspects of both the advertised and the comparison brands enhanced believability of the ad claim, generated more favorable attitudes toward the advertised brand, and resulted in fewer negative attributions about the advertiser.

Claim structure may also differ based on whether the claim presents a clear and definitive conclusion (close-ended or explicit) or allows consumers to draw their own conclusion (open-ended or implicit). Results regarding type of conclusion have been mixed and not well explored. While open-ended conclusions may eliminate many of the negative outcomes associated with comparative advertisements and encourage greater processing, these results are dependent on whether the perceivers are motivated to attend to the message and the extent to which they comprehend it (Sawyer 1988). In a study of incomplete comparatives, Shimp (1978) found that open-ended messages elicited multiple plausible interpretations, some of which were potentially misleading.

Market Share of the Featured Brand(s)

The effectiveness of comparative advertising has also been found to be moderated by *market share*. Comparative advertising is more effective for new or low-share advertised brands than for the leading brand. Shimp and

Dyer (1978) discovered that comparative advertisements increased believability of the advertisement and the associated purchase intention for a
new brand, while noncomparative advertisements were more effective for
the established brand. In the same vein, Pechmann and Ratneshwar (1991)
argued that direct comparative advertisements are most effective for new
brands entering the market. They also showed that indirect comparatives
increase purchase intentions for moderate-share brands, while direct comparatives not only increase awareness of the comparison brand but also
result in a greater likelihood for sponsor misidentification. Conversely, for
low-share brands, direct comparative claims are more effective at increasing
attention and purchase intentions for the advertised brand without increasing top-of-mind awareness of the comparison brand or leading to sponsor
misidentification.

In summary, identifying various stimulus factors associated with comparative advertisements and creating ad executions based on a consideration
of these factors may be of utility in influencing several dependent measures
(including, but not restricted to, brand attitudes). Importantly, while inquiries
examining the effectiveness of direct versus indirect comparisons are contex-
tually relevant and deserve more attention, findings pertaining to the featured
attributes and the claims themselves (in terms of verifiability and structure)
may also carry weight in influencing consumer processing and judgments.
For instance, message effectiveness may be enhanced if the (comparative)
ad claim relies on a moderate number of alignable attributes at the product-
type level, is substantiated and verifiable prior to consumption, is made by
relatively low-share brands, and is generally perceived as more positive by
disclaiming superiority on at least one attribute or holding back on attacking
the comparison brand.

Situational Factors

In addition to stimulus factors, the efficacy of comparative advertising may be
contingent on situational factors, including product involvement, situational
involvement, types of information processing situations, situational induce-
ment of mind-sets, and market share of the featured brands.

Product Involvement

Comparatives are believed to require greater cognitive resources than non-
comparatives, especially when competitors are explicitly named. As a
result, comparative advertising tends to be processed to a greater extent via
a central processing route (Dröge 1989). In line with this research, Putrevu

and Lord (1994) argue that information pertaining to some products tends to be processed centrally, while information associated with some other products tends to be processed peripherally. These authors found that the relative effectiveness of comparative and noncomparative advertising was moderated by *product-specific cognitive and affective involvement*. More specifically, a comparative attribute-based ad format elicited favorable attitude toward the advertised brand when products were high in both cognitive and affective involvement. In contrast, noncomparative attribute-based appeals led to more positive attitude to the ad only when affective involvement was low. A conflicting finding is that obtained by Pfau (1994), who found that comparative appeals were more effective for the advertised brands when product involvement was low than when it was high. Even though Putrevu and Lord (1994) had a more nuanced set of predictions, the reasons for the conflict are not clear and deserve deeper examination.

Situational Involvement

Pechmann and Esteban (1993) examined how situational involvement moderated the relation between comparative advertising and the persuasion processing routes, brand attitude, and purchase intention. Situational involvement influences situational goals and the level of distraction associated with ad exposure. Pechmann and Esteban (1993) manipulated the extent of message processing by varying argument strength to examine the persuasion processes by which comparative and noncomparative advertising were routed. Under moderate involvement, strong (versus weak) arguments led to favorable brand evaluation with comparative advertising that was processed centrally, but not with noncomparative advertising that was processed peripherally. Specific to the persuasion outcomes (brand attitude and purchase intentions), they found that under low or moderate involvement, when comparative advertising was processed centrally, it elicited positive attitudes toward the ad, which in turn enhanced purchase intention but not brand attitude. In contrast, under high involvement, consumers evaluated brands on the basis of the strength of the message argument rather than peripheral cues, and thus comparative advertising did not lead to positive brand evaluation.

Type of Information Processing

Thompson and Hamilton (2006) demonstrated that consumers using analytical processing were persuaded more by comparative advertising, while consumers using imagery processing were persuaded more by noncomparative advertising. Matching (versus mismatching) between advertisement format and processing mode improved processing fluency, which in turn enhanced message persuasiveness, attitude toward the advertisement, attitude toward the advertised brand, and purchase intentions.

Situationally Induced Mind-Sets

Jain and colleagues (2006) investigated the moderating role of regulatory focus on persuasiveness of a "maximal" comparison that claimed superiority to a comparison object and a "minimal" comparison that claimed parity with a comparison object. Promotion-focused consumers were found to maximize gains and were driven away from nongains, while prevention-focused consumers tended to avoid losses or were driven toward nonlosses. The authors situationally activated self-regulation goals (prevention/promotion) and found that when a brand was compared to another brand or a minimal standard, promotion-focused consumers evaluated the advertised brand more favorably when they viewed maximally framed comparisons. On the other hand, prevention-focused consumers evaluated the advertised brand as equivalent regardless of the comparative advertisement frame. In contrast, when a brand was compared to a recommended standard, promotion-focused consumers continued to be more persuaded by the maximal frames. However, under these circumstances, prevention-focused consumers were persuaded more by the minimal frames. Claiming that a brand exceeded a recommended standard in maximal frames was perceived as a deviation from the norm by prevention-focused consumers. Thus, prevention-focused consumers regarded such message frames as a possible loss that should be avoided.

Based on the situational factors proposed here, comparative advertising may engender more positive brand attitudes when situational involvement is low or moderate and when products require high cognitive and affective involvement in decision making. Comparative advertising may also be more effective for consumers who use analytical- versus imagery-based processing. Finally, for promotion-oriented consumers, maximal-framed comparative advertisements may be more effective than minimal-framed messages in general, while for prevention-oriented consumers, message frame effectiveness may in part depend on the extent to which the claim represents a normative deviation and, consequently, a potential loss.

Individual Factors

The final set of moderators we propose relates to differences among message recipients. These factors include expertise, implicit theory orientation, brand loyalty, willingness to switch from a comparison brand, gender, and culture.

Expertise

The relative effectiveness of comparative and noncomparative advertising appears to depend on message perceivers' expertise. Experts who have more knowledge about the advertised product or service domain tend to use more specific attribute knowledge to evaluate advertisements. Sujan and Dekleva (1987) found that for experts, comparative advertisements led to greater amounts of informativeness, higher extremity of evaluation, and greater distinctiveness than noncomparative advertisements made at both the product-class and product-type levels. In contrast, for novices, comparative advertisements resulted in greater informativeness and distinctiveness than noncomparative advertisements that were made at the product-class level but not at the product-type level.

Implicit Theory Orientation

The persuasiveness of comparative adverting appeals may also be a function of the consumers' implicit theory orientations. Jain, Mathur, and Maheswaran (2009) found that incremental theorists who hold the worldview of malleability (where the worldview may be domain specific) evaluated the advertised brand more favorably when they viewed approach-framed comparative advertisements (messages that featured positive aspects of the advertised brand) than when they viewed avoidance-framed advertisements (messages featuring the negative aspects of the comparison brand) unless they were exposed to information that violated their theories. In contrast, entity theorists were equally persuaded by approach and avoidance comparative frames unless they were exposed to information that violated their theories.

Brand Loyalty

Putrevu and Lord (1994) found that a comparative ad format was effective for brand switchers but had a negative consequence for individuals who were already loyal to the comparison brand. Brand switchers favorably evaluated the comparative appeal that claimed superiority over a comparison brand, while loyal consumers disliked the appeal that targeted against their preferred brand. Jain and Maheswaran (2000) similarly found that consumers were more resistant to a preference-inconsistent than to a preference-consistent message. This resistance was manifested in the extent to which they counterargued the message and the need for stronger arguments to support a preference-inconsistent message for such consumers to be persuaded.

Gender

Some research has shown that consumer *gender* moderates the effectiveness of comparative advertising. Males, being more selective processors, seem to have low elaboration thresholds, while females, who are more likely to be comprehensive processors, possess a higher elaboration threshold (Meyers-Levy 1989; Meyers-Levy and Maheswaran 1991; Meyers-Levy and Sternthal 1991). In the context of comparative advertisements, males regarded moderately intense direct comparative appeals as more persuasive for high-involvement products than high-intensity appeals featuring attribute-by-attribute comparisons. In contrast, for females, moderately intense comparative appeals were more effective when an advertised brand belonged to a low-involvement product category (Pfau 1994). Chang (2007) further demonstrated that comparative adverting was more effective for males, while noncomparative advertising was more effective for females. Specifically, for males, comparative advertising enhanced brand-evaluation involvement, which in turn led to more favorable ad and brand evaluations and greater purchase intentions as compared to noncomparative advertising. In contrast, for females, comparative advertising increased inferences of manipulative intent, which in turn led to less favorable ad and brand evaluations. In addition, attribute alignability moderated this relationship. Males evaluated comparative ads featuring alignable attributes more favorably than those featuring nonalignable attributes, while females expressed more favorable attitudes toward comparative ads featuring non-alignable attributes than those featuring alignable attributes.

Culture

Cross-cultural research has classified consumers based on the extent to which they are individualistic or collectivistic (Triandis 1988); whether they are from high- or low-context communication cultures (Hall 1976); and whether they have independent or interdependent self-construal (Markus and Kitayama 1991). Choi and Miracle (2004) found that when exposed to (direct and indirect) comparative advertisements, consumers in the United States had more positive attitudes toward the advertisement and the advertised brand but did not have higher purchase intention than Korean consumers. The two cultures did not differ in their brand attitude and purchase intention when evaluating noncomparative advertisements. Self-construal was found to mediate the effect of national culture on the effectiveness of indirect comparative and noncomparative advertising but not on the effectiveness of direct comparative advertising. Jeon and Beatty (2002) further found that Korean consumers, who were not familiar with the direct comparative advertising format, responded to direct comparative advertising more favorably than indirect comparative advertising in terms of brand attitude and purchase intentions. In contrast, consumers in the United States, who were familiar with the direct comparative advertising format, viewed indirect comparative advertising as more persuasive than direct comparative advertising. However, Donthu (1998) found that comparative advertising engendered more negative attitudes toward the ad, especially in countries where comparative adverting was rarely used (e.g., Great Britain) or not used at all (e.g., India) than those where a comparative ad format was widely or moderately used (e.g., United States and Canada). Low-context communication cultures rely on explicit messages and verbal communication, while high-context communication cultures (such as Japan, Korean, China, and Arab countries) rely on contextual elements or nonverbal communication (Ferraro 1994; Hall 1976). Shao, Bao, and Gray (2004) found that comparative advertising was more effective in the low-context communication cultures. Among low-context communication cultures, direct comparative advertising was more persuasive than indirect comparative advertising. No differences were found in the attitude toward direct and indirect comparative ads.

In summary, experts seem to have more favorable attitudes toward comparative ads than noncomparative ads at both the product-class and product-type level, while novices have more favorable attitudes toward comparative ads, but only at the product-class level. Approach-framed comparative ads have been found to be more effective than avoidance-framed comparative ads for incremental theorists who hold a malleable worldview, while entity theorists have equivalent evaluations regardless of the ad frame. Finally, comparative advertising seems to be more effective for brand switchers, for males, and for consumers in low-context communication cultures.

Thus far, we have integrated past findings to propose a set of conceptual moderators that capture several variables that have been examined in the comparative advertising literature. These moderators relate to the stimulus, the situation, and the individuals receiving the message. The main goal of this section has been to compartmentalize extant research into a streamlined framework. A less central purpose has been to offer integrative propositions relating to each of these factors that can be tested to advance our understanding of comparative advertising. In the next section, we propose a research agenda consisting of several additional factors that have yet to receive attention in the comparative advertising literature.

Future Research

Based on an extensive review of the literature on comparative advertising, we find that a broad spectrum of important psychological constructs have not been discussed in the literature. Our goal in this section is to garner some interest and raise awareness of many variables for further exploration. In conjunction with the foregoing section, we structure this section using the stimulus, situational, and individual trifecta of factors.

Stimulus Variables

Type of Appeal

The link between the nature of the stimuli and comparative advertising effectiveness is worthy of further exploration. One variable that has been demonstrated to influence the persuasiveness of an appeal is the extent to which it is affective or cognitive. In general, affective versus cognitive appeals have been found to be more persuasive when the basis for attitude formation is similarly affective or cognitive (Fabrigar and Petty 1999). This notion of matching appeal with the attitude-formation basis should be investigated in the comparative ad context. Because of the consistent finding that comparative ads elicit greater cognitive activity, it is possible that comparative ads are perceived as cognitive appeals. If this speculation holds, then according to the matching hypothesis, comparative ads should be more effective when the attitude formation is based on cognitive appeals. This expectation is aligned with Thompson and Hamilton's (2006) finding—that in analytical processing situations, comparative ads are more persuasive, while in imagery-processing situations, noncomparative ads are more persuasive.

Message Repetition

Another area for further research is the impact of message repetition on comparative advertising effectiveness. For example, all else being equal, low levels of repetition may foster a more positive attitude to comparative ads than to noncomparative ads, while moderate numbers of repetitions may not render such a difference. As noted in Cacioppo and Petty (1989), moderate numbers of repetitive exposures (e.g., listening to an appeal about a comprehensive exam policy three times) generated more positive attitude when listening to strong arguments in the appeal than when listening to weak arguments. Further, low exposure (listening to the appeal one time) did not produce attitudinal differences between strong and weak arguments. This finding led Cacioppo and Petty to conclude that message repetition (up to a point) increases the "opportunity to scrutinize the argument" (Cacioppo and Petty 1989) and enhances elaboration (Cacioppo and Petty 1979, 1989). To the extent that comparative ads are elaborated more than noncomparative ads, repetition should enhance elaboration of noncomparative ads. Assuming that at moderate levels of repetition, the two types of ads may be elaborated about equally, the cognitive activity advantage that comparative ads have should be neutralized. On the other hand, if a comparative ad seeks to retain its elaboration advantage at moderate repetition levels, the advertiser may try and feature multiple comparisons.

Self-Referencing

Another fruitful direction for research is to examine the role of self-referencing in ad comprehension. Self-referencing activates cognitive generalizations about the self that are stored in memory and applies meaning to the incoming information within the self-schemata (Markus 1977, 1980; Rogers 1981). Symons and Johnson's (1997) meta-analysis on self-referencing revealed that self-referencing promoted better recall (as compared to information about others or semantic information) because it was easy to remember and attracted more attention. Therefore, ads that contain self-referencing information may lead to high recall for both comparative ads and noncomparative ads. Therefore, it is possible that the large amount of knowledge retrieved in self-schemata may render differences between self-reference–based comparative ads and noncomparative ads nonsignificant.

Combinational Directives

Our review on attribute specificity reveals that attributes that are comparable along some aspects have a higher recall than attributes that are common to both brands and/or attributes that do not correspond (Zhang and Markman 1998). If comparative ads feature both typical and atypical attributes, such a combination will have attributes that are comparable to some extent but are neither identical nor drastically different. Thus, ads that compare alternatives on typical as well as atypical attributes may be better recalled than ads that compare brands only on typical or on atypical attributes. Using too many noncomparable attributes may lead to difficulty in comprehension, while too few may fail to achieve the salience threshold necessary for recall (Zhang and Markman 1998).

Situational Variables

Mood

As stated earlier, research suggests that comparative ads are more likely to be processed via a central route as compared to noncomparative ads, and as a result elicit greater attention and elaboration (Dröge 1989). Further, Bless and colleagues (1990) suggest that negative emotions may induce central processing whereas positive emotions may lead to peripheral processing. Thus, people in a positive mood may not evaluate comparative and noncomparative ads differently, and those in a negative mood may favor the advertiser more when exposed to comparative ads. In Bless and colleagues' (1990) study, participants in a negative mood generated a higher proportion of favorable cognitive responses to a tape recording about an increase in student service fees and greater attitude change when exposed to strong arguments than to weak arguments. In contrast, participants in the positive mood condition did not exhibit such differences in cognitive responses and/or attitude change. In the second study, when distracted during message exposure, participants in different mood conditions did not differ in their cognitive responses and/or attitude change. Thus, positive mood appears to interfere with information processing in a manner similar to distraction.

Construal Level

Another situational factor that deserves research attention in comparative advertising contexts is construal level (Trope and Liberman 2003). People respond to near-future and distant-future events differently because near-future events are represented more concretely while distant-future events are represented in more abstract terms. Ads that feature products in the distant future may place people in abstract mind-sets, making comparisons based on product attributes appear distant and consequently of less importance from a temporally proximate perspective. Thus, consumers may not differ in their responses to comparative and noncomparative ads in temporally distant situations. In contrast, a temporally proximal product may induce concrete thinking and render the comparisons meaningful and salient. Therefore, consumers may favor an advertised brand featured in comparative ads over the advertised brand in noncomparative ads. This interaction between ad type (comparative/noncomparative) and temporal construal may further interact with the type of attribute(s) featured in the messages (abstract/concrete). Other factors that influence construal levels may also be interesting to comparative advertising research. Bar-Anan and colleagues (2007), using

Stroop-like tasks, found that spatial distance was automatically associated with other types of psychological distance. They argue that psychological distance (e.g., temporal distance) is automatically activated upon exposure to any other type of psychological distance (e.g., spatial distance). Therefore, the placement of advertisements in stores, whether spatially distant or proximal from the consumers, may influence the effectiveness of comparative ads. If the ads are spatially distant, the comparison between products in the ads may not be perceived to be meaningful and may not be favored over noncomparative ads. If the ads are spatially proximal, the comparison being made may appear more meaningful and elicit more favorable responses relative to noncomparative ads.

Selectivity Motivation

An interesting situational variable that may help extend the research on comparative ads is socioemotional selectivity motivation. Different motivations assume primacy depending on the perception of time. When time is perceived as open-ended (and therefore relatively unconstrained), the goal of knowledge acquisition is activated. When time is perceived as limited, the goal of emotion regulation becomes salient. A study by Carstensen, Isaacowitz, and Charles (1999) found that HIV-positive participants, with lower life expectancy, held representations of prospective social partners significantly more along affective dimensions than HIV-negative participants. Therefore, people who perceive time as open-ended may prefer comparative ads to noncomparative ads because the richer information in comparative ads is better aligned with their goal of knowledge acquisition. In contrast, people who perceive time as limited may prefer noncomparative ads to comparative ads because the emotional-laden attribute trade-off (Luce, Payne, and Bettman 1999) inherent in comparative ads may be perceived as inconsistent with their emotion regulation goal.

Individual Variables

Need for Closure

Our review reveals that brand specificity influences the effectiveness of comparative ads. People varying in need for closure (Webster and Kruglanski 1994) may also differ in their responses to different types of comparative ads. People who are high (versus low) in need for closure may have a lower tolerance for ads that contain less specific comparisons due to their discomfort with ambiguity.

Risk Propensity

It will be useful to understand how people with varying risk-taking propensities (Levenson 1990; Zuckerman and Kuhlman 2000) differ in the manner in which they process information contained in comparative ads. This line of inquiry will be especially meaningful for public policy makers who are interested in understanding how to promote healthy behavior through marketing messages. It is possible that risk-averse consumers may be more persuaded by comparisons that are more objective (Darley and Smith 1993), while consumers who are more risk-seeking may be dubious about claim objectivity and may in fact prefer comparisons between the advertiser and an ambiguous leading brand.

Consumer Ideology

Future research may also explore whether people with varying ideologies perceive comparative ads differently. Forsyth (1980) contends that individuals differ in the degree to which they endorse idealism versus relativism. Such differences may not only be reflected in moral judgment but may also influence how people perceive and process information contained in comparative ads. For example, relativistic people may perceive comparative ads to be more persuasive because of their worldview (i.e., "everything is relative"). Idealistic people may prefer noncomparative ads to comparative ads because they uphold universalist beliefs, while conditional beliefs such as "A is good only when compared to B" are less consistent with their values.

Social Orientation

Our review finds gender to be a moderator of the effectiveness of comparative ads. With diminishing stereotypical gender roles, individual differences relating to gender should receive more attention in research on comparative ads. Research suggests that individuals differ in their agentic and communal orientations (Hupfer 2001; Hupfer and Detlor 2006). Agentic orientation is measured by items such as *self-sufficient, make my own choices, am my own person, self-reliant,* and *independent,* whereas *nurturing, understanding, compassionate, sympathetic,* and *sensitive to the needs of others* characterize communal orientation. Direct comparison between brands in an ad, especially if the comparison implicates social meaning, may be favored by people high in communal orientation over ads without social comparison content. In contrast, people high in agentic orientation may prefer ads without direct (social) comparisons.

Locus of Control

People also differ in their perceived locus of control (Miller and Minton 1969; Rotter 1966) and thus may vary in their perceptions of locus of control process for comparative ads. For example, comparative ads that contain attributions to the product (e.g., "You can lose more weight by taking pill A over pill B") may be more favored by people who believe in internal control rather than by those who believe in external control. This may be so because the attribution information is meaningful to people who attribute experience to controllable factors but not to those who attribute experience to factors beyond their control. For example, if people believe that the ability to lose weight is beyond their control (e.g., genetic), they will find comparative product information irrelevant.

Concluding Remarks

Our forgoing review and research agenda focus on comparative advertising in general marketing domains. We do not investigate two specific types of comparisons: political advertising (Ansolabehere and Iyengar 1995) and price comparisons (Barone, Manning, and Miniard 2004; Grewal, Marmorstein, and Sharma 1996). Political persuasion that takes place typically in person-perception settings is replete with the use of comparative messages almost as a norm. Indeed, a vast literature exists in this domain that examines various issues pertinent to political advertising. Comparing insights obtained from political advertising research and those documented in product/service advertising may lead to a more generalizable and enriched model of comparative advertising effectiveness that cuts across person and object perception. We also do not examine message-based persuasion in the area of a routine managerial pursuit-price comparisons. A literature review of price comparison research is overdue. Such a review could assist in discovering (a) best practices in price comparison communication, and (b) potential avenues for future research.

References

Ansolabehere, S., and S. Iyengar. 1995. *Going Negative: How Political Advertisements Shrink and Polarize the Electorate.* New York: Free Press.

Bar-Anan, Y., N. Liberman, Y. Trope, and D. Algom. 2007. "Automatic Processing of Psychological Distance: Evidence from a Stroop Task." *Journal of Experimental Psychology: General* 136: 610–22.

Barone, M.J., K.C. Manning, and P.W. Miniard. 2004. "Consumer Response to Retailers' Use of Partially Comparative Pricing." *Journal of Marketing* 68: 37–47.

Barry, T.E. 1993. "Twenty Years of Comparative Advertising in the United States." *International Journal of Advertising* 12: 325–50.

Barry, T.E., and R.L. Tremblay. 1975. "Comparative Advertising: Perspectives and Issues." *Journal of Advertising* 4: 15–20.

Belch, G.E. 1981. "An Examination of Comparative and Noncomparative Television Commercials: The Effects of Claim Variation and Repetition on Cognitive Response and Message Acceptance." *Journal of Marketing Research* 18: 333–49.

Bless, H., G. Bohner, N. Schwarz, and F. Strack. 1990. "Mood and Persuasion." *Personality and Social Psychology Bulletin* 16: 331–45.

Boush, D.M., and I. Ross. 1986. "The Influence of Substantiation Details on Perceptions of Comparative Advertising Claims: An Exploratory Investigation." In *1986 AMA Educators' Proceedings,* ed. T.A. Shimp, 340–44. Chicago: American Marketing Association.

Cacioppo, J.T., and R.E. Petty. 1979. "Effects of Message Repetition and Position on Cognitive Response, Recall, and Persuasion." *Journal of Personality and Social Psychology* 37: 97–109.

———. 1989. "Effects of Message Repetition on Argument Processing, Recall, and Persuasion." *Basic and Applied Social Psychology* 10: 3–12.

Campbell, M.C., and A. Kirmani. 2000. "Consumer's Use of Persuasion Knowledge: The Effects of Accessibility and Cognitive Capacity on Perceptions of an Influence Agent." *Journal of Consumer Research* 27: 69–83.

Carstensen, L.L., D.M. Isaacowitz, and S.T. Charles. 1999. "Taking Time Seriously: A Theory of Socioemotional Selectivity." *American Psychologist* 54: 165–81.

Chang, C. 2007. "The Relative Effectiveness of Comparative and Noncomparative Advertising: Evidence for Gender Differences in Information-Processing Strategies." *Journal of Advertising* 36: 21–35.

Choi, Y.K., and G.E. Miracle. 2004. "The Effectiveness of Comparative Advertising in Korea and the United States: A Cross-Cultural and Individual-Level Analysis." *Journal of Advertising* 33: 75–87.

Darley, W.K., and R.E. Smith. 1993. "Advertising Claim Objectivity: Antecedents and Effects." *Journal of Marketing* 57: 100–13.

Demirdjian, Z.S. 1983. "Sales Effectiveness of Comparative Advertising: An Experimental Field Investigation." *Journal of Consumer Research* 10: 362–64.

Donthu, N. 1992. "Comparative Advertising Intensity." *Journal of Advertising Research* 32: 53–58.

———. 1998. "A Cross-Country Investigation of Recall of and Attitude Toward Comparative Advertising." *Journal of Advertising* 27: 111–22.

Dröge, C. 1989. "Shaping the Route to Attitude Change: Central Versus Peripheral Processing Through Comparative Versus Noncomparative Advertising." *Journal of Marketing Research* 26: 193–204.

Dröge, C., and R.Y. Darmon. 1987. "Associative Positioning Strategies Through Comparative Advertising: Attribute Versus Overall Similarity Approaches." *Journal of Marketing Research* 24: 377–88.

Etgar, M., and S.A. Goodwin. 1982. "One-Sided Versus Two-Sided Comparative Message Appeals for New Brand Introductions." *Journal of Consumer Research* 8: 460–65.

Fabrigar, L.R., and R.E. Petty. 1999. "The Role of the Affective and Cognitive Bases of Attitudes in Susceptibility to Affectively and Cognitively Based Persuasion." *Personality and Social Psychology Bulletin* 25: 363–81.

Ferraro, G.P. 1994. *The Cultural Dimension of International Business.* Englewood Cliffs, NJ: Prentice Hall.

Forsyth, D.R. 1980. "A Taxonomy of Ethical Ideologies." *Journal of Personality and Social Psychology* 39: 175–84.

Golden, L.L. 1979. "Consumer Reactions to Explicit Brand Comparisons in Advertisements." *Journal of Marketing Research* 16: 517–32.

Goodwin, S., and M. Etgar. 1980. "An Experimental Investigation of Comparative Advertising: Impact of Message Appeal, Information Load, and Utility of Product Class." *Journal of Marketing Research* 17: 187–202.

Gorn, G.J., and C.B. Weinberg. 1984. "The Impact of Comparative Advertising on Perception and Attitude: Some Positive Findings." *Journal of Consumer Research* 11: 719–27.

Grewal, D., S. Kavanoor, E.F. Fern, C. Costley, and J. Barnes. 1997. "Comparative Versus Noncomparative Advertising: A Meta-Analysis." *Journal of Marketing* 61: 1–15.

Grewal, D., H. Marmorstein, and A. Sharma. 1996. "Communicating Price Information Through Semantic Cues: The Moderating Effects of Situation and Discount Size." *Journal of Consumer Research* 23: 148–55.

Grossbart, S., D.D. Muehling, and N. Kangun. 1986. "Verbal and Visual References to Competition in Comparative Advertising." *Journal of Advertising* 15: 10–23.

Hackleman, E.C., and S.C. Jain. 1979. "An Experimental Analysis of Attitudes Toward Comparison and Non-Comparison Advertising." *Advances in Consumer Research* 6: 90–94.

Hall, E.T. 1976. *Beyond Culture.* Garden City, NY: Anchor Press.

Hupfer, M.E. 2001. "Self-Concept Orientation and Response to Agentic and Communal Advertising Messages." Ph.D. diss., University of Alberta, Edmonton.

Hupfer, M.E., and B. Detlor. 2006. "Gender and Web Information Seeking: A Self-concept Orientation Model." *Journal of the American Society for Information Science and Technology* 57: 1105–15.

Iyer, E.S. 1988. "The Influence of Verbal Content and Relative Newness on the Effectiveness of Comparative Advertising." *Journal of Advertising* 17: 15–21.

Jackson Jr., D.W., S.W. Brown, and R.R. Harmon. 1979. "Comparative Magazine Advertisements." *Journal of Advertising Research* 19: 21–26.

Jain, S.C., and E.C. Hackleman. 1978. "How Effective Is Comparison Advertising for Stimulating Brand Recall?" *Journal of Advertising* 7: 20–25.

Jain, S.P., N. Agrawal, and D. Maheswaran. 2006. "When More May Be Less: The Effects of Regulatory Focus on Responses to Different Comparative Frames." *Journal of Consumer Research* 33: 91–98.

Jain, S.P., B. Buchanan, and D. Maheswaran. 2000. "Comparative Versus Noncomparative Advertising: The Moderating Impact of Prepurchase Attribute Verifiability." *Journal of Consumer Psychology* 9: 201–11.

Jain, S.P., and D. Maheswaran. 2000. "Motivated Reasoning: A Depth-of-Processing Perspective." *Journal of Consumer Research* 26: 358–71.

Jain, S.P., P. Mathur, and D. Maheswaran. 2009. "The Influence of Consumers' Lay Theories on Approach/Avoidance Motivation." *Journal of Marketing Research* 46: 56–65.

Jain, S.P., and S.S. Posavac. 2004. "Valenced Comparisons." *Journal of Marketing Research* 41: 46–58.

Jeon, J.O., and S.E. Beatty. 2002. "Comparative Advertising Effectiveness in Different National Cultures." *Journal of Business Research* 55: 907–13.

Johnson, M.D., and D.A. Horne. 1988. "The Contrast Model of Similarity and Comparative Advertising." *Psychology & Marketing* 5: 211–32.

Kirmani, A., and R. Zhu. 2007. "Vigilant Against Manipulation: The Effect of Regulatory Focus on the Use of Persuasion Knowledge." *Journal of Marketing Research* 44: 688–701.

Lamb Jr., C.W., W.M. Pride, and B.A. Pletcher. 1978. "A Taxonomy for Comparative Advertising Research." *Journal of Advertising* 7: 43–47.

Levenson, M.R. 1990. "Risk Taking and Personality." *Journal of Personality and Social Psychology* 58: 1073–80.

Levine, P. 1976. "Commercials That Name Competing Brands." *Journal of Advertising Research* 16: 7–14.

Liaukonyte, J. 2009. "Empirical Essays on Advertising Content." Ph.D. diss., University of Virginia, Charlottesville.

Luce, M.F., J.W. Payne, and J.R. Bettman. 1999. "Emotional Trade-off Difficulty and Choice." *Journal of Marketing Research* 36: 143–59.

Macarthur, K. 2007. "Why Big Brands Are Getting into the Ring." *Advertising Age* 78: 6.

MacKenzie, S.B., R.J. Lutz, and G.E. Belch. 1986. "The Role of Attitude Toward the Ad as a Mediator of Advertising Effectiveness: A Test of Competing Explanations." *Journal of Marketing Research* 23: 130–43.

Manning, K.C., P.W. Miniard, M.J. Barone, and R.L. Rose. 2001. "Understanding the Mental Representation Created by Comparative Advertising." *Journal of Advertising* 30: 27–39.

Markus, H.R. 1977. "Self-Schemata and Processing Information About the Self." *Journal of Personality and Social Psychology* 35: 63–78.

———. 1980. "The Self in Thought and Memory." In *The Self in Social Psychology,* ed. D.M. Wegner and R.R. Vallacher, 102–30. New York: Oxford University Press.

Markus, H.R., and S. Kitayama. 1991. "Culture and the Self: Implications for Cognition, Emotion, and Motivation." *Psychological Review* 98: 224–53.

McDougall, G.H.G. 1978. "Comparative Advertising: The Effect of Claim Type and Brand Loyalty." *Current Issues & Research in Advertising* 1: 39.

Meyers-Levy, J. 1989. "Priming Effects on Product Judgments: A Hemispheric Interpretation." *Journal of Consumer Research* 16: 76–86.

Meyers-Levy, J., and D. Maheswaran. 1991. "Exploring Differences in Males and Females Processing Strategies." *Journal of Consumer Research* 18: 63–70.

Meyers-Levy, J., and B. Sternthal. 1991. "Gender Differences in the Use of Message Cues and Judgments." *Journal of Marketing Research* 28: 84–96.

Miller, A.G., and H.L. Minton. 1969. "Machiavellianism, Internal-External Control, and the Violation of Experimental Instructions." *Psychological Record* 19: 369–80.

Miniard, P.W., R.L. Rose, M.J. Barone, and K.C. Manning. 1993. "On the Need for Relative Measures when Assessing Comparative Advertising Effects." *Journal of Advertising* 22: 41–57.

Muehling, D.D. 1987. "Comparative Advertising: The Influence of Attitude-Toward-the-Ad on Brand Evaluation." *Journal of Advertising* 16: 43–49.

Muehling, D.D., and N. Kangun. 1985. "The Multi-Dimensionality of Comparative Advertising: Implications for the Federal Trade Commission." *Journal of Public Policy and Marketing* 4: 112–28.

Muehling, D.D., J.J. Stoltman, and S. Grossbart. 1990. "The Impact of Comparative Advertising on Levels of Message Involvement." *Journal of Advertising* 19: 41–50.

Neese, W.T., and R.D. Taylor. 1994. "Verbal Strategies for Indirect Comparative Advertising." *Journal of Advertising Research* 34: 56–70.

Pechmann, C., and G. Esteban. 1993. "Persuasion Processes Associated with Direct Comparative and Noncomparative Advertising and Implications for Advertising Effectiveness." *Journal of Consumer Psychology* 2: 403–32.

Pechmann, C., and S. Ratneshwar. 1991. "The Use of Comparative Advertising for Brand Positioning: Association Versus Differentiation." *Journal of Consumer Research* 18: 145–60.

———. 1992. "Consumer Covariation Judgments: Theory or Data Driven?" *Journal of Consumer Research* 19: 373–86.

Pechmann, C., and D.W. Stewart. 1990. "The Effects of Comparative Advertising on Attention, Memory, and Purchase Intentions." *Journal of Consumer Research* 17: 180–91.

Pfau, M. 1994. "Impact of Product Involvement, Message Format, and Receiver Sex on the Efficacy of Comparative Advertising Messages." *Communication Quarterly* 42: 244–58.

Prasad, V.K. 1976. "Communications-Effectiveness of Comparative Advertising: A Laboratory Analysis." *Journal of Marketing Research* 13: 128–37.

Pride, W.M., C.W. Lamb, and B.A. Pletcher. 1979. "The Informativeness of Comparative Advertisements: An Empirical Investigation." *Journal of Advertising* 8: 29–48.

Putrevu, S., and K.R. Lord. 1994. "Comparative and Noncomparative Advertising: Attitudinal Effects Under Cognitive and Affective Involvement Conditions." *Journal of Advertising* 23: 77–91.

Rogers, J.C., and T.G. Williams. 1989. "Comparative Advertising Effectiveness: Practitioners' Perceptions Versus Academic Research Findings." *Journal of Advertising Research* 29: 22–37.

Rogers, T.B. 1981. "A Model of the Self as an Aspect of the Human Information Processing System." In *Personality, Cognition, and Social Interaction,* ed. N. Cantor and J.F. Kihlstrom, 193–214. Hillsdale, NJ: Lawrence Erlbaum.

Rose, R.L., P.W. Miniard, M.J. Barone, K.C. Manning, and B.D. Till. 1993. "When Persuasion Goes Undetected: The Case of Comparative Advertising." *Journal of Marketing Research* 30: 315–30.

Rotter, J.B. 1966. "Generalized Expectancies for Internal Versus External Control of Reinforcement." *Psychological Monographs* 80: 1–28.

Sawyer, A.G. 1988. "Can There be Effective Advertising Without Explicit Conclusions? Decide for Yourself." In *Nonverbal Communication in Advertising,* ed. S. Hecker and D.W. Stewart, 159–84. Lexington, MA: Lexington Books.

Shao, A.T., Y. Bao, and E, Gray. 2004. "Comparative Advertising Effectiveness: A Cross-Cultural Study." *Journal of Current Issues & Research in Advertising* 26: 67–80.

Shimp, T.A. 1978. "Do Incomplete Comparisons Mislead?" *Journal of Advertising Research* 18: 21–27.

Shimp, T.A., and D.C. Dyer. 1978. "The Effects of Comparative Advertising Mediated by Market Position of Sponsoring Brand." *Journal of Advertising* 7: 13–19.

Snyder, R. 1989. "Misleading Characteristics of Implied-Superiority Claims." *Journal of Advertising* 18: 54–61.

Stutts, M.A. 1982. "Comparative Advertising and Counterargument." *Journal of the Academy of Marketing Science* 10: 302–13.

Sujan, M., and C. Dekleva. 1987. "Product Categorization and Inference Making: Some Implications for Comparative Advertising." *Journal of Consumer Research* 14: 372–78.

Swinyard, W.R. 1981. "The Interaction Between Comparative Advertising and Copy Claim Variation." *Journal of Marketing Research* 18: 175–86.

Symons, C.S., and B.T. Johnson. 1997. "The Self-Reference Effect in Memory: A Meta-Analysis." *Psychological Bulletin* 121: 371–94.

Thompson, D.V., and R.W. Hamilton. 2006. "The Effects of Information Processing Mode on Consumers' Responses to Comparative Advertising." *Journal of Consumer Research* 32: 530–40.

Triandis, H.C. 1988. "Collectivism vs. Individualism: A Reconceptualization of a Basic Concept in Cross-Cultural Psychology." In *Cross-Cultural Studies of Personality, Attitudes and Cognition,* ed. G. Verma and C. Bagley, 60–95. London: Macmillan.

Trope, Y., and N. Liberman. 2003. "Temporal Construal." *Psychological Review* 110: 403–21.

Webster, D.M., and A.W. Kruglanski. 1994. "Individual Differences in Need for Cognitive Closure." *Journal of Personality and Social Psychology* 67: 1049–62.

Wilkie, W.L., and P.W. Farris. 1975. "Comparison Advertising: Problems and Potential." *Journal of Marketing* 39: 7–15.

Wilson, R.D. 1976. "An Empirical Evaluation of Comparative Advertising Messages: Subjects' Responses on Perceptual Dimensions." *Advances in Consumer Research* 3: 53–57.

Wilson, R.D., and A. Muderrisoglu. 1980. "An Analysis of Cognitive Responses to Comparative Advertising." *Advances in Consumer Research* 7: 566–71.

Zhang, S., F.R. Kardes, and M.L. Cronley. 2002. "Comparative Advertising: Effects of Structural Alignability on Target Brand Evaluations." *Journal of Consumer Psychology* 12: 303–11.

Zhang, S., and A.B. Markman. 1998. "Overcoming the Early Entrant Advantage: The Role of Alignable and Nonalignable Differences." *Journal of Marketing Research* 35: 413–26.

Zuckerman, M., and D.M. Kuhlman. 2000. "Personality and Risk-Taking: Common Bisocial Factors." *Journal of Personality* 68: 999–1029.

8

Brand Experience

Managerial Applications of a New Consumer Psychology Concept

J. Joško Brakus, Bernd Schmitt, and Lia Zarantonello

Consider some of the intriguing new products and brands that have appeared in the market during the first decade of the twenty-first century: Apple with its iPod and iPhone products. The Mini Cooper and Nintendo's Wii. These products all boast innovative design and promise superior function. But focusing on their innovative product features tells only part of the story. Even more creative and innovative is the way the brands are marketed to consumers—through appeals to their senses, feelings, intellect, curiosity, and self-image rather than to more rational, analytical notions of value. Such marketing techniques are turning up in all sorts of industries, from consumer electronics and automotive to telecommunications and retailing. What they have in common is a focus on the brand experience.

Brand experience is a new and exciting consumer psychology concept. And it is not exciting only to academics. Marketing practitioners have come to realize that understanding how consumers experience brands and, in turn, how to provide appealing brand experiences for them, is critical for differentiating brands in the competitive environment. As a result, numerous trade writings have appeared that present useful frameworks, concepts, and tools for managing experiences (Chattopadhyay and Laborie 2005; Pine and Gilmore 1999; Schmitt 1999, 2003; Shaw and Ivens 2002; Smith and Wheeler 2002). Moreover, in the academic branding literature, several emotion- and experience-related concepts have been developed, such as brand personality, brand community, brand trust, brand attachment, brand engagement, and brand love (Aaker 1997; Carroll and Ahuvia 2006; Delgado-Ballester, Munuera-Alemán, and Yagüe-Guillén 2003; McAlexander, Schouten, and Koenig 2002; Thomson, MacInnis, and Park 2005).

In this chapter, we describe the concept of brand experience and its dimensions. We will alternate throughout the chapter between marketing practice and research conducted on this topic. Our own thinking and research was influenced, in part, by experiential marketing campaigns and managerial projects that we worked on with several companies. Thus, we will discuss key characteristics of experiential branding as we show how the concept of brand experience may be used to address relevant marketing issues. Finally, we present a project-based management framework for managing experiences.

Traditional Versus Experiential Marketing

In their book *The Experience Economy,* Pine and Gilmore (1999) argued that economies went through different stages of economic value creation, starting with commodities, then consumer goods, and then services. The most recent way to create value, according to the authors, occurs by "staging experiences." It is questionable whether the U.S. economy and other highly developed economies should be dubbed "experience economies," given that more than two-thirds of their GDP is still created through services and only a minor part through the type of staged experiences described by Pine and Gilmore (1999), such as theme restaurants. However, there is no doubt that in the twenty-first century products and services, and even some commodities (e.g., coffee, water, salt), are increasingly branded and marketed by using experiences. Schmitt (1999) referred to this new marketing approach as experiential marketing.

Branding and marketing in prior to the twenty-first century was quite different. Marketers did not care about the experiences their brands provided to customers. Marketing approaches focused instead on functional features and performance characteristics of products, such as hardware and memory in electronics products, gas mileage in cars, durability in major appliances, or cleaning power in detergents. Traditional marketers viewed customers as rational decision makers who weighed these features and benefits against one another and carefully selected products with the highest overall utility. It was the marketing of the industrial and consumer age. The dominant paradigm in consumer research viewed the consumer as a kind of information processor that made comparisons and generated decisions—a very rational creature that would systematically consider alternatives, weigh pros and cons, and make appropriate judgments (Bettman 1979). Marketers subscribing to this approach looked at their consumers as engineers might: they treated them as analytical and rational creatures. Applied to branding, the rational approach stressed the importance of choice models and perceptual maps and advertising as the key persuasion tool, because through advertising marketers could present—and tweak—product features and benefits most easily to consumers.

The Brand Experience Construct

In a paper that we published in the *Journal of Marketing,* we conceptualized brand experience as, "subjective, internal consumer responses (sensations, feelings, and cognitions) as well as behavioral responses that are evoked by brand-related experiential attributes when consumers interact with brands, shop for them and consume them" (Brakus, Schmitt, and Zarantonello 2009, 53). An experience is thus essentially a private event that occurs in response to some kind of stimulus. Experiences are usually not self-generated but induced; experiences are "of" or "about" something external to the subject (Schmitt 1999). The goal for experiential marketers, then, is to provide stimuli that will result in experiences for consumers; and marketers and brand managers are doing just that.

Brand experience, as we define it, extends far beyond the realm of advertising (Rust and Oliver 1994). Public relations, events, and online communications and new media are increasingly important (Ries and Ries 2004). In fact, in some cases advertising may be irrelevant for building brand experiences, and may not even be used. Google is an example. Google's brand value has been built without spending a cent on advertising. Or think of how Starbucks and other designer coffee shops have transformed the mundane experience of having a cup of coffee. Starbucks has built its brand through its in-store experience and not through mass media advertising. Bottled water is another example. Many bottled water companies do not advertise. Instead, they rely on creative package design to evoke feelings and associations: Poland Spring, the unpolluted wilds of Maine; Fiji, the island paradise of the South Pacific; and Spa, the pristine beauty of the Alps.

Experiences happen in diverse settings. Consumer and marketing research has shown that brand experiences occur when consumers search, examine, and evaluate products; when they shop for them and receive service; and when they consume them (Arnould, Price, and Zinkhan 2002; Brakus, Schmitt, and Zhang forthcoming; Holbrook 2000). When consumers search for, examine, and evaluate products, the experience can be *direct,* when there is physical contact with the product, or *indirect,* when a product is presented on a website or in an ad (Hoch 2002). Shopping and service experiences occur when a consumer interacts with a store's physical environment, its personnel, and its policies and practices (Hui and Bateson 1991; Kerin, Jain, and Howard 1992). Atmospheric variables and salespeople play a key role in the shopping experience (Arnold et al. 2005; Boulding et al. 1993; Grace and O'Cass 2004; Jones 1999; Ofir and Simonson 2007).

Most important, experiences occur when consumers use products. Consumption experiences are often multidimensional, including a variety of feelings and hedonic dimensions (Holbrook and Hirschman 1982). With respect to feelings, prior consumer research had limited itself to the study of affect—that is, whether a consumer "liked" or "disliked" a product. Holbrook and Hirschman (1982), however, argued that there were many other emotions relevant to the consumption experience that had been ignored—joy, envy, anger, and fear, for example. Moreover, before Holbrook and Hirschman, consumer researchers had focused on consumer satisfaction. The theory was that if you were satisfied with the product, that is, if it fulfilled or exceeded your functional expectations, then you would buy it again and loyalty would be built from there. Holbrook and Hirschman made the point that there were other important responses involved in consumers' interactions with products; such as fun, play, and aesthetic responses. This recognition changed the study of customer value. Much of the interpretive research on consumption experiences following the pioneering work by Holbrook and Hirschman focused on hedonic goals that occur during and after the consumption of, for example, jazz, movies, museums, river rafting, baseball, and skydiving (Arnould and Price 1993; Celsi, Rose, and Leigh 1993; Holt 1995; Joy and Sherry 2003).

Differences Between Brand Experience and Other Brand Constructs

Brand experience is a new brand construct that is distinct from others. In particular, brand experience differs from evaluative, affective, and associative constructs such as brand attitudes, brand involvement, brand attachment, customer delight, and brand personality.

Brand Experiences Versus Brand Attitudes

Attitudes are general evaluations that are based on beliefs (Fishbein and Ajzen 1975), while experiences result from exposure to attributes that result from consumer interactions with brands. Brand experiences are not belief-based, but can result in evaluations and may develop into an attitude that consumers can retrieve when asked about their brand experiences (e.g., "I like the experience"). Overall brand evaluations are therefore more general and do not elucidate the very nature of brand experience.

Brand Experience Versus Consumer Involvement

Involvement is based on needs, values, and interest that motivate a consumer toward an object such as a brand (Zaichkowsky 1985). Moreover, antecedents of involvement include the perceived importance and personal relevance of a brand. Brand experience, in contrast, does not presume a motivational state. Experiences can happen even when consumers do not show interest or have a personal connection with the brand. Moreover, brands that consumers are highly involved with are not necessarily brands that evoke the strongest experiences.

Brand Experience Versus Brand Attachment

Brand attachment refers to a strong emotional bond (i.e., "hot affect") between a consumer and a brand, as evidenced by its three dimensions—affection, passion, and connection (Park and MacInnis 2006; Thomson et al. 2005). In contrast to brand attachment, brand experience is not an emotional relationship concept. Experiences are sensations, feelings, cognitions, and behavioral responses evoked by brand-related stimulation. Over time, brand experiences may result in emotional bonds, just as they may result in an overall attitude; but emotions are only one possible internal outcome of the stimulation that evokes experiences.

Brand Experience Versus Customer Delight

Customer delight is characterized by arousal and positive affect; it may be considered the affective component of satisfaction (Oliver, Rust, and Varki 1997). Customer delight results from disconfirming, surprising consumption (Oliver et al. 1997). In contrast to customer delight, brand experiences do not occur only after consumption; they occur whenever there is a direct or indirect interaction with the brand. Moreover, a brand experience does not have to be surprising; it may be either expected or unexpected.

Brand Experience Versus Brand Personality

Consumers endow brands with human characteristics that result in a brand personality. The five dimensions that may related to a brand are sincerity, excitement, competence, sophistication, and ruggedness (Aaker 1997). Consumers endow brands with these five traits in a higher-order, inferential process (Johar, Sengupta, and Aaker 2005); that is, consumers do not feel sincere or excited about the brand, but project these traits onto brands. In contrast, brand experiences are actual sensations, feelings, thoughts, and behavioral responses arising from brand-based firm-consumer interactions. As a result, just as we expect brand experience to differ from brand evaluations, brand involvement, brand attachment, and customer delight, we expect brand experience to be conceptually and empirically distinct from brand personality.

The Dimensions of Brand Experience

In our research, we conceptualized brand experience as a *multidimensional construct*. Based on writings in philosophy (Dewey 1922, 1925); cognitive science (Pinker 1997); and applied research on experience marketing and management (Pine and Gilmore 1999; Schmitt 1999), we identified five dimensions of brand experience: sensory, affective, intellectual, behavioral, and social (Brakus et al. 2009, 53). Sensory experience refers to the stimulation of the five human senses and includes aesthetics and sensory qualities. Affective experience includes moods and emotions. Intellectual experience includes convergent/analytical and divergent/imaginative thinking. Behavioral experience refers to motor actions and behavioral experiences. Social experience refers to relational experiences, such as relating to a reference group.

It is important to note that experience dimensions can be evoked by various specific brand-related stimuli (for example, colors, shapes, typefaces, designs, slogans, mascots, and brand characters). There is, however, no one-to-one correspondence such that a certain stimulus type would trigger only a specific experience dimension. For example, while colors, shapes, typefaces, and designs usually result in sensory experience, they may also result in emotions (e.g., red for Coca-Cola) or in intellectual experiences (e.g., when designs use complex patterns). Similarly, slogans, mascots, and brand characters, while they may result in imaginative thoughts, may trigger emotions (e.g., "Bibendum," the Michelin Man) or stimulate actions (e.g., Nike's "Just Do It").

Deciding which experience dimension a brand should be focused on is a complex management decision. It requires an understanding of consumer preferences, competitive approaches, and social and cultural trends. We will discuss each dimension further by providing practical examples for each one.

Sensory experiences result from the stimulation of consumers' multiple senses—sight, sound, touch, smell, and taste. Sensory experiential marketing thus concerns the marketing of design and aesthetics—creating a unique experience via arousing interest and engaging the five senses (Schmitt and Simonson 1997).

Makers of PDAs and consumer electronics devices use a multisensory approach in the design of their products, including the color scheme of the product line and the sound and touch elements of the "user experience." This so-called sense marketing plays an increasingly important role in creating a brand experience. In the car industry, sight, sound, touch, and even smell are important considerations when designing the interior of a car. Small differences in smell and taste can make or break a food product (e.g., wine or chocolates), or determine whether the brand is experienced as mass-market or up-market. Sight and touch are also important for food products. For example, the packaging of many "luxury" chocolates is extravagant. Packaging for Richart, one of the most expensive chocolate brands, is pure glossy white, with gold or silver embossed lettering. Red cloth ribbons seal the packages. The chocolates are shaped and decorated with patterns, colors, and other ornamentation (a special line displays children's drawings). Special chocolate plaques can be made to customers' specifications. Richart even sells a burlwood chocolate vault with temperature and humidity gauges.

Affective experiences result from feelings and emotions. Affective experiential marketing thus must be guided by the objective of creating experiences that range from mild moods linked to a brand (e.g., for a noninvolving, nondurable grocery brand or service or industrial product) to strong emotions (e.g., for a consumer durable, technology, or social-marketing campaign). The impact of mild moods and emotions should not be underestimated. They are not just "information" as the cognitive view would argue. Experiencing positive moods and emotions on an ongoing basis may be essential for consumer happiness.

Intellectual experiences appeal to the mind with the objective of creating cognitive, problem-solving experiences that engage customers creatively. Intellectually focused experiential marketing thus can target customers' thinking through surprise, intrigue and provocation. Such marketing is common for new technology products but has even been used for inexpensive apparel. In its classic campaign, Benetton, the Italian casual wear retail brand, presented images that alluded to race, war, and disease (such as a black horse mounting a white horse, a blood-stained T-shirt of a soldier killed in action, a dying AIDS patient) to really shake up customers, perhaps even offend them in order to get them to think about societal issues.

Behavioral experiences refer to bodily experiences, individual actions and behaviors, interactions with others involving the brand, and more general lifestyle choices. This type of experiential marketing requires a close understanding of how consumers view their bodies as well as, more generally, how they like to live. Nike's "Just Do It" campaign is a classic example of this type of branding. Frequently depicting famous athletes in action, the campaign transformed the brand experience by appealing to the need to identify with celebrity role models, thus enticing the customer to action.

Finally, social experiences contain aspects of other experiences, in particular affective experiences. Indeed, empirically, social experiences, because they involve people, are hard to distinguish from affective experiences. However, conceptually, social experiences and marketing and branding focused on relations expand beyond the individual's personal, private feelings, thus relating the individual to something outside his or her present state. They relate the person to a broader social system (a subculture, a country, and so on), thus establishing strong brand relations. The motorcycle brand Harley-Davidson, by now commonplace in marketing textbooks, is an experiential brand focused on relations. From the physical experience of riding a Harley to the psychological devotion that the product commands, Harley transcends the consumption experience to a way of life for bikers. Individual users thus become members of a brand community (Muniz and O'Guinn 2001).

Experiential appeals rarely result in only one type of experience. Many brand managers strive to employ experiential hybrids that combine two or more experiences at the same time in order to broaden the experiential appeal. Ideally, marketers should strive to create holistically integrated experiences that possess qualities of all five experience dimensions.

Empirical Studies

To explore whether consumers had a conception of experience that was similar to the conceptualization that we just presented, we asked young adults (MBA students) to describe their experience with a brand of their choice. In this qualitative study, participants were instructed to choose a brand that provides a strong experience for them and one in the same category that does not. Consumers considered the following brands to be "experiential brands": Abercrombie & Fitch, American Express, Apple (iPod), The Body Shop, BMW, Crest, Disney, Google, HBO, Home Depot, MasterCard, Nike, Starbucks, Target, W Hotel, Washington Mutual, and Williams-Sonoma (see Table 8.1). The following were considered "nonexperiential brands": Aéropostale, Canon, Dell, Dick's Sporting Goods, Dunkin' Donuts, Hilton, Macy's, Microsoft, Reebok, Sony, Sur la Table, Tim Horton's, True Value, Visa, Volkswagen, and Walmart. We expect that the intuitions of the readers of this article, by and large, correspond to those of our sample. In other words, the concept has face validity.

Importantly, the qualitative results confirmed many of the tenets of experiential branding described earlier. The content analysis of the open-ended responses indicated that, in line with our conceptualization, all consumers had a concept of brand experience and viewed brand experiences as being evoked by brand-related firm/customer interactions. For each experiential brand, we asked two raters to select descriptions that corresponded with our conceptualization of sensory, affective, cognitive, behavioral, and social experiences. Indeed, participants gave descriptions of sensations (e.g., "touch and feel," "appeal to different senses," "smells nice and is visually warm");

feelings (e.g., "fun," "refreshed," "inspired," "nostalgia," "in a good mood"); analytical and imaginative thoughts (e.g., "the brand intrigues me," "I think of topics like animal testing, purity and wellness," "reminds me to use my imagination," "makes me think about precious things in life"); behaviors (e.g., "enjoy playing with all the products," "I change the way I organize and interact with information," "I want to work out," "It's a place I want to go"); and the social context of branded experiences (e.g., "It's like a membership in an exclusive, country-clubish community," "I am part of a 'smarter' community," "I feel like an athlete").

This was not the case for the nonexperiential brands. In those cases participants responded to price and promotions, functionality, and utility. Here is what they said about Walmart, Visa, and Aéropostale: "They focus on price as low as price can be; their retail stores are incredibly basic"; "Visa is solely about service and not about experience. Visa promotes being accepted everywhere. Visa is about convenience and reliability and less about how I as a customer feel about the brand"; "Aéro's brand stands for little more than cheap clothing."

We also developed a brand experience scale (Brakus et al. 2009). To do that, we followed the standard scale construction procedures suggested in the literature (Nunnally 1978). The final scale consisted of only four of the dimensions that we conceptualized here, because affective and relational experiences needed to be combined based on the empirical results (see Table 8.2). We showed that our brand experience scale was reliable internally across samples and over time and that it was distinct from general brand evaluations. We also showed that the brand experience scale possessed discriminant validity from motivational and affective brand scales, such as brand involvement, brand attachment, and customer delight. This means the scale measures something different from what is measured by other existing marketing and branding scales. After developing the brand experience scale, we tested its accuracy at predicting two key marketing outcomes: satisfaction and loyalty.

Next, we show how the brand experience scale can be applied empirically. We look how brand experience can be used to differentiate branded products and how it can contribute to brand equity in a marketing event.

Experiential Differentiation

As shown in the beginning of this chapter, many brands try to provide experiential differentiation rather than functional differentiation because in many categories products are functionally similar and it is difficult for consumers to differentiate between products based on functional attributes (Brakus et al. 2009; Chang and Chieng 2006; Schmitt 1999). Marketers can differentiate

Table 8.1

Consumers' Descriptions of Experiential Brands

Abercrombie & Fitch
- It's a complete experience when you enter the store
- Stimulates me; sexy
- It's like a membership in an exclusive, country-clubish community

American Express
- It's an interactive experience
- Part of luxury, sophistication, exclusivity
- Because of sponsoring activities, I feel fun, excitement, and entertainment

Apple iPod
- I love the touch and feel of the products
- I enjoy playing with all the products
- I am part of a "smarter" community
- This brand intrigues me
- I really feel Apple products go with my way of life
- I use the iPod when I am jogging and I exercise more because of the iPod

The Body Shop
- Appeals to different senses
- I think of topics like animal testing, purity, and wellness
- I want to be with people that share the values that the brand promotes

BMW
- I feel young; I feel stylish
- It's just great to drive
- A BMW is a symbol of my success

Crest
- I feel refreshed
- Don't really like the smell
- Feels clean, fresh, and healthy

Disney
- Stimulates my senses
- I feel like a child; I feel warm and safe; I want to discover things; the brand reminds me to use my imagination
- I feel part of the magic

Google
- The search is elegant; it creates a mood of playfulness and curiosity
- I feel happy and proud because I am "smart" and "in-the-know"
- With Google, I change the way I organize and interact with information

HBO
- Puts me in a good mood
- It's "discussion inducing"; I want to discuss the shows with others
- I enjoy the entertainment

Home Depot
- I did not know anything about construction, but I felt really comfortable
- I felt confident and in good hands
- Provides the experience that any customer can tackle any home improvement project

MasterCard
- Makes me think about precious things in life
- I feel more youthful than when I use AmEx or Visa
- Initially the Priceless campaign was emotive, but it's now simply a way of identifying the brand for me

Table 8.1 *(continued)*

Nike
• Makes me think of how to live an active lifestyle
• Makes me feel powerful
• I want to work out
• I feel inspired to start working out
• I feel like an athlete
• The store incites me to act, like swing the baseball bat or put on the running shoes
• I enjoy designing my own shoe that perfectly fits my personality
Starbucks
• Smells nice and is visually warm
• It's comfortable and puts me in a better mood
• It's like being around a Barnes and Nobles crowd
Target
• Shopping experience is very pleasant
• Products are displayed to please the eye
• Many stores are putting in Starbucks for an even more enhanced shopping experience
W Hotel
• Being part of something fun, happening and exciting
• It was an amazing feeling to hang out in the lobby
• Service is disappointing
Washington Mutual
• I have positive feelings because of their friendliness
• It's a place I want to go and do not have to go
• I also had a negative one-time experience
Williams Sonoma
• I had a feeling of nostalgia
• Full of memories of home
• It's relaxed and unhurried

Source: Brakus, Schmitt, and Zarantonello 2009.

products by emphasizing experiential, nonfunctional product characteristics or certain aspects of the judgment context. In an unpublished manuscript, two of the authors (Brakus and Schmitt), together with Sir Shi Zhang, focused on two types of experiential attributes—sensory and affective attributes—and investigated how they could result in differentiation and a compelling experience for customers.

While the term "experiential" may be considered as referring to any attribute that can be literally experienced, Brakus et al. (forthcoming) focused on sensory and affective attributes presented in a nonverbal way (e.g., as is often done in marketing communications by presenting a color or shape rather than naming that color; or by presenting an emoticon of a smiley face rather than the word "smile") or presented through imagery-invoking words (e.g., "Hello Sunshine," as a VW Beetle ad did). Whereas functional attributes are utilitarian and, in both consumer reports and in marketing research, presented in a feature-based, informative verbal format (cf. *Consumer Reports*-style

Table 8.2

The Brand Experience Scale

Dimension	Items
Sensory	• This brand makes a strong impression on my visual sense or other senses. • I find this brand interesting in a sensory way. • This brand does not appeal to my senses.*
Affective	• This brand induces feelings and sentiments. • I do not have strong emotions for this brand.* • This brand is an emotional brand.
Intellectual	• I engage in a lot of thinking when I encounter this brand. • This brand does not make me think.* • This brand stimulates my curiosity and problem solving.
Social	• I engage in physical actions and behaviors when I use this brand. • This brand results in bodily experiences. • This brand is not action oriented.*

Source: Brakus, Schmitt, and Zarantonello 2009.
Note: Items marked with an * are negatively phrased and reverse-coded.

"alternative by attribute" tables, e.g., "gas mileage: 22 miles per gallon"), experiential attributes do not provide "means to an end" and, in that sense, are not utilitarian (Zeithaml 1988). Experiential attributes appear on products, packages, logos, as part of ads, or as backgrounds on websites (Henderson et al. 2003; Mandel and Johnson 2002; Schmitt and Simonson 1997; Spies, Hesse, and Loesch 1997).

Drawing on processing fluency theory (Schwarz and Clore 1996; Winkielman et al. 2003), Brakus and colleagues (forthcoming) showed that consumers processed sensory and affective attributes more fluently (i.e., with less effort) than functional attributes under certain conditions, which in turn led to a more positive evaluation of alternatives described with sensory and affective attributes compared to those described with functional attributes only. Most important, once experiential product attributes—sensory or affective—differentiated products in the choice set and the incidental cues in the choice context—again sensory or affective—managed to draw consumers' attention to those experiential product attributes, consumers would infer that there was value in those experiential attributes, over and above the functional value of the product. Consequently, that experiential value would increase the likelihood of choice of a functionally inferior alternative that was differentiated with experiential attributes relative to a functionally superior alternative that did not posses experiential attributes and was differentiated with functional attributes only. (Note: Brakus, Schmitt, and Zhang obtained this result for low-involvement, cheap everyday necessities.)

Brakus and colleagues (forthcoming) showed that experiential attributes could be a source of compelling experiences for consumers, which, in turn, could affect consumer judgment. Their findings also indicate the operation of different processes in diverse situations and contexts. Nonfluent processing of experiential attributes occurs when consumers pragmatically decide whether experiential attributes can offer value in addition to what functional attributes provide. Fluent processing occurs when functional attributes are nondiagnostic (i.e., a consumer cannot make a decision based on functional attributes because functional attribute values are similar for all alternatives in the choice set). In such cases, consumers engage in a visual categorization process to match the experiential contextual cue with an experiential attribute of the same type.

In another experiment, Brakus and colleagues showed more directly that the experiential sensory and affective attributes cold be processed more fluently than functional attributes. One way of demonstrating this is to vary the speed of information presentation. Because nonfluent processing occurs in steps and takes more time than fluent processing, Brakus and colleagues predicted that positive functional attribute information would result in more positive judgments when the information was presented slowly. When the speed of presentation was increased, it would restrict consumers' reasoning about functional attributes. They would therefore not be able to assess all the positive attributes of the new product.

In contrast, when individuals spontaneously match experiential stimuli, speed limitations should affect experiential attributes much less than functional attributes, if the former are processed fluently. In that case, sensory and affective attributes such as colors, shapes, or emoticons could be comprehended instantly based on their surface characteristics, without paying close attention to certain features of sensory and affective stimuli (Ekman 1993; Rosch 1972).

To test this prediction Brakus and colleagues conducted an experiment using animated online Flash ads in which they manipulated the speed of information presentation. They showed that evaluations of product displays described by functional features were significantly affected by different speeds of attribute presentation (i.e., they were less positive for fast rather than for slow speed of attribute information presentation), while evaluations of product displays described by experiential features (sensory or affective) were not affected significantly.

Application of the Brand Experience Scale to Event Marketing

Two of the authors have also applied the brand experience concept to the relatively under-researched area of event marketing. In particular, Zarantonello and Schmitt (forthcoming) wanted to demonstrate that brand experience contributes to brand equity, in addition to brand attitude, in a marketing event. Attitudes toward brands have traditionally been considered among the most important outcomes of advertising communication (e.g., Greene and Stock 1966) and, more recently, of event marketing (Kinney and McDaniel 1996; Lacey et al. 2007; Sneath, Finney, and Close 2005). However, the importance of the emotional impact of events has also been highlighted recently (Drengner, Gaus, and Jahn 2008; Martensen et al. 2007). Based on these contributions, Zarantonello and Schmitt (forthcoming) proposed that brand experiences—which include not only emotions, but also sensory, intellectual and interactive stimulations—are a key concept to understanding how events affect consumers.

To test whether sponsored events are sources of experiences for consumers and whether those experiences contribute to brand equity, Zarantonello and Schmitt conducted a field study that was structured as a one-group pretest/posttest quasi-experimental design (Cook and Campbell 1979). The experimental treatment was "participation in an event" and the events considered include the following: an event sponsored by Gatorade; a trade fair in which Nokia participated with its own stand; three street events, two of which were organized by Red Bull and one by Nokia; two pop-up shops, one by Fiat and one by Baci Perugina. The study was conducted in a non-university setting with more than three hundred regular consumers who were approached on the street by research assistants. Before and after participating in one of the events considered, consumers were asked about their brand experience and brand equity related to the brand organizing the event; after participating in the event, they were also asked about their attitude toward the brand.

Zarantonello and Schmitt (forthcoming) showed that events contribute to brand equity both directly and indirectly through brand attitude and brand experience. They found a strong direct effect of events on brand equity. Events must thus be viewed as enhancing existing brand equity. Most importantly, they found significant indirect effects involving brand attitude and brand experience, indicating that brand attitudes and experiences occurring at events enhance brand equity. They also found that the indirect effect that occurs through brand experience is stronger and more significant than the indirect effect that occurs through brand attitudes. Both the direct and indirect effects do not seem to depend on the type of event.

The studies that we have discussed so far had mostly scholarly objectives. Next, we discuss how the concept of brand experience can help managers to formulate and implement a branding strategy.

A Project-Based Framework

Managing the brand experience, and not just researching it, requires a step-by-step process (a "how-to" approach) that includes research, strategy development, and implementation. One of the authors (Schmitt) has developed and presented a managerially focused project framework called Customer Experience Management (CEM) (Schmitt 2003). He also applied it in many company projects. The managerial process and the practical ideas are closely related to the concepts presented in this chapter.

The original CEM framework had five steps. For the purpose of this chapter, which focuses specifically on brand experiences, we can simplify the framework into three steps:

1. Analyzing the experiential world of the customer (analysis step)
2. Building the experience platform (strategy step)
3. Designing the brand experience (implemenation step)

Next we briefly explain the steps (with relevent examples included).

Analyzing the Experiential World of the Customer

The first step of the CEM framework requires original insight into the consumer's world and his or her perception of a brand. The research and analysis of step 1—referred to as "customer insight"—is done from a broad perspective by analyzing and researching not only the brand but also consumption and usage patterns of customers and the sociocultural context that affects consumers' experiential needs and wants. For example, in the beauty and cosmetics industry, the sociocultural analysis may include trends such as "wellness," "spiritualism," which affect consumer lifestyles, and, ultimately, perceptions of skin care and cosmetics products.

Customer-insight research can include focus groups, surveys, and interviews, and is frequently supplemented by ethnographic and interpretive research techniques.

Building the Experience Platform

The second step, the experience platform, includes the formulation of a core experience concept that can be used as a guiding principle for subsequent implementations. An experience platform is different from a positioning statement or a typical perceptual map. The experiential platform includes a multisensory, multidimensional depiction of the desired experience (referred to as "experiential positioning") and a specification of the experiential value that the customer can expect from the product in terms of the experience dimensions discussed earlier. The experiential platform culminates in an overall implementation theme that can be used to coordinate subsequent marketing and communication efforts as well as future innovation.

To be useful, the platform must be simple; it may be one intriguing concept or idea (e.g., "energy" for a beauty brand; or "authenticity" for a car brand) or it may be captured in a phrase or brand line. Frequently, it is also expressed visually (e.g., on a visual board or via a brief "brand video.") The concept must be compatible with the brand's values and personality (D. Aaker 1996; J. Aaker 1997).

Designing the Brand Experience

Finally, the experience platform must be implemented so that it results in a brand experience. Designing the brand experience includes, among other things, the selection of experiential features that can serve as experience providers. Experiential features may include some functionality, but their main purpose is to create an experience, which is why we find silk in a shampoo, gold in a liquor, or green in a skin cream.

The experience also includes an appealing "look and feel" in visual identity, packaging, websites, and in environments or stores. Experiential messages and imagery in advertising and collaterals, as well as online, complete the brand experience. Finally, in service businesses, face-to-face exchanges and contact points (e.g., via call centers) are important for designing the right experience.

The design of the brand experience is often outsourced. It thus becomes the domain of corporate identity and design firms, graphic and interior designers, as well as media and advertising agencies. Various agencies communicate with each other to guarantee consistency and integration. Also, more and more firms are appointing "customer experience" or "brand experience" managers that make sure that the integration takes place. For new brands, the task of designing the brand experience also requires creativity to differentiate the brand in unusual ways in the marketplace. Outside-industry benchmarking can be a useful tool for creating innovative solutions (Schmitt 2007).

Before a firm embarks on a brand experience project, it must be clear about its objective, which is critical in any business project, including a CEM project. Two characteristics differentiate good objectives from bad ones. First, the objective should be measurable, and the measurement criteria need to be specified (for example, for an experience project, criteria include satisfaction scores; loyalty increases by a certain percentage point, premium pricing above a certain threshold, a certain number of new customers; increased trial by a certain percentage). Second, a simple empirical model should be built that lays out how the quantitative objective is supposed to be reached via the experience project.

Brand experience projects in major companies usually last up to twelve months. After the experience project is finished, the project should be managed on a continuous basis, upgrading and updating as necessary. Ideally, the experience philosophy needs to be "institutionalized."

Using Brand Experience to Address Marketing Issues

So far, we have presented concepts, empirical studies, and a project management framework. Throughout the chapter, we have illustrated our concepts and findings with practical examples. We discuss now how the concept is useful in addressing classic marketing issues: segmentation and targeting, positioning, innovation management, and how it can provide a fresh and new perspective on these issues.

Segmentation and Targeting

The brand experience concept is most useful for segmentation and targeting. Most segmentation is not done from the customer's point of view, but from the perspective of products (segmenting by features, price or distribution channel, for example). Similarly, companies often believe that targeting decisions are sound as long as their analysts have engaged in massive data mining to search for structures in geographically and demographically prepared datasets. Given immense computing power and data mining capabilities, this temptation is understandable. However, adequate segmentation and targeting decisions should acknowledge the experiential world of customers and segmentation must also be based on customers' current or desired experience with a brand.

Positioning

Another key strategic issue for companies is how to position the corporate brand and individual product brands in a competitive context. For that purpose, many companies perform brand-architecture analyses and commission perceptual maps, which are based on similarity data and analyzed using multidimensional scaling techniques. The maps are usually based on verbal input and are generally not representative of customers' daily experiences. Dimensions are often generic (e.g., "expensive-cheap," or "high quality-low quality," or "innovation-traditional"). Even when the labeling is a bit more specific (for instance, "fresh-processed" for a food product, or "more durable-faster setting" for an industrial adhesive), we still often lack an understanding of what exactly these terms mean to the customer; what value they provide; and how they are supposed to affect packaging, advertising, service, and innovations. The alternative from an experience perspective is the introduction of a customer-relevant new concept or a new dimension. Moreover, a creative and innovative implementation theme may be used to execute the new positioning. Both the concept and the theme may be developed based on customer insight and may be related to the experience platform discussed earlier.

Service Management

Service quality is every company's priority. However, most service management is not experience-focused, which can hurt the brand experience. Moreover, service management is based on prior assumptions made about customer preferences about service and universal service procedures—for example, customers want to be treated in an intimate and personalized manner, or customers prefer self-service. As a result, most service systems are either personnel- or technology-intensive, but not customer-focused. To create a desirable brand experience through service, people and technologies need to be brought together to deliver outstanding, memorable, and unique service experiences.

Innovation Management

Innovation is often viewed as residing in the R&D department and focused on technical innovation. From a brand experience perspective, this view is narrow. Technical innovation is only part of the story; there is also brand and marketing innovation, especially when the brand is experienced in new ways. That is, customers value innovation, but not just features-and-benefits–oriented technical innovation. Minor improvements in product design can be major brand-experience innovations. A brand extension that changes the product form slightly can be a breakthrough innovation if it contributes to customer experience in a positive and meaningful way. Even innovation in communications can be viewed as an innovation because brand experiences are built not only through actual branded products, but also through communications for those products. Managers often overlook such innovation opportunities because they are focused on technical innovation and not on the brand experience. Thus, many issues that are framed as innovation challenges are, in fact, challenges to better understand and communicate the brand experience.

Conclusion

Brand experiences arise in a wide variety of consumer settings when consumers search for, shop for, and consume brands. Accordingly, we conceptualized brand experience as subjective consumer responses that are evoked by brand-related experiential attributes in such settings. We showed that brand experience can be broken down empirically into four dimensions (sensory, affective, intellectual, and behavioral), which are differentially evoked by various brands.

The brand experience scale that we constructed is short and easy to administer, consisting of only twelve items. The scale can be used, and has been used, in academic research and in company projects. It is internally consistent, reliable, and valid, as we found through conducting various tests. Most important, brand experience has behavioral impact; it affects consumer satisfaction and loyalty directly and indirectly through brand personality judgments.

Brand experience offers a unique academic perspective (especially vis-à-vis more functionally focused approaches in consumer psychology). And we feel it is relevant for brand management and other brand- and marketing-related issues. To facilitate managerial decision making, we have introduced key experience concepts and provided a project-based framework for managing brand experiences.

References

Aaker, D. 1996. *Building Strong Brands*. New York: Free Press.

Aaker, J.L. 1997. "Dimensions of Brand Personality." *Journal of Marketing Research* 34: 347–56.

Arnold, M.J., K.E. Reynolds, N. Ponder, and J.E. Lueg. 2005. "Customer Delight in a Retail Context: Investigating Delightful and Terrible Shopping Experiences." *Journal of Business Research* 58: 1132–45.

Arnould, E.J., and L. Price. 1993. "River Magic: Extraordinary Experience and the Extended Service Encounter." *Journal of Consumer Research* 20: 24–45.

Arnould, E.J., L. Price, and G.L. Zinkhan. 2002. *Consumers*, 2d ed. New York: McGraw-Hill/Irvin.

Bettman, J. 1979. *An Information Processing Theory of Choice*. Reading, MA: Addison-Wesley.

Boulding, W., A. Kalra, R. Staelin, and V. Zeithaml. 1993. "A Dynamic Process Model of Service Quality: From Expectations to Behavioral Intentions." *Journal of Marketing Research* 30: 7–27.

Brakus, J.J., B. Schmitt, and L. Zarantonello. 2009. "Brand Experience: What Is It? How Do We Measure It? And Does It Affect Loyalty?" *Journal of Marketing* 73: 52–68.

Brakus, J.J., B. Schmitt, and S. Zhang. "Experiential Attributes, Brand Experiences, and Preference Judgments: The Role of Processing Fluency." Working paper, Leeds University Business School.

Carroll, B.A., and A. Ahuvia, A. 2006. "Some Antecedents and Outcomes of Brand Love." *Marketing Letters* 17: 79–89.

Celsi, R.L., R.L. Rose, and T. Leigh. 1993. "An Exploration of High-Risk Leisure Consumption through Skydiving." *Journal of Consumer Research* 20: 1–23.

Chang, P.L., and M.H. Chieng. 2006. "Building Consumer-Brand Relationship: A Cross-Cultural Experiential View." *Psychology and Marketing* 23: 927–59.

Chattopadhyay, A., and J.L. Laborie. 2005. "Managing Brand Experience: The Market Contact Audit™." *Journal of Advertising Research* 45: 9–16.

Cook, T.D., and D.T. Campbell. 1979. *Quasi-Experimentation: Design and Analysis Issues for Field Settings.* Boston: Houghton Mifflin.

Delgado-Ballester, E., J.L. Munuera-Alemán, and M.J. Yagüe-Guillén. 2003. "Development and Validation of a Brand Trust Scale." *International Journal of Market Research* 45: 35–53.

Dewey, J. 1922. *Human Nature and Conduct.* New York: The Modern Library.

———. 1925. *Experience and Nature,* rev. ed. New York: Dover Publications.

Drengner, J., H. Gaus, and S. Jahn. 2008. "Does Flow Influence the Brand Image in Event Marketing?" *Journal of Advertising Research* 48: 138–47.

Ekman, P. 1993. "Facial Expression and Emotion." *American Psychologist* 48: 384–92.

Fishbein, M., and I. Ajzen. 1975. *Belief, Attitude, Intention, and Behavior: An Introduction to Theory and Research.* Reading, MA: Addison-Wesley.

Grace, D., and A. O'Cass. 2004. "Examining Service Experiences and Post-Consumption Evaluations." *Journal of Services Marketing* 18: 450–61.

Greene, J.D., and J.S. Stock. 1966. "Brand Attitudes as Measures of Advertising Effects." *Journal of Advertising Research* 6: 14–22.

Henderson, P.W., J.A. Cote, S.M. Leong, and B. Schmitt. 2003. "Building Strong Brands in Asia: Selecting the Visual Components of Image to Maximize Brand Strength." *International Journal of Research in Marketing* 20: 297–313.

Hoch, S.J. 2002. "Product Experience Is Seductive." *Journal of Consumer Research* 29: 448–54.

Holbrook, M.B. 2000. "The Millennial Consumer in the Texts of Our Times: Experience and Entertainment." *Journal of Macromarketing* 20: 178–92.

Holbrook, M.B., and E.C. Hirschman. 1982. "The Experiential Aspects of Consumption: Consumer Fantasies, Feelings, and Fun." *Journal of Consumer Research* 9: 132–40.

Holt, D.B. 1995. "How Consumers Consume: A Typology of Consumption Practices." *Journal of Consumer Research* 22: 1–16.

Hui, M.K., and J.E.G. Bateson. 1991. "Perceived Control and the Effects of Crowding and Consumer Choice on the Service Experience." *Journal of Consumer Research* 18: 174–84.

Johar, G., J. Sengupta, and J. Aaker. 2005. "Two Roads to Updating Brand Personality Impressions: Trait vs. Evaluative Inferencing." *Journal of Marketing Research* 42: 458–69.

Jones, M.A. 1999. "Entertaining Shopping Experiences: An Exploratory Investigation." *Journal of Retailing and Consumer Services* 6: 129–39.

Joy, A., and J.F. Sherry Jr. 2003. "Speaking of Art as Embodied Imagination: A Multi-sensory Approach to Understanding Aesthetic Experience." *Journal of Consumer Research* 20: 259–82.

Kerin, R.A., A. Jain, and D.J. Howard. 1992. "Store Shopping Experience and Consumer Price-Quality-Value Perceptions." *Journal of Retailing* 68: 376–97.

Kinney, L., and S.R. McDaniel. 1996. "Strategic Implications of Attitude-toward-the-Ad in Leveraging Sponsorships." *Journal of Sport Management* 10: 250–61.

Lacey, R., J.Z. Sneath, Z.R. Finney, and A.G. Close. 2007. "The Impact of Repeat Attendance on Event Sponsorship Effects." *Journal of Marketing Communications* 13: 243–55.

Mandel, N., and E.J. Johnson. 2002. "When Web Pages Influence Choice: Effects of Visual Primes on Experts and Novices." *Journal of Consumer Research* 29: 235–45.

Martensen, A., L. Grønholdt, L., Bendtsen, and M.L. Jensen. 2007. "Application of a Model for the Effectiveness of Event Marketing." *Journal of Advertising Research* 47: 283–301.

McAlexander, J.H., J.W. Schouten, and H.F. Koenig. 2002. "Building Brand Community." *Journal of Marketing* 66: 38–54.

Muniz, Jr., A.M., and T.C. O'Guinn. 2001. "Brand Community." *Journal of Consumer Research* 27: 412–32.

Nunnally, J.C. 1978. *Psychometric Theory.* New York: McGraw-Hill.

Ofir, C., and I. Simonson. 2007. "The Effect of Stating Expectations on Consumer Satisfaction and Shopping Experience." *Journal of Marketing Research* 44: 164–74.

Oliver, R.L., R. Rust, and S. Varki. 1997. "Customer Delight: Foundations, Findings, and Managerial Insight." *Journal of Retailing* 73: 311–36.

Park, C.W., and D.J. MacInnis. 2006. "What's In and What's Out: Questions over the Boundaries of the Attitude Construct." *Journal of Consumer Research* 33: 16–18.

Pine II, J.B., and J.H. Gilmore. 1999. *The Experience Economy: Work Is Theatre and Every Business a Stage.* Cambridge, MA: Harvard Business School Press.

Pinker, S. 1997. *How the Mind Works.* New York: Norton.

Ries, A., and L. Ries. 2004. *The Fall of Advertising and the Rise of PR.* New York: HarperCollins.

Rosch, E. 1972. "Universals in Color Naming and Memory." *Journal of Experimental Psychology* 93: 311–30.

Rust, R.T., and R.W. Oliver. 1994. "The Death of Advertising." *Journal of Advertising* 23: 72–77.

Schmitt, B.H. 1999. *Experiential Marketing: How to Get Customers to Sense, Feel, Think, Act, Relate to Your Company and Brands.* New York: Free Press.

———. 2003. *Customer Experience Management.* New York: Wiley.

———. 2007. *Big Think Strategy.* Cambridge, MA: Harvard Business School Press.

Schmitt, B.H., and A. Simonson. 1997. *Marketing Aesthetics: The Strategic Management of Brands.* New York: Free Press.

Schwarz, N., and G.L. Clore. 1996. "Feelings and Phenomenal Experiences." In *Social Psychology: Handbook of Basic Principles,* ed. E.T. Higgins and A.W. Kruglanski, 433–65. New York: Guilford Press.

Shaw, C., and J. Ivens. 2002. *Building Great Customer Experiences.* New York: Palgrave Macmillan.

Smith, S., and J. Wheeler. 2002. *Managing the Customer Experience: Turning Customers into Advocates.* Upper Saddle River, NJ: Financial Times Prentice Hall.
Sneath, J.Z., R.Z. Finney, and A.G. Close. 2005. "An IMC Approach to Event Marketing: The Effects of Sponsorship and Experience on Customer Attitudes." *Journal of Advertising Research* 45: 373–81.
Spies, K., F. Hesse, and K. Loesch. 1997. "Store Atmosphere, Mood, and Purchasing Behavior." *International Journal of Research in Marketing* 14: 1–17.
Thomson, M., D.J. MacInnis, and C.W. Park. 2005. "The Ties That Bind: Measuring the Strength of Consumers' Emotional Attachments to Brands." *Journal of Consumer Psychology* 15: 77–91.
Winkielman, P., N. Schwarz, T.A. Fazendeiro, and R. Reber. 2003. "The Hedonic Marking of Processing Fluency: Implications for Evaluative Judgment." In *The Psychology of Evaluation: Affective Processes in Cognition and Emotion,* ed. J. Musch and K.C. Klauer, 189–217. Mahwah, NJ: Lawrence Erlbaum.
Zaichkowsky, J.L. 1985. "Measuring the Involvement Construct." *Journal of Consumer Research* 12: 341–52.
Zarantonello, L., and B.H. Schmitt. "Understanding Event Marketing: The Role of Brand Experience." Working paper, Bocconi University.
Zeithaml, V.A. 1988. "Consumer Perceptions of Price, Quality and Value: A Means-End Model and Synthesis of Evidence." *Journal of Marketing* 52: 2–22.

9

Success Stories

How Marketing Managers Can Leverage the Psychology of Narratives

Jennifer Edson Escalas

In this chapter, I advocate the use of narratives as part of a brand's positioning strategy and in advertising campaigns, because stories are able to persuade, create meaning, and demonstrate product usage experiences. More important, stories are able to involve, captivate, and entertain consumers, which is critical in today's marketplace, with ubiquitous advertising and the rise of social media. I begin with a discussion of narratives in general, focusing on the specific aspects of stories that make them useful to marketers. Next, I explore the role of narratives in branding and advertising. I propose that marketers can use narratives to construct a compelling brand biography to create emotional connections to brands and serve as a guide for an integrated marketing communication program. This is followed by a discussion of narrative advertising, which can generate emotion, is persuasive, and models the way products may be used. Finally, I discuss specific reasons why a narrative approach to marketing can reap benefits in social media–based marketing campaigns.

Narratives

Scholars in psychology who study narratives use the analogy of science and literature to propose two different modes of thought: the rigorous world of logical deduction, labeled paradigmatic thought, and the imprecise world of aesthetic intentions, labeled narrative thought (Bruner 1986). Narrative thought creates stories that are coherent accounts of particular experiences, temporally structured, and context-sensitive (Baumeister and Newman 1994). The narrative mode of thought does not necessitate that individuals form elaborate, complex novels in their minds. Rather, under conditions of narrative processing, people think about incoming information as if they were trying to create a story. In day-to-day living, individuals continuously attempt to impose narrative structure on occurrences in order to understand them. They do not experience life as a random series of unrelated events, but rather as a comprehensible, meaningful chronology.

The Structure of Narratives

What makes a story a story? An important aspect of narrative thought is its structure. This structure consists of two important elements: chronology and causality. First, narrative thought organizes events in terms of a temporal dimension; that is, things occur over time. The human perception of time is configured as episodes, whereas time in reality is an undifferentiated, continuous flow. The general objective of narrative thought is to achieve closure by framing episodes with a beginning, middle, and end, and this is considered to be the fundamental way in which human events are understood (Kerby 1991; Polkinghorne 1991). For example, think about a movie or novel that is presented in a series of complex flashbacks. The satisfaction of comprehension occurs when one is able to understand the underlying temporal order of events. This is the point at which the story begins to "make sense" to the reader or audience member.

Second, narrative thought structures elements into an organized framework that establishes relationships between a story's elements and allows for causal inferencing. Narrative story organization revolves around general knowledge about human goal-oriented action sequences. Episode schemas are one way to characterize narrative structure (Pennington and Hastie 1986, 1992), representing a standard sequence of events in both the real world and in stories. In an episode schema, an event, or series of events, initiates a psychological reaction and activates goals in a main character. The goals may be formulated in response to the initial event or may be preexisting goals that are activated by the initial event. The protagonist's psychological state and goals provide reasons for his or her subsequent actions. These actions, in turn, lead to an outcome or result. Accompanying physical states may be the main character's state at the time of the initiating events or the result of the initiating events and may also contribute to the activation of mental states or goals. Because these narrative elements are organized through time, causal inferences can be made. What happens in time one (for example, the protagonist feels jealous) causes what happens in time two (he kills his rival).

The Function of Narrative Thought

In order to make sense of what goes on in the world, people naturally think about things, people, and events in the form of narratives. By constructing stories, individuals organize their experiences, create order, explain unusual events, gain perspective, and make evaluations (Bruner 1990). Narratives place events into framing contexts so that the parts can be understood in relation to the whole. For example, the meaning of an event is the result of its being a part of a plot (Polkinghorne 1991). As a result of this emplotment, people can make meaningful evaluations (Pennington and Hastie 1992), form judgments (Gergen and Gergen 1988), and inform action (Olson 1990). Understanding experienced events as part of a narrative also makes them memorable and sharable (Olson 1990).

Many scholars now assert that people naturally tend to think about and interpret the world around them through narrative thought (Bruner 1986, 1990; Kerby 1991). Narrative is the mode of thought that best captures the experiential aspect of human intention, action, and consequences; it involves reasons and goals (Reissman 1993). The narrative process is so pervasive that people spontaneously create stories to explain the random movement of colored rectangles, attributing causality to the movement (Michotte 1963). Bruner (1986) suggests a genetic proclivity for narrative. He proposes that the reason people have no early infancy memories is that they are unable to organize events in narrative form at that stage of development.

Thus, the human mind can be thought of as a creative storybuilder. Forming stories is an ongoing process; people fit characters and episodes together in a narrative form to render the world and their lives meaningful. As storybuilders, people do not record the world but rather create it, mixing in cultural and individual expectations and combining sensory input and preexisting knowledge (Chafe 1990). Narratives are also a social and cultural construction. They are influenced by the social setting in which a person exists (Kerby 1991). The stories that people tell one another are determined, in part, both by shared language and the genre of storytelling inherited from traditions (Olson 1990).

Story Quality

Beyond the basic structure of narrative, other theories have identified story characteristics that contribute to a narrative's quality. These characteristics answer the question, "what makes a *good* story?" Clearly, there are many theories about narrative quality. Here, I outline three approaches to understanding what makes a compelling story. All three study story quality from the perspective that a good story is one that increases one's mental engagement and evokes an emotional response.

First, Bruner (1986) proposes two dimensions to narrative: the landscape of action and the landscape of consciousness. The former is the causal sequence of events, while the latter is the degree to which the viewer is made aware of the protagonist's psychological state. The landscape of action consists of events that are visible to the casual observer: the initiating event, resulting action(s), and outcome(s). The landscape of consciousness allows the reader/ viewer to "get inside the head" of the story's character(s). The audience learns what the character is thinking and feeling. There is an emphasis on attitudes, motivations, goals, and personal development. Whereas a landscape of action is necessary for any narrative, a landscape of consciousness has been shown to make a narrative more compelling. Readers make more inferences and exert a greater effort to construct an interpretation when a story has a well-developed landscape of consciousness (Feldman et al. 1990). Thus a story with both a landscape of action and consciousness is a better story than one that contains only a landscape of action.

Another aspect of narrative that has been identified as a contributor to a story's quality is based on the idea of an evaluative slope. Gergen and Gergen (1988) theorize that the dramatic engagement of a narrative depends on the evaluative slope of the story, which represents the events in a story evaluated over time (as it occurs in the narrative) for the degree to which they improve or worsen the state of the protagonist. Stories that have a steep incline or decline in their evaluative slope and those that alternate (e.g., rising, falling, then rising again) evoke the most emotion. The classical tragedy *Oedipus Rex* is an example of a narrative with rapidly deteriorating events, from the perspective of the protagonist. Gergen and Gergen would contend that this steep downward evaluative slope creates drama and generates emotion.

Finally, a narrative imbalance has also been shown to improve a story's quality (Feldman et al. 1990; Lucariello 1990). This imbalance can take the form of a breach in canonical expectations about how people should behave or how stories should unfold (e.g., throwing water on birthday cake candles breaches one's cultural expectations about birthday party behavior). Narratives often pay attention to unusual events, with the goal of explaining such events in a way that conforms to accepted standards. A narrative imbalance can also be tension between story elements, such as actions that fail to achieve goals (e.g., the love of Romeo and Juliet fails to bring them and their feuding families together). These narrative imbalances lead to increased elaboration by readers as they attempt to explain the imbalance (Feldman et al. 1990; Lucariello 1990).

Narratives and Persuasion

Marketers are in the business of improving consumers' attitudes toward their products, that is, the persuasion business. Narrative processing has been shown to affect persuasion through a process called transportation, defined as "immersion into a text" (Green and Brock 2000, 702; see also Gerrig 1994). Most marketers are aware of persuasion theories based on analytical thought, for example, where "elaboration leads to attitude change via logical consideration and evaluation of arguments" (Green and Brock 2000, 702). In these models, the amount of thought given to the persuasive stimulus affects which message components will be most effective at changing attitudes and how long such changes will persist.

However, narrative processing is different from analytical processing. When a person thinks in the form of a story, he or she may be "transported" by the narrative. Transportation leads to persuasion through reduced negative cognitive responding (i.e., less counterarguing); realism of experience; and strong affective responses (Green and Brock 2000). Being immersed or lost in a story enhances persuasion without increasing critical evaluation of the message (Escalas 2007). Narrative transportation affects brand evaluation and persuasion through several mechanisms. First, strong feelings associated with the story may be transferred to the attitude object (Escalas 2007). Second, the scenes presented in the text (or visually in the case of a movie or advertisement) evoke imagery that links the experience of entering the narrative world to the meaning of the story, building beliefs about the characters and objects presented in the story (Escalas 2004b; Green and Brock 2002). Furthermore, transportation makes a narrative experience feel more real, and because real experiences can strongly influence attitudes (Fazio and Zanna 1981; Green and Brock 2000), narrative processing can also have a strong influence on attitudes.

Capitalizing on Narrative Research

With this background on how people naturally think in terms of stories to make sense of the world around them, I now move on to the practical implications of this information for marketers. It makes sense for marketers to speak to consumers in the language they understand, the language they use to interpret incoming information and communicate with others. Consumers use stories to understand their personal experiences with people and the world around them, which includes products and brands. Furthermore, we now know a bit about what makes a story captivating and persuasive, so we should be able to apply this knowledge to creating compelling marketing campaigns.

Brand Biographies

Consumers value products and brands for different reasons. One reason may be for a product's instrumental features or attributes, which provide tangible benefits (e.g., cars provide transportation and salt adds flavor to food). A second major reason is that, in some cases, consumers form an emotional connection with products or brands so that these products come to signify more than just the sum of their features. As an example of special meaning, many people become particularly attached to their first car. The car provides freedom and independence; it is part of a rite of passage into adulthood. Important memories become associated with the car, for example, going to the prom or high school graduation. In many cases, the brand of car acquires special meanings for the consumer and he or she exhibits brand loyalty, continuing to buy that brand well into the future.

Brand equity research often refers to the value of a brand being derived from its associations, symbols, or meanings (Keller 1993; Levy 1959; McCracken 1989). Strong brands are those that form an emotional connection with consumers, going beyond functional product features and benefits. These brands symbolize characteristics that consumers believe are important to them personally. How are emotional connections formed? How does symbolic meaning become associated with a brand? One mechanism is through the construction of narratives or stories. Research has shown that brand stories can present brand images that consumers integrate with their personal brand experiences, building a special, emotional connection between the self and the brand (Escalas 2004b). When consumers have a self-brand connection, then the company behind the brand can gain an enduring competitive advantage. Although competitors may easily copy a positively regarded product attribute or feature, a self-brand connection creates a bond that may be difficult to break.

The brand biography is an unfolding story that chronicles the brand's origins, experiences, and evolution over time (Paharia et al. 2011). These stories are constructed by managers to create a brand's personality, symbolism, and meaning. For example, Nike is a strong brand whose marketing communications revolve around a well-crafted brand biography. While some attention may occasionally be paid to features and benefits, the bigger picture in Nike ads revolves around a story of hard work, sweat, and perseverance; the result of the story is that Nike enables people to achieve their very best. Thus, Nike's story is about supporting consumers on their personal quest for excellence. This story resonates with Nike's target consumers, who are athletic, fitness-conscious individuals. Using Nike sports gear, the consumer can build his or her own personal story of accomplishment. Nike is now more than a bundle of high-tech sports features. It is connected to the consumer's ideal self; the brand represents hard work that leads to personal accomplishment. Even consumers who are not athletic or fitness conscious can use this meaning from Nike's brand biography to communicate an idealized image of themselves to others. Thus, Nike's brand biography has a clear plot in which the brand plays a role in actions that lead to favorable outcomes, it reflects the history and culture of the brand, it models how consumers can use the brand, and it even allows the consumer to become part of the narrative. Nike's brand story is the centerpiece of its entire marketing communication strategy.

In addition to the brand story creating meaning through narrative context, a well-crafted brand biography can help the brand be perceived of as authentic, despite the increasingly skeptical consumer of our modern age. Brand heritage has been identified as one driver of brand authenticity. Heritage is a function of a brand having a relevant and engaging brand story. Authenticity is about practicing what one preaches; being totally clear about who one is and what one does best. When a brand's rhetoric gets out of sync with customers' actual experiences, the brand's integrity and future persuasiveness suffers. Thus, the brand story must be believable and compelling enough to convince consumers to suspend disbelief about the brand's fundamentally commercial nature in order to be considered authentic (Grayson and Martinec 2004).

Advertising Narratives

Many advertisements tell stories. Most often, an ad is a self-contained narrative. For example, the "Priceless" campaign by MasterCard has all the narrative elements in an episode schema. In a recent instantiation of this campaign, the initiating event shows some people in front of a scenic overlook, which inspires them to take pictures. The main character, a blond man, pulls out his camera to take a picture. The narrator describes the camera, including its price. The secondary characters, an African-American couple, pulls out their camera, which the narrator describes as being exactly the same as the first camera, but purchased online for 30 percent less. This causes concern in the protagonist, who breaks the "fourth wall" between the actors and the audience, and begins talking to the narrator. The action begins when the protagonist is so distracted by the narrator's information that he falls off the cliff the group is photographing. The narrator describes each ensuing action by how much the remedies will cost (ibuprophen, x-ray, and chiropractor). The other couple takes their pictures (accomplishing the goal, which the protagonist is unable to complete, due to the complicating actions of falling off the cliff). In the end, the protagonist is uninjured, but the actual outcome is that MasterCard marketplace is a cheaper way to shop, which is "priceless."

In addition to ads that are complete stories in and of themselves, ad campaigns can have varying degrees of storytelling. For example, some ad campaigns tell the same basic story over and over again with different characters and in different settings. In addition to the MasterCard campaign mentioned earlier, the painkiller Aleve uses this structure in its ads. In each ad, the protagonist is a hardworking individual who suffers from arthritis. He or she needed multiple doses of other pain-relief medicine to make it through the day, but with Aleve he or she is able to take just two pills in the morning and work pain free for the entire day. The characters may be cowboy hat manufacturers, electricians, or seamstresses, but the narrator is always a caring loved one.

Other ad campaigns tell ongoing stories in serial form. These are the melodramas of advertising. Again, there are varying degrees of this structure. The quintessential continuing story campaign was that of Taster's Choice in the 1980s. These ads were nearly soap operas, with each successive ad building on the storyline presented in the previous ad (or episode). The ads all ended on a suspenseful note: for example, what will happen to the couple who fell in love over Taster's Choice coffee when the woman's ex-husband appears on the scene? The success of the Taster's Choice campaign has led to other continuing story campaigns, including Hallmark cards (a young woman tries to teach her boyfriend the importance of looking at the back of cards) and Nissan's Seven Days in a Sentra campaign (comedian Marc Horowitz spent a week living in his Sentra automobile).

While these examples of storied advertisements show some variety, they all contain the basic narrative elements of chronology and causality. The definition of a narrative ad is simply an ad that tells a story. The extent to which an ad tells a story, however, is a matter of degree (Mick 1987). Some ads may not have all the elements required to be a story. Others may focus on what happens but not why. Others may not allow viewers into the hearts and minds of the characters. Thus, the narrative structure of advertising runs along a continuum, with completely nonnarrative ads on one end, and well-developed, complete, and moving stories on the other.

Narrative ads have been studied by some consumer researchers looking at drama in advertising, which I would argue is synonymous with the definition of narrative ads presented in this chapter. Deighton, Romer and McQueen (1989) find that drama advertising affects persuasion by evoking feelings and by verisimilitude, which they operationalize as drawing the viewer into the ad and the ad being perceived with authenticity. Dramatic ads work by generating affect, personally involving the viewer in the ad, and appearing to be realistic or believable stories. Stern (1994) theorizes that classical dramas are persuasive because they provide consumers with a coherent cause-effect progression. In response, consumers are able to make causal attributions about the product/person/situation interaction. Additionally, she claims that classical dramas work through empathy. Consumers are actively drawn into classical dramas and therefore experience affective reactions. This is consistent with Green and Brock's (2000) transportation theory of persuasion.

Story Quality in Advertisements

Although many advertisements tell stories, some ads tell "better" stories than others. The MasterCard ad described earlier is likely to be judged as a better story than many story ads that demonstrate simple product usage scenarios. For example, a typical pain-relief product ad shows a character in pain (the initial event, or the result of some other initial event). To solve this problem, the character uses the pain-relief product (goal and action). The outcome is a happy, pain-free protagonist. Even though this ad is in the form of a story, it is not very compelling.

Why is one advertising narrative better than another? The answer is, for the same reason that one story is more compelling than another. Providing the consumer with a landscape of consciousness is one way that an advertising narrative can be more interesting and entertaining. When people are able to relate to a character's thoughts and feelings and observe personal development, they are more likely to be drawn into the ad story. Furthermore, ads that evoke emotion can move or touch consumers in a personal way. Gergen and Gergen's (1988) research on dramatic engagement suggests that an advertising narrative in which the protagonist's situation rapidly improves or worsens, or alternates between the two, should be especially good at generating emotional responses in consumers.

Another aspect of ad story quality is the extent to which the ad is novel. Story ads with a narrative imbalance should be more interesting and provocative than those that conform too rigidly to expectations. Additionally, ads that follow repetitive storylines may become abstractions to consumers. Rather than focusing on the particular events, the story may be perceived as mechanistic. Narrative research has shown that scripts score low on measures of story quality (Brewer and Lichtenstein 1981). Therefore, overdependence on the use of story "formulas" may eliminate the benefits of advertising narratives. However, if a story ad is too novel, or if it departs from expectations too much, then the advertiser may sacrifice ease of understanding (Mandler 1984). People have expectations about how stories will unfold, and too large a breach in those expectations can lead to incomprehensibility, particularly in a 30- to 60-second ad.

Story quality has a direct impact on the extent to which narrative transportation occurs, with higher-quality stories leading to more transportation and therefore more persuasion (Green, Garst, and Brock 2004). Consumer research finds that complex advertising narratives lead to higher levels of transportation and greater persuasion due to the consumer's deployment of more cognitive and imaginative resources (Nielsen and Escalas 2010). Studies found that consumers are willing to invest more resources to understand a difficult-to-read story, which in real-life settings may be highly complex. This idea is consistent with psychological research on story quality, which treats high-quality stories as those that evoke more processing effort. The underlying assumption is that a complex, thought-provoking story is a good story. Again, the caveat with advertising is that the ad must be comprehensible in a 30- to 60-second time frame.

Priming Narrative Thought Using Advertising

There are a variety of methods by which an ad can invoke narrative thought. Ads may be presented to consumers in the form of a story, which is likely to prime narrative processing of the ad. For example, a recent FedEx commercial shows an employee explaining to his boss that he has solved the company's shipping problem using carrier pigeons. He shows the boss the extremely large pigeons developed for heavy packages, however, the birds drop their packages on cars below them, wreaking havoc on the city. The ad concludes with the boss telling the employee to use FedEx to solve the problem. The fact that the ad is in the form of a story may prime the ad viewer to think in narrative form, processing the ad's events in keeping with the episode schema presented above, by piecing the elements together over time and focusing on causality. Or the individual may be drawn into the story, imagining himself or herself as the employee or perhaps even as the boss, and experiencing the story events through that character's perspective. Or, the consumer may relate the externally presented story to a personal story and begin to think in a self-generated, narrative way about the shipping problems at their workplace or even just general shipping problems (e.g., with online shopping or sending of gifts). In the first case, the ad is processed narratively, but the story is external to the ad viewer. The interaction is quite distant. In the second case, the viewer is drawn into the story, becoming personally caught up in the events. Self-referencing occurs as the viewer imagines himself or herself to be one of the characters. In this third case, the external narrative provides what can be considered a narrative shell or script; it provides an initial narrative direction or starting point for self-generated thought.

Another way in which advertising can elicit narrative thought is by directly encouraging self-generated narratives, for example stimulating autobiographical memories or mental simulation of product use. Both autobiographical memories and mental simulations are usually in the form of stories (Fiske 1993; Polkinghorne 1991). Here, rather than presenting a complete story, the ad may present songs or images designed to evoke memories of the past (Sujan, Bettman, and Baumgartner 1993), or the ad may be filmed from the first-person perspective, encouraging imaginings about the future (Escalas 2004a; Meyers-Levy and Peracchio 1996). Ads also present direct exhortations to think about the past (e.g., "Remember the times of your life," for Kodak film) or to imagine the future (e.g., "Imagine yourself in a Mercury"). Thus, ads may prime mental simulation and autobiographical memory retrieval indirectly with images, music, and so forth, or directly with specific instructions or cues for the consumer to follow.

What Advertising Narratives Can Do for Ad Responses

Based on the assertion that advertising narratives prime narrative thought, there are a variety of ways in which ads that tell stories can affect consumers. First, narrative advertisements can influence viewers' cognitive responses. They may be able to capture a viewer's attention and draw him or her into an ad, leading to transportation. Narrative transportation can be the result of an interesting and relevant plot, a familiar setting, or characters with whom the viewer can relate (Escalas, Moore, and Britton 2004). Similarly, advertising narratives can enhance character identification. Research has shown that the quality of a story in general leads to increased elaboration by the readers or listeners (Feldman et al. 1990). Ad viewers will engage in the cognitive activities necessary to comprehend the story, such as establishing relationships among the narrative elements and developing causal inferences. This increased elaboration is likely to result in better recall about the ad and the brand.

Narrative thought also leads to emotional responses. In advertising research, four types of feelings have been identified as capturing the majority of affective responses to ads: upbeat feelings, warm feelings, uneasy feelings, and disinterested feelings (Goodstein, Edell, and Moore 1990). On the one hand, upbeat feelings, warm feelings, and uneasy feelings have been shown to be positively related to narrative structure: a compelling story can be favorably received when it has a happy ending, evokes compassion for characters, or even makes one uneasy due to a downward sloping evaluative slope (Escalas et al. 2004). These emotions are linked to positive brand evaluations. On the other hand, narrative thought has been shown to be negatively related to disinterested feelings, which lead to negative brand evaluations. As narrative structure improves, so does story quality, and hence subjects may be more interested in the ad, rather than distancing themselves and becoming skeptical (Escalas et al. 2004).

Through transportation, advertising narratives and narrative responses in consumers should have an impact on attitudes toward the ad itself and the brand being advertised. Story ads are often judged to be good ads (with correspondingly high attitudes toward the ad) because stories are an interesting and entertaining form of communication. Furthermore, narrative thought may provide a more enjoyable form of processing. These factors may favorably influence consumers' assessments of story ads. Favorable attitudes toward an ad have been shown to positively influence attitudes toward the advertised brand (see Brown and Stayman 1992). As discussed earlier, narrative transportation leads to persuasion; that is, favorable brand attitudes. First, transportation leads to positive emotions that may be transferred to the brand. Second, transported individuals do not engage in criticism of the ad and brand. Third, consumers may understand and appreciate the way that the brand is to be used based on an advertising narrative, building favorable beliefs about the brand. These are especially powerful if the ad evokes vivid imagery and realistic experiences.

Finally, given that people naturally create meaning based on stories, it is logical to assume that advertising narratives will help to create brand meaning for consumers. Narrative research has shown that people are very good at establishing the relationship between story elements and extrapolating meaning (Carr 1986; Polkinghorne 1991). Thus, a story ad that provides a brand with a series of linkages to certain types of characters, settings, and usage scenarios creates meaning for that brand. If one of the connections built through the advertising narrative is to the consumer, then the brand's meaning may be especially compelling. Because people often think of themselves in the form of narratives, narrative thought may create a link between the brand and the self, which contributes to a brand's meaning and value. In this case, consumers come to value the psychological and symbolic brand benefits because these benefits help them construct and cultivate their self-identity and express their self-concepts, publicly or privately. In the process of using brands to construct and communicate self-identities, brand associations may become linked to the consumer's mental representation of self, forming a self-brand connection, which builds brand equity.

What Advertising Narratives Can Do for Product Experiences

The stories provided in narrative ads may do more than influence ad viewers' cognitive, affective, and attitudinal responses. The content of a narrative ad may set up a narrative shell or script that the viewer can use in subsequent purchase situations. Many beer ads show stories of young men who end up having a good time drinking beer, even after overcoming some problem, such as losing a sporting event or having an argument with a wife or girlfriend. These ads show the men feeling better and having a lot of fun while drinking beer together. In real life, men may come to believe that they will have a better time if they drink beer. Beer campaigns may have, over time, increased the primary demand for beer in general as consumers have seen story after story highlighting the positive results of drinking beer in social settings. When these consumers think about drinking beer, their own narrative enactment may be favorably inclined. Thus an ad can influence viewers' construction of narratives in the future. This ability to affect consumer narratives may allow marketers to make their brands more valuable.

Narrative ads can also serve as "generic plots" that actually frame or influence subsequent consumption experiences with the brand. The externally provided narratives serve as a template enabling consumers to evaluate and make sense of their later experiences with the brand. For example, as a result of MasterCard's "priceless" campaign, one instantiation of which was described earlier, consumers have seen many stories about spending money to achieve "priceless" benefits. As a result, the consumer may begin to spend more money on credit, with the goal of achieving the "priceless" benefits depicted in the ads' stories. This is more than mere recall of an advertising narrative in a purchase setting; what I propose here is an effect on actual usage evaluations. A generic plot may affect the way that consumers cognitively interpret their experiences. For example, consumers in the MasterCard ads are all very happy. This is not interpreted as a random event if the story in the ad indicates that this happiness was caused by the "priceless" benefits associated with purchases enabled by MasterCard. But more than that, the next time the consumer buys something with his or her MasterCard, he or she may actually feel more happiness and satisfaction while making the purchase. Thus, consumers may come to construct their personal consumption experiences using the generic plots presented in narrative ads.

Many consumer behavior researchers have alluded to the power of stories in guiding and constructing subsequent consumption experiences. For example, Puto and Wells (1984) assert that transformational ads can "transform" product usage experiences, and Deighton (1984) argues that advertising suggests a hypothesis for consumers regarding what their consumption experiences will be like. When consumers later encounter ambiguous evidence (the consumption experience), confirmatory biases (Slovic, Fischoff, and Lichtenstein 1977) may lead them to evaluate those experiences in keeping with the hypotheses created in the advertising. Since many consumption experiences are subjective and ambiguous, consumers may construct stories to interpret such experiences using narratives suggested in advertising.

I do not mean to imply that only narrative ads are able to transform or guide consumption experiences. Other advertising structures may accomplish the same thing via different processes. However, story ads may be particularly well suited for "teaching" consumers what they should expect to experience (which then becomes what they actually perceive they experience though narrative interpretation). Scott (1994) asserts that narratives are more palatable than exhortation for changing beliefs. Narratives provide parables or exemplary stories that embody cultural expectations and values. Thus, advertising narratives can show consumers how to use the brand, how they will feel when they use the brand, and how they should evaluate their brand experience.

Narratives and Social Media

If one thinks about the history of advertising, early on, advertisers simply had to communicate directly with consumers about their new and innovative products, highlighting the features and benefits that differentiated them from the competition. As advertising became ubiquitous in our society and products achieved high quality parity, the goals of advertising shifted toward the objectives of breaking through the clutter and building emotional connections to consumers, in order to be heard and achieve differentiation. Now we are at another crossroads, where social media has entered the advertising panorama. Distrustful consumers, after years of advertising exposure, are skeptical of marketers. Facilitated by technological advancements, they can now turn to other consumers for product information and recommendations. Word-of-mouth communication, which is very difficult for marketers to control, is now coming to the forefront. The psychology of narratives can help marketing managers contribute to, guide, and encourage consumer dialogues about their brands.

When companies engage in social media marketing, a primary objective is to engage consumers in a conversation about their products, services, and brands. These consumers in turn spread positive word of mouth communication about the company to others. Thus, companies often hope to create brand "evangelists" or "missionaries" who actively advocate for the company. Consumer research can shed light on some best practices for how to create engagement with consumers in order to foster brand advocacy. Two areas in particular are relevant to this discussion: first, creating compelling brand stories to engage consumers, and second, building self-brand connections to enhance evangelism.

The communication that the company sends out into the social media network must be interesting, engaging, and memorable. Otherwise, consumers will not notice the brand, let alone promote the brand to others. Stories are a natural way to have impact because they have the structure, context, and detail necessary to be relevant and memorable. Narrative research demonstrates that a good story involves the listener/reader, increasing the amount of thought about the characters, events, and even brands in that story. A good narrative provides the characters and situations necessary to evoke positive feelings, which in turn spill over onto the brand being promoted. What makes a compelling story? Stories consist of a plot, with actors engaged in actions to achieve their goals, where they often have to overcome obstacles. In order to be compelling, a plot typically includes something unusual or unexpected. A good plot also provides insight into the protagonist's psychological state; that is, his or her thoughts and feelings. Thus it is important for companies to build a compelling brand biography, which guides social media interaction, and also to tell a compelling story whenever they communicate with consumers.

One of the big issues facing marketers moving from traditional campaigns to those that include social media venues is the question of content. Simply posting a 30- or 60-second ad on the Internet, even if that ad tells a compelling story, is not enough. Social media creates an ongoing conversation with consumers. Content must evolve and change as part of the continuous dialogue. So rather than condensing a story down to a very short commercial, marketers can now develop longer, more complex narrative arcs. These longer stories can be presented through social media in serialized form, harkening back to the Taster's Choice commercials of the 1980s. In a serialized narrative, small pieces of the story are presented to consumers over time, with each episode ending at a point that creates interest, often leaving off with a narrative imbalance or mini-cliffhanger. Thus, compelling content can extend over time, giving consumers a reason to stay in conversation with the brand. A key advantage of this approach is the longer-term, brand-building aspect of the company-consumer dialogue. This is in direct contrast to the discounts, coupons, and free goods and services approach to maintaining consumer engagement, which leads to a reduction in brand value rather than building brand equity.

Second, brand evangelists need to be emotionally involved with the brand. The brand has to matter to them, so that they are motivated to "spread the word." We know people use products and brands in part to create and represent desired self-images and to present these images to others or to themselves. That is, consumers value the brand because it helps them construct and cultivate their self-identity and express their self-concepts, to themselves and to others. Brands can be used as tools for social integration or to connect people to their past. Brands act as symbols of personal accomplishment, provide self-esteem, allow one to differentiate oneself and express individuality, and help people through life transitions. In the process of using brands to construct and communicate self-identities, brand associations may become linked to the consumer's mental representation of self, forming a self-brand connection, a unique relationship with the brand. These powerful connections between the brand and the consumer's self-identity lead to impassioned brand advocacy. These are the brands that matter to consumers; these are the brands they want to talk about.

A good example of one such social media oriented campaign is Pedigree dog food and the Pedigree Foundation to promote shelter dog adoption. The campaign is organized around the story of adopting shelter dogs, an issue that is very important to an active subset of Pedigree's target market. The website and commercials tell an adoption story, which states that, "Every dog that finds itself in a shelter has a story. Our goal is to make sure those stories have a happy ending." This story provides compelling content for the website and the commercials built around this issue. Coupled with cute pictures of dogs and moving music, the Pedigree narrative evokes strong emotions in anyone who cares about animals, even slightly. The brand has started a fund to help shelter dogs, which, when added to the story, builds authenticity. When consumers become fans of Pedigree on Facebook, a bowl of dog food is donated to a shelter. Those consumers who are especially passionate about dogs can get additional information on shelter programs and events by following Pedigree on Twitter. Thus, the brand's meaning is not based on nutritional dog food features, rather, it comes from the identity built through the shelter dog adoption storyline. This meaning engages consumers, helping to create missionaries who spread the word through social media about the adoption program and the Pedigree brand.

Conclusion

In general, narrative structure helps individuals organize and understand situations, others, and themselves. People think in terms of stories, imposing a temporal and relational structure on events. This chapter extends narrative research to the realm of brand building, advertising, and social media. I propose that brand biographies can be an effective tool in positioning a brand in the mind of the target audience, creating emotional connections with consumers, and building brand equity. A coherent and compelling brand narrative should be used to guide a marketing communications campaign. Advertising narratives evoke narrative processing in consumers, which positively affects their cognitive, affective, attitudinal, and behavioral responses to the ad and the brand. Given that narratives are the natural way that consumers think and communicate about brands, brand and advertising narratives can engage consumers so that they communicate about brands in their social networks. In the emerging world of social media, where consumers influence each other's brand evaluations as much as or more than companies are able to, having authentic, involving brand and advertising stories can be an effective way to engage consumers so that they are motivated to communicate favorably about brands to other consumers. As a result of understanding and applying the psychology of narratives, marketers should be in a better position to differentiate their brands in today's marketplace.

References

Baumeister, R.F., and L.S. Newman. 1994. "How Stories Make Sense of Personal Experiences: Motives That Shape Autobiographical Narratives." *Personality and Social Psychology Bulletin* 20: 676–90.

Brewer, W.F., and E.H. Lichtenstein. 1981. "Event Schemas, Story Schemas, and Story Grammars." In *Attention and Performance,* ed. J. Long and A. Baddeley, 363–79. Hillsdale, NJ: Lawrence Erlbaum.

Brown, S. P., and D.M. Stayman. 1992. "Antecedents and Consequences of Attitude Toward the Ad: A Meta-analysis." *Journal of Consumer Research* 19: 34–51.

Bruner, J. 1986. *Actual Minds, Possible Worlds.* Cambridge, MA: Harvard University Press.

———. 1990. *Acts of Meaning.* Cambridge, MA: Harvard University Press.

Carr, D. 1986. *Time, Narrative, and History.* Bloomington: Indiana University Press.

Chafe, W. 1990. "Some Things That Narratives Tell Us About the Mind." In *Narrative Thought and Narrative Language,* ed. B.K. Britton and A.D. Pelligrini, 79–98. Hillsdale, NJ: Lawrence Erlbaum.

Deighton, J. 1984. "The Interaction of Advertising and Evidence." *Journal of Consumer Research* 11: 763–70.

Deighton, J., D. Romer, and J. McQueen. 1989. "Using Drama to Persuade." *Journal of Consumer Research* 16: 335–43.

Escalas, J.E. 2004a. "Imagine Yourself in the Product: Mental Simulation, Narrative Transportation, and Persuasion." *Journal of Advertising* 33: 37–48.

———. 2004b. "Narrative Processing: Building Consumer Connections to Brands." *Journal of Consumer Psychology* 14: 168–79.

———. 2007. "Narrative Versus Analytical Self-Referencing and Persuasion." *Journal of Consumer Research* 34: 421–29.

Escalas, J.E., M.C. Moore, and J.E. Britton. 2004. "Fishing for Feelings: A Hook Helps!" *Journal of Consumer Psychology* 14 (1&2): 105–13.

Fazio, R.H., and M.P. Zanna. 1981. "Direct Experience and Attitude-Behavior Consistency." In *Advances in experimental social psychology,* ed. L. Berkowitz, 161–202. New York: Academic Press.

Feldman, C.F., J. Bruner, B. Renderer, and S. Spitzer. 1990. "Narrative Comprehension." In *Narrative Thought and Narrative Language,* ed. B.K. Britton and A.D. Pelligrini, 1–78. Hillsdale, NJ: Lawrence Erlbaum.

Fiske, S.T. 1993. "Social Cognition and Social Perception." *Annual Review of Psychology* 44: 155–94.

Gergen, K.J., and M.M. Gergen. 1988. "Narrative and the Self as Relationship." *Advances in Experimental Social Psychology* 21: 17–56.

Goodstein, R.C., J.A. Edell, and M.C. Moore. 1990. "When Are Feelings Generated? Assessing the Presence and Reliability of Feelings Based on Storyboards and Animatics." In *Emotion in Advertising: Theoretical and Practical Explorations,* ed. S.J. Agres, J.A. Edell, and T.J. Dubitsky, 175–93. Westport, CT: Quorum Books.

Grayson, K., and R. Martinec. 2004. "Consumer Perceptions of Iconicity and Indexicality and Their Influence on Assessments of Authentic Market Offerings." *Journal of Consumer Research* 31: 296–312.

Gerrig, R.J. 1994. "Narrative Thought?" *Personality and Social Psychology Bulletin* 20: 712–15.

Green, M.C., and T.C. Brock. 2000. "The Role of Transportation in the Persuasiveness of Public Narratives." *Journal of Personality and Social Psychology* 79: 701–21.

———. 2002. "In the Mind's Eye: Transportation-Imagery Model of Narrative Persuasion." In *Narrative Impact: Social and Cognitive Foundations,* ed. M.C. Green, J.J. Strange, and T.C. Brock, 315–42. Mahwah, NJ: Lawrence Erlbaum.

Green, M.C., J. Garst, and T.C. Brock. 2004. "The Power of Fiction: Persuasion via Imagination and Narrative." In *The Psychology of Entertainment Media: Blurring the Lines Between Entertainment and Persuasion,* ed. L. J. Shrum, 161–76. Mahwah, NJ: Lawrence Erlbaum.

Keller, K.L. 1993. "Conceptualizing, Measuring, and Managing Customer-Based Brand Equity." *Journal of Marketing* 57: 1–22.

Kerby, A.P. 1991. *Narrative and the Self.* Bloomington: Indiana University Press.

Levy, S.J. 1959. "Symbols for Sale." *Harvard Business Review* 37: 117–24.

Lucariello, J. 1990. "Canonicality and Consciousness in Child Narrative." In *Narrative Thought and Narrative Language,* ed. B.K. Britton and A.D. Pelligrini, 131–50. Hillsdale, NJ: Lawrence Erlbaum.

Mandler, J.M. 1984. *Stories, Scripts, and Scenes: Aspects of Schema Theory.* Hillsdale, NJ: Lawrence Erlbaum.

McCracken, G. 1989. "Who Is the Celebrity Endorser? Cultural Foundations of the Endorsement Process." *Journal of Consumer Research* 16: 310–21.

Meyers-Levy, J., and L. Peracchio. 1996. "Moderators of the Impact of Self-Reference on Persuasion." *Journal of Consumer Research* 22: 408–23.

Michotte, A. 1963. *The Perception of Causality,* trans. by T.R. Miles and E. Miles. London: Methuen.

Mick, D.G. 1987. "Toward a Semiotic of Advertising Story Grammars." In *Marketing and Semiotics: New Directions in the Study of Signs for Sale,* ed. J. Umiker-Sebeok, 249–78. Berlin: Walter de Gruyter.

Nielsen, J., and J.E. Escalas. 2010. "Easier Is Not Always Better: The Moderating Role of Processing Type on Preference Fluency." *Journal of Consumer Psychology* 20: 295–305.

Olson, D.R. 1990. "Thinking About Narrative." In *Narrative Thought and Narrative Language,* ed. B.K. Britton and A.D. Pelligrini, 99–112. Hillsdale, NJ: Lawrence Erlbaum.

Paharia, N., A. Keinan, J. Avery, and J.B. Schor. 2011. "The Underdog Effect: The Marketing of Disadvantage and Determination Through Brand Biography." *Journal of Consumer Research* 37: 775–790.

Pennington, N., and R. Hastie. 1986. "Evidence Evaluation in Complex Decision Making." *Journal of Personality and Social Psychology* 51: 242–58.

———. 1992. "Explaining the Evidence: Tests of the Story Model for Juror Decision Making." *Journal of Personality and Social Psychology* 62: 189–206.

Polkinghorne, D.E. 1991. "Narrative and Self-Concept." *Journal of Narrative and Life History* 1: 135–53.

Puto, C.P., and W.D. Wells. 1984. "Informational and Transformational Advertising: The Differential Effects of Time." In *Advances in Consumer Research* (vol. XI), ed. T.C. Kinnear, 572–76. Provo, UT: Association for Consumer Research.

Reissman, C.K. 1993. *Narrative Analysis.* Newbury Park, CA: Sage.

Scott, L.M. 1994. "The Bridge from Text to Mind: Adapting Reader-Response Theory to Consumer Research." *Journal of Consumer Research* 21: 461–80.

Slovic, P., B. Fischoff, and S. Lichtenstein. 1977. "Behavioral Decision Theory." *Annual Review of Psychology* 28: 1–39.

Stern, B.B. 1994. "Classical and Vignette Television Advertising Dramas: Structural Models, Formal Analysis, and Consumer Effects." *Journal of Consumer Research* 20: 601–15.

Sujan, M., J.R. Bettman, and H. Baumgartner. 1993. "Influencing Judgments Using Autobiographical Memories: A Self-Referencing Perspective." *Journal of Marketing Research* 30: 422–36.

10

The Consumer-Generated Product Review

Its Effect on Consumers and Marketers

Ohyoon Kwon and Yongjun Sung

The advent of user-centric Web technologies and platforms has enabled the efficient creation and distribution of user-generated content. As a result, the landscape of online media has changed dramatically. The proliferation of user-generated content has launched the participation, massive and direct, of consumers in marketing communications. This participation is through electronic word of mouth (hereafter eWOM). Traditional word of mouth (hereafter WOM), based on prior relationships, generally takes place in face-to-face communication settings. eWOM, however, requires no strong ties and occurs mostly in the form of many-to-many communications among remote contacts (Chatterjee 2001; Dellarocas 2003). With the aid of eWOM, consumers have abundant venues (e.g., blogs, virtual brand communities, social networking sites, instant messaging, and discussion forums) to share their own consumption-related experiences. Such forums are unrestricted by time or location (Ha 2004; Hennig-Thurau and Walsh 2003). Therefore, eWOM has provided unprecedented opportunities for consumers to seek out and share product and service information in the interactive media environment (Dwyer 2007).

Of the various eWOM forms, one intended to facilitate information exchanges from its origin is the consumer-generated online product review. In 1995, Amazon.com first began offering options for its customers to post their purchase and usage experiences. As a result, millions of product reviews have been written and read by consumers. In fact, such product reviews are regarded as one of the most popular and successful features of Amazon (Harmon 2004). Since then, a number of websites have provided consumer-centric platforms to help consumers post and share their reviews on products and services, such a portal websites (Yahoo.com), retailer websites (Amazon.com), manufacturer websites (Dell.com), search engines (Google.com) and product review websites (epinions.com).

In the fields of marketing and consumer behavior, a growing body of academic literature and recent popular press articles highlight the proliferation and importance of the consumer-generated online product review. The purpose of this chapter is, therefore, to provide an extensive review of key academic research regarding consumer-generated online product reviews. First, we discuss the popularity and importance of the consumer-generated product review in today's new media and marketing communication environment. Second, we provide a literature review of some factors that have been identified as important variables of the success of product review. Subsequently, we discuss how consumers process product information and reach final decisions in a virtual environment context. Finally, this chapter concludes with managerial implications for marketers and brand managers.

The Popularity and Importance of the Consumer-Generated Online Product Review

The proliferation of product reviews appears to be associated with the growth of e-commerce. As consumers increasingly turn to the Internet to purchase a variety of products, they are likely, now more than ever, to be exposed to a number of product reviews. And they do take notice. Nearly nine out of ten U.S. online shoppers read consumer-generated product reviews before making a purchase. Of those online shoppers who spend more than five hundred dollars per year, 96 percent usually read at least two product reviews before making a purchase (Freedman 2008). More than 55 percent of U.S. online shoppers rely on consumer-generated online product reviews more than any other online information source. Sixty-two percent of American consumers seek advice from consumer-generated product reviews (Forrester Research 2008). Taken together, these figures indicate that consumers are now relying on peer consumers' opinions and experiences before making a purchase decision.

Other research shows which products or services motivate consumers to seek peer consumers' opinions and suggestions (and when). In one study, more than eight out of ten consumers reported needing such advice for travel/recreation/leisure and electronic goods (Opinion Research Corp. 2008). Household products/services motivated about two out of three consumers (66 percent); followed by clothing (55 percent); automotive (55 percent); and personal care (40 percent) (Opinion Research Corp. 2008). More than half of consumers (53 percent) sought reviews while trying to make decisions between two or three products, and 40 percent said they would read online reviews when beginning their shopping research (Freedman 2008). These reviews, it appears, become more influential when consumers try to make final purchase decisions between a few alternatives and when they struggle to understand all the attributes or features of the products.

The key for businesses is whether these consumer reviews impact product/ service sales. Studies on sales impact have been conducted based on the review valence and the volume of the review. Chevalier and Mayzlin (2006) investigated Amazon.com and barnesandnoble.com. First, focusing on the average review score for a book, Chevalier and Mayzlin (2006) found that there was a positive association between product ratings by consumers and the book's sales. The impact of the lowly one-star reviews, however, was more powerful than of five-star reviews in final purchase decisions (Chevalier and Mayzlin 2006). Hu, Liu, and Zhang (2008) also found that favorably reviewed products sold more than those that receive unfavorable reviews. Second, the volume of product reviews generated by peer consumers significantly influences product/service sales (Chen, Wu, and Yoon 2004; Park and Park 2008). A large number of product reviews indicates that more peer consumers have already purchased and used the product. This drives down the perceived risk related to purchasing the product (Chen et al. 2004; Park and Park 2008). As consumers' discussions about specific products via online product reviews become more available, consumers are more likely to purchase the products.

In sum, consumer-generated online product reviews have clearly gained in popularity. The primary reason is that they provide product information from a users' perspectives and are more conveniently accessible to consumers (Bickart and Shindler 2001). A vast number of consumer-generated online product reviews reflect diverse consumer experiences with products, allow consumers to evaluate products or services from peer consumers' viewpoints, and eventually result in increased sales. In the following section, we look at the factors contributing to the popularity and importance of consumer-generated online product reviews.

Factors Affecting the Growth of Consumer-Generated Online Product Reviews

As the evidence makes plain, consumer-generated online product reviews are an important source of information for consumers (e.g., Chevalier and Mayzlin 2006; Hennig-Thurau and Walsh 2003; Liu 2006). An extensive body of literature has explored several factors that have affected the growth of consumer-generated product reviews online. Of these, we'll discuss three: (1) consumers' motives; (2) perceived credibility; and (3) perceived helpfulness.

Consumer Motives

Research has identified several sources used by consumers to obtain information relevant to their purchase needs. The importance of prepurchase information in the purchase process has been clearly documented. Interpersonal sources of information are recognized as especially weighty; they are considered neither biased nor exaggerated (Arndt 1967; Brown and Reingen 1987; Herr, Kardes, and Kim 1991; Kiel and Layton 1981). Given their wide dissemination and high levels of acceptance, when we understand the motives behind them we'll collect insights into how our peers influence our consumer purchases and communication behavior, and eventually, the market success of products (Stauss 2000).

Hennig-Thurau and Walsh (2003) examined motives that explain why consumers, at the individual level, look for product reviews from their peers. They classify reviews according to consumption stage—prepurchase versus postpurchase. A prospective buyer uses reviews at the prepurchase stage first and foremost to make better buying decisions and to reduce their search time (Hennig-Thurau and Walsh 2003). They also found that consumers read fellow consumers' opinions to learn about how to use products and services in the postpurchase stage. Indeed, the consumer-generated online product review serves as the infrastructure of a virtual community. It provides social and information utility by helping consumers compare their product experiences (Hennig-Thurau and Walsh 2003).

At the prepurchase stage, another significant force determining the degree and depth of external information search is choice confusion (Punj and Staelin 1983). When consumers learn of many attractive alternatives, they are confused about which is the best option; they perceive a higher level of purchased-related risk under economic and time constraints and seek more product-related information by expanding the amount of external search (Claxton, Fry, and Portis 1974; Punj and Staelin 1983; Srinivasan and Ratchford 1991). Kwon, Chu, and Choi (2010) showed that consumers faced with choice confusion rely on their peers' opinions via online product reviews to select the best option and to obtain peace of mind about their choice. Their findings are consistent with the results from industry that consumers are most likely to read other consumers' opinions when they are trying to decide between two or three products (Freedman 2008). Further, Kwon and colleagues (2010) found that product reviews are perceived as providing qualified product information, reducing search costs, and influencing purchase decisions.

Consumers at the prepurchase stage seek their fellow consumers' opinions, suggestions, and experiences for three reasons: (1) to get more qualified product information; (2) to do it in less time; and (3) to get help in making a decision. The findings clearly suggest that consumers perceive such information as credible and helpful. Hence, we focus on these two important issues—credibility and helpfulness—in the following sections.

Perceived Information Credibility

A long history of research finds that perceived credibility in persuasive communications consists of perceptions of a source's expertise, trustworthiness, or attractiveness, as well as judgments of information quality or accuracy (Freeman and Spyridakis 2004). In the traditional media context, authority and the ability to produce information were given to a limited number of sources and information was subject to filtering through professional gatekeepers (Metzger 2007). However, the Internet enables anyone to be an author of information and to disseminate it on a mass scale. Web-based information is not always accurate or impartial, which results in issues of credibility due to the lack of editorial reviews and traditional authority or established reputation (Fritch and Cromwell 2001; Johnson and Kaye 2000; Rieh 2002). Yet people generally consider Web-based information to be equally credible as that obtained from traditional media (Flanagin and Metzger 2000). Therefore, researchers are increasingly interested in information credibility in the interactive media environment (Johnson and Kaye 2004; Kaye and Johnson 2006).

Product reviews were once considered suspect because anyone can post them without filtering through professional gatekeepers and they take place between reviewers and readers who have no previous relationship. But in the current marketplace, more than 70 percent of consumers regard online product reviews as credible (Nielsen 2009). So the manner in which readers construe the credibility of online product reviews is of paramount importance. In this section, we approach the perceived information credibility of product reviews created by peer consumers with a focus on perceived source credibility, information content, and review experiences.

An extensive body of literature on source credibility posits that when the source is considered as more credible, message recipients are more likely to be persuaded (Hovland, Janis, and Kelley 1953; Hovland and Weiss 1951; Petty and Cacioppo 1986). Further, considerable research has repeatedly documented that characteristics of a message source exert direct influence on message recipients' attitudes and behaviors (Chaiken and Maheshwaran 1994; Mackie, Worth, and Asuncion 1990; Ohanian 1990; Petty, Wegener, and White 1998). Therefore, when focusing on the characteristics of peer reviewers, some researchers have investigated how reviewers' source credibility was construed and how the perceived credibility of peer reviewers affects the processing of product information. In particular, Forman, Ghose, and Wiesenfeld (2008) assumed that in their product reviews, reviewers provide identity-descriptive information that involves how they behave and what products they purchase. These researchers then explored how and why, in a real setting, reviewer disclosure of identity-descriptive information influenced other consumers' product evaluations. According to Forman et al. (2008), consumer reviewers tend to disclose their identity-descriptive information when prior product reviews convey reviewer identity-descriptive information. Online consumer reviews that convey reviewers' identity-descriptive information tend to be rated as more helpful than those without identity-descriptive information (Forman et al. 2008). Therefore, identity-description information associated with reviewers' purchase and usage situations directly influences the level of their credibility. Also, review readers appear to process the peer reviewers' credibility based on the identity-description information (Forman et al. 2008).

Using an experimental setting, Smith, Menon, and Sivakumar (2005) investigated the dimensions of reviewer credibility and the effects of credibility on consumer choice with an exceptional emphasis on consumer trust. To this end, they focused on and manipulated reviewer expertise and rapport as significant constructs that would have greater influence on consumer trust and purchase choice. Reviewer expertise is associated with reviewer qualifications for review (Mayer, Davis, and Schoorman 1995; Sitkin and Roth 1993). Reviewer rapport is defined as the affective bond toward peer reviewers (Smith et al. 2005). Reviewer expertise was cued through the following information: the number of restaurants that the reviewer had visited in an area, the length of experience, and the breadth of exposure to restaurants as a product category. Reviewer rapport was cued by means of providing information related to the reviewer's personal taste, lifestyle, and hobbies, which enabled the subjects to identify with the reviewer. Both the reviewer expertise and rapport had a significant and positive association with trust as well as perceived influence on purchase decisions (Smith et al. 2005).

Another determinant in the interactive media environment that influences perceived credibility appears to be associated with information content (Flanagin and Metzger 2000). Similar to traditional media sources, the Internet provides a wide range of information to its users. The perceived credibility of Web-based information is determined by its content (Flanagin and Metzger 2000). We can apply this finding to the context of consumer-generated product reviews. Given that concrete and self-validated information is found to be the most credible (Rosenthal 1971), first-hand consumption experiences reflected in online product reviews appear to have been self-verified, central to making them credible. Consumer-generated product reviews usually offer product assessment from a consumer's perspective generally based on direct purchase and usage experiences, so it is plausible for review readers to rate the online product reviews as credible in spite of the lack of relationships with peer reviewers.

Media scholars have also explored and found a positive relationship between Web experiences and credibility perceptions (Johnson and Kaye 2000; Kiousis 2001). In line with this notion, online product reviews seem highly credible by the very fact of their proliferation. As more consumers become accustomed to using online product reviews, the perception of their credibility spreads. In addition, the fact that online retailers allow their customers review their experiences with the retailer also contributes to the review's credibility.

In sum, review readers face certain risks associated with product purchase, such as uncertainty and higher search cost. These readers appear to pay attention to the self-descriptive information of peer reviewers, including their lifestyles, purchase experience, and knowledge concerning product categories. In doing so, review readers might evaluate reviewer expertise or rapport even if they do not have strong ties with the peer reviewers. Once the review readers perceive relatively greater reviewer expertise or rapport, they are more likely to show greater trust in the peer reviewers and put faith in their product reviews. Information content also appears to play an important role as a determinant in the perceived credibility of online product reviews. Actual experiences with products and assessments based on experience provide self-verification for product reviews by peer consumers and contribute to the perceived credibility of information. As consumers search for their peers' suggestions and opinions to reduce purchase-related risks, their experiences with the reviews can, in turn, increase trust in using them and extend the perceived credibility of product information.

Perceived Helpfulness

Online product reviews are used by consumers to help them decide on purchases. This helpfulness appears to be important (Kumar and Benbasat 2006). Some scholars approach the perceived helpfulness factor using diagnosticity (Mudambi and Schuff 2010) and conformity (Danescu-Niculescu-Mizil et al. 2009).

Mudambi and Schuff (2010) use diagnosticity to emphasize extremity and depth of review. Review extremity is evaluated based on numerical star ratings for consumer-generated online product reviews, which usually range from one to five stars at Amazon.com. A one-star rating reflects an extremely negative review, a three-star rating reflects a modest review, and five stars indicate an extremely positive review. Review depth is associated with the review's length, as measured in words. According to Mudambi and Schuff

(2010), online product reviews with extreme ratings were less helpful than product reviews reviewed with moderate ratings. Consumers generally regard lengthier online product reviews as being more helpful.

Focusing on average ratings, Danescu-Niculescu-Mizil and colleagues (2009) explored how consumers evaluated peer consumers' reviews in terms of perceived helpfulness. They used a dataset of four million Amazon.com book reviews and tested the effect of conformity by calculating the average number of stars for all reviews. Book reviews closer to the average rating were perceived as more helpful than reviews with extremely negative or extremely positive ratings. The perceived helpfulness of a book review by peer consumers is based upon whether its star rating converges with the average star rating of the book (Danescu-Niculescu-Mizil et al. 2009). This result indicates that a consumer's willingness to conform to other consumers' general evaluations plays a pivotal role in evaluating a product review.

In terms of the perceived helpfulness of a review, empirical studies consistently point to the importance of a converging evaluation of a product (Danescu-Niculescu-Mizil et al. 2009; Mudambi and Schuff 2010). Platforms for sharing consumer opinions and experiences continually evolve to provide user-centric product information (i.e., average rating, most helpful product reviews, cons and pros). Because of this, consumers, without extensive effort, are able to get a feel for other consumers' integrated evaluations. Consequently, consumers can make faster decisions when product reviews are helpful. The bottom line is a better purchase decision done more efficiently.

The Process of Consumer-Generated Product Reviews

Given that consumer-generated product reviews have a great impact on final purchase decisions, it is important to investigate how consumers process information found in online product reviews. As many scholars have noted, consumers' processing of product information is quite complicated and hard to predict. In order to explore how individuals process product information in persuasive messages, three variables have been widely employed: product categories, message valences, and motivational orientations (e.g., Aaker and Lee 2001; Brown and Reingen 1987; Ford, Smith, and Swasy 1988). We will discuss these in relation to online consumer-generated product reviews.

Product Category

Considerable research utilizes the search/experience framework and investigates how the characteristics of a product affect consumers' information-seeking behaviors and information processing (e.g., Hsieh, Chiu, and Chiang

2005; Klein 1998). In particular, the term "search goods" refers to products with features that can be easily known prior to purchasing (Klein 1998; Nelson 1974). By contrast, so-called experience goods are products with attributes that can be known only after purchasing (Klein 1998; Nelson 1974). Some scholars postulate that it can be quite costly to figure out product attributes of experience goods before purchasing (Ford, Smith, and Swasy 1988; Klein 1998). When consumers have difficulty in discovering product qualities and attributes prior to purchase and use, they rely more on fellow consumers' purchase and usage experiences to reduce the ambiguity of judgmental criteria (Bone 1995). In the context of consumer-generated product reviews, Park and Lee (2009) found that consumers rely more on reviews for experience goods than for search goods in making purchase decisions.

A considerable amount of research has also applied the utilitarian/hedonic framework to the processing of product information (Strahilevitz and Meyers 1998). Utilitarian products are those that maximize consumers' instrumental goals, delivering more cognitively oriented benefits (Batra and Ahtola 1991; Hirschman and Holbrook 1982). For example, cell phones, digital cameras, PDAs, computer monitors, and printers are all utilitarian products. Hedonic products are those that maximize emotional or sensory gratification. For example, music, novels, magazines, and DVDs are all hedonic products. According to Sen and Lerman (2007), in terms of using product reviews, consumers process utilitarian products differently from hedonic ones. Take a consumer considering a (utilitarian) cell phone for purchase. In reading consumer-generated product reviews, he will focus more on avoiding a negative purchase result (Sen and Lerman 2007). Take another consumer shopping for a (hedonic) DVD. In reading consumer-generated product reviews, she will pay more attention to finding positive benefits (Sen and Lerman 2007).

Product type, in summary, moderates the effects of online product reviews. Peer consumers' online product reviews convey diverse usage situations and experiences. Because of this, consumers focus more heavily on product reviews for experience goods. In purchasing such products, consumers appear to read the reviews to avoid negative outcomes. Consumers who read product reviews for search goods appear to do so to secure positive (emotionally satisfying) outcomes.

Message Valence

In the literature on message processing, researchers have emphasized the role of message valence (negative vs. positive). Research on WOM communication has consistently shown that consumers give negative information more weight than positive information. Negative reports wield more influence on a recipient's judgment and decision-making tasks (Brown and Reingen 1987; Kanouse and Hanson 1972; Skowronski and Carlston 1987). A consumer generally finds these reports credible because peer consumers who generate negative reports have nothing to gain by giving a negative opinion (Mizerski 1982).

Consumers process negative information in consumer-generated online product reviews differently than positive information. They process such information according to product type. As we saw above, reviews of utilitarian products are more impactful than those for hedonic products (Sen and Lerman 2007). Consumers attribute negative reviews of hedonic products to the individual reviewer's idiosyncrasies rather than to the product's aspects (Sen and Lerman 2007). Park and Lee (2009) explored the negative effects of the consumer-generated online product review across product type (search vs. experience goods). They worked from the notion that negative effects are more likely to prevail when a consumer cannot know a product's attributes before purchasing it. What they found bore out this notion. Product reviews on experience goods made a greater impact on purchase decisions due to the increased uncertainty about the purchase (Park and Lee 2009).

Empirical research findings indicate that an interaction between product type and message valence influences how consumers process product reviews. Researchers have found that consumers respond differently to negative information according to what they are hoping to purchase. Therefore, we may assume that consumers make different cognitive efforts for three reasons: (1) to avoid uncertainty associated with purchases according to product type; (2) to discern why peer reviewers posted their reviews; and (3) to realize the biggest benefit on the basis of peer reviewers' experiences.

Motivational Orientations

Past studies have suggested that consumers make decisions based on their specific motivational orientations or goals (Aaker and Lee 2001; Agrawal and Maheswaran 2005; Lee and Aaker 2004). Regulatory focus theory postulates that people have two different types of goals (see Higgins 1997). It explains why some people are motivated by goals such as advancement, achievement, and aspirations through approaching positive outcomes (promotion-focused); and why others are motivated by responsibilities, obligations, and security, which can be attained through avoiding negative outcomes (prevention-focused) (Higgins 1997, 1998). What appears to be of some importance, according to research, is how these promotion and prevention goals predict consumer behaviors (e.g., Aaker and Lee 2001; Pham and Avnet 2004). In terms of message processing, a considerable number of studies have postulated that the compatibility between persuasive messages and motivational orientations has a significant influence on consumers' levels of engagement in the messages, attitude formation, and behavioral change (e.g., Petty and Cacioppo 1986). More specifically, when an appeal is compatible with their goal, consumers pay more attention and engage in higher elaboration and have more favorable attitude toward the appeal (Aaker and Lee 2001; Lee and Aaker 2004).

In this respect, how consumers' different consumption goals are formulated and attained through either the promotion focus or the prevention focus provides insights to understanding their responses to different types of consumer-generated product reviews (Kwon and Sung 2010). In an experimental setting Kwon and Sung (2010) investigated how consumers' different consumption goals affect their processing of online product reviews and how this processing impacts their purchase intention. When a consumer's promotion (or prevention) goal becomes more dominant, a promotion-framed (or prevention-framed) consumer-generated product review is more likely to have a greater impact on the consumer's favorable attitudes toward the reviewed brand and purchase intention for the brand. As a result, consumers' desired goals are important predictors of what sort of reviews influence their attitudes.

Managerial Implications

This overview of the recent literature on the consumer psychology of consumer-generated online product reviews provides insight into how consumer-generated product reviews have become popular and how consumers process product information in online reviews in this new media age. In addition, the proliferation and credibility of the consumer-generated online product review also provide marketers with great opportunities to reap benefits and communicate with their customers. Managerial implications for marketers include (1) benefits from consumer-generated product reviews; (2) issues associated with negative feedback in the online reviews; (3) ways to increase the number of the reviews; and (4) strategies to communicate with consumers via the reviews.

Can Giving Consumers a Voice Pay Off?

In today's competitive market, a customer's willingness to recommend a product or service can be crucial to success (Reichheld 2003). Referral value articulated through positive consumer product reviews might predict the performance of companies better than traditional measures, including reports of customer satisfaction. Therefore, consumers' referral value expressed via product reviews could contribute significantly to the sales of products and to brand evaluation.

Consumer-generated product reviews provide product information in terms of usage situations and measures product performance from a user's perspective (Bickart and Shindler 2001). Given this, a growing body of literature has demonstrated that there is a positive association between consumers' evaluations of products and sales (Chevalier and Mayzlin 2006; Dellarocas, Zhang, Awad 2007). Furthermore, some scholars have drawn attention to how the volume of consumer-generated online product reviews affects the sales of the product. They have found a positive relationship between review volume and sales (Liu 2006; Park and Park 2008). Park and Park (2008) show us that a more diverse pool of consumer-generated online product reviews enhance brand evaluations under high-risk contexts. Review readers were more likely, they found, to engage in more message elaboration, which led to greater sales.

Also, consumer-generated product reviews are integral to disseminating information concerning a wide variety of new products. Clemons, Gao, and Hitt (2006) found that more informed consumers have greater opportunities to choose what they want by relying on the aid of the diverse opinions and experiences of peer consumers. In addition, products distinguish themselves from their competitors through diverse consumer opinions and ratings (Clemons et al. 2006). These researchers argue that product reviews from different perspectives enable small brands to compete with other big brands due to hyperdifferentiation and resonance marketing.

Consumer-generated online product reviews reflect product attributes recognized through purchase situations and usage experiences (Bickart and Schindler 2001). Marketer-generated information, on the other hand, emphasizes attributes such as technical specifications and product performance. These two sources of information (consumer vs. marketer) supplement each other for consumers searching for the best product. Consumers are cognitive misers. They are not likely to spend extensive time figuring out product attributes based on marketer-generated information, nor will they always engage in extensive information search efforts (Payne, Bettman, and Johnson 1993). Instead, they might rely on fellow consumers' purchase and usage experiences to reduce uncertainty pertaining to product purchases to reduce perceived purchase risks (Chen and Xie 2008; Kwon et al. 2010). A diverse pool of positive consumer-generated product reviews significantly contributes to a favorable evaluation of a reviewed brand (Park and Park 2008) and is associated with higher sales of reviewed products (Clemons et al. 2006). For instance, PETCO added a platform for consumers to post reviews of PETCO products. Following this move, top-rated products were converted at a 49 percent higher rate (Holland 2007). Further, PETCO customers who relied on peer customers' product reviews in shopping for PETCO products spent 63 percent more than those using other tools. Such evidence clearly indicates that consumer-generated online product reviews have enabled consumers to facilitate their final purchase processes. Consumer product reviewers appear to work, for free, as a marketer's sales assistants.

Consequently, the online presence of consumer-generated product reviews has facilitated consumers' purchase decision processes as well as helped online retailers improve interactions with their customers (Kumar and Benbasat 2006). In particular, by means of setting up the platform for consumer-generated product reviews online, retail companies have been able to increase consumers' loyalty to their websites, overall conversion rates, and their customers' average order values (Bazaarvoice 2007b).

Do Marketers Have to Fear Negative Consumer-Generated Product Reviews?

Marketers are concerned, of course, about the negative effects of consumer-generated product reviews. Yet the tone of consumer-generated product reviews is extremely positive with an average rating of 4.3 out 5 (Bazaarvoice 2007a). This finding may be associated with the motives of consumer reviewers. According to Hennig-Thurau and Walsh (2004), consumer reviewers are motivated by self-enhancement—a tendency to take credit for good outcomes—so positive reviews predominate. Products about which consumers post their experiences, opinions, and suggestions might sell better than those without such postings.

Not all negative online product reviews harm brand evaluations and sales. The coexistence of positive and negative consumer-generated product reviews appears to be more realistic, reflecting different types of consumer interests and needs (Clemons et al. 2006). Together, both types of reviews provide consumers with peer consumers' diverse opinions and experiences, and provide a brand with a great opportunity to differentiate itself from competing products (Clemons et al. 2006). Furthermore, readers of both positive and negative reviews may consider themselves better informed, which may increase the likelihood that they'll make a purchase.

Negative consumer product reviews can sometimes work as direct feedback from consumers. For instance, Land of Nod, which was acquired by Crate & Barrel, discovered through reviews that their activity table for kids was vulnerable to indentations when kids wrote on them. Land of Nod changed to a harder wood and contacted their reviewers, offering them new tables (Fredrickson 2009). Consumer response was phenomenal and customers generated numerous positive reviews.

Online reviews can lead to product improvement, better communications with customers, and greater customer satisfaction. Marketers, it would seem, should focus on increasing the presence of consumer-generated product reviews.

How Can Marketers Increase the Volume of Consumer-Generated Product Reviews?

The presence of numerous online product reviews not only provides diverse information for a specific product, but reflects the popularity of that product. Thus, marketers should increase the volume of these reviews and consider them as new elements in their marketing communication mix. Accordingly, they should look to the motives of consumer reviewers. As postulated by Hennig-Thurau and Walsh (2004), consumer reviewers are more likely to post their experiences, opinions, and suggestions concerning products when they can obtain economic incentives. Some companies offer incentives to motivate their customers to write reviews. PETCO, for example, launched a sweepstakes campaign to boost consumer-generated product reviews. In two months PETCO saw an 800 percent increase in volume of posted reviews. However, the ratings and the quality of the reviews showed little change (Fredrickson 2009). Marketers can evidently increase the number of consumer product reviews by luring people to write reviews with economic incentives, but it is important to note that consumer reviewers are not likely to change their ratings and reviews for incentives. Their motivation is to give others the opportunity to buy the right product or warn them away from the wrong ones (Hennig-Thurau and Walsh 2004).

In addition, in the new media environment, reviewers have virtually no prior relationship with readers of their reviews. Nevertheless, the reviewers wish to communicate through their product reviews and enjoy meeting peer consumers (Hennig-Thurau and Walsh 2004). Therefore, marketers should offer customers a customer-centric communication tool, one that allows them to communicate with each other and that increases community coherence and activity. In this way marketers can help their customers build a sense of community and increase their familiarity with others based on shared interests and needs. Accordingly, customers with a sense of community might have greater brand commitment and spread product information for potential customers.

How Can Marketers Use Consumer-Generated Online Product Reviews?

By tapping into the diverse opinions, ideas, and experiences found in online product reviews, marketers are able to constantly assess how consumers perceive the benefits of their products and services. More specifically, by inspecting a wide range of consumer-generated product reviews, marketers are able to ensure that their intended benefits are successfully delivered to their target audiences. Furthermore, by examining consumer-generated product reviews, marketers can re-evaluate their products from the consumer's perspective without investing a huge amount of financial and human resources. Accordingly, marketers are able to develop marketing and communication strategies that are compatible with the consumption goals of their target audiences. For example, Oriental Trading Company evaluated their products on the basis of consumer-generated product reviews and then changed or removed 700 of its products. Based on this same notion, Canon launched an online advertising campaign focusing on consumer-generated product reviews.

In conclusion, consumer-generated online product reviews that reflect various consumption experiences can provide marketers with an opportunity to communicate interactively with their customers. Therefore, consumer-generated product reviews can play an important role as a new and important factor in implementing new types of marketing communication strategies. In addition to boosting short-term sales, such communications with customers might, in the long term, build better customer relationships with brands.

References

Aaker, J.L., and A.Y. Lee. 2001. "'I' Seek Pleasures and 'We' Avoid Pains: The Role of Self-Regulatory Goals in Information Processing and Persuasion." *Journal of Consumer Research* 28: 33–49.

Agrawal, N., and D. Maheswaran. 2005. "The Effects of Self-Construal and Commitment on Persuasion." *Journal of Consumer Research* 31: 841–49.

Arndt, J. 1967. "Role of Product-Related Conversations in the Diffusion of a New Product." *Journal of Marketing Research* 4: 291–95.

Batra, R., and O.T. Ahtola. 1991. "Measuring the Hedonic and Utilitarian Sources of Consumer Attitudes." *Marketing Letters* 2: 159–70.

Bazaarvoice. 2007a. "Keller Fay Group and Bazaarvoice Study Finds Altruism Drives Online Reviewers. November 26." Available at www.bazaarvoice.com/about/press-room/keller-fay-group-and-bazaarvoice-study-finds-altruism-drives-online-reviewers, accessed March 9, 2011.

———. 2007b. "Social Commerce Statistics." Available at www.bazaarvoice.com/resources/stats, accessed March 9, 2011.

Bickart, B., and R.M. Schindler. 2001. "Internet Forums as Influential Sources of Consumer Information." *Journal of Interactive Marketing* 15: 31–40.

Bone, P.F. 1995. "Word-of-Mouth Effects on Short-Term and Long-Term Product Judgments." *Journal of Business Research* 32: 213–23.

Brown, J.J., and P.H. Reingen. 1987. "Social Ties and Word-of-Mouth Referral Behavior." *Journal of Consumer Research* 14: 350–62.

Chaiken, S., and D. Maheswaran. 1994. "Heuristic Processing Can Bias Systematic Processing: Effects of Source Credibility, Argument Ambiguity, and Task Importance on Attitude Judgment." *Journal of Personality and Social Psychology* 66: 460–73.

Chatterjee, P. 2001. "Online Reviews: Do Consumers Use Them?" In *Advances in Consumer Research,* ed. M.C. Gilly and J. Myers-Levy, 129–34. Provo, UT: Association for Consumer Research.

Chen, P., S. Wu, and J. Yoon. 2004. "The Impact of Online Recommendations and Consumer Feedback on Sales." Proceedings of the International Conference on Information Systems, 711–24.

Chen, Y., and J. Xie. 2008. "Online Consumer Review: Word-of-Mouth as a New Element of Marketing Communication Mix." *Management Science* 54: 477–91.

Chevalier, J.A., and D. Mayzlin. 2006. "The Effect of Word of Mouth on Sales: Online Book Reviews." *Journal of Marketing Research* 43: 345–54.

Claxton, J.D., J.N. Fry, and B. Portis. 1974. "A Taxonomy of Prepurchase Information-gathering Patterns." *Journal of Consumer Research* 1: 35–42.

Clemons, E., G. Gao, and L. Hitt. 2006. "When Online Reviews Meet Hyperdifferentiation: A Study of the Craft Beer Industry." *Journal of Management Information Systems* 23: 149–71.

Danescu-Niculescu-Mizil, C., G. Kossinets, J. Kleinberg, and L. Lee. 2009. "How Opinions Are Received by Online Communities: A Case Study on Amazon.com Helpfulness Votes." Proceedings of the 18th International Conference on World Wide Web, 141–150. Madrid: ACM.

Dellarocas, C. 2003. "The Digitization of Word of Mouth: Promise and Challenges of Online Feedback Mechanisms." *Management Science* 49: 1407–24.

Dellarocas, C., X. Zhang, & N.F. Awad. 2007. "Exploring The Value of Online Product Reviews in Forecasting Sales: The Case of Motion Pictures." *Journal of Interactive Marketing* 21: 23–45.

Dwyer, P. 2007. "Measuring the Value of Electronic Word of Mouth and Its Impact in Consumer Communities." *Journal of Interactive Marketing* 21: 63–79.

Flanagin, A.J., and M.J. Metzger. 2000. "Perceptions of Internet Information Credibility." *Journalism & Mass Communication Quarterly* 77: 515–40.

Ford, G.T., D.B. Smith, and J.L. Swasy. 1988. "An Empirical Test of the Search, Experience and Credence Attributes Framework." In *Advances in Consumer Research,* ed. M.J. Houston, 239–44. Provo, UT: Association for Consumer Research.

Forman, C., A. Ghose, and B. Wiesenfeld. 2008. "Examining the Relationship between Reviews and Sales: The Role of Reviewer Identity Disclosure in Electronic Markets." *Information Systems Research* 19: 291–313.

Forrester Research. 2008. "North American Technographics Customer Experience Online Survey, Q3 2007f." Available at www.forrester.com/er/research/survey/excerpt/1,5449,630,00.html, accessed March 9, 2011.

Fredrickson, C. 2009. "The Social Power of User-Generated Content." eMarketer, October 20. Available at www.emarketer.com/blog/index.php/social-power-usergenerated-content, accessed March 9, 2011.

Freedman, L. 2008. "Merchant and Customer Perspectives on Customer Reviews and User-generated Content." Available at www.e-tailing.com/content/wp-content/uploads/2008/12/2008_WhitePaper_0204_4FINAL-powerreviews.pdf, accessed March 9, 2011.

Freeman, K.S., and J.H. Spyridakis. 2004. "An Examination of Factors that Affect the Credibility of Online Health Information." *Technical Communication* 51: 239–63.

Fritch, J.W., and R.L. Cromwell. 2001. "Evaluating Internet Resources: Identity, Af-filiation, and Cognitive Authority in a Networked World." *Journal of the American Society for Information Science and Technology* 52: 499–507.

Ha, H.Y. 2004. "Factors Influencing Consumer Perceptions of Brand Trust Online." *Journal of Product and Brand Management* 13: 329–42.

Harmon, A. 2004. "Amazon Glitch Unmasks War of Reviewers." *New York Times,* February 14, A1. Available at www.nytimes.com/2004/02/14/us/amazon-glitch-unmasks-war-of-reviewers.html, accessed March 9, 2011.

Hennig-Thurau, T., and G. Walsh. 2003. "Electronic Word-of-Mouth: Motives for and Consequences of Reading Customer Articulations on the Internet." *International Journal of Electronic Commerce,* 8: 51–74.

———. 2004. "Electronic Word-of-Mouth via Consumer-Opinion Platforms: What Motivates Consumers to Articulate Themselves on the Internet?" *Journal of Interactive Marketing* 18: 38–52.

Herr, P.M., F.R. Kardes, and J. Kim. 1991. "Effects of Word-of-Mouth and Product-Attribute Information on Persuasion: An Accessibility-Diagnosticity Perspective." *Journal of Consumer Research* 17: 454–62.

Higgins, E.T. 1997. "Beyond Pleasure and Pain." *American Psychologist* 52: 1280–1300.

———. 1998. "Promotion and Prevention: Regulatory Focus as a Motivational Principle." *Advances in Experimental Social Psychology* 30: 1–46.

Hirschman, E.C., and M.B. Holbrook. 1982. "Hedonic Consumption: Emerging Concepts, Methods and Propositions." *Journal of Marketing* 46: 92–101.

Holland, A. 2007. "Adding Customer Reviews Increases Conversions—Dramatically." Marketing Sherpa, May 21. Available at www.marketingsherpa.com/article.php?ident=29968, accessed March 9, 2011.

Hovland, C.I., I.L. Janis, and H.H. Kelley. 1953. *Communication and Persuasion.* New Haven, CT: Yale University Press.

Hovland, C.I., and W. Weiss, W. 1951. "The Influence of Source Credibility on Communication Effectiveness." *Public Opinion Quarterly* 15: 635–50.

Hsieh, Y., H. Chiu, and M. Chiang. 2005. "Maintaining a Committed Online Customer: A Study Across Search-Experience-Credence Products." *Journal of Retailing* 81: 75–82.

Hu, N., L. Liu, and J. Zhang. 2008. "Do Online Reviews Affect Product Sales? The Role of Reviewer Characteristics and Temporal Effects." *Information Technology and Management* 9: 201–14.

Johnson, T.J., and B.K. Kaye. 2000. "Using Is Believing: The Influence of Reliance on the Credibility of Online Political Information Among Politically Interested Internet Users." *Journalism & Mass Communication Quarterly* 77: 865–79.

———. 2004. "Wag the Blog: How Reliance on Traditional Media and the Internet Influence Credibility Perceptions of Weblogs Among Blog Users." *Journalism & Mass Communication Quarterly* 81: 622–42.

Kanouse, D.E., and R.L. Hanson. 1972. "Negativity in Evaluations." In *Attribution: Perceiving the Causes of Behavior,* ed. E.E. Jones et al., 47–62. Morristown, NJ: General Learning Press.

Kaye, B.K., and T.J. Johnson. 2006. "The Age of Reasons: Motives for Using Different Components of the Internet for Political Information." In *The Internet Election: Perspectives on the Web in Campaign* 2006, ed. A.P. Williams and J.C. Tedesco, 147–67. Lanham, MD: Rowman & Littlefield.

Kiel, G.C., and R.A. Layton. 1981. "Dimensions of Consumer Information-Seeking Behavior." *Journal of Marketing Research* 18: 233–42.

Kiousis, S. 2001. "Public Trust or Mistrust? Perceptions of Media Credibility in the Information Age." *Mass Communication & Society* 4: 381–403.

Klein, L.R. 1998. "Evaluating the Potential of Interactive Media through a New Lens: Search Versus Experience Goods." *Journal of Business Research* 41: 195–203.

Kumar, N., and I. Benbasat. 2006. "The Influence of Recommendations and Consumer Reviews on Evaluations of Websites." *Information Systems Research* 17: 425–39.

Kwon, O., S. Chu, and S.M. Choi. 2010. "Factors Influencing the Use of Consumer-Generated Product Reviews: An Information Search Perspective." In *Proceedings of the 2010 American Marketing Association Summer Marketing Educators' Conference,* ed. E. Iyer and R.A. Coulter. Boston, MA: American Marketing Association.

Kwon, O., and Y. Sung. 2010. "The Interplay of Self-Construal and Regulatory Focus on Consumer Evaluation of Online Product Reviews." In *Proceedings of the 2010 American Academy of Advertising,* ed. W. Lee, 73. Minneapolis, MN: American Academy of Advertising.

Lee, A.Y., and J.L. Aaker. 2004. "Bringing the Frame into Focus: The Influence of Regulatory Fit on Processing Fluency and Persuasion." *Journal of Personality and Social Psychology* 86: 205–18.

Liu, Y. 2006. "Word of Mouth for Movies: Its Dynamics and Impact on Box Office Revenue." *Journal of Marketing* 70: 74–89.

Mackie, D.M., L.T. Worth, and A.G. Asuncion. 1990. "Processing of Persuasive In-group Messages." *Journal of Personality and Social Psychology* 58: 812–22.

Mayer, R.C., J.H. Davis, and F.D. Schoorman. 1995. "An Integrative Model of Organizational Trust." *Academy of Management Review* 20: 709–34.

Metzger, M.J. 2007. "Making Sense of Credibility on the Web: Models for Evaluating Online Information and Recommendations for Future Research." *Journal of the American Society for Information Science and Technology* 58: 2078–91.

Mizerski, R.W. 1982. "An Attribution Explanation of the Disproportionate Influence of Unfavorable Information." *Journal of Consumer Research* 9: 301–10.

Mudambi, S.M., and D. Schuff. 2010. "What Makes a Helpful Online Review? A Study of Customer Reviews on Amazon.com." *MIS Quarterly* 34: 185–200.

Nelson, P. 1974. "Advertising as Information." *Journal of Political Economy* 82: 729–54.

Nielsen. 2009. "Nielsen Global Online Consumer Survey." Available at http:// content/uploads/2009/07/pr_global-study_07709.pdf, accessed April 3, 2011.

Ohanian, R. 1990. "Construction and Validation of a Scale to Measure Celebrity Endorsers' Perceived Expertise, Trustworthiness, and Attractiveness." *Journal of Advertising* 19: 39–52.

Opinion Research Corp. 2008. "Online Consumer Reviews Significantly Impact Consumer Purchasing Decisions." June 23. Available at www.opinionresearch.com/filesave/online_feedback_pr_final_6202008.pdf, accessed March 10, 2011.

Park, C., and T.M. Lee. 2009. "Information Direction, Website Reputation and eWOM Effect: A Moderating Role of Product Type." *Journal of Business Research* 62: 61–67.

Park, D., and S. Park. 2008. "The Multiple Source Effect of Online Consumer Reviews on Brand Evaluations: Test of the Risk Diversification Hypothesis." *Advances in Consumer Research* 35: 744–45.

Payne, J.W., J.R. Bettman, and E.J. Johnson. 1993. *The Adaptive Decision Maker.* New York: Cambridge University Press.

Petty, R.E., and J.T. Cacioppo. 1986. *Communication and Persuasion: Central and Peripheral Routes to Attitude Change.* New York: Springer-Verlag.

Petty, R.E, D.T. Wegener, and P.H. White. 1998. "Flexible Correction Processes in Social Judgment: Implications for Persuasion." *Social Cognition* 16: 93–113.

Pham, M.T., and T. Avnet. 2004. "Ideals and Oughts and the Reliance on Affect Versus Substance in Persuasion." *Journal of Consumer Research* 30: 503–18.

Punj, G.N., and R. Staelin. 1983. "A Model of Consumer Information Search Behavior for New Automobiles." *Journal of Consumer Research* 9: 366–80.

Reichheld, F.F. 2003. "The One Number You Need to Grow." *Harvard Business Review* 81: 46–54.

Rieh, S.Y. 2002. "Judgment of Information Quality and Cognitive Authority in the Web." *Journal of the American Society for Information Science and Technology* 53: 145–61.

Rosenthal, P.I. 1971. "Specificity, Verifiability, and Message Credibility." *Quarterly Journal of Speech* 57: 393–401.

Sen, S., and D. Lerman. 2007. "Why Are You Telling Me This? An Examination into Negative Consumer Reviews on the Web." *Journal of Interactive Marketing* 21: 76–94.

Sitkin, S.B., and N.L. Roth. 1993. "Explaining the Limited Effectiveness of Legalistic "Remedies" for Trust/Distrust." *Organization Science* 4: 367–92.

Skowronski, J.J., and D.E. Carlston. 1987. "Social Judgment and Social Memory: The Role of Cue Diagnosticity in Negativity, Positivity, and Extremity Biases." *Journal of Personality and Social Psychology* 52: 689–99.

Smith, D., S. Menon, and K. Sivakumar. 2005. "Online Peer and Editorial Recommendations, Trust, and Choice in Virtual Markets." *Journal of Interactive Marketing* 19: 15–37.

Srinivasan, N., and B.T. Ratchford. 1991. "An Empirical Test of a Model of External Search for Automobiles." *Journal of Consumer Research* 18: 233–42.

Stauss, B. 2000. "Using New Media for Customer Interaction: A Challenge for Relationship Marketing." In T. *Relationship Marketing,* ed. T. Hennig-Thurau and U. Hansen, 233–53. Berlin: Springer.

Strahilevitz, M., and J.G. Myers. 1998. "Donations to Charity as Purchase Incentives: How Well They Work May Depend on What You Are Trying to Sell." *Journal of Consumer Research* 24: 434–46.

11

Improving the Predictive Power of Consumer Research by Measuring Naturally Occurring Judgments

Maria L. Cronley, Frank R. Kardes,
Susan Powell Mantel, and Hélène Deval

When market researchers investigate consumers' attitudes toward their products, brands, or marketing tactics they typically collect written responses to standard attitude questions. While this method is a good measure of capturing the attitude reported, it does not address the process by which that attitude is created. How does the researcher know, for example, if the reported attitude is one that was formed naturally and simply reported or was created in response to the measurement question itself (i.e., measurement-induced)? Further, if the method cannot differentiate between naturally occurring attitudes and measurement-induced attitudes, how can we determine the behavioral implications of the attitude formation process? That is not to say that question-induced attitudes do not happen in the real world, but rather that it is important to understand the difference between the two formation processes in order to understand how attitudes affect behavior.

To put this into context, imagine a hypothetical shopping trip. Tyler is shopping for a party that he and his roommates, John and Allen, are having in a few days. When he gets to the store, he notices a new brand of salsa and calls home to ask for advice. Now, consider two possible endings to this story. In the first ending, John picks up the phone, upon hearing the question "What do you think about the new brand of X Salsa?" John responds immediately, "Oh, I really wanted to try that brand." Conversely, in the second ending, Allen picks up the phone. In response to the same question, Allen takes a few seconds to remember elements of an advertisement that he recently saw for the brand including the spokesperson, the look of the salsa, and the apparent delight of the actors eating the salsa. As he thinks about the advertisement, he decides that Brand X Salsa would be a good brand to try and says, "Let's try it." In the first case, John is reporting an existing attitude that was naturally formed prior to the attitude question, but in the second case Allen is reporting an attitude that is question-induced and may never have been formed if the question had not been posed. If instead of a roommate calling from the store, the request for an attitude came from a market researcher, the two responses would be indistinguishable, and yet Allen's attitude may never have been formed without the researcher's question.

In industry and in academia, attitude researchers frequently assume that their results reflect the operation of naturally occurring judgment processes rather than measurement-induced judgment processes. Nonetheless, measurement effects are fairly common in attitude research (Feldman and Lynch 1988; Machin and Fitzsimons 2005; Weaver and Schwarz 2008). Hence, a procedure is needed for discriminating between naturally occurring versus measurement-induced judgment processes. Unfortunately, marketing academics often prefer to believe that their research is uncontaminated by measurement-induced effects, and consequently marketing academics are highly resistant to research on spontaneous or naturally occurring judgment processes. In our experience, marketing practitioners are much more open to this type of research. Hence, we wrote this chapter for marketing practitioners who seek to derive greater predictive and explanatory power from their attitude research by discriminating between naturally occurring and measurement-induced judgment processes.

Measuring Naturally Occurring Attitudes

Fazio, Lenn, and Effrein (1983; see also Kardes, Cronley, and Kim 2006) developed a useful procedure for discriminating between naturally or spontaneously formed versus measurement-induced attitudes that utilizes a two-step response latency method. This procedure involves randomly assigning participants to separate attitude consolidation versus no consolidation conditions and measuring the speed with which participants can indicate their evaluations of an attitude object (e.g., a product, service, ad, spokesperson, salesperson). Response speed is measured in milliseconds and is recorded automatically by a computer in a response latency task. In attitude consolidation conditions, consumers indicate their attitudes on standard attitude scales presented in a paper-and-pencil questionnaire before responding to a computer-based response latency task. This procedure requires consumers to think about, reflect on, and integrate information and knowledge about the attitude object and thus crystallize their attitudes before their response times are measured. By contrast, in no-consolidation conditions, consumers perform the computer-based response latency task before responding to the paper-and-pencil standard attitude scales. Response times are faster in consolidation than in no-consolidation conditions when measurement-induced attitudes are formed. However, response latencies do not differ as a function of the consolidation manipulation when spontaneously or naturally occurring attitudes are formed.

Fazio is best known for his work on attitude accessibility (i.e., the speed and ease with which existing attitudes are drawn from memory) and attitude-behavior correspondence (Fazio 1989, 1995; Fazio, Powell, and Williams 1989). This research also requires the use of a computer-based response latency methodology. However, a consolidation manipulation is not used because the focus is on familiar attitude objects that are associated with a previously formed evaluation. As the strength of the object-evaluation association increases, response latencies to attitudinal inquiries decrease and attitude-behavior correspondence increases. There is no need to perform a consolidation manipulation for familiar attitude objects that have been evaluated previously.

For novel objects and for relatively unfamiliar objects, however, a consolidation manipulation is crucial for distinguishing between spontaneously formed attitudes and measurement-induced attitudes. This distinction is important because spontaneous naturally formed attitudes have a greater influence on related judgments and behaviors, relative to measurement-induced attitudes (Fazio et al. 1983). Measurement-induced attitudes are mere epiphenomena that would not exist if participants had not been exposed to standard attitude scales. Fazio and colleagues (1983) refer to measurement-induced attitudes as non-attitudes due to their artificial status. It should be emphasized that different computer-based response latency tasks are needed to measure attitude accessibility and to measure spontaneous, naturally occurring attitude formation. An attitude consolidation manipulation is needed to measure spontaneous attitude formation, but not to measure attitude accessibility.

The Attitude Formation Debate

The marketing academic literature exhibits a great deal of confusion and conflicting ideas about how attitudes are formed. As a way of framing some of this debate, the process by which an attitude is formed has been described by two conflicting hypotheses: automaticity versus functionality. The first hypothesis (automaticity) assumes that attitudes are formed quickly, easily, and routinely, and the second hypothesis (functionality) assumes that attitude formation requires the goal-dependent expenditure of cognitive resources. We will review the literature that supports each hypothesis as well as discuss four experiments that test the two hypotheses against each other (Cronley, Mantel, and Kardes 2010). Strong support for the functionality hypothesis was found across all four experiments.

The Automaticity Hypothesis

Several streams of marketing academic research seek to explain how attitudes are formed. Most of these models, such as the Elaboration Likelihood Model (ELM), the Heuristic-Systematic Model (HSM), and the System 1-System 2 Model, suggest that consumers generally desire to form attitudes and do so spontaneously or naturally via a dual information processing system. Most dual-process models (Chaiken and Trope 1999; Evans 2008; Kahneman 2003; Kahneman and Frederick 2002; Stanovich and West 2000, 2002) assume that information processing is sometimes performed quickly and effortlessly (the peripheral, heuristic, or system 1 routes), and sometimes performed slowly and deliberately (the central, systematic, or system 2 routes). For example, quick and effortless system 1 processes are assumed to operate routinely and continuously, like perceptual processes, whereas slow and deliberate high-effort system 2 processes are assumed to monitor and override system 1 processes when the output conflicts with those of system 2. According to Kahneman, "Because the overall capacity for mental effort is limited, effortful processes tend to disrupt each other, whereas effortless processes neither cause nor suffer much interference when combined with other tasks" (2003, 698). Kahneman suggests that because system 1 is effortless and difficult to disrupt, it is typically the default process. By contrast, effortful system 2 operations occur only given sufficient motivation and ability to deliberate.

To the extent that system 1 processes map onto the peripheral route of the Elaboration Likelihood Model (Petty, Cacioppo, and Schumann 1983; Petty and Wegener 1999; Wheeler, Petty, and Bizer 2005), and the heuristic route of the Heuristic-Systematic Model (Chen and Chaiken 1999; Maheswaran, Mackie, and Chaiken 1992; Ratneshwar and Chaiken 1991), the peripheral route and the heuristic route should be followed automatically and these low-effort, shallow-processing routes should be the default routes to persuasion. Hence, peripheral cues (e.g., moods, feelings) and persuasion heuristics (e.g., "length implies strength," "experts are usually correct," "consensus implies validity") should always influence attitudes, except when high-effort processes override their influence. Inasmuch as system 2 processes map onto the central route of the ELM and the systematic route of the HSM, high levels of motivation (e.g., involvement, need for cognition, need to evaluate) and ability to elaborate (e.g., time, knowledge, repetition) should increase the influence of strong message arguments and decrease the influence of weak peripheral cues.

Consistent with this analysis, Bargh and colleagues (1992) suggest that all attitudes, regardless of their accessibility, are activated automatically on the mere presence or mention of an attitude object. Thus, according to all of these models, a person forms some kind of attitude spontaneously or naturally at the time of stimulus presentation. Using the priming procedure developed by Fazio and colleagues (1986) and Bargh and colleagues (1992) found that evaluative response latencies to adjectives with unambiguous evaluative implications were faster when those adjectives were immediately preceded by attitude objects with similar (versus dissimilar) evaluative implications. Bargh and colleagues (1992) concluded that automatic attitude activation occurs for all attitudes, and that the effect is not limited to attitudes high in accessibility. However, Fazio (1993) reanalyzed these results and demonstrated that automatic attitude activation occurs only for highly accessible attitudes, consistent with the implications of the functionality hypothesis.

The Functionality Hypothesis

According to the functionality hypothesis, consumers form attitudes spontaneously or naturally only when it is functional or beneficial for them to do so (Fazio 1995; Fazio et al. 1983). Attitudes can reduce ambiguity and confusion, orient consumers toward important objects and events, simplify decision making, and increase the likelihood of having pleasant everyday experiences. Having a previously formed evaluation of a product or brand stored in memory provides consumers with a "ready aid" for decision making whenever the product is encountered (the knowledge function of Katz [1960] or the object appraisal function of Smith, Bruner, and White [1956]). Instead of reflecting on their evaluations, consumers saved the time- and energy-consuming process of deciding how to respond each and every time the product is encountered.

Research shows that objects associated with previously formed, highly accessible attitudes draw attention automatically and facilitate quick and efficient orienting responses (Roskos-Ewoldsen and Fazio 1992). Previously formed attitudes also facilitate categorization of multiply categorizable objects (Smith, Fazio, and Cejka 1996). Many objects can be categorized in multiple ways. For example, yogurt can be categorized as a health food or a dairy product. Sunbathing can be categorized as a fun activity or as an activity that can lead to cancer. Categories associated with previously formed accessible attitudes are more influential than categories associated with inaccessible or unformed attitudes. Hence, when attitudes toward health food products are primed via repeated questioning, yogurt is more likely to be categorized as a health food. The implication here is that the context information available at the time that the attitude is formed is likely to influence the perception and categorization of the attitude object. Therefore, understanding the processes by which the attitude is formed is helpful in understanding how that attitude will be perceived and, in turn, how that attitude will influence subsequent judgments and behavior.

Stored attitudes also facilitate preference and choice while reducing autonomic reactivity due to the expenditure of cognitive effort (Blascovich et al. 1993; Fazio, Blascovich, and Driscoll 1992). In one study, subjects either indicated their attitudes toward several abstract paintings or performed a color-naming task for the same set of paintings. Later, subjects were asked to indicate their preferences between pairs of paintings. Decision times were faster and stress levels were lower when attitudes were previously reported and therefore previously formed compared to those who did not form an attitude (due to color-naming task).

Previously formed attitudes also free up cognitive resources for other more important concerns (Fazio and Powell 1997). Freshman having previously formed attitudes toward academic topics (i.e., possible majors, possible courses to take) enjoyed better mental and physical health, compared to their counterparts without previously formed attitudes. Hence, consistent with the functionality hypothesis, previously formed attitudes (a) orient attention toward hedonically relevant objects (Roskos-Ewoldsen and Fazio, 1992); (b) facilitate categorization (Smith et al. 1996); (c) simplify decision making and reduce the stress associated with it (Blascovich et al. 1993; Fazio, Herr, and Powell 1992); and (d) improve coping (Fazio and Powell 1997).

The distinction between spontaneous or natural versus measurement-induced attitude formation is based on the distinction between the automaticity hypothesis and the functionality hypothesis. While the former suggests that, at the least, some form of low-effort processing is the default and is always active, thereby producing attitudes spontaneously and effortlessly, the latter suggests that people may not always generate an attitude about an object the moment it is encountered and forming an attitude spontaneously or naturally requires consumers to reflect on and integrate information and knowledge bearing on the attitude object. The functionality hypothesis suggests that consumers are likely to perform these cognitive activities only when they expect the resulting attitude to facilitate performance on a future judgment or choice task. For example, spontaneous attitude formation is more likely when consumers expect to receive future inquiries about their attitudes toward an object or when consumers expect to receive future opportunities to consume, talk about, or use the object (Fazio et al. 1983).

To distinguish between spontaneously or naturally formed versus measurement-induced attitudes, Fazio and colleagues (1983) gave participants descriptions of five novel word-game puzzles. Half of the participants were led to expect that it would be useful or functional to form attitudes toward each of the puzzles and half were given no expectation of functional need. In consolidation conditions, participants were asked to indicate their attitudes toward each of the five puzzles on standard paper-and-pencil attitude scales prior to performing the response latency task. This task forced participants to consolidate their responses, feelings, and knowledge about each puzzle type (i.e., form an attitude). In no-consolidation conditions participants did not perform this consolidation exercise, but instead performed the response latency task before receiving the standard attitude scales. For the response latency task, participants received inquiries about each puzzle type displayed on a monitor and were asked to indicate how much they liked or disliked each puzzle type by pressing a key labeled "yes" or a key labeled "no" to evaluative yes/no questions as quickly and as accurately as possible. Response latencies in milliseconds were recorded automatically. The results showed that when spontaneous attitude formation was unlikely, response latencies were faster in consolidation conditions than in no-consolidation conditions. However, when spontaneous attitude formation was likely, either due to the expectation of future questioning (experiment 1) or due to the expectation of future usage of the puzzle (experiment 2), response latencies did not differ as a function of the consolidation versus no-consolidation manipulation.

This paradigm (Fazio et al. 1983) provides a useful technique for determining the conditions under which naturally occurring attitude formation is likely to occur, and, thus, to investigate the two opposing hypotheses: automaticity versus functionality. As issue relevance increases, the functional utility of naturally forming an attitude (Fazio 1989, 1995) and the likelihood of following the central route to persuasion should also increase (Chen and Chaiken 1999; Maheswaran et al. 1992; Petty et al. 1983; Petty and Wegener 1999; Ratneshwar and Chaiken 1991; Wheeler et al. 2005). Therefore, the functionality hypothesis (but not the automaticity hypothesis) would suggest that as the perceived issue relevance increases, the likelihood that an attitude will be formed spontaneously or naturally (rather than being measurement-induced) should also increase.

One way to increase issue relevance is via accuracy motivation (Chaiken 1980; Cronley et al. 2005; Maheswaran et al. 1992; Petty, Harkins, and Williams 1980; Stapel, Koomen, and Zeelenberg 1998). When consumers expect to share, explain, or justify their judgments and decisions to others, they are more likely to process information extensively and deeply, and are therefore more likely to follow the central route to persuasion and form subsequent attitudes spontaneously.

Issue relevance is also influenced by dispositional variability in the need to evaluate, a personality trait that reflects a persons' tendency to create and hold attitudes. Need to evaluate is "the chronic tendency to engage in evaluative responding" (Jarvis and Petty 1996, 172). When the need to evaluate is high, consumers generate a greater number of evaluative thoughts and hold clearly defined attitudes on a greater variety of topics. Such individuals are quick to judge, opinionated, and likely to view their opinions as functional or useful. Therefore, they are more likely to follow the central route to persuasion and naturally form attitudes compared to their low need to evaluate counterparts (Tormala and Petty 2001).

The route to persuasion is also influenced by the ability or opportunity to process information carefully (Cacioppo and Petty 1985; Moore, Hausknecht, and Thamodaran 1986; Petty, Wells, and Brock 1976; Sanbonmatsu and Kardes 1988). Time pressure, distraction, high levels of physiological arousal, and multiple task demands have been shown to decrease the likelihood of elaborative processing even when consumers are motivated to deliberate. Thus, according to the functionality hypothesis, internal motivation to evaluate will only lead to spontaneous, natural attitude formation when participants also have the ability to fully process the available information.

Hence, to summarize, the automaticity hypothesis suggests that the consolidation manipulation should have no effect on response latencies regardless of the level of issue relevance or opportunity to process. This is because naturally occurring or spontaneous attitude formation is assumed to occur regardless of which route to persuasion consumers are likely to follow. The presumed default route to persuasion (system 1, peripheral route, or heuristic route) suggests that consumers process the information quickly and effortlessly in order to spontaneously form attitudes even though the stimulus is not deeply processed. Similarly, the effortful route to persuasion (system 2, central route, systematic route) suggests that consumers process data fully and deeply in order to spontaneously form attitudes. Conversely, the functionality hypothesis suggests that the consolidation manipulation should have a significant effect on response latencies when issue relevance is low, when the need to evaluate is low, or when the ability to elaborate is low, because natural, spontaneous attitude formation is unlikely to occur when consumers follow the low-effort peripheral or heuristic routes to persuasion. The functionality hypothesis also suggests that the consolidation manipulation will have no effect on response latencies when consumers are likely to follow the high-effort central or systematic routes to persuasion.

Naturally Occurring Judgment Processes in Persuasion

Cronley and colleagues (2010) set out to test the automaticity hypothesis versus the functionality hypothesis using the (no) consolidation, response latency procedure created by Fazio and colleagues (1983; see also, Kardes et al. 2006). Using mock ads for Breathe Right clear nasal strips and for the KitchenAid stand mixer, a 2 (high or low accuracy motivation) × 2 (celebrity or noncelebrity endorser) × 2 (consolidation or no-consolidation) with a continuous variable (need to evaluate) mixed design was used in conjunction with a response latency task. Results were pooled across replicates because similar results were observed for both products. The attitudes reported were consistent with past research on the dual process models of persuasion. When accuracy motivation was high, participants followed the central/systematic route to persuasion and type of endorser had no effect on brand attitudes. When accuracy motivation was low, participants followed the peripheral/heuristic route to persuasion and more favorable brand attitudes were formed when celebrity (versus noncelebrity) endorsers were presented.

More importantly, response latencies were consistent with the functionality hypothesis. That is, response times were slower in the no-consolidation/low accuracy motivation/low need to evaluate condition than in the remaining conditions. This pattern of results indicates that when the motivation to process information carefully is low, either due to low accuracy motivation or due to a low need to evaluate, measurement-induced brand attitudes are formed. When the motivation to process information carefully is high, consumers are likely to form brand attitudes spontaneously. Although extensive prior research has shown that peripheral cues and heuristic cues influence attitude favorableness when peripheral/heuristic route processing is likely (for a review, see Chaiken and Trope 1999), prior research has not examined whether attitude formation occurs naturally or due to the measurement task when consumers follow the peripheral/heuristic route to persuasion. Consistent with the implications of the functionality hypothesis, these results suggest that naturally occurring or spontaneous attitude formation is likely when consumers follow the high-effort central/systematic route, but not when they follow the low-effort peripheral/ heuristic route.

To test the generalizability of these results, Cronley and colleagues (2010) conducted a follow-up experiment, manipulating cognitive load (full attention versus divided attention) to vary the ability to process information carefully. The dispositional variable of need to evaluate was again included. Different products (Internet website home pages for PayPal.com and NewJob.com) and a different peripheral/heuristic cue were used. Also, similar results were again observed for both products. The peripheral/heuristic cue was manipulated via a website counter that provided information about the popularity of the service. A high counter number (878,965 visits) was used in high popularity conditions, and a low counter number (513 visits) was used in low popularity conditions. All the other elements of the home pages were held constant.

A divided-attention distraction task was used to manipulate cognitive load (Gilbert 1989; Gilbert, Tafarodi, and Malone 1993). In high cognitive load conditions, while viewing each website for 30 seconds, participants were instructed to press a button whenever the number "5" appeared in a number string at the bottom of the monitor. In low cognitive load conditions, participants were not instructed to perform this digit detection task.

Results that were consistent with previous research on the dual process models of persuasion were found. Specifically, a significant cognitive load by peripheral/heuristic cue interaction was found on brand attitude favorableness. In high cognitive load conditions, participants followed the peripheral/heuristic route to persuasion, and more favorable brand attitudes were formed in high popularity than in low popularity conditions. In low cognitive load conditions, participants followed the central/systematic route to persuasion, and no effect for the peripheral/heuristic cue was found.

More importantly, the response latencies were consistent with the functionality hypothesis (not the automaticity hypothesis). That is, slower response latencies were found in the no-consolidation/high cognitive load/low need to evaluate condition than in the remaining experimental conditions. This pattern suggests that when consumers follow the peripheral/heuristic route to persuasion, either due to high cognitive load or due to a low need to evaluate, they are unlikely to form attitudes unless they are forced to do so by exposure to standard attitude scales provided in the consolidation task. This suggests that attitudes formed via the peripheral/heuristic route to persuasion are measurement-induced. When consumers follow the central/systematic route to persuasion, however, spontaneous attitude formation is likely. Considered together, the results of both experiments imply that attitude formation requires cognitive resources and naturally occurring or spontaneous attitude formation is likely only when consumers expect attitudes to be useful for some future task.

Naturally Occurring Judgment Processes in Consumer Choice

The two experiments described above are consistent with the functionality hypothesis and suggest that attitudes are only formed spontaneously when consumers are motivated and able to process brand information via slow, deliberative, and effortful central/systematic processing. Conversely, reported attitudes are measurement-induced when the dual process model predicts quick, effortless, peripheral/heuristic processing. However, this does not mean that the peripheral/heuristic route to persuasion is irrelevant to the brand manager. Remember the hypothetical shopping trip described at the beginning of this chapter. In the second ending to the story, Allen constructed his attitude in response to the question posed by Tyler. In this case, the peripheral route, question-induced attitude formation is relevant to the buying behavior because Tyler's purchase is likely to have been influenced by Allen's measurement-induced attitude. Therefore, the brand manager is likely to be interested in how the timing of attitude formation, whether naturally occurring or measurement-induced, influences both the attitude itself and the subsequent purchase behavior. Specifically, will attitudes formed spontaneously influence purchase decisions differently than attitudes that are only formed in response to an inquiry? For question-induced attitudes, will the attitude be based on information available at the time of stimulus presentation or information available at the time of attitude formation? Extending the functionality hypothesis, we suspect that spontaneously formed attitudes should be formed based on information available at the time of stimulus presentation and have a greater influence on consumer choice than measurement-induced attitudes, which should be formed based on recallable memories of the stimulus presentation as well as information present at the time of attitude measurement.

To test this hypothesis, U.S. consumers were shown two unfamiliar but real Canadian candy bars, Jersey Milk and Indulge (Cronley et al. 2010). Jersey Milk was a flat rectangular candy bar that was slightly larger than the oblong block chocolate bar, Indulge. Participants were shown both bars early in the experiment, then the bars were removed from the immediate area and the consolidation/response latency method was used to collect attitude and response latency measures. At the beginning of the response latency task (without the candy bars in sight), the consumers were provided the two brand names and asked to choose one of the two chocolate bars to take home as payment for their time.

Consistent with the results of the first two experiments, a significant consolidation by need to evaluate interaction was found. When the need to evaluate was low, response latencies were faster in consolidation than in no-consolidation conditions. When the need to evaluate was high, the consolidation manipulation had no effect on response latencies. This pattern suggests that measurement-induced attitudes were formed when the need to evaluate was low, and naturally occurring attitudes were formed when it was high.

More importantly, the results also showed a difference in actual choice behavior depending on when the attitude was formed. Specifically, those who were likely to have spontaneously formed their attitudes during product examination chose the candy bar that was perceptively larger (i.e., Jersey Milk). Conversely, those who were not likely to have formed their attitude prior to the candy selection question were 2.4 times more likely to choose the candy bar with the more pleasant-sounding name (i.e., Indulge). Thus it appears that information present at the time of choice (i.e., the more appealing brand name) was more influential than information only present during the viewing of the candy bars (i.e., the relative size) in determining the outcome of the choice for those who had not previously formed an attitude. The reverse is true (i.e., size appears to be more important) for those who spontaneously formed their attitude when they viewed the candy bars.

Furthermore, analyses of attitude-choice correlations (i.e., the positive relationship between the reported brand attitude and the subsequent candy bar choice) showed that the correlations were greater in conditions of spontaneously formed (versus measurement-induced) attitudes across both small and large candy bars. This suggests that spontaneously formed attitudes resulted in strong, significant attitude-behavior correlations, while measurement-induced attitudes resulted in weak, nonsignificant correlations. Hence, measurement-induced attitudes have little or no influence on choice, whereas spontaneously formed attitudes have a strong impact on choice.

In a follow-up experiment, a new within-subject manipulation of consolidation was developed and tested in order to examine the effects of attitude relevance, attitude accessibility, and incidental processing on spontaneous versus measurement-induced attitude formation and on recall. In the high attitude relevance condition, participants were asked to imagine that they recently moved to a new house and needed to choose a brand of interior house paint (adapted from Snyder and Kendzierski 1982). Further, they were told that a manufacturer was trying to decide whether or not to launch a new brand of house paint and was seeking their input on the brand and that their opinion was extremely important and relevant and would potentially affect whether the new brand was marketed. In the high attitude accessibility condition, participants were asked to organize their thoughts and views (adapted from Snyder and Kendzierski 1982). In this condition, participants typed out their thoughts about interior wall paint before examining the advertisement. In the incidental processing condition (or the low attitude relevance/low attitude accessibility control condition), participants were asked to examine an advertisement for an interior house paint and to count the different aesthetic elements used in the ad (e.g., the typefaces, colors, pictures, words). They were told that the advertiser was interested in the aesthetic appeal of the advertisement.

The within-subject manipulation of consolidation was performed by asking participants to indicate their brand evaluations on four five-point attitude scales, which were rotated (good/bad, like/dislike, satisfied/unsatisfied, favorable/unfavorable). Response latencies in milliseconds were recorded automatically. Mean response latencies to attitudes scales 2 through 4 were compared to the response latency to attitude scale 1. When naturally occurring or spontaneous brand attitudes are formed during ad evaluation, the difference in response latencies should approach zero. That is, relatively fast response latencies should be observed across all four attitude scales. On the other hand, relatively large differences in response times should be observed when measurement-induced attitudes are formed because slow response latencies should be observed for attitude scale 1, and faster response latencies should be observed on the subsequent attitude scales (2 through 4) because repeated measurement produces consolidation.

The results revealed that the difference in response latencies between the first attitude and the latter attitudes asked were nonsignificant when attitude relevance was high. However, this difference was significant when attitude accessibility was high, and an even larger difference was found in the incidental processing control condition. This pattern suggests that spontaneous attitude formation is likely when attitude relevance is high, but not in the remaining conditions. This effect was qualified by an interaction with the need to evaluate. When attitude relevance was high, the need to evaluate had no effect on response latencies. When attitude accessibility was high, differences in response latencies were greater when the need to evaluate was low rather than high. These differences were even more pronounced in incidental processing conditions. This pattern of results suggests that when attitude accessibility is high or when incidental processing is likely, spontaneous attitude formation is more likely only when the need to evaluate is high, rather than low.

Next, reported recall was evaluated and coded as being brand-related (i.e., elements relevant to the attributes of the paint) or ad-related (i.e., elements relevant to the execution of the advertisement). Brand-related recall was four times more likely to be reported when spontaneous attitude formation was likely (high attitude relevance or high need to evaluate) or when attitude accessibility was high. Only the low need to evaluate/incidental processing participants were more likely to report ad-focused recall. Finally, there was a significant correlation between the reported attitude and the reported recall among consumers with measurement-induced attitudes, suggesting that the reported attitude is formed, at least partially, based on memories that were recalled during the measurement task. Conversely, there was a low correlation between the reported attitudes and the reported recall for those who spontaneously formed their attitude, indicating that they did not specifically recall elements of the original stimulus in order to report their attitude.

Combining the response latency results with the recall results, the conclusion that can be drawn is that when attitude accessibility is high, consumers are likely to engage in and think about the advertisement and store information about the brand; however, if the category is not relevant to that consumer, they will not naturally form an attitude about the brand. This indicates that attitude relevance, attitude accessibility, and spontaneous attitude formation are conceptually and empirically distinct.

Conclusion

Considered together, the results of research by Cronley and colleagues (2010) provide strong support for the functionality hypothesis and contradict the implications of the automaticity hypothesis. Attitude formation toward novel or unfamiliar products and services requires effort and is influenced heavily by information processing goals and by cognitive ability to process information. Spontaneous or naturally occurring attitude formation is likely when consumers follow the high-effort central/systematic route to persuasion, but not when they follow the low-effort peripheral/heuristic route to persuasion.

Naturally occurring or spontaneously formed attitudes are also consequential, and they exert a powerful influence on choice. Measurement-induced attitudes, on the other hand, have little or no influence on choice. Furthermore, whereas spontaneously formed attitudes are more likely to be formed on information available at the time of stimulus presentation, question-induced attitudes are likely to be constructed on the basis of information available at the time of measurement in addition to information recalled. Thus marketers must be creative in order to influence these constructed attitudes.

The finding that the central/systematic route to persuasion produces spontaneously formed attitudes, and that the peripheral/heuristic route to persuasion produces measurement-induced attitudes might suggest to some that there is only one route to attitude change: the central route. This strong interpretation is consistent with Kruglanski and Orehek's (2007) view that dual-process models have outlived their usefulness and that a single-process model—the if-then reasoning rule-based unimodel—captures persuasion processes in all of their richness and complexity. We prefer a weaker interpretation, and suggest that question-induced or measurement-induced attitudes can occur in natural settings. The formation of question-induced attitudes does not just require exposure to a battery of survey instruments administered in a marketing research setting. In natural settings, including both face-to-face interactions (e.g., at point of sale or in recommendation situations) and online interactions (e.g., blogging, third-party review sites, social networking contexts), consumers frequently ask other consumers about their opinions about various products and services. Rather than voicing no opinion, many consumers are willing and eager to construct a new opinion, on the spot, in response to such inquiries.

Although these new opinions did not exist in any a priori fashion and were not retrieved from memory, they can, under some circumstances, influence subsequent judgments and behaviors (Machin and Fitzsimons 2005).

The research reviewed in this chapter also demonstrates that Fazio and colleagues' (1983) consolidation procedure can be applied gainfully to determine the effects of marketing variables on spontaneous versus measurement-induced attitude formation. It should be emphasized that this procedure assesses attitude formation processes rather than attitude strength. The within-subject consolidation manipulation (used in experiment 4 of Cronley et al. 2010) has little effect on attitude strength because the development of attitude strength requires direct experience (Fazio 1989, 1995); extensive knowledge (Fabrigar et al. 2006), and high levels of attitude certainty due to resistance to counterattitudinal information (Petrocelli, Tormala, and Rucker 2007). Furthermore, this experiment demonstrated that attitude accessibility alone does not produce a higher likelihood of spontaneous attitude formation. Instead, a motivation to process (e.g., a personally relevant category or a high need to evaluate) is needed before spontaneous attitude formation is likely. Said more simply, attitude relevance, attitude accessibility, and spontaneous attitude formation are conceptually and empirically distinct. Hence, other procedures are more appropriate for assessing attitude strength (see Fabrigar et al. 2006; Fazio 1989, 1995; Petrocelli et al. 2007).

Marketers can use these results in evaluating their communication plans. For example, some manufacturers pay a premium to place their advertisement in proximity of an article or news story that references the product category. The marketer assumes that the article or news story will prime the category and the advertisement will be easier to process—thus producing central route processing and more thoughtful attitude formation. This research suggests that priming of the category may make the processing easier and encourage brand based information to be stored in memory, but the consumer is no more likely to form an attitude about the product unless they see the product as relevant. Further, without a spontaneously formed attitude, choice is unlikely to be correlated with attitudes that are formed later. Therefore, manufacturers may want to reconsider paying a premium to place advertisements in proximity to a category reference and instead focus on making the product relevant to the viewer.

The Fazio and colleagues' (1983) consolidation and response latency procedure should be used to determine what types of advertising executions are likely to stimulate thinking about the functional benefits of attitudes and to encourage spontaneous attitude formation. Thought-provoking ad executions, such as comparative advertising (Dröge 1989); mystery ads (Fazio et al. 1992); self-referencing (Escalas 2007); and the use of curiosity-arousing rhetorical questions (Ahluwalia et al. 2004) might be particularly effective in eliciting spontaneous attitude formation.

Discriminating between naturally occurring and measurement-induced attitude can also enhance the ability to predict consumer choices in the marketplace. Recent research shows that standard attitude scales predict shareholder value (Mizik and Jacobson 2008). Our research suggests that naturally occurring attitudes should be even more predictive of shareholder value, and that measurement-induced attitudes should be less predictive. In principle, the consolidation and response latency paradigm can be adapted to any type of judgment. For example, customer satisfaction scores have also been shown to predict stock prices (Fornell et al. 2006). Because satisfaction scores are also susceptible to measurement effects, it would be useful to distinguish between naturally occurring satisfaction judgments and measurement-induced satisfaction judgments. The consolidation and response latency procedure enables marketers to distinguish between naturally occurring judgments and measurement-induced judgments. The former type of judgment predicts and controls behavior, whereas the latter type introduces noise that diminishes predictive accuracy and reduces explanatory power. The consolidation and response latency procedure also enables marketers to determine if a particular marketing variable is effective in producing naturally occurring judgment processes that occur in samples exposed to judgment measures and to segments receiving no such measures. Hence, the procedure affords marketers the ability to address questions that cannot be addressed through the use of standard scales and measures.

References

Ahluwalia, R., R.E. Burnkrant, D.G. Mick, and M. Brucks 2004. "Answering Questions About Questions: A Persuasion Knowledge Perspective for Understanding the Effects of Rhetorical Questions." *Journal of Consumer Research* 31: 26–42.

Bargh, J.A., S. Chaiken, R. Govender, and F. Pratto. 1992. "The Generality of the Automatic Attitude Activation Effect." *Journal of Personality and Social Psychology* 62: 893–912.

Blascovich, J., J.M. Ernst, J. Tomaka, R.M. Kelsey, K.L. Salomon, and R.H. Fazio. 1993. "Attitude Accessibility as a Moderator of Autonomic Reactivity During Decision Making." *Journal of Personality and Social Psychology* 64: 165–76.

Cacioppo, J.T., and R.E. Petty. 1985. "Central and Peripheral Routes to Persuasion: The Role of Message Repetition." In *Psychological Processes and Advertising Effects: Theory, Research, and Application,* ed. L.F. Alwitt and A.A. Mitchell, 91–111. Hillsdale, NJ: Lawrence Erlbaum.

Chaiken, S. 1980. "Heuristic Versus Systematic Information-Processing and the Use of Source Versus Message Cues in Persuasion." *Journal of Personality and Social Psychology* 39: 752–66.

Chaiken, S., and Y. Trope, eds. 1999. *Dual-Process Theories in Social Psychology.* New York: Guilford Press.

Chen, S., and S. Chaiken. 1999. "The Heuristic-Systematic Model in Its Broader Context." In *Dual-Process Theories in Social Psychology*, ed. S. Chaiken and Y. Trope, 73–96. New York: Guilford Press.

Cronley, M., S.P. Mantel, and F.R. Kardes. 2010. "Effects of Accuracy Motivation and Need to Evaluate on Mode of Attitude Formation and Attitude-Behavior Consistency." *Journal of Consumer Psychology* 20: 274–81.

Cronley, M.L., S.S. Posavac, T. Meyer, F.R. Kardes, and J.J. Kellaris 2005. "A Selective Hypothesis Testing Perspective on Price-Quality Inference and Inference-Based Choice." *Journal of Consumer Psychology* 15: 159–69.

Dröge, C. 1989. "Shaping the Route to Attitude Change: Central Versus Peripheral Processing Through Comparative Versus Noncomparative Advertising." *Journal of Marketing Research* 26: 193–204.

Escalas, J.E. 2007. "Self-Referencing and Persuasion: Narrative Transportation Versus Analytical Elaboration." *Journal of Consumer Research* 33: 421–29.

Evans, J.S.B.T. 2008. "Dual-Processing Accounts of Reasoning, Judgment, and Social Cognition." *Annual Review of Psychology* 59: 255–78.

Fabrigar, L.R., R.E. Petty, S.M. Smith, and S.L.J. Crites. 2006. "Understanding Knowledge Effects on Attitude-Behavior Consistency: The Role of Relevance, Complexity, and Amount of Knowledge." *Journal of Personality and Social Psychology* 90: 556–77.

Fazio, R.H. 1989. "On the Power and Functionality of Attitudes: The Role of Attitude Accessibility." In *Attitude Structure and Function,* ed. A.R. Pratkanis, S.J. Breckler, and A.G. Greenwald, 153–79. Hillsdale, NJ: Lawrence Erlbaum.

———. 1993. "Variability in the Likelihood of Automatic Attitude Activation: Data Reanalysis and Commentary on Bargh, Chaiken, Govender, and Pratto (1992)." *Journal of Personality and Social Psychology* 64: 753–58.

———. 1995. "Attitudes as Object-Evaluation Associations: Determinants, Consequences, and Correlates of Attitude Accessibility." In *Attitude Strength: Antecedents and Consequences,* ed. R.E. Petty and J.A. Krosnick, 247–82. Hillsdale, NJ: Lawrence Erlbaum.

Fazio, R.H., J. Blascovich, and D.M. Driscoll. 1992. "On the Functional Value of Attitudes: The Influence of Accessible Attitudes on the Ease and Quality of Decision Making." *Personality and Social Psychology Bulletin* 18: 388–401.

Fazio, R.H., P.M. Herr, and M.C. Powell. 1992. "On the Development and Strength of Category-Brand Associations in Memory: The Case of Mystery Ads." *Journal of Consumer Psychology* 1: 1–13.

Fazio, R.H., T.M. Lenn, and E.A. Effrein. 1983. "Spontaneous Attitude Formation." *Social Cognition* 2: 217–34.

Fazio, R.H., and M.C. Powell. 1997. "On the Value of Knowing One's Likes and Dislikes: Attitude Accessibility, Stress, and Health in College." *Psychological Science* 8: 430–36.

Fazio, R.H., M.C. Powell, and C.J. Williams. 1989. "The Role of Attitude Accessibility in the Attitude-to-Behavior Process." *Journal of Consumer Research* 16: 280–88.

Fazio, R.H., D.M. Sanbonmatsu, M.C. Powell, and F.R. Kardes. 1986. "On the Automatic Activation of Attitudes." *Journal of Personality and Social Psychology* 50: 229–38.

Feldman, J.M., and J.G. Lynch. 1988. "Self-Generated Validity and Other Effects of Measurement on Belief, Attitude, Intention, and Behavior." *Journal of Applied Psychology* 73: 421–35.

Fornell, C., S. Mithas, F.V. Morgeson III, and M.S. Krishnan. 2006. "Customer Satisfaction and Stock Prices: High Returns, Low Risk." *Journal of Marketing* 70: 3–14.

Gilbert, D.T. 1989. "Thinking Lightly About Others: Automatic Components of the Social Inference Process." In *Unintended Thought,* ed. J.S. Uleman and J.A. Bargh, 189–211. New York: Guilford Press.

Gilbert, D.T., R.W. Tafarodi, and P.S. Malone. 1993. "You Can't Not Believe Everything You Read." *Journal of Personality and Social Psychology* 65: 221–33.

Jarvis, W.B.G., and R.E. Petty. 1996. "The Need to Evaluate." *Journal of Personality and Social Psychology* 70: 172–94.

Kahneman, D. 2003. "A Perspective on Judgment and Choice: Mapping Bounded Rationality." *American Psychologist* 58: 697–720.

Kahneman, D., and S. Frederick. 2002. "Representativeness Revisited: Attribute Substitution in Intuitive Judgment." In *Heuristics and Biases: The Psychology of Intuitive Judgment,* 49–81. New York: Cambridge University Press.

Kardes, F.R., M. L. Cronley, and J. Kim. 2006. "Construal-Level Effects on Preference Stability, Preference-Behavior Correspondence, and Suppression of Competing Brands." *Journal of Consumer Psychology* 16: 135–44.

Katz, D. 1960. "The Functional Approach to the Study of Attitudes." *Public Opinion Quarterly* 24: 163–204.

Kruglanski, A.W., and E. Orehek. 2007. "Partitioning the Domain of Social Inference: Dual Mode and Systems Models and Their Alternatives." *Annual Review of Psychology* 58: 291–316.

Machin, J.E., and G.J. Fitzsimons. 2005. "Marketing by Mistake: The Unintended Consequences of Consumer Research." In *Applying Social Cognition to Consumer-focused Strategy,* ed. F.R. Kardes, P.M. Herr, and J. Nantel, 81–95. Mahwah, NJ: Lawrence Erlbaum.

Maheswaran, D., D.M. Mackie, and S. Chaiken. 1992. "Brand Name as a Heuristic Cue: The Effects of Task Importance and Expectancy Confirmation on Consumer Judgments." *Journal of Consumer Psychology* 1: 317–36.

Mizik, N., and R. Jacobson. 2008. "The Financial Value Impact of Perceptual Brand Attributes." *Journal of Marketing Research* 45: 15–32.

Moore, D.L., D. Hausknecht, and K. Thamodaran. 1986. "Time Compression, Response Opportunity, and Persuasion." *Journal of Consumer Research* 13: 85–99.

Petrocelli, J.V., Z.L. Tormala, and D.D. Rucker. 2007. "Unpacking Attitude Certainty: Attitude Clarity and Attitude Correctness." *Journal of Personality and Social Psychology* 92: 30–41.

Petty, R.E., J.T. Cacioppo, and D. Schumann. 1983. "Central and Peripheral Routes to Advertising Effectiveness—The Moderating Role of Involvement." *Journal of Consumer Research* 10: 135–46.

Petty, R.E., S.G. Harkins, and K.D. Williams. 1980. "The Effects of Group Diffusion of Cognitive Effort on Attitudes: An Information-Processing View." *Journal of Personality and Social Psychology* 38: 81–92.

Petty, R.E., and D.T. Wegener. 1999. "The Elaboration Likelihood Model: Current Status and Controversies." In *Dual-Process Theories in Social Psychology,* ed. S. Chaiken and Y. Trope, 37–72. New York: Guilford Press.

Petty, R.E., G.L. Wells, and T.C. Brock. 1976. "Distraction Can Enhance or Reduce Yielding to Propaganda: Thought Disruption Versus Effort Justification." *Journal of Personality and Social Psychology* 34: 874–84.

Ratneshwar, S., and S. Chaiken. 1991. "Comprehension's Role in Persuasion: The Case of Its Moderating Effect on the Persuasive Impact of Source Cues." *Journal of Consumer Research* 18: 52–62.

Roskos-Ewoldsen, D.R., and R.H. Fazio. 1992. "On the Orienting Value of Attitudes: Attitude Accessibility as a Determinant of an Object's Attraction of Visual Attention." *Journal of Personality and Social Psychology* 63: 198–211.

Sanbonmatsu, D.M., and F.R. Kardes. 1988. "The Effects of Physiological Arousal on Information Processing and Persuasion." *Journal of Consumer Research* 15: 379–85.

Smith, E.R., R.H. Fazio, and M.A. Cejka. 1996. "Accessible Attitudes Influence Categorization of Multiply Categorizable Objects." *Journal of Personality and Social Psychology* 71: 888–98.

Smith, M.B., J.S. Bruner, and R.W. White. 1956. *Opinions and Personality.* Oxford, UK: John Wiley and Sons.

Snyder, M., and D. Kendzierski. 1982. "Acting on One's Attitudes: Procedures for Linking Attitude and Behavior." *Journal of Experimental Social Psychology* 18: 165–83.

Stanovich, K.E., and R.F. West. 2000. "Individual Differences in Reasoning: Implications for the Rationality Debate?" *Behavioral and Brain Sciences* 23: 645–726.

———. 2002. "Individual Differences in Reasoning: Implications for the Rationality Debate?" In *Heuristics and Biases: The Psychology of Intuitive Judgment,* ed. T. Gilovich, D. Griffin, and D. Kahneman, 421–40. New York: Cambridge University Press.

Stapel, D.A., W. Koomen, and M. Zeelenberg. 1998. "The Impact of Accuracy Motivation on Interpretation, Comparison, and Correction Processes: Accuracy Knowledge Accessibility Effects." *Journal of Personality and Social Psychology* 74: 878–93.

Tormala, Z.L., and R.E. Petty. 2001. "Online Versus Memory-Based Processing: The Role of 'Need to Evaluate' in Person Perception." *Personality and Social Psychology Bulletin* 27: 1599–1612.

Weaver, K., and N. Schwarz. 2008. "Self-Reports in Consumer Research." In *Handbook of Consumer Psychology,* ed. C.P. Haugtvedt, P.M. Herr, and F.R. Kardes, 1081–1102. New York: Taylor and Francis Group/Lawrence Erlbaum.

Wheeler, S.C., R.E. Petty, and G.Y. Bizer. 2005. "Self-Schema Matching and Attitude Change: Situational and Dispositional Determinants of Message Elaboration." *Journal of Consumer Research* 31: 787–97.

12

Negativity and Customer Satisfaction

Its Managerial Implications

Keiko I. Powers

How to satisfy our customers? This has been a key managerial question for organizations in various sectors, and its importance has become greater in today's more competitive market. As organizations continue improving ways to satisfy their customers, having a competitive edge in customer satisfaction has become an increasingly more complex goal, requiring advanced strategic planning and execution from the managerial to the operational level (Denove and Power 2006). Such complexity calls for on-going introduction and dissemination of solid theories from various psychological perspectives for a better and more in-depth understanding of customer satisfaction. As the quality of products and services continues to improve in various industries, many organizations address the customer relationship with terms such as "delighting customers" or "exceeding customer expectations" rather than simply satisfying customers or meeting expectations; another indication of how competitive the market has become (Matzler et al. 2004).

Just as the market has been raising the bar for customer satisfaction, various research studies in consumer psychology and related disciplines have focused on the concept of satisfaction from the positive perspective. However, fewer studies have focused on the concept of dissatisfaction; that is, how consumers act when they are dissatisfied or "unhappy" with the product or service. Assessments for unhappy customers are often limited to complaining behaviors (e.g., Halstead and Page 1992; Tax and Chandrashekaran 1992). A possible explanation from the research perspective is that it is more difficult to empirically identify those who are dissatisfied because survey questionnaire items are often organized to measure the extent of how satisfied customers are. As a result, it limits the ability to accurately capture detailed information regarding dissatisfaction. In addition, customer satisfaction is often addressed from a more general marketing perspective in the industry (see, for example,

Anderson and Sullivan 1993; Johnson, Anderson, and Fornell 1995), and a more disaggregate approach to satisfaction versus dissatisfaction based on consumer psychology theories has not been typically implemented as the mainstream strategy. As a result, dissatisfied customers tend to be considered residing on the opposite end of the satisfaction continuum from satisfied customers when marketing strategies are developed. However, ample research studies in consumer psychology suggest that dissatisfaction is not merely a mirror image of satisfaction (e.g., see Giese and Cote 2000; Mano and Oliver 1993; Oliver 1993).

Many researchers advocate the multifactor theory of satisfaction (Mano and Oliver 1993). This implies that behavioral outcomes closely linked to satisfaction (e.g., repurchase, word of mouth [WOM]) are often key drivers to company success and do not exhibit a linear relationship with satisfaction. Therefore, simply applying reversed strategies for improving customer satisfaction may not offer approaches that lead to successful handling of dissatisfied customers. Considering the potentially very high negative impacts of dissatisfaction (e.g., WOM, intention not to repurchase) on business success (Mittal, Ross, and Baldasare 1998), it is critical to identify dissatisfied customers and assess their psychological and behavioral characteristics. The main purpose of this chapter is twofold: First, to develop a quantitative approach to identify emotionally dissatisfied customers based on application of a psychological theory on negativity. Second, to compare and contrast psychological and behavioral characteristics of emotionally dissatisfied with those of satisfied customers. The empirical investigation is based on a large-scale customer satisfaction survey on car purchases in the United States. Theoretical and managerial implications of the empirical findings from the psychological perspective are discussed.

Literature Review

Negativity Versus Positivity

Past studies on negativity versus positivity have investigated these opposing constructs in various contexts (Folkes and Patrick 2003; Ito et al. 1998; Skowronski and Carlston 1989; Smith et al. 2006; Vaish, Grossman, and Woodward 2008). Ito and colleagues' (1998) psychophysiological experiments based on positive and negative visual stimuli demonstrated that negativity bias takes place at the evaluation-categorization stage, reflecting an automatic evaluative processing of negative information. Skowronski and Carlston (1989) compared negativity and positivity biases in the context of impression formation, and stated that negativity biases are associated with morality judgments whereas positivity biases are linked to ability judgments. More recently, Folkes and Patrick (2003) examined how negative and positive information from one employee affects perceptions of other employees of the same company in the case of service industry. Their empirical analysis demonstrated existence of positivity bias where positive evaluation of one employee led to more favorable evaluations of other employees. Smith and colleagues (2006) claimed that where attention bias exists toward negative information, the bias can be eliminated if positive constructs are introduced. From the developmental psychology perspective, Vaish, Grossman, and Woodward (2008) stated that negativity bias has an evolutionary foundation, citing its existence among infants and children.

In addition to this work on various empirical investigations, the concept of negativity has gained much attention in attempts to better understand the construct from the psychological perspective, and it has been the focus of various theoretical reviews (for extensive reviews on negativity see Baumeister et al. 2001; Rozin and Royzman 2001; Skowronski and Carlston 1989). Among the many negativity entities cited, one of the key aspects of negativity bias, or negativity dominance, is considered most robust and common (Rozin and Royzman 2001). This principle states that the holistic evaluation of negative events, objects, and so forth is more negative than the sum of subjective assessments of the individual factors. Baumeister and colleagues (2001) described the bias in the context of the positive-negative asymmetry effect where the no-sum pattern is observed for negative cues but not for positive ones. In reviewing the nature of negativity in various psychological domains, such as learning, information processing, and emotion, they postulated the existence of negative dominance with emotion, stating that, "events involving bad emotions remain more salient on peoples' minds than events involving good emotions" (333). Skowronski and Carlston (1989) mentioned extreme cues in addition to negative cues as the source of the no-sum phenomenon. Based on their category diagnosticity approach, they stated that both "negative and extreme cues are more influential because of people's implicit hypotheses concerning the relationships between behavioral cues and trait categories" (139).

Satisfaction, Emotion, and Negativity

For many years, satisfaction has been the focus of research efforts in various marketing-related disciplines. Some studies have investigated consumer satisfaction from a broader marketing or industry perspective (e.g., Anderson and Sullivan 1993; Johnson et al. 1995; Matzler et al. 2004). Satisfaction has also been one of the most extensively researched concepts in the psychology field, and many studies have investigated the construct from various perspectives over the years (for reviews, see Giese and Cote 2000; Yi 1990). One of the key approaches to the concept of satisfaction is to compare cognitive versus affective components (e.g., Jun et al. 2001; Mano and Oliver 1993; Oliver 1993). These studies have emphasized the importance of the role of the affective component when discussing satisfaction. More recently, emotion, which is closely related to affect, has been the focus of more research studies on satisfaction. The link between emotion and consumption has been well documented (Bagozzi, Gopinath, and Nyer 1999; Huang 2001; Koenig-Lewis and Palmer 2008; Ladhari 2009; Machleit and Mantel 2001; Westbrook and Oliver 1991; White 2006; White and Yu 2005). Bagozzi and colleagues (1999) and Huang (2001) depicted the importance of emotion in marketing from various perspectives, including via several psychological and marketing subdisciplines, such as an appraisal theory of emotions, cognitive processes, consumer behavior, and advertising. Westbrook and Oliver (1991) investigated the relationship between consumption emotion and consumer satisfaction and concluded that, "a number of qualitatively different affective experiences coexist and are related to the common unidimensional satisfaction continuum" (89). White and Yu (2005) investigated satisfaction emotions in the context of consumer behavioral intentions and stated that emotions play a key role in influencing consumer satisfaction and intentions. Koenig-Lewis and Palmer (2008), based on their longitudinal study, found that the satisfaction level at the time of an event was not related to the likelihood to recommend a product six months after an event, but the level of positive emotions at the event was strongly associated with recommendation likelihood. These findings have important implications to marketers regarding the timing of satisfaction assessment. Machleit and Mantel (2001) studied the relationship between satisfaction and emotion during shopping and found that the effect of emotions on satisfaction is greater when the emotions are attributed to the store. Based on the findings, they stated that stores can benefit from encouraging shoppers to attribute positive feelings toward the store but not negative feelings. Finally, and particularly relevant to the present study, is the statement by Baumeister and colleagues (2001) regarding the effect of bad emotions (see above).

Based on the literature on negativity, emotion, satisfaction, and their interrelationships, the main purpose of the present study is to examine whether the negativity dominance pattern is in fact identified among consumers. To test this hypothesis, I conducted empirical analysis of consumer satisfaction utilizing customer service surveys where satisfaction is closely linked to emotionally involving experiences (Ladhari 2009; White 2006; White and Yu 2005). When consumers were asked to provide overall evaluation as well as specific ratings on various aspects of customer service (e.g., courtesy of salesperson, waiting time for service, and so on), their response patterns to rating scales for measuring the satisfaction level allowed quantitative assessment/disentanglement of negativity dominance among the respondents. Given the theoretical foundation on emotion and negative dominance, the empirical study demonstrates how the quantitative methodology allows differential assessments of dissatisfied customers.

Empirical Study

Data

Our study was based on large-scale survey data on dealer service satisfaction collected from more than 28,000 customers who purchased or leased a new car in 2008. Customers were asked to respond to questions regarding the car purchase experience and then to rate specific items for each factor—such as the sales representative, facility features, and so on—as well as an overall satisfaction item at the factor level. For example, various performance measures, such as friendliness or product knowledge, served as specific rating items for the sales representative. The overall rating scale for evaluating the sales representative in general was also provided to assess customer satisfaction at the factor level. In addition, the questionnaire included various behavioral experience measures (e.g., test drive experience, the time taken for negotiation, and interactions with the sales representative) and reason items (e.g., reasons for choosing the dealer or the vehicle). The survey was conducted for the U.S. market, and the questionnaire was mailed out to those who purchased or leased a new car in a two-month period of 2008.

Methodology

The quantitative methodology, based on the theory of negative dominance, was developed utilizing the satisfaction ratings based on 10-point rating scales at the factor and the specific item levels. As noted in the previous section, the questionnaire consisted of rating scales for overall satisfaction of a particular service-related factor (subOSAT), such as service representative and corresponding specific items (attributes) such as friendliness. As shown in Figure 12.1, the questionnaire contained multiple factor-attributes combinations, with each combination asking various service-related key features at both more general and more specific levels. In addition, the questionnaire included a rating scale for the overall satisfaction (OSAT) on the service in general. This three-level hierarchical structure with overall satisfaction (OSAT), overall satisfaction for each factor (subOSAT), and corresponding specific items (attributes), allows a quantitative assessment of negative dominance.

Figure 12.2 depicts examples of a negative dominance response pattern and a response pattern that does not display negative dominance. As can be seen

Figure 12.1   **Three-Level Hierarchical Structure for Satisfaction Assessment**

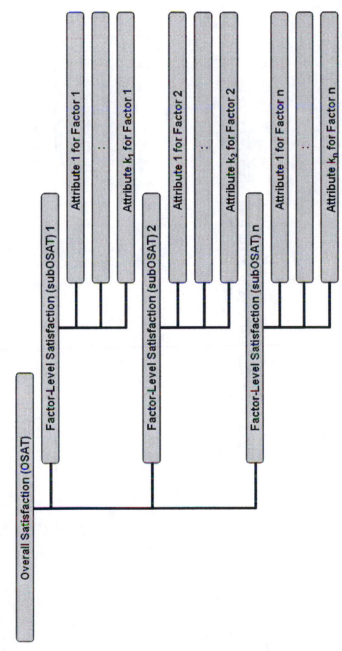

Note: The number of attributes could vary from subOSAT to subOSAT.
Item Examples:
Overall satisfaction (OSAT): Overall satisfaction with service during car purchase.
Factor-level or sub-overall satisfaction (subOSAT): Overall satisfaction with sales representative.
Attributes: Sales representative's knowledge, responsiveness, understanding of your vehicle needs, etc.

Figure 12.2 **Illustrative Examples of Negative Dominance Versus Non-Negative Dominance Response Patterns**

Negative Dominance Case

	Unacceptable 1	2	3	4	Average 5	6	7	8	9	Outstanding 10	Dont Know/ Not Applicable
Attribute A	○	○	○	○	●	○	○	○	○	○	○
Attribute B	○	○	○	●	○	○	○	○	○	○	○
Attribute C	○	○	●	○	○	○	○	○	○	○	○
Attribute D	○	○	○	●	○	○	○	○	○	○	○
Overall Satisfaction (subOSAT)	○	○	●	○	○	○	○	○	○	○	○

The mean attribute score = 5+4+3+4 = 4, whereas the subOSAT rating score = 3. In this case, subOSAT is smaller than the mean attribute score by one full point, or it is a negative dominance case.

Non-Negative Dominance Case

	Unacceptable 1	2	3	4	Average 5	6	7	8	9	Outstanding 10	Dont Know/ Not Applicable
Attribute A	○	○	●	○	○	○	○	○	○	○	○
Attribute B	○	○	○	●	○	○	○	○	○	○	○
Attribute C	○	○	●	○	○	○	○	○	○	○	○
Attribute D	○	●	○	○	○	○	○	○	○	○	○
Overall Satisfaction (subOSAT)	○	○	●	○	○	○	○	○	○	○	○

The mean attribute score = 3+4+3+2 = 3, and the subOSAT rating score = 3. In this case, subOSAT is equal to the mean attribute score, or it is a non-negative dominance case.

in the top example for negative dominance, the rating scores for attributes 1 through 4 are 5, 4, 3, and 4, with the sum (or the mean for quantitative derivation of negative dominance) of 4. The rating score for the corresponding subOSAT is 3, which is one full point lower than the mean of attributes. On the other hand, the bottom example for nonnegative dominance gives the same value for the attribute mean and subOSAT. In positive dominance, the response pattern displays a mirror image of the negative dominance case with the subOSAT score at least one full point higher than the average score for the corresponding attributes.

Equations (12.1) and (12.2) provide the operational definition of negative dominance (ND) and positive dominance (PD), respectively.

$$\text{ND} = 1 \text{ if subOSAT} < Int\left(\sum_{i=1}^{k} \frac{A_i}{k}\right); \text{ND} = 0 \text{ otherwise} \qquad (12.1)$$

$$\text{PD} = 1 \text{ if subOSAT} > Int\left(\sum_{i=1}^{k} \frac{A_i}{k}\right) + 1; \text{PD} = 0 \text{ otherwise} \qquad (12.2)$$

where

$subOSAT$ = Overall satisfaction rating score for each factor (range 1–10)
A_i = Attribute i rating score (range 1–10)
k = Total number of attributes
Int = Integer operator (e.g., 2.3 = 2, 8.9 = 8, and so on)

The quantitative definitions in Equations (12.1) and (12.2) state that if the mean of attribute ratings is at least one full point lower (or higher) than the rating score for subOSAT, then it is a negative (or positive) dominance case. The questionnaire for the present study contained four response sets of overall satisfaction (subOSAT) and corresponding specific questions (e.g., overall satisfaction on the sales representative factor and a corresponding set of items asking specific service performance by sales representative). Applying Equation (12.1) and (12.2), each of the response sets was tested for existence of negative dominance or positive dominance at the respondent level. "Negative dominance" respondents are defined as those who display at least one response set that satisfied Equation (12.1) with no response sets that satisfied the condition for positive dominance, i.e., Equation (12.2). "Positive dominance" respondents are defined similarly, reversing the conditions for Equations (12.1) and (12.2). When a respondent displayed both the negative dominance pattern and the positive dominance pattern among the four response sets (mixed case) or had no dominance patterns, the respondent was assigned to the base group.

After the negative dominance and positive dominance respondents were identified, their demographic background was first compared with the base group. The main purpose of the comparisons was to examine whether the negativity dominance pattern was in fact identified among consumers and to understand their background characteristics. The three groups were then compared with respect to the number of negative experience episodes, WOM measured with the number of positive and negative recommendations, and repurchase intention.

Results

Negativity/Positivity Dominance: Demographic Comparisons

The negative/positive dominance methodology identified approximately 11 percent ($n = 3,839$) and 16 percent ($n = 5,568$) of the respondents as those who displayed the negative dominance and positive dominance pattern, respectively. To examine whether the dominance pattern was associated with any of the respondents' characteristics, their demographic background was compared among the negative dominance (ND) group, the positive dominance (PD) group, and the base group. The latter group did not clearly display either dominance pattern. Table 12.1 shows the results of demographic comparisons.

Significance-test results are not included in Table 12.1, since statistical testing based on large sample sizes as in this case results in statistical significance even for very small differences. Therefore, comparing and interpreting substantive differences among the three groups is more meaningful. Overall, the three groups display similar patterns with respect to demographic backgrounds. There are no characteristics that stand out as considerably different; there seems to be a minor difference in the mean age, with the negative dominance group being younger (i.e., 48.3 versus 50.7 years old for the other two groups), but there are no other demographic characteristics with interpretable differences.

Negativity/Positivity Dominance: Validity Assessment

To assess soundness of the negative dominance methodology, a few steps were taken to check validity. First, the patterns associated with negative and positive dominance were compared with the response pattern associated with the overall satisfaction (OSAT). Figure 12.3 shows frequency distributions of the ND, PD, and base groups for each of the OSAT rating scores. The number of respondents for the ND group is fairly evenly distributed across different

Table 12.1

Demographic Comparisons Among Negative/Positive Dominance and Base Groups

Category	Negative dominance group	Positive dominance group	Base group
Sample size	3,839	5,568	25,232
(% sample size)	11.0	16.0	73.0
% of male	60.0	56.0	59.0
Mean age	48.3	50.7	50.7
Education			
% High school	15.6	21.6	19.6
% Trade school	30.2	32.0	29.9
% 4-yr college	28.1	23.7	26.8
% Graduate degree	26.0	22.7	23.7
Marital status			
% Married	72.6	69.8	73.7
% Single	14.7	13.5	12.6
% Widowed	2.1	6.3	4.2
% Divorced	10.5	10.4	9.5
Race			
% White/Caucasian	86.2	84.2	88.3
% Black/African American	3.2	4.2	3.2
% Asian	4.3	3.2	3.2
% Hispanic	4.3	6.3	4.3
% Other	2.1	2.1	1.1
Income			
% under $40K	13.5	16.1	12.5
% $40K–under $70K	23.6	28.7	25.0
% $70K–under $100K	24.7	23.0	25.0
% $100K–$175K	28.1	23.0	26.1
% greater than $175K	10.1	9.2	11.4
Vehicle type			
% of premium car owner	10.0	10.0	12.0

OSAT scores, but there is a small spike at the score of 8. Both PD and base groups display a monotonic distribution, with the OSAT rating score of 10 having the highest number of respondents compared to the other scores. This is due to the fact that many consumers in the United States tended to give relatively high ratings in satisfaction surveys. Figure 12.3 clearly shows that the ND group consists of respondents with various OSAT rating scores, and there are many respondents with a higher level of satisfaction (OSAT), suggesting that the negative dominance pattern is being driven by separate dynamics from the OSAT-related satisfaction continuum.

To test the hypothesis that the negative dominance group consists of consumers who had more negative experiences, each respondent's pattern to vari-

Figure 12.3   **Frequency Distribution of Respondents by Overall
                Satisfaction Rating**

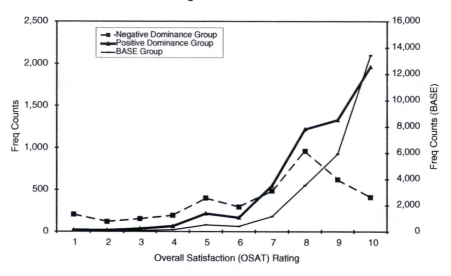

ous service performance measures was examined. These measures consisted
of such items as "dealer staff did not spend enough time" or "dealer put a lot
of pressure to pay more for my vehicle than I wanted to," and a composite
score based on these measures was created as a proxy to assess the intensity
of episode experiences that triggered a negative emotional reaction to the
service. As shown in Figure 12.4, the percentage of respondents with negative emotion episodes is substantially higher than the other two groups, with
49 percent versus 18 percent, 8 percent for ND group, PD group, and base
group, respectively. These differences support the notion that the methodology successfully identified the group of respondents with strongly negative
reaction to the service received at the time of car purchase.

Negativity/Positivity Dominance: WOM and Repurchase Intention

When selected outcome measures were compared among the three groups,
the resulting patterns clearly displayed consistent patterns for the negative
dominance group. The incidence rate of negative comments (i.e., WOM) was
substantially higher for the negative dominance respondents (15 percent versus 2 to 3 percent for the ND group and the other two groups, respectively),
whereas the incidence rate for positive comments was the lowest for the ND
group with 34 percent, compared to 55 to 65 percent for the other two groups
(see Figure 12.5). As shown in Figure 12.6, the mean number of negative/
positive recommendations among the three groups showed consistent pat-

Figure 12.4 **Percent of Respondents Experiencing "Negative Emotion" Episodes**

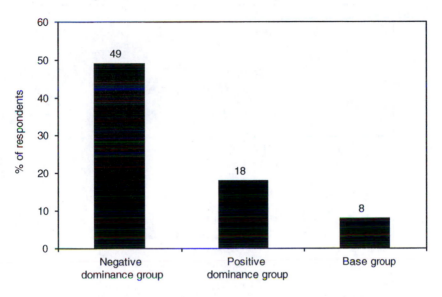

Figure 12.5 **Percent of Respondents with Positive/Negative Recommendations**

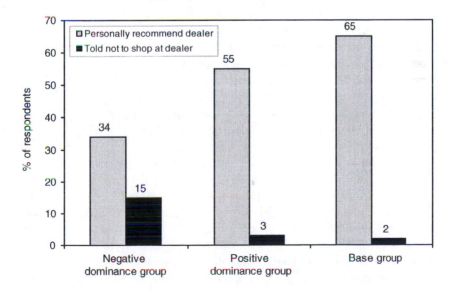

Figure 12.6   **Mean Number of Positive/Negative Recommendations**

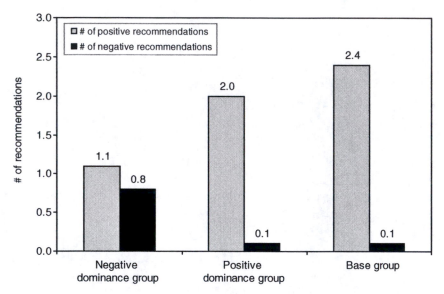

terns as the incidence rates, with the ND group having the mean number of negative recommendations of 0.8 compared to 0.1 comments for the other two groups.

The differences in the number of negative recommendations among the three groups can be further highlighted at the aggregate level. When the total number of negative recommendations is compared by summing up the results for each group, the number is the highest for the ND group, with 3,018 negative recommendations (see Table 12.2). This number is slightly higher than the combined number of the other two groups, (i.e., 658 + 2336 = 2994). This indicates that the ND group is responsible for more than 50 percent of all the negative recommendations regarding dealer service for car purchase when the group size is just 11 percent of the total sample.

Repurchase intention for this study was assessed in terms of the respondents' intention to go back for maintenance and repair services of their purchased or leased new vehicle. Respondents were asked to respond on a 4-point rating scale: definitely will, probably will, probably will not, or definitely will not return to the same dealer for service. Figure 12.7 shows the percentage of respondents who chose "definitely will not return for service" or "probably will not return for service." For both categories, the negative dominance group has the highest percentages with 14 percent for definitely will not and 23 percent for probably will not. Combining these two categories, 37 percent of the negative dominance group stated that they do not wish to go back to

Table 12.2

Aggregate-Level Total Number of Negative Recommendations by Group

Group	Total # of negative recommendations
Negative dominance group	3,018
Positive dominance group	658
Base group	2,336

Note: The number of recommendations was derived by summing up all the recommendations among the respondents within each group. The numbers may be slightly different from the values obtained by multiplying the mean numbers by the sample sizes due to rounding.

Figure 12.7   **Percent of Respondents with Intention *Not* to Return to Dealer for Service**

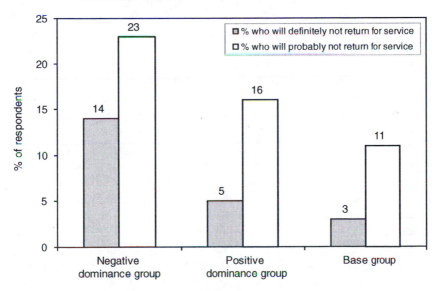

the dealer, which is substantially higher than 21 percent and 14 percent for positive dominance group and base group, respectively. This implies a higher probability of lost business due to lower service-related revenues from negative dominance consumers.

Discussion

By applying the psychological theory of negative dominance to a real-life large-scale satisfaction survey, the current study developed a quantitative

approach to negative dominance and successfully identified a group of respondents who had car purchase experiences with negative emotion evaluation. When consumers were asked to provide an overall evaluation as well as
specific ratings on various aspects of customer service (e.g., courtesy of sales
person, waiting time for service), their response patterns allowed quantitative
assessment/disentanglement of negativity dominance. The verification analysis
results clearly indicate that the negative-dominance–triggered responses to
the satisfaction survey were based on underlying psychological dynamics that
are separate from the explicitly stated satisfaction level represented by rating
scores in the questionnaire.

First, the theory of negative dominance stated that the holistic evaluation
of negative events, objects, and so forth—is more negative than the sum
of subjective assessments of individual events or objects, and the theory
was empirically supported in the real-life satisfaction rating context. Approximately 11 percent of the respondents were found to display a pattern in
which the overall satisfaction rating is lower (more negative) than the mean
of corresponding attribute ratings. The quantitative approach also identified
the positive dominance for approximately 16 percent of respondents. The
dominance pattern appears to be symmetric between negativity and positivity as far as the sizes of these two groups are concerned; however, only the
negative dominance group displayed behavioral and attitudinal responses that
were consistent with the core definitions of negative/positive dominance of
these two groups. In this regard, the results clearly support the principle of
negative dominance (Rozin and Royzman 2001) and its asymmetric nature
(Baumeister et al. 2001). These findings are different from those in the study
by Ahluwalia (2002), who stated that the negativity effect may be overstated
in consumer environments. The results of her empirical study indicated no
clear negativity. It is possible that the difference might be due to the difference
in the evaluation target between the product and the service.

The comparisons of demographic backgrounds among the three groups
did not find any unique profiles specific to the negative dominance group.
However, when their experiences during car purchase were compared, the
negative dominance group showed a substantially higher incidence of negative episode experiences. These results suggest that the psychological process
associated with negative dominance is more likely to be driven by service
experiences rather than the consumer profile differences. The comparisons
between negative dominance distribution and overall satisfaction in Figure
12.3 further strengths the notion of negative dominance, as the negative dominance pattern existed among those whose overall rating was 8 or higher (i.e.,
satisfied customers). These findings strongly support the existence of negative
dominance in the context of satisfaction evaluation for customer service.

The assessments of WOM and repurchase intention exhibited consistent patterns with the theory of negative dominance, further supporting the soundness of the theory and the methodology. Both the incidence rate of negative WOM and the number of negative recommendations are substantially higher than in the other two groups. In fact, as shown in Table 12.2, the number of negative recommendations originated from the negative dominance group was more than 50 percent of all the negative comments, though the size of this group accounts for only 11 percent of the total sample. This has important implications from a marketing perspective. Despite its small size in terms of market share, the negative dominance group is responsible for more than 50 percent of negative influence due to WOM. While it is difficult to accurately quantify this by simply comparing the differences in the number of negative recommendations, the potential damage to the firm's marketing efforts cannot be ignored considering the magnitude of the differences in the incidence rate of WOM (15 percent for the negative dominance group compared to 2 percent and 3 percent for the positive dominance and base groups).

The patterns observed in repurchase intention also imply negative impact on business performance. The repurchase intention item measured the customer's intention to return to the same dealer for future maintenance or repair services, and the proportion of respondents who definitely or probably will not return for the negative dominance group was 37 percent, substantially higher than the other two groups. The financial implications to the dealerships cannot be understated. From a separate satisfaction survey on auto dealer services, the average amount that U.S. car owners spent for repair or maintenance services in 2008 was approximately $180 per visit. Focusing on those who responded "definitely will not," 14 percent of the negative dominance group, or 537 car buyers, would not return to the dealer from whom they purchased their cars. This translates to approximately $97,000 in lost revenue for this group. The same estimation steps applied to the base group, which is more than 6 times larger than the ND group, result in a loss of approximately $136,000 or less than 1.5 times that of the ND group, when potential revenue losses are compared.

These findings suggest that the consumers with negative emotions identified with the methodology (i.e., those who displayed the negative dominance pattern), though a relatively small group, can hinder marketing efforts by corporations as well as service providers. Mittal and colleagues (1998) claim it is essential to assess the negative aspect of satisfaction, by stating that, "To maximize overall satisfaction and repurchase intentions, managers should optimize and not maximize attribute-level performance . . . eliminate negative performance first and then focus on increasing performance in the positive direction" (45). Similarly, Anderson and Sullivan (1993) state, "an important component of managing satisfaction is the ability to control the impact of negative disconfirmation through complaint handling and effective customer service" (141). Applications of psychological theories based on the negativity concept can help managers derive customer profiling/segmentation that allows more strategic and differentiated approaches to service, which would result in more cost-effective marketing and customer intervention efforts. As many organizations become more competitive in customer satisfaction strategies, it is critical for these organizations to incorporate advanced approaches based on sophisticated psychological theories. Thorough investigations of various marketing activities and behavioral measures surrounding this group of consumers, and comparisons to other consumer groups, would provide insights that could provide a better understanding of what the true definition of customer satisfaction is for each organization, which in turn allows more effective strategic planning and execution.

Future research can explore in depth the applicability of negative dominance theory by applying the quantitative methodology to survey data in other industries as well as in other markets. Preliminary investigations based on surveys in European markets have resulted in consistent findings for identifying the negative dominance group in all the markets being tested. Accumulation of more empirical evidence will help us better understand the intricate relationships among negativity, emotion, and satisfaction. In addition, it is important to continue addressing the validity of the negative dominance methodology with various analysis approaches. For example, a key question is whether the attributes are lacking information in asking about service-related performance; the incomplete information could affect the negative dominance pattern between the attributes and subOSAT in an unexpected manner. The survey used for our study went through rigorous assessments and revisions to ensure all the key information was covered. In addition, this study provided ample evidence that the negative dominance methodology successfully identified a group of consumers expressing their dissatisfaction with respect to various criteria, such as negative WOM, or repurchase intention. It would still be interesting to carry out an in-depth investigation of the attribute-response patterns of the negative dominance respondents at a disaggregate level, which could provide more insights into understanding this group's characteristics.

Conclusion

Among researchers and practitioners in the field of marketing, psychological aspects of emotion have gained more attention in various related disciplines, such as behavioral economics, behavioral finance, and game theory. (e.g., Andrade and Van Boren 2010; Ariely 2010; Lerner, Small and Loewenstein 2004; Levav and McGraw 2009; Seo and Barrett 2007). For example, from the behavioral economics perspective, Ariely (2009) cited the long-term effects of emotions on making financial decisions. Similarly, the other studies reported effects of the emotional state on economic decisions in various settings, such as stock investment, gambling, and endowment. These studies are clear testimony to the growing interest in and the importance of emotion for understanding phenomena and dynamics that have in the past typically relied on theories addressing more rational and cognitive processing. It is evident that one of the key psychological constructs, emotion, has important impacts on marketing efforts at various levels, and related psychological theories can continue playing a key role in understanding the underlying dynamics of customer satisfaction.

References

Ahluwalia, R. 2002. "How Prevalent Is the Negativity Effect in Consumer Environments?" *Journal of Consumer Research* 29: 270–79.

Anderson, E.W., and M.W. Sullivan. 1993. "The Antecedents and Consequences of Customer Satisfaction for Firms." *Marketing Science* 12: 125–43.

Andrade, E.B., and L. Van Boven. 2010. "Feelings Not Forgone: Underestimating Affective Reactions to What Does Not Happen." *Psychological Science* 21: 706–11.

Ariely, D. 2010. "The Long-Term Effects of Short-Term Emotions." *Harvard Business Review* (January–February): 38.

Bagozzi, R.P., Gopinath, M., and Nyer, P.U. 1999. "The Role of Emotions in Marketing." *Journal of the Academy of Marketing Science* 27: 184–206.

Baumeister, R.F., E. Bratslavsky, C. Finkenauer, and K.D. Vohs. 2001. "Bad Is Stronger." *Review of General Psychology* 5: 323–70.

Denove, C., and J.D. Power. 2006. *Satisfaction: How Every Great Company Listens to the Voice of the Customer.* New York: Portfolio.

Folkes, V.S., and V.M. Patrick. 2003. "The Positivity Effect in Perceptions of Services: Seen One, Seen Them All?" *Journal of Consumer Research* 30: 125–37.

Giese, J.L., and J.A. Cote. 2000. "Defining Consumer Satisfaction." *Academy of Marketing Science Review* 1: 1–26.

Halstead, D., and T.J. Page. 1992. "The Effects of Satisfaction and Complaining Behavior on Consumer Repurchase Intentions." *Journal of Consumer Satisfaction, Dissatisfaction and Complaining Behavior* 5: 1–11.

Huang, M.H. 2001. "The Theory of Emotions in Marketing." *Journal of Business and Psychology* 16: 239–47.

Ito, T.A., J.T. Larsen, N.K. Smith, and J.T. Cacioppo. 1998. "Negative Information Weighs More Heavily on the Brain: The Negativity Bias in Evaluative Categorizations." *Journal of Personality and Social Psychology* 75: 887–900.

Johnson, M.D., E.W. Anderson, and C. Fornell. 1995. "Rational and Adaptive Performance Expectations in a Customer Satisfaction Framework." *Journal of Consumer Research* 21: 695–707.

Jun, S., Y.J. Hyun, J.W. Gentry, and C.S. Song. 2001. "The Relative Influence of Affective Experience on Consumer Satisfaction Under Positive Versus Negative Discrepancies." *Journal of Consumer Satisfaction, Dissatisfaction and Complaining Behavior* 14: 141–53.

Koenig-Lewis, N., and A. Palmer. 2008. "Experiential Values over Time—A Comparison of Measures of Satisfaction and Emotion." *Journal of Marketing Management* 24: 69–85.

Ladhari, R. 2009. "Service Quality, Emotional Satisfaction, and Behavioral Intentions: A Study in the Hotel Industry." *Managing Service Quality* 19: 308–31.

Lerner, J.S., D.A. Small, and G. Loewenstein. 2004. "Heart Strings and Purse Strings Carryover Effects of Emotions on Economic Decisions." *Psychological Science* 15: 337–41.

Levav, J., and P. McGraw. 2009. "Emotional Accounting: How Feelings About Money Influence Consumer Choice." *Journal of Marketing Research* 46: 66–80.

Machleit, K.A., and S.P. Mantel. 2001. "Emotional Response and Shopping Satisfaction Moderating Effects of Shopper Attributions." *Journal of Business Research* 54: 97–106.

Mano, H, and R.L. Oliver. 1993. "Assessing the Dimensionality and Structure of the Consumption Experience: Evaluation, Feeling, and Satisfaction." *Journal of Consumer Research* 20: 451–66.

Matzler, K., F. Bailom, H.H., Hinterhuber, B. Renzl, and J. Pichler. 2004. "The Asymmetric Relationship Between Attribute-Level Performance and Overall Customer Satisfaction: A Reconsideration of the Importance-Performance Analysis." *Industrial Marketing Management* 33: 271–77.

Mittal, V., W.T. Ross, and P.M. Baldasare. 1998. "The Asymmetric Impact of Negative and Positive Attribute-Level Performance on Overall Satisfaction and Repurchase Intentions." *Journal of Marketing* 62: 33–47.

Oliver, R.L. 1993. "Cognitive, Affective, and Attribute Bases of the Satisfaction Response." *Journal of Consumer Research* 20: 418–30.

Rozin, P., and E.B. Royzman. 2001. "Negativity Bias, Negativity Dominance, and Contagion." *Personality and Social Psychology Review* 5: 296–320.

Seo, M.G., and L.F. Barrett. 2007. "Being Emotional During Decision Making—Good or Bad? An Empirical Investigation." *Academy of Management Journal* 50: 923–40.

Skowronski, J.J., and D.E. Carlston. 1989. "Negativity and Extremity Biases in Impression Formation: A Review of Explanations." *Psychological Bulletin* 105: 131–42.

Smith, N.K., J.T. Larsen, T.L. Chartrand, and J.T. Cacioppo. 2006. "Being Bad Isn't Always Good: Affective Context Moderates the Attention Bias Toward Negative Information." *Journal of Personality and Social Psychology* 90: 210–20.

Tax, S.S., and M. Chandrashekaran. 1992. "Consumer Decision Making Following a Failed Service Encounter: A Pilot Study." *Journal of Consumer Satisfaction, Dissatisfaction and Complaining Behavior* 5: 55–68.

Vaish, A., T. Grossmann, and A. Woodward. 2008. "Not All Emotions Are Created Equal: The Negativity Bias in Social-Emotional Development." *Psychological Bulletin* 134: 383–403.

Westbrook, R.A., and R.L. Oliver. 1991. "The Dimensionality of Consumption Emotion Patterns and Consumer Satisfaction." *Journal of Consumer Research* 18: 84–91.

White, C. 2006. "Towards an Understanding of the Relationship Between Mood, Emotions, Service Quality and Customer Loyalty Intentions." *Service Industries Journal* 26: 837–47.

White, C., and Y.T. Yu. 2005. "Satisfaction Emotions and Consumer Behavioral Intentions." *Journal of Services Marketing* 19: 411–20.

Yi, Y. 1990. "A Critical Review of Consumer Satisfaction." In *Review of Marketing*, ed. V.A. Zeithaml, 68–123. Chicago: American Marketing Association.

13

Nonconscious Processes in Consumer Behavior

A Review of Prior Literature and
Implications for Marketing

*Israel Martinez, Raquel Castaño,
Claudia Quintanilla, and Martin Reimann*

As early as the 1950s, market researcher James Vicary claimed an increase in sales in both soft drinks and popcorn after flashing the messages "Drink Coca-Cola" and "Eat popcorn" for a few milliseconds between scenes in a movie theater (Karremans, Stroebe, and Claus 2006). After several unsuccessful attempts to independently replicate these findings, Vicary conceded in 1962 that he had never actually proven the effects of these subliminal advertisements (Egermann, Kopiez, and Reuter 2006). However, several decades later, research showed that it is possible to modify behavior outside of the individuals' awareness using nonconscious primes. Although both subliminal primes (i.e., stimuli of which the individual is not aware) and supraliminal primes (i.e., stimuli of which the existence but not the potential influence is apparent to the individual) happen on a nonconscious level, they do not operate in the way that Vicary supposed (Karremans et al. 2006).

Research on nonconsciousness continues to make important progress (e.g., Bargh 1990; Chartrand et al. 2008), but this was not always the case. In psychology, where choice was first assumed to be conscious and deliberate, consciousness (as opposed to nonconsciousness) was initially the major focus of research (Fitzsimons et al. 2002). Similarly, in consumer research, previous studies have focused on consumer behavior largely as a conscious process (Cohen and Chakravarti 1990). However, most of consumers' everyday lives may not be determined by conscious intentions and deliberate choices, but by psychological processes that are put in motion by stimuli from the environment and that operate outside of conscious awareness and guidance (Bargh and Chartrand 1999). Research on learning has also shown that skills, especially those related to reward and punishment, may become routine through practice and repetition such that their operation becomes nonconscious (Bechara et al. 1997; Kihlstrom 1987; Vera and Simon 1993; Wegner and Bargh 1998).

In general, nonconscious processes are, by definition, beyond conscious awareness or voluntary control (Epley and Gilovich 1999). Two concepts are central to understanding nonconscious processes: priming and goal pursuit. *Priming*—that is, using recent experiences to create internal readiness without an intervening act of will (see Bargh and Chartrand 2000)—has been used to nonconsciously modify individuals' judgments (Greenwald and Banaji 1995); alter their moods (Monahan, Murphy, and Zajonc, 2000); modify their levels of conformity (Epley and Gilovich 1999); and even increase their creativity (Fitzsimons, Chartrand, and Fitzsimons 2008). Thus, the focus of priming research is to study the effects of situational context and the manner in which certain environmental stimuli cause the consumer to think, feel, and behave differently than he or she might have done otherwise (Bargh and Chartrand 2000). Specifically, prior research indicates two ways to deliver primes: subliminally, in which the primes are not accessible to an individual's awareness; and supraliminally, in which the individual is aware of the primes but not of their potential influence (Bargh 2002). Both subliminal and supraliminal priming produce significant differences in consumers' perception, goals, and decision making, but the effects of subliminal priming are said to be stronger (Tom et al. 2007). Previous research on nonconscious processes has also shown that preference for an object can be increased by increasing the consumer's exposure to that object (Zajonc 1968). In other words, when primes are repeated, the activated psychological mechanism becomes more likely to influence conscious judgments and problem solving (Bargh and Chartrand 2000).

Goal pursuit, the second key concept in the understanding of nonconscious processes, involves deliberation, weighing of pros and cons, and assessing how a goal fits one's other goals, norms, and values (Hassin, Bargh, and Zimerman 2009). In general, goals are mental representations of a future state that one either consciously or nonconsciously believes one wants to attain (Aarts and Hassin 2005). Of particular interest to this research is the fact that goal pursuit may be triggered outside of conscious awareness (Bargh et al. 2001) because goals can (a) alter the way incoming information is encoded (Bettman 1979); (b) modify behavior (Bargh 1990; Chartrand et al. 2008); (c) guide decisions (Bettman, Luce, and Payne 1998); (d) affect actions based on the perceived progress toward them (Fishbach and Dhar 2005); and (e) become stronger when progress is made toward attaining them (Kivetz,

Urminsky, and Zheng 2006). Once a desired outcome enters the mind of the decision maker, an end point is visualized toward which the individual's actions are then directed. For example, consumers make purchases in order to achieve one or more goals (Bagozzi and Dholakia 1999). Most consumer decisions are said to result from a set of automated response patterns rather than from a reflective or considered search (Zaltman 2000). In other words, consumers often have goals that are activated nonconsciously but are pursued consciously (Bagozzi and Dholakia 1999). They are unaware that the goals have been activated or of their operation, yet their behavior changes to attain the goal (Bargh 2002).

The purpose of this chapter is to shed light on the effects of nonconscious priming stimuli on goal pursuit and to highlight how our knowledge of nonconscious processes of consumption can be used to improve marketing. We categorize these stimuli into the five basic senses: vision, audition, olfaction, taste, and touch. First, we review the literature on nonconscious processes from the fields of consumer psychology and general psychology. Second, building on this literature, we derive implications for marketing.

Literature Review

Our literature review was based on two disciplines: consumer psychology and general psychology. We reviewed papers published between 1968 and 2009 in the *Journal of Consumer Research, Journal of Marketing Research,* and *Journal of Marketing.* We also reviewed articles from *Science, Journal of Personality and Social Psychology, Journal of Experimental Psychology, Psychological Science,* and *Journal of Experimental Social Psychology.* Even though the purpose of this chapter is to highlight the latest research on nonconscious processes of consumer behavior, it is also important to highlight classical research that contributed significantly to the literature. Table 13.1—sorted by sense and year—summarizes the state of the field. Most of the works listed were published in the last decade.

Visual Primes

Conceptual Overview

Images and words have been used as both subliminal and supraliminal visual primes in prior research. A method called backward stimulus masking has been used to prime a certain behavior subliminally. In this technique, a visual stimulus is presented very briefly (e.g., a happy face

Table 13.1

Literature Review of Nonconscious Processes

Author(s)	Year	Journal	Focal topic	Stimulus type	Sample size	Independent variable	Dependent variable	Findings
Bargh, Chen, and Burrows	1996	*Journal of Personality and Social Psychology*	Social interaction behavior	Visual	34	Rude, polite, or neutral	Interruptions	Faster interruption of the experimenter in the rude condition than in the polite or neutral conditions
			Elderly stereotype	Visual	30	Elderly prime condition or neutral	Walking speed	Slower walking speed in the elderly condition
			Awareness	Visual	19	Elderly prime condition or neutral	Awareness	Priming manipulation occurred nonconsciously
			Mood	Visual	33	Elderly prime condition or neutral	Mood	Same level of sadness and arousal in both the elderly and neutral conditions
Epley and Gilovich	1999	*Journal of Experimental Social Psychology*	Conformity	Visual	34	Conformity or nonconformity	Conformity index	More similar ratings between the participants and the confederates in the conformity condition
			Asymmetry	Visual	120	Conformity, nonconformity, or control	Conformity index	Priming nonconformity inadvertently also primes conformity

Bargh, Gollwitzer, Lee-Chai, Barndollar, and Trötschel, 2001	Journal of Personality and Social Psychology						
		Achievement	Visual	78	High or neutral performance	Performance	Found more words in performance condition
		Cooperation	Visual	60	Supraliminal high cooperation (or neutral) and conscious high cooperation (or neutral)	Cooperation	Cooperated more in the cooperation and the conscious condition
		Achievement	Visual	288	Priming: high or neutral performance × task (impression formation or word search) × delay (none or 5 min) × gender	Performance	Priming effect increased with time in the performance-priming condition
		Obstacles	Visual	76	High or neutral performance	Performance	More participants continued working after they were told to stop in the performance condition
		Resumption of interrupted goals	Visual	65	High performance or neutral	Performance	More participants continued working after they were interrupted in the performance condition

(continued)

Table 13.1 (continued)

Study	Year	Journal	Topic	Modality	N	Manipulation	Dependent variable	Findings
Strahan, Spencer, and Zanna	2002	Journal of Experimental Social Psychology	Drinking behavior and subliminal primes	Visual	81	Thirst condition (thirsty vs. not thirsty) × prime (thirst-related vs. neutral words)	Milliliters consumed	More liquid consumed in the thirst-related prime condition when individuals were thirsty, but not when satiated
			Drinking behavior and subliminal primes	Visual	35	Prime (thirst-related or neutral)	Sport beverage rating	Higher rating of thirst-quenching beverage in the thirst-related prime condition
			Subliminal and sadness	Visual	90	Prime (sad face vs. neutral prime) × future task expectation (expectation to interact with other person or not)	Rating of compact discs, number of songs chosen	More persuasive effect of an advertisement to restore mood in the sadness condition
Morrin and Ratneshwar	2003	Journal of Marketing Research	Brand attention, brand recall, brand recognition, brand evaluation, mood and arousal	Visual	90	Ambient scent and brand familiarity	Brand attention, brand recall, brand recognition, brand evaluation, mood and arousal	More attention to brands, better brand recall and recognition in the pleasant ambient scent condition

			Brand attention, brand recall, brand recognition, brand evaluation, mood and arousal	Visual	60	Ambient scent at encoding, brand familiarity, and ambient scent at retrieval	Brand attention, brand recall, brand recognition, brand evaluation, mood and arousal	Higher brand memory in the pleasant ambient scent at encoding condition
Killgore and Yurgelun-Todd	2004	NeuroImage	Emotion	Visual	12	Prime: happy or sad faces	Amygdala and anterior cingulate gyrus	More activation of the anterior cingulate gyrus and amygdala in the happy faces condition
Fishbach and Dhar	2005	Journal of Consumer Research	Choice and progress	Visual	45	Type of scale: narrow (−5 lbs and +5 lbs) or wide (−25 lbs and +25 lbs)	Product choice	Higher goal-consistent choices in the lower progress condition
			Interest	Visual	40	Social comparison standard (high vs. low)	Interest in nonacademic activities	Greater interest in nonacademic activities in the low social standard condition
			Action choice, commitment, and progress	Visual	50	Goal focus: commitment or progress	Inconsistent action choice	More choice of inconsistent actions in the progress than in the commitment evaluation condition

(continued)

Table 13.1 *(continued)*

Authors	Year	Journal	Measures	Method	N	Manipulation	DV	Results
Karremans, Stroebe, and Claus	2006	*Journal of Experimental Social Psychology*	Choice and perceived progress	Visual	52	Time: before or after exercising	Food choice	Higher choice of tasty and fatty dinner in the prior-to-workout condition
			Motivation and choice	Visual	61	Lipton iced tea or neutral prime	Thirst and product choice	Higher choice for specific drink in the primed drink condition only when individuals were thirsty
			Motivation and choice	Visual	105	Thirsty or not thirsty × Lipton iced tea vs. control	Product choice	Higher choice for specific drink in the primed drink condition only when individuals were thirsty
Chartrand, Huber, Shiv, and Tanner	2008	*Journal of Consumer Research*	Product choice	Visual	51	Prestige or thrift	Prestigious choice	Higher choice of higher-priced products in the prestige condition than in the thrift condition
			Product choice and time	Visual	249	Goal prime: prestige or thrift and time delay (high or low)	Prestigious choice	Greater effect of the prime in the high delay condition

Authors	Year	Journal	Construct	Method	N	Prime	DV	Results
			Real choice and satiation	Visual	180	Goal prime: prestige, thrift or neutral × goal satiation (high satiation or real choice vs low satiation or hypothetical choice)	Prestigious choice	Satiation of the goal only in the real, not in the hypothetical, choice
			Brands as primes	Visual	107	Prestige retail brands or thrift retail brands	Prestigious choice	Higher choice of thrift products in the thrift-oriented brands condition
Fitzsimons, Chartrand, and Fitzsimons	2008	Journal of Consumer Research	Creativity and brands as primes	Visual	341	Prime: Apple or IBM logos and delay: delay or no delay	Creativity	More creativity in the Apple than in the IBM condition
			Honesty, progress, and brands as primes	Visual	63	Prime: Disney channel or E! channel logos and progress (low, high or neutral)	Honesty	Higher honesty in the Disney channel than in the E! channel condition
			Creativity, chronic creativity motivation, and brands as primes	Visual	73	Prime: Apple, IBM or neutral and chronic creativity motivation	Creativity	More creativity in the Apple than in the IBM condition only when they had a chronic goal to be creative
Hassin, Bargh, and Zimerman	2009	Social Cognition	Performance and flexibility	Visual	42	Prime: high performance or neutral	Performance	Better score at a task in the high performance condition

(continued)

Table 13.1 (continued)

							Flexibility	
Ferraro, Bettman, and Chartrand	2009	Journal of Consumer Research	Performance and flexibility	Visual	64	Prime: high performance or neutral	Product choice	More flexibility at a task in the high performance condition
			Choice and exposure	Visual	126	Frequency of exposure (0, 4, or 12 photos showing Dasani water)	Product choice	Higher choice likelihood with higher exposure frequency
			Choice, exposure, and misattribution	Visual	271	Frequency of exposure (0, 4, or 12 photos showing Dasani water) and misattribution (yes or no)	Product choice	Higher choice of product in the no-misattribution condition
			Choice, exposure, and pre-exposure	Visual	199	Frequency of exposure (0, 4, or 12 photos showing Dasani water) and pre-exposure (yes or no)	Product choice	Higher product choice in the pre-exposure condition
			Choice and group membership	Visual	163	In-group or out-group	Product choice	Higher product choice in the in-group condition
Gorn	1982	Journal of Marketing	Music in advertisement	Auditory	244	Liked or disliked music	Product choice	Greater product choice when the product is associated with liked music

						Advertised with music or advertised with information	Product choice	Greater product choice when the product is advertised with information
				Auditory	122			
Egermann, Kopiez, and Reuter	2006	*Journal of Articles in Support of the Null Hypothesis*	Subliminal messages in music	Auditory	66	Word list and choice of drink	Word choice and product choice	Same behavior in both subliminal and neutral messages condition
Spangenberg, Crowley, and Henderson	1996	*Journal of Marketing*	Effect on ambient scent in a retail environment	Olfactory	308	Scent affect (neutral or pleasing) × scent intensity (low, medium, high) and control condition	Evaluations of the store, the store environment, the merchandise, specific products, intentions to visit the store, purchase intention for specific products, actual vs. perceived time spent, number of products examined	Higher evaluations of store, store environment, merchandise, intent to visit store and number of products examined, and lower perceived time spent in the pleasant ambient scent condition

(continued)

Table 13.1 (continued)

Authors	Year	Journal	Construct	Modality	N	Manipulation	Measure	Finding
Holland, Hendriks, and Aarts	2005	Psychological Science	Scents and response time	Olfactory	50	Prime: cleaner scent or control	Lexical decision task	Faster response time to cleaning-related words in the citrus scent condition
			Scents and expected behavior	Olfactory	56	Prime: cleaner scent or control	Activities planned for the rest of the day	More cleaning activities planned in the citrus scent condition
			Scents and behavior	Olfactory	22	Prime: cleaner scent or control	Cleanliness behavior	More cleaning behavior in the citrus scent condition
Zhong and Leonardelli	2008	Psychological Science	Social inclusion and warmth	Haptic	65	Social exclusion or social inclusion	Perceived room temperature	Lower estimated room temperature in the socially excluded condition
			Social inclusion and warmth	Haptic	52	Social exclusion or social inclusion	Product choice	Higher preference for warm foods and drinks in the social exclusion condition
Williams and Bargh	2008	Science	Social perception and warmth	Haptic	41	Temperature (cup of hot coffee or iced coffee)	Personality impression questionnaire	Warmer perception of a person when individuals hold a hot cup of coffee than a cup of iced coffee
			Social activities and warmth	Haptic	53	Temperature (hot or cold therapeutic pad)	Product choice	Higher choice of gift for a friend in the warm condition

for 20 milliseconds) and is immediately followed by a different visual stimulus, which is shown for a longer duration (e.g., a neutral face for 100 ms). Under such conditions, participants are unaware of the initial target stimulus and report perceiving only the second masking stimulus (Killgore and Yurgelun-Todd 2004).

Images and words can also be presented supraliminally. For example, the scrambling sentence task (Srull and Wyer 1979) uses words supraliminally to nonconsciously activate either an impression formation or a memory-processing goal (Chartrand and Bargh 1996). In this task, participants are asked to construct grammatical sentences out of a series of words presented in scrambled order, where one of the words in the sentence is the target concept. Srull and Wyer (1979) found that once the trait concept or schema is made more accessible by this task, the likelihood that the same schema will be used to encode new information increases. The literature also reveals several other examples in which behavior is modified using different supraliminal primes. For example, participants who were supraliminally primed with words related to the elderly walked more slowly afterward than they did in the neutral condition (Bargh, Chen, and Burrows 1996), and participants primed with achievement-related words performed better on a task (Bargh et al. 2001).

In consumer psychology, actual product choice has been modified using primes of either prestige or thrift (Chartrand et al. 2008), or by varying the frequency of supraliminal exposure (Ferraro, Bettman, and Chartrand 2009). However, it has also been shown that priming affects participants' behavior primarily when they are motivated to pursue a certain goal, not when the goal has been satiated (Strahan, Spencer, and Zanna 2002). For example, subliminally priming participants with the name of a thirst-quenching drink is more likely to increase the choice of this drink and the intention to drink it if participants are thirsty (Karremans, Stroebe, and Claus 2006). Package design, shape, and size have also been shown to have an effect on consumers outside their awareness. For example, prior research has shown that aesthetic package designs significantly increase the reaction time to choose a product compared to standardized packages (Reimann et al. 2010); taller shapes are perceived to contain more than shorter ones; and consumers prefer taller packages (Raghubir and Krishna 1999).

Managerial Implications

Words and images have been used as visual primes in prior research and have been shown to affect behavior nonconsciously. Building on this research, marketing managers should carefully consider the location of their products (e.g., in a specific store environment) and advertisements (e.g., on a billboard) since previously viewed, nonconsciously processed stimuli may change consumers' perception of their products. For example, consumers may prefer an inexpensive product alternative if they have been previously exposed to stimuli related to thrift and savings, but will choose more prestigious alternatives if they have been previously exposed to stimuli related to prestige (Chartrand et al. 2008). Similarly, brands can serve as visual primes that nonconsciously activate goal pursuit; if not in terms of the brand itself, at least attributes related to the brand. For example, if a consumer sees a brand that emphasizes value, she or he may buy an inexpensive product, even in an unrelated product category. Therefore, marketing managers should be aware of the context in which their products are presented in case there are external and incidental exposures that could encourage or discourage consumers' preference for their product. Managers should also carefully consider package design and shape since it has been demonstrated that size attracts attention and that consumers tend to choose products in packages that appear taller than other products (Raghubir and Krishna 1999).

Auditory Primes

Speech

Conceptual Overview

Previous research efforts have tried to develop auditory-masking procedures, including speech stimuli implanted in white noise or synchronized messages (Harris et al. 1996). This procedure was also applied in subliminal audiotapes, which transmitted relaxing subliminal audio messages, supposedly to enhance memory and boost self-esteem (Kouide and Dupoux 2005). Another method for subliminal speech priming used auditory prime stimuli that are time-compressed and concealed within a spectrally similar, incomprehensible sound (Dupoux, Kouider and Mehler 2003). However, evidence has indicated that subliminal audiotapes do not produce any effects associated with subliminal content (Greenwald et al. 1991).

Managerial Implications

Since the literature presents contradictory evidence on the effects of subliminal messages, further research is needed. However, marketing managers should be aware that the potentially highly deceptive nature of these stimuli means that they may not be in the consumers' interest (Federal Communications Commission 2008). Therefore, it may be recommended that marketing managers use different auditory stimuli, such as music.

Music

Conceptual Overview

Previous research has indicated that varying the musical elements (e.g., mode, tempo, pitch, rhythm, harmony, or volume) can nonconsciously alter affective states (e.g., happiness, sadness, or amusement) (Bruner 1990). For example, Alpert and Alpert (1989) showed that happy music resulted in elevated moods in consumers, but sad music generated higher purchase intentions. Prior research has also used music to mask subliminal primes, such as spoken messages. At least five strategies can be used to embed messages in music (Egermann et al. 2006). First, the message can be placed in the music under the auditory limit, where it is masked by the music. Second, words with a reversed time structure (e.g., backward messages) can be mixed with music above the perceptual threshold; such messages have allegedly been recorded backward into rock music (Moore 1988). Third, the first two techniques can be combined as subliminal backward masked messages, such as a message recorded backward and played at very low volumes. Fourth, messages containing frequencies above 15 kHz can be recorded; for example, subliminal audio self-help tapes often contain information at high frequencies that is allegedly disentangled by the human auditory system, even though these acoustic signals are not revealed by spectrographic analysis (Merikle 1988). Finally, time-shrunk subliminal messages can be hidden in music, such as messages that are played back twice as fast as recorded. However, the use of subliminal words in music has not been shown to have an effect on choice behavior (Egermann et al. 2006). Furthermore, background music in restaurants has been shown to nonconsciously affect behavior. For example, when slow-tempo background music was played in a restaurant, customers stayed longer and consumed more alcoholic beverages (Milliman 1986).

Managerial Implications

Music is likely to have its greatest behavioral effect when consumers have high affective and/or low cognitive involvement with the product (Bruner 1990). However, figuring out the appropriate background music for different store settings can be complicated, especially because happy music produces elevated moods, yet sad music results in greater purchase intentions (Alpert and Alpert 1989).

Olfactory Primes

Conceptual Overview

Prior research has also studied the nonconscious effects of olfactory primes on behavior. Specifically, some studies have reported effects of scent on approach-avoidance tendencies. For example, previous research has suggested that scents increase gambling in casinos (Chase 1998), the time spent on a decision task (Bone and Ellen 1999; Mitchell, Kahn, and Knasko 1995), and intentions to visit a store (Spangenberg, Crowley, and Henderson 1996). Furthermore, consumers may form associations between scents and memory (Holland, Hendriks and Aarts 2005). For example, the smell of pine trees may trigger the memory of the holiday season and the scent of citrus may be associated with cleaning.

Marketers and retailers use fragrance in a wide variety of circumstances because consumers are likely to devote more attention to stimuli encountered in pleasantly scented environments (Morrin and Ratneshwar 2000). Prior research has shown that scent also extends to improved brand memory (Morrin and Ratneshwar 2003). Therefore, ambient scents can be used in settings such as retail stores, automobile showrooms, trade shows, and product demonstrations to increase the amount of time spent in the retail environment and the amount of mental attention devoted to relevant stimuli (e.g., products and brands). Congruency of the scent with the product category does not seem to be a highly relevant factor in improving brand memory (Morrin and Ratneshwar 2003), thus if marketing management's goal is to induce consumers to pay attention to and remember the products and brands they see in a particular setting, the use of virtually any pleasant scent should help to achieve this objective.

Managerial Implications

According to Spangenberg, Crowley, and Henderson (1996), the presence of an affectively neutral (e.g., lavender or ginger) or a pleasing (e.g., orange or spearmint) scent in a store is an inexpensive and effective way to enhance consumers' reactions to the store and its merchandise. Further, adding scent-emitting devices to in-store displays or scent strips to print advertisements could considerably enhance brand awareness and brand recall (Morrin and Ratneshwar 2003). Although a wide array of pleasant scents may work effectively, marketing managers can consider using a characteristic or "signature" scent for their brand to differentiate it from competing offerings.

Gustatory Primes

Consumers generally experience profound sensory confusion when eating or drinking (Rozin 1982). Even though this process involves at least two senses (taste and smell), perceptions while eating or drinking are usually attributed solely to taste; for example, the "sweet smell" experienced when sniffing a pie generates the sweet sensation of sugar on the tongue (Stevenson 2001). Despite the fact that gustatory stimuli affect consumers' everyday lives, from "taste promotions" in supermarkets to wine tastings, research on the nonconscious effects of gustatory primes are literally nonexistent in prior research. As such, further work is necessary on this potentially highly effective prime.

Haptic Primes

Conceptual Overview

Finally, haptic (touch) stimuli have also been shown to serve as primes that trigger nonconscious mechanisms and subsequently impact behavior. For example, temperature perceptions have been linked nonconsciously to social exclusion/inclusion. Specifically, participants who recalled the experience of being socially excluded estimated lower room temperatures than those who recalled being included (Zhong and Leonardelli 2008). Tactile reactions to either hot or cold temperature have also been used as nonconscious primes. For example, participants who held a hot coffee cup rated an unfamiliar person as being nicer and more generous (Williams and Bargh 2008) than did those who held an ice-cold coffee cup. Similarly, people who briefly held a hot therapeutic pad chose a gift for a friend more often than did people who held a cold therapeutic pad, extending these temperature-related priming effects into the realm of decision making (Williams and Bargh 2008).

Touch also plays an important part in product evaluation. For example, Krishna and Morrin (2008) suggested that the haptic characteristics of product containers may be transferred to the products they contain. Thus, the perceived haptic properties of products and their packaging could have important implications for consumer behavior.

Managerial Implications

More research is needed to suggest to managers a proper course of action regarding haptic primes. For example, understanding whether slight temperature variations in a store have an effect on brand perception and choice behavior may increase customer satisfaction. Regarding product packaging, using haptically inferior packaging could affect consumers' perceptions of the quality of the products the packages contain (Krishna and Morrin 2008).

Conclusion

In this chapter, we have reviewed the effects of nonconscious processes on diverse consumer behaviors. For three of the five human senses—vision, audition, and olfaction—we provided a conceptual overview of how specific consumer behaviors have been primed nonconsciously in prior research. On the basis of the resulting insight, we derived implications for marketing, shedding more light on the practical relevance of research on nonconsciousness in consumer behavior. Our literature review also revealed that little is known on the nonconscious effects of taste and touch, so further research is necessary in this area.

References

Aarts, H., and R.R. Hassin. 2005. "Automatic Goal Inference and Contagion: On Pursuing Goals One Perceives in Other People's Behavior." In *Social Motivation: Conscious and Unconscious Processes,* ed. J.P. Forgas and K.D. Williams, 153–67. New York: Cambridge University Press.

Alpert, J.I., and M.I. Alpert. 1989. "Background Music as an Influence in Consumer Mood and Advertising Responses." *Advances in Consumer Research* 16: 485–91.

Bagozzi, R.P., and U. Dholakia. 1999. "Goal Setting and Goal Striving in Consumer Behavior." *Journal of Marketing* 63: 19–32.

Bargh, J.A. 1990. "Auto-Motives: Preconscious Determinants of Social Interaction." In *Handbook of Motivation and Cognition: Foundations of Social Behavior,* ed. E.T. Higgins and R.M. Sorrentino, vol. 2, 93–130. New York: Guilford Press.

———. 2002. "Losing Consciousness: Automatic Influences on Consumer Judgment, Behavior, and Motivation." *Journal of Consumer Research* 29: 280–85.

Bargh, J., and T.L. Chartrand. 1999. "The Unbearable Automaticity of Being." *American Psychologist* 54: 462–79.

———. 2000. "The Mind in the Middle: A Practical Guide to Priming and Automaticity." In *Handbook of Research Methods in Social and Personality Psychology,* ed. H.T. Reis and C.M. Judd, 253–85, Cambridge, UK: Cambridge University Press.

Bargh, J.A., M. Chen, and L. Burrows. 1996. "Automaticity of Social Behavior: Direct Effects of Trait Construct and Stereotype Activation on Action." *Journal of Personality and Social Psychology* 71: 230–44.

Bargh, J.A., P.M. Gollwitzer, A. Lee-Chai, K. Barndollar, and R. Trötschel. 2001. "The Automated Will: Nonconscious Activation and Pursuit of Behavioral Goals." *Journal of Personality and Social Psychology* 81: 1014–27.

Bechara, A., H. Damasio, D. Tranel. and A.R. Damasio. 1997. "Deciding Advantageously Before Knowing the Advantageous Strategy." *Science* 275: 1293–95.

Bettman, J.R. 1979. "Memory Factors in Consumer Choice: A Review." *Journal of Marketing* 43: 37.

Bettman, J.R., M.F. Luce, and J.W. Payne. 1998. "Constructive Consumer Choice Processes." *Journal of Consumer Research* 25: 187–217.

Bone, P.F., and P.S. Ellen. 1999. "Scents in the Marketplace: Explaining a Fraction of Olfaction." *Journal of Retailing* 75: 243–62.

Bruner II, G.C. 1990. "Music, Mood, and Marketing." *Journal of Marketing* 54: 94–104.

Chartrand, T.L., and J.A. Bargh. 1996. "Automatic Activation of Impression Formation and Memorization Goals: Nonconscious Goal Priming Reproduces Effects of Explicit Task Instructions." *Journal of Personality and Social Psychology* 71: 464–78.

Chartrand, T.L., J. Huber, B. Shiv, and R.J. Tanner. 2008. "Nonconscious Goals and Consumer Choice." *Journal of Consumer Research* 35: 189–201.

Chase, V.D. 1998. "Making Stereophonic Scents." *Appliance Manufacturer* 46: 12.

Cohen, J.B., and D. Chakravarti. 1990. "Consumer Psychology." *Annual Review of Psychology* 41: 243–88.

Dupoux, E., S. Kouider, and J. Mehler. 2003. "Lexical Access Without Attention? Explorations Using Dichotic Priming." *Journal of Experimental Psychology, Human Perception and Performance* 29: 172–84.

Egermann, H., R. Kopiez, and C. Reuter. 2006. "Is There an Effect of Subliminal Messages in Music on Choice Behavior?" *Journal of Articles in Support of the Null Hypothesis* 4: 7–11.

Epley, N., and T. Gilovich. 1999. "Just Going Along: Nonconscious Priming and Conformity to Social Pressure." *Journal of Experimental Social Psychology* 35: 578–89.

Federal Communications Commission. 2008. Press Statement. Available at http://www.fcc.gov/mb/audio/decdoc/public_and_broadcasting.html#_Toc202587568.

Ferraro, R., J.R. Bettman, and T.L. Chartrand. 2009. "The Power of Strangers: The Effect of Incidental Consumer Brand Encounters on Brand Choice." *Journal of Consumer Research* 35: 729–41.

Fishbach, A., and R. Dhar. 2005. "Goals as Excuses or Guides: The Liberating Effect of Perceived Goal Progress on Choice." *Journal of Consumer Research* 32: 370–77.

Fitzsimons, G.M., T.L. Chartrand, and G.J. Fitzsimons. 2008. "Automatic Effects of Brand Exposure on Motivated Behavior: How Apple Makes You Think Different.'" *Journal of Consumer Research* 35: 21–35.

Fitzsimons, G.J., J.W. Hutchinson, P. Williams, J.W. Alba, T.L. Chartrand, J. Huber, and others. 2002. "Non-Conscious Influences on Consumer Choice." *Marketing Letters* 13: 269–79.

Gorn, G.J. 1982. "The Effects of Music in Advertising on Choice Behavior: A Classical Conditioning Approach." *Journal of Marketing* 46: 96–104.

Greenwald, A.G., and M.R. Banaji. 1995. "Implicit Social Cognition: Attitudes, Self-esteem, and Stereotypes." *Psychological Review* 102: 4–27.

Greenwald, A.G., E.R. Spangenberg, A.R. Pratkanis, and J. Eskenazi. 1991. "Double-Blind Tests of Subliminal Self-Help Audiotapes." *Psychological Science* 2: 119–22.

Harris, J.L., D. Salus, R. Rerecich, and D. Larsen. 1996. "Distinguishing Detection from Identification in Subliminal Auditory Perception: A Review and Critique of Merikle's Study." *Journal of General Psychology* 123: 41–50.

Hassin, R.R., J.A. Bargh, and S. Zimerman. 2009. "Automatic and Flexible: The Case of Non-Conscious Goal Pursuit." *Social Cognition* 27: 20–36.

Holland, R.W., M. Hendriks, and H. Aarts. 2005. "Smells Like Clean Spirit." *Psychological Science* 16: 689–93.

Karremans, J.C., W. Stroebe, and J. Claus. 2006. "Beyond Vicary's Fantasies: The Impact of Subliminal Priming and Brand Choice." *Journal of Experimental Social Psychology* 12: 1–7.

Kihlstrom, J.F. 1987. "The Cognitive Unconscious." *Science* 237: 1445–52.

Killgore, W.D.S., and D.A. Yurgelun-Todd. 2004. "Activation of the Amygdala and Anterior Cingulate During Nonconscious Processing of Sad Versus Happy Faces." *NeuroImage* 21: 1215–23.

Kivetz, R., O. Urminsky, and Y. Zheng. 2006. "The Goal-Gradient Hypothesis Resurrected: Purchase Acceleration, Illusionary Goal Progress, and Customer Retention." *Journal of Marketing Research* 43: 39–58.

Kouide, S., and E. Dupoux. 2005. "Subliminal Speech Priming." *Psychological Science* 16: 617–25.

Krishna, A., and M. Morrin. 2008. "Does Touch Affect Taste? The Perceptual Transfer of Product Container Haptic Cues." *Journal of Consumer Research* 34: 807–18.

Merikle, P. 1988. "Subliminal Auditory Messages: An Evaluation." *Psychology and Marketing* 5: 355–72.

Milliman, R. 1986. "The Influence of Background Music on the Behavior of Restaurant Patrons." *Journal of Consumer Research* 13: 286–90.

Mitchell, D.J., B.E. Kahn, and S.C. Knasko. 1995. "There's Something in the Air: Effects of Congruent or Incongruent Ambient Odor on Consumer Decision Making." *Journal of Consumer Research* 22: 229–39.

Monahan, J.L., S.T. Murphy, and R.B. Zajonc. 2000. "Subliminal Mere Exposure: Specific, General, and Diffuse Effects." *Psychological Science* 11: 462–66.

Moore, T.E. 1988. "The Case Against Subliminal Manipulation." *Psychology and Marketing* 5: 297–316.

Morrin, M., and S. Ratneshwar. 2000. "The Impact of Ambient Scent on Evaluation, Attention, and Memory for Familiar and Unfamiliar Brands." *Journal of Business Research* 49: 157–65.

———. 2003. "Does It Make Sense to Use Scents to Enhance Brand Memory?" *Journal of Marketing Research* 40: 10–25.

Raghubir, P., and A. Krishna. 1999. "Vital Dimensions in Volume Perception: Can the Eye Fool the Stomach?" *Journal of Marketing Research* 36: 313–26.

Reimann, M., J. Zaichkowsky, C. Neuhaus, T. Bender, and B. Weber. 2010. "Aesthetic Package Design: A Behavioral, Neural, and Psychological Investigation." *Journal of Consumer Psychology* 20: 431–41.

Rozin, P. 1982. "Taste-Smell Confusions and the Duality of the Olfactory Sense." *Perception and Psychophysics* 31: 397–401.

Spangenberg, E.R., A.E. Crowley, and P.W. Henderson. 1996. "Improving the Store Environment: Do Olfactory Cues Affect Evaluations and Behaviors?" *Journal of Marketing* 60: 67–81.

Srull, T.K., and R.S. Wyer. 1979. "The Role of Category Accessibility in the Interpretation of Information About Persons: Some Determinants and Implications." *Journal of Personality and Social Psychology* 37: 1660–72.

Stevenson, R.J. 2001. "The Acquisition of Odor Qualities." *Quarterly Journal of Experimental Psychology* 54: 561–77.

Strahan, E.J., S.J. Spencer, and M.P. Zanna. 2002. "Subliminal Priming and Persuasion: Striking While the Iron Is Hot." *Journal of Experimental Social Psychology* 38: 556–68.

Tom, G., C. Nelson, T. Srzentic, and R. King. 2007. "Mere Exposure and the Endowment Effect on Consumer Decision Making." *Journal of Psychology* 141: 117–25.

Vera, A.H., and H.A. Simon. 1993. "Situated Action: A Symbolic Interpretation." *Cognitive Science* 17: 7–48.

Wegner, D.M., and J.A. Bargh. 1998. "Control and Automaticity in Social Life." In *Handbook of Social Psychology,* ed. S.T. Fiske, D.T. Gilbert, and G. Lindzey, vol. 1, 446–96. Boston: McGraw-Hill.

Williams, L.E., and J.A. Bargh. 2008. "Experiencing Physical Warmth Promotes Interpersonal Warmth." *Science* 322: 606–11.

Zajonc, R. 1968. "Attitudinal Effects of Mere Exposure." *Journal of Personality and Social Psychology* 9: 1–27.

Zaltman, G. 2000. "Consumer Researchers: Take a Hike!" *Journal of Consumer Research* 26: 423–28.

Zhong, C., and G.J. Leonardelli. 2008. "Cold and Lonely: Does Social Exclusion Literally Feel Cold?" *Psychological Science* 19: 838–42.

14

Marketing Insights from a Model of Action and Empirical Findings

Geraldine Fennell

Imagine a group of marketers sixty years ago sitting across the table from a group of behavioral scientists eager to learn what managers seek from behavioral science. What one model would the marketers ask for?

Everyday Tasks and Interests

To answer that question, we need look no further than what industry is all about. Aside from investment for national defense, what goes on in all the offices and conference rooms of the business world is planning by entrepreneurs and employees for producing, distributing, and announcing availability of goods and services to assist people in pursuing the tasks and interests that maintain their life and quality of life (QOL). Goods and services are produced to be used in conjunction with, or instead of, individual human action in pursuit of everyday tasks and interests. As the business function that advises management on what to produce and offer, what marketers need most from behavioral science is to understand the nature of such human action. It would seem obvious that a model of everyday human action must be at the top of marketers' request list. In this chapter, to state some practical managerial guidelines for marketers, always with an eye to satisfactory return on investment (ROI) I draw on Fennell's (e.g., 1978, 1980, 1997) work in psychology and consumer behavior developing models of human action.

A request to guide marketers as they advise management with a view to obtaining a satisfactory ROI from producing goods and services brings behavioral scientists into somewhat unfamiliar terrain. Psychologists may assume that variables in the physical environment are likely to be givens and, while not lacking in interest, are unlikely to be the dependent variable in their studies. Plainly, however, such a task involves marketers guiding those who create aspects of the environment, namely, the goods and services available for sale and promoted via the media. The task calls for an unaccustomed degree of involvement with the environment, specifically with the kind of impact that action makes; for example, whether or not it achieves what was intended and identifying what was it intended to achieve. Action as environmental impact focuses attention upstream to the conditions that made taking action seem desirable. How is the upstream terrain to be conceptualized? Such is the task that a model of action must address. Accordingly, the assignment that marketers' request to behavioral science implicates is to come to grips with the nature of action, having regard to the conditions upstream as well as the outcome of environmental impact downstream, which constitute the contexts for action in pursuit of interests and accomplishing of tasks (Fennell 1991). Fortunately, Lewin (1936, 11) explicitly included the environment in his behavioral formulation: $B = f(S)$; $S = f(P\ E)$. Behavior (B) is a function of the situation (S). The situation—for Lewin, the situation as perceived—is a function of the person (P) and the environment (E). It is useful to think of action as a function of intersecting personal and environmental systems upstream, as perceived (Fennell 1987).

Modeling Everyday Action

The range of behavioral relevance of an individual good or service points to the scope of the model of action that marketers need. A good or service is intended to address a small slice of the array of activities in which individuals engage daily as they strive to maintain life and QOL. Since marketers advise management on what choice objects to make available, that is, what attributes to offer for an adequate ROI, the needed behavioral model must include upstream terms that specify for an individual the attributes to search for, that is, which attributes qualify choice objects as desirable. At issue here is understanding the process that disposes individuals to use their behavioral resources, in turn making them ready to pay for goods and services to assist them as they pursue the tasks and interests of their daily lives. Action conceived as counterchange, that is, an environmental impact to restore imbalance following an upstream change (Fennell 1988a) is appropriate for those who would offer managerial guidance. Such a model will include upstream terms to represent the originating change that initiates a behavioral episode that is directed by the nature of that upstream change and leads to downstream action that the individual expects or hopes will effect appropriate counterchange. As marketers guide the firm to offer saleable goods and services, a model of action focuses attention on the nature of the upstream imbalance in the prospect's current state that provides direction for attributes of a good or service designed to help the actor effect the necessary counterchange.

The Relevant Universe

To benefit from economy of scale, in each venture industry aims to address one kind of activity across many individuals and over time. Accordingly, marketers' need for a second model—a model of the relevant universe—becomes apparent. Given management's focus on ROI, the naturally occurring domestic population in its home country is not necessarily the relevant universe, even if management is not interested in engaging in international business. As is known from syndicated services such as the Simmons Study of Media and Markets, the tasks and interests that industry serves have a range of population incidence from, for example, 3 percent (for motion sickness remedies) to 95 percent (for toothpaste)[1] (Fennell, Saegert, and Gilbride 2002). Engaging in the activity that is focal for a particular venture is an obvious criterion for management to use when assigning population members to a universe relevant for the focal venture. In so doing, management is regarding them as prospects whose particular circumstances it studies with a view to an eventual decision, in a competitive environment, regarding the conditions to target with a responsive offering. Plainly, nonprospects are unlikely to be a source of information on the upstream conditions for engaging in the focal activity. People who do not own or care for a dog, for example, can have little relevant insight to impart to a producer regarding dog care products that dog owners would value enough to acquire for money. Moreover, ROI considerations make it unlikely that management would try to induce nonprospects to engage in the focal activity, for example, to start owning or caring for a dog. To the contrary, they suggest that management's resources are better spent searching for upstream conditions as yet unaddressed by existing brands—its own and its competitors.' For inclusion in management's "market as defined," the criterion of engaging in the focal activity needs refining, however. In any one instance, management will want to specify whether inclusion criteria should comprise, for example, people who engage in, or buy for, or influence purchase in regard to, the focal activity (e.g., caring for a dog). Frequency of engaging in the focal activity and other considerations may also be relevant (Fennell 1985, 110).

Behavioral Demand

Consider prospects on their way to the supermarket bent on acquiring certain kinds of goods. They have in mind the nature of the upstream conditions in which the planned purchases will be used, which directs their search for specific items to consider buying and their eventual choice among what is available in the marketplace. Building on Lewin, it is useful to think of the upstream conditions as personal and environmental systems, each of which may be transitory or enduring (enduring being understood within the relevant context), coexisting independently, sometimes intersecting to form a "situation as perceived" (Fennell 1980). Consider the following illustration:

> I am working at my laptop and find myself finally putting my work aside to acknowledge and act upon my realization that I have become uncomfortably cold. I review various ways of becoming warm, including closing the window fully, reaching for a sweater, getting a hot drink. From a range of actions and objects that I consider in such circumstances, I choose those that appear appropriate to the present prevailing conditions, consider further what has served me well on similar occasions in the past, and choose one such option to try to put into effect. If I am successful in doing so, after some moments back at work, I check my state of being. If I am back to normal comfort, I continue and the episode is over. If I am still uncomfortably cold, I try another option. In either case, I add my experience on this latest occasion to what I have learned in the past about options to deal with this kind of situation.

In the illustration, personal and environmental systems intersect to allocate my behavioral resources, initiating a behavioral episode by specifying the attribute (e.g., warm-making) that guides the actions and objects I search for and consider; in the present instance, actions and objects designed to increase the adjacent air temperature or more directly to make me feel warm. In living creatures, behavioral resources are available to be accessed as needed. Intersecting systems (e.g., air temperature, the setup of my office, my discomfort threshold, time since last meal) combine to tap into behavioral resources, making environmental impacts available for specific ends that are already specified in the systems that are operative. In the illustration, they direct me to search for what will bring about a state of affairs in which I have become warmer. They create demand for actions and objects with the capacity to "make warmer," thus specifying the criterion for admitting actions and objects into my consideration set for the present behavioral episode. The attribute "making warmer" now has value for me. In the behavioral economy, what has value is something to which the individual is ready to allocate resources (Fennell 1997). Human sensitivities and the prevailing environmental conditions combine to deploy behavioral demand, making individuals ready to spend their resources in particular ways, which industry hopes to tap into. Plainly, management's resources are best used for ROI when they can build on the way people are ready to deploy their behavioral resources.

Selecting Within a Population

Considering any domestic population, countless occasions of intersecting systems occur in any period—year, month, day—each with its own particulars of personal and environmental conditions. Human language has already brought a degree of order to such occurrences under the names of everyday activities and routines, for example, caring for a dog, dressing warmly, office designing, furnishing an office, taking nourishment. Moreover, broadly corresponding to activity names, industry has provided a degree of order through the product categories that it has created, for example, dog food, dog collars, warm clothing, hot drinks, heating appliances. Activity names as found in language and product categories as they have evolved in the marketplace are handy means of grouping and addressing the countless specific instances of intersecting personal and environmental systems that result in people engaging in the tasks and interests of everyday life. They provide handy criteria for management to use when selecting individuals in a naturally occurring population to regard as prospects, that is, individuals who engage in an activity for which they could use some version of a corresponding product category that management is interested in producing or who already are product category users. To make best use of its resources with an eye to ROI, management excludes from consideration for the focal venture individuals who do not qualify on such an initial criterion of relevance. Note that the present concept of prospect rejects as unnecessarily narrow, and largely inappropriate for consumer markets, a focus on one's existing customers as the relevant universe. Instead, it includes within management's purview, as the outside reach of its interest within a naturally occurring population, all who could conceivably use an offering within the firm's product category by virtue of their engaging in the focal activity, whether current customers or not. In this regard, for example, research shows that compared with nonprospects, more prospects process advertising messages about the focal activity and corresponding product category (Fennell and Saegert 1999). Relying on communicating at a distance, as is so often a feature of today's business, management has some expectation that its message will resonate with prospects more than nonprospects to rise above the pervading babble.

Selecting Within a Market

Marketers know, however, that activity names (feeding a dog) and the product categories (dog food) that correspond to them comprise highly diverse conditions across individuals and even within individuals over time. In fact, the rule—repeatedly documented in industry marketing research—is a finding of diversity *within* activity and product category. The diversity at issue here is diverse personal and environmental conditions in the context for the focal activity, which can be investigated as prospects' diverse concerns and interests on an occasion of engaging in the focal activity. Marketers study such diversity in what they refer to as market segmentation research. They first carve a market out of a naturally occurring population by selecting as prospects individuals who engage in the focal activity. Then, through qualitative research, they identify diverse conditions in which prospects engage in the focal activity, thus identifying candidate segments of demand, which, in turn, are candidate targets of marketing strategy. In the absence of a model of the kinds of condition that may exist, management has been compelled to undertake a subsequent quantification phase in a vacuum—on a purely empirical basis—having had to rely on the skill of focus group moderators to elicit useful descriptions of the context in which prospects engage in the focal activity. Items suggested by the qualitative phase proliferate well into the hundreds, and management remains without guidance regarding comprehensiveness or possible redundancy. Lacking a model, management lives in uncertainty about the extent to which the existing diverse conditions are adequately covered or, indeed, may be present redundantly, in questionnaire items that address essentially the same behavioral issue.

Unit of Analysis

A task for marketing scientists is to address such diversity by conceptualizing different kinds of condition that can guide qualitative research and subsequent quantification. Such a conceptualization permits marketers to study diversity systematically within activity domain and product category. Note that, as discussed elsewhere (Fennell and Saegert 2004), "diversity," as reflected in the well-known demographic and socioeconomic categories, describes population subgroups. Such variables show a modest relationship with activity engaged in and product category used, but do not differentiate conditions *within* activity or product use. What is needed then is to conceptualize kinds of situation as perceived in the Lewinian sense, where $S = f (P, E)$, as noted above. A relevant conceptualization has not been available in mainstream psychology, due, doubtless, to the narrow behavioral scope that the range of relevance of a good or service imposes—a range whose specificity has not been in focus within the mainstream. Correspondingly, the appropriate unit of analysis is a *single occasion* for an activity, given that people use and assess the performance of goods and services on individual occasions of use. With regard to the relevant universe, considerations of putting resources to best use for ROI require management to identify and deploy its resources on prospects in the naturally occurring population within its chosen region of geographic space, and with regard to an appropriate period of time, for example, day, week, season, or year. For a focal venture, then, the relevant universe may be, for example, all occasions for feeding the dog in the United States in a calendar year. Plainly, such a formal statement of the relevant universe serves a useful purpose, if only as a framework for fruitful discussion and argument at product planning sessions, where it can suggest, for example, alternative sampling plans for collecting information on the range of upstream elements potentially relevant for product design. It does not, of course, impose any particular research design, but permits the research team to choose a design, realistically oriented to the big picture.

Kinds of Situations as Perceived

Available constructs in mainstream psychology are not well suited to the task of bringing order to the myriad instances in which intersecting systems allocate an individual's resources to considering action. "Traits" addresses only one of the four classes of relevant variables, that is, enduring personal, and thus fails to allow for transitory personal, or enduring or transitory environmental. "Attitude" presupposes an attitude object imbued with attributes, where what is needed is a construct that facilitates *specifying* valued attributes. Objectively stated "kinds of occasion" are unsuitable by definition as the construct must reflect a situation *as perceived*. Moreover, research shows that objective specification, for example, demographic and socioeconomic variables and also objectively stated "occasions of use," are heterogeneous in regard to subjective perceptions (Yang, Allenby, and Fennell 2002). A construct such as motive, although it has the required motivational quality, is unsuitable when construed as a trait, as it fails to reflect transitory personal, and environmental states, enduring and transitory, pertaining on occasions of use. Moreover, even the "consumer-"oriented construct of lifestyles is unsuitable, because its scope, which extends beyond that of a single good or service, cannot reflect components of personal and environmental systems as they intersect to form an occasion of an activity for which a specific version of a product category is intended to be appropriate. The needed construct is one that facilitates reporting elements of the intersecting personal and environmental systems that (a) have the capacity to selectively engage the individual's attention while (b) allocating his or her behavioral resources to effecting an appropriate adjustment.

Marketers must conceptualize, or find a model of, qualitatively distinct kinds of *situation as perceived*. Since action is a means of adjusting person-environment relations, the variable required here is one that can be viewed as allocating the individual's resources to effecting an environmental impact that the individual expects or hopes will improve his or her state of being in the given context. We are making the usual assumption that resources, in this case behavioral resources including time, will be expended only if there is an expectation that to do so passes a cost-benefit test. Such a criterion indicates that what is needed here is to conceptualize kinds of condition that require the individual to consider expending behavioral resources to effect a favorable change in state of being as experienced. Such resource allocating conditions demand that behavioral resources be deployed in a manner appropriate to the prevailing, activating conditions.

To model such demand-creating conditions (DCC), in earlier work Fennell turned to the classic experimental operations that students of learning and motivation have used in the laboratory, as described elsewhere (e.g., Fennell 1978, 1980, 1988a). The outcome is seven qualitatively different classes of DCC, five of which are simple and two are complex—complex meaning that more than one source of motivation is present, that is, approach-avoidance and approach-frustration. Figure 14.1 illustrates the classes as applied to four activities.

A behavioral episode begins when elements in the person and the environment combine to allocate an individual's resources to making an adjustment in existing person-environment relations. The elements may combine in any of the seven forms of DCC. In the five simple cases, one source of motivation is present. In all five cases, the individual imagines a state of affairs that is more desirable than the current state. The first three are cases in which the present state is unpleasant in some way. The imagined state lacks the unpleasant element of the current state. In classes 4 and 5 the current state is acceptable until the individual perceives that it can be better. The imagined state contains a desirable attribute that is absent in the current state. It may be useful to think of these two kinds of motivating condition as reflecting the "stick and carrot" long recognized by folk wisdom. The stick is a prod that prompts the donkey to move away from a source of unpleasantness to a state where the prod is no more. The carrot, or more accurately, anticipating the pleasure of enjoying the carrot, represents moving toward a state of being that is more desirable than the current state. Through the ages, folk wisdom has recognized these two kinds of motivation in various ways, including "bread and circuses," and "bread and roses." Most texts in consumer behavior present these two kinds of motivation. However, authors illustrate them with reference to specific, existing goods and services rather than attributes. For example, stick-type motivation is illustrated by positing that the TV has broken down (unpleasant state of affairs) and the individual is motivated to enter the marketplace to replace it. Carrot-type motivation is illustrated by positing an advertiser claiming avail-

Figure 14.1 **Motivations for Selected Activities**

Motivational class	Brushing teeth	Daily swimming	Attending live theater	Feeding the cat
	The individual may be …	Daily swimmer may be engaging in …	Individual may attend live theater …	Leslie may be …
1. Problem solving	escaping from the unpleasant process of bacteria in the mouth creating bad breath, or from damaging teeth, or from the ugliness of teeth discolored or stained from smoking cigarettes/drinking coffee/eating blueberries	ameliorating a medical condition	seeking restoration for a weary body and overtaxed mind; or relief from boredom, drudgery, banality, stultifying routine, or from absorption with the concerns of young or ailing charges; escaping from an environment that is oppressive or distracting or lacking in privacy	troubled by Cat's sluggish movements, dry skin, overweight body, or lack of appetite
2. Problem prevention	preventing imagined criticisms from oneself/ significant others on grounds that one is lazy, careless of personal hygiene, lacking in consideration for others	expressing self image as an individual who knows how to care for themselves, who maintains the fitness of younger person	considering the implications of attending the performance for his or her self-concept as a (discerning) cultivator of the good life, a generous provider/host, a thoughtful lover/spouse/parent/child	catering to a spoiled child, nurturing a loyal friend, tending an expensive status symbol
3. Routine maintenance	maintaining a system that needs only routine attention	a routine activity as a matter of course	engaging in a routine with minimal investment of thought and interest	mindlessly performing a routine chore

4. Exploratory opportunity	exploring an interesting question related to brushing techniques	a skilled activity whose continued improvement is a subject of absorbing interest	intrinsically interested in theater as a student of human condition or the aficionado fascinated by the complexities and finer points of the theater arts	"into" cat nutrition, finding interest in learning ever more and more about the functions of various ingredients in Cat's diet
5. Sensory opportunity	enjoying the sensory experiences associated with bristle on gums, taste and tingle of dentifrice, and the sight of glistening pearly teeth	an opportunity for a multitude of sensory pleasures, of moving water and physical movements of the body	considering the theater as an opportunity to feast the senses	empathizing with Cat, Leslie may take pleasure in presenting an array of delectable meals to please Cat's palate
6. Product-related problems	in addition to one or more of the preceding orientations, worrying about possible damage to enamel, irritation and strong taste	any of the preceding with, nevertheless, a range of unpleasant aspects, such as cold changing rooms, chlorine smells, exposing one's body to comparative evaluation by self and others	Additionally perceiving attendance as entailing some troubling elements, such as expense, inconvenience, possibilities for embarrassment, for feeling more "out of it" than if one stayed home	doing any of the preceding while worried about cost, trouble, waste, smell, and other considerations
7. Frustration	With one or more of the preceding orientations, frustrated that toothpastes aren't strong enough to prevent cavities or claim more than they can deliver	where currently available physical conditions, suits, accessories, and gear are poorly designed and hindrances to realizing the swimmer's desired outcome from the activity	finding available theatre less enjoyable than one would wish	"making do" with food delivery systems that are deficient in some respect

ability of a "new, improved" version of some existing good or service. Here, however, the application applies to an upstream current state that initially assumes away existing goods and services to focus at the level of a specific, relevant attribute whose absence (stick) or presence (carrot) is desired.

As becomes evident later, the distinction between simple and complex DCC is important in that it recognizes that the thought of engaging in action may give rise to a second, countervailing, source of motivation, namely, contemplated action introduces its own source of unpleasantness, for example, expected cost, in the widest sense; not only monetary cost, but excessive effort, stress, embarrassment, pain, injury, or discomfort. Producers, in fact, are well aware of such a source of motivation *away from* the marketplace, as reflected in the numerous offerings that provide a desirable attribute while removing a countervailing one, such as, decaffeinated coffee, low-calorie foods, nonharmful cleaning products, and childproof packaging. The claims that producers make for their offerings are of two basic kinds: attributes are desirable because they (1) remove stick-type or offer carrot-type conditions or (2) remove possible undesirable consequences of attempting to do so. Note, however, that when a product claim offers attributes of only the second kind, no information is provided on the nature of the stick- or carrot-type conditions to which the offering is responding. Producers facing the task of designing offerings must have access to information about not only what to avoid in a desirable offering but, more basically, the nature of the conditions to which their offering must be responsive if it is to possess value that prompts prospects to approach the market in the first place. We return to this point later when discussing a largely unrecognized aspect of obtaining information on user wants from prospects' reactions to the attribute/benefits of offerings or candidate offerings.

A General Model of Action and Its Adaptation as a Model of Brand Choice

In Figure 14.2, features of the general model of action represented to the right of the DCC are similar to the well-known components of expectancy value models of attitude. An adaptation of the general model of action for brand choice is shown in Figure 14.3. Superimposed on the figure is a distinction between ex post and ex ante approaches to marketing strategy. The distinction at issue here is whether or not existing goods and services are posited. Much that is written about marketing strategy assumes that goods and services are already in existence and are the subject of investigation and analysis— very often with a view to attempting to extract information concerning what prospects want from the product. Referred to here as an ex post approach, it makes use of a model that lacks a DCC component. Accordingly, only the model to the right of the ex post line is in use. In effect, such an approach can be viewed as attempting to gain understanding of the DCC but without access to a model of their likely structure. Such research usually must proceed in the form of analysis of respondent reactions to attributes/benefits of existing or candidate offerings. In contrast, a general model of action permits an ex ante approach in which the objective is to study directly the nature of the upstream conditions including the attributes that such conditions specify as valuable, and the extent to which offerings or candidate offerings are appropriate to such conditions in light of the firm's strengths and weaknesses and those of the competition.

Two Approaches to Studying Wants

It is plain from Figure 14.3 that two approaches are available to study prospects' wants as they engage in the focal activity and use brands in the corresponding focal product category: Marketers can study wants as (1) features of the DCC upstream and (2) reactions to attributes of the brands or candidate brands of goods and services available for sale or under consideration. In the former case, at issue are aspects of the intersecting personal and environmental systems that result in behavioral demand. Wants are readily identified in the form of concerns and interests (CI) in the context for engaging in the focal activity. In the latter case and more traditionally, wants have been studied downstream in the form of reactions to attributes of marketplace goods and services, often referred to in research as "attributes/benefits" (AB) of existing or candidate offerings. Plainly, these are different approaches to studying wants. Concern/Interest (CI) items reflect prospects' reports of their experience of the context the last time they engaged in the focal activity, i.e., an activity (e.g., planning a holiday) that corresponds to a product category in which management is interested in producing or continuing to produce an offering (e.g., organized tours). Attribute/Benefit (AB) items reflect prospects' reports of their reactions to the features of goods and services that claim to help as prospects engage in the focal activity. Evidence is available that wants identified in the form of reactions to AB items are ambiguous in regard to the concerns /interests to which producers would want their offerings to be responsive—the motivational ambiguity of product benefits/attributes that Fennell (1978) referred to. For example, repeatedly, we have found zero correlation between rank ordering among prospects of items reflecting CIs in the context for the focal activity and items reflecting reactions to ABs (e.g., brushing one's teeth [Fennell and Saegert 2010a]; coloring the edges of the eyelids [Fennell, Saegert, and Hoover 1997]; or choosing a vacation destina-

Figure 14.2 **Model of Action**

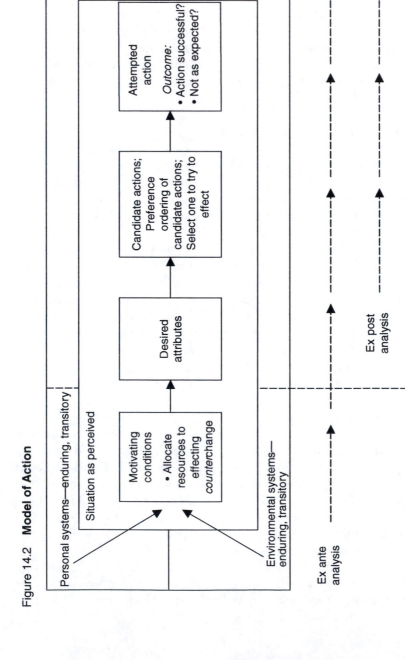

Source: Adapted from Fennell 1988b.

Figure 14.3   **Model of Brand Use**

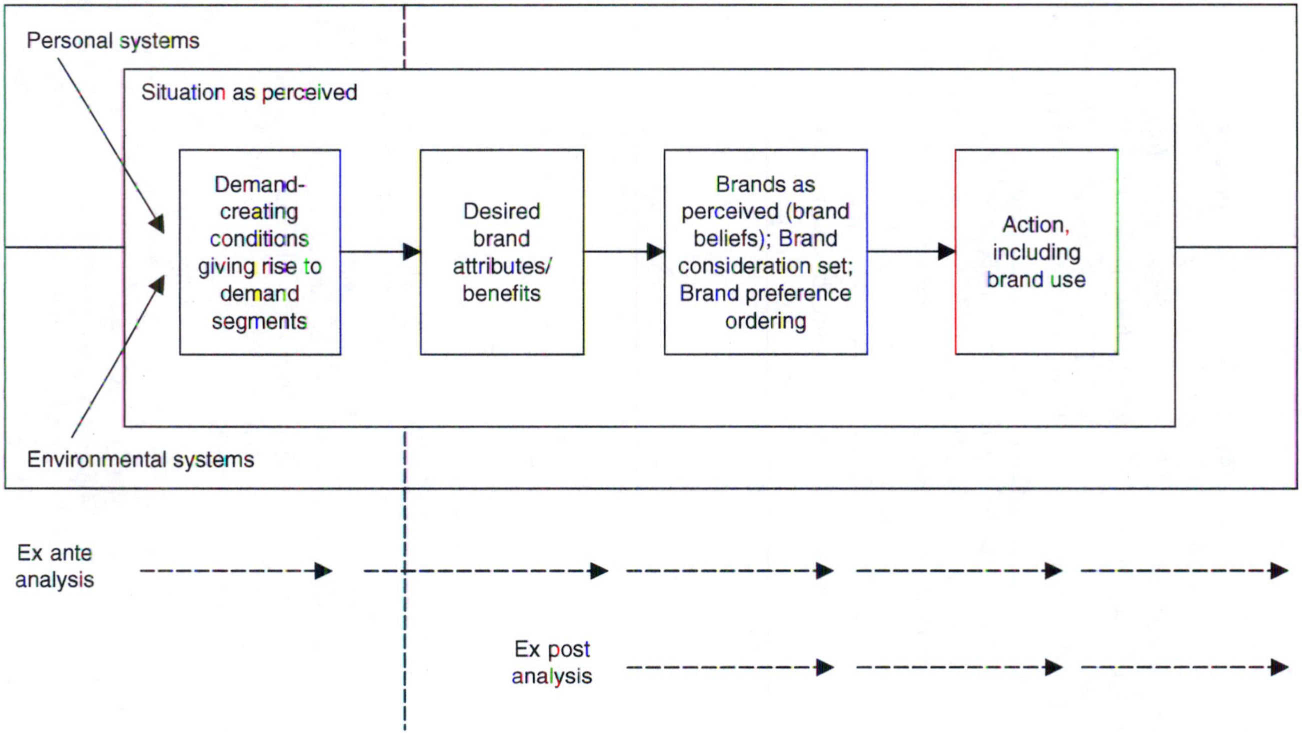

Personal systems

Situation as perceived

| Demand-creating conditions giving rise to demand segments | → | Desired brand attributes/benefits | → | Brands as perceived (brand beliefs); Brand consideration set; Brand preference ordering | → | Action, including brand use |

Environmental systems

Ex ante analysis

Ex post analysis

Source: Adapted from Fennell 1988b.

tion [Saegert and Hoover 2005]). In the next section, I report further evidence regarding the distinction between CIs and ABs.

Pilot Investigation: CIs and ABs for Taking Photographs

To pursue the outcome of earlier studies of CIs and ABs, Joel Saegert and I have engaged in a pilot project to explore the nature of these two approaches to understanding prospects' wants. From qualitative research conducted among camera users, we generated a set of eighteen CIs that camera users reported they had experienced in the context for taking photographs. Corresponding to each CI, we wrote an AB item in the form of a claim that a camera producer could make for a brand of camera. Subjects for the study were 100 students in introductory marketing classes in a large southwestern U.S. university who identified themselves as camera users. In a three-stage procedure, subjects were first asked to indicate the extent to which each CI was present on the last occasion when they were taking photographs, and to then indicate which was "Your Top One." In a second stage, they were asked to respond to a personality questionnaire designed to serve as a filler task to minimize recall of their CI responses when making their subsequent AB responses in stage three. In the third stage they were asked to choose their "Most Important" choice criterion from the eighteen AB items we had constructed to be responsive to the CI items. In a debriefing interview, no respondents indicated that they had viewed the stage 3 questions as a test of the reliability of their responses to the stage 1 items.

Findings

In the analysis that is of interest here, respondents' reports of Most Important AB were examined for congruence or otherwise with the CI that they reported as Your Top One on the most recent occasion when they were taking photographs. In Tables 14.1 and 14.2, we examine the outcome in detail for the six AB items most often chosen as Most Important. The same format is followed throughout. Each table heading shows an AB item selected as Most Important by respondents, the number of whom is shown on the row titled Base. In the body of the table we show the CI item that those respondents chose as Your Top One in the context of the most recent occasion on which they were taking photographs. On the last line of the table, we show the original CI item, for which the AB item in the table heading was written as a claim that management could tailor a responsive brand to support.

Items reported in Tables 14.1 and 14.2 differ as follows: In Table 14.1, the AB items are responsive to a CI in a complex DCC, that is, class 6 or 7 in

Table 14.1

CIs Chosen as "Your Top One" for AB (Complex) Chosen as "Most Important"

(1) AB: Photos Will Turn Out Just as You Want

Base (Ss choosing the AB as Most Important) =	13
CI chosen as Your Top One	
I wanted to photograph the beauty I saw in the world.	4
I took photos just for the fun of it.	3
I wanted to save some of my life's experiences photographically.	3
I needed photos to record my work/hobby.	1
I wanted to capture the beauty of family members and friends in my pictures.	1
I wanted to document my vacation experiences.	1

Original CI: I worried the photos I took wouldn't show what I expected.

(2) AB: Not Complicated to Use

Base (Ss choosing the AB as Most Important) =	12
CI chosen as Your Top One	
I took photos just for the fun of it.	5
I wanted to save some of my life's experiences photographically.	3
I wanted to capture the beauty of family members and friends in my pictures.	1
I wanted to photograph the beauty I saw in the world.	1
I wanted to document my vacation experiences.	1
I wanted to capture the beauty of family members and friends in my pictures.	1

Original CI: I was irritated that the camera was so technical to use.

(3) AB: Compact and Light

Base (Ss choosing the AB as Most Important) =	7
CI chosen as Your Top One	
I wanted to document my vacation experiences.	2
I was worried that a special event (for example, birthday, ceremony or get-together), would be lost if I didn't record it.	2
I wanted to save some of my life's experiences photographically.	1
I took photos just for the fun of it.	1
Taking photos was something I did routinely without much thought.	1

Original CI: I hated the bother of carrying around a big camera.

Table 14.2

CIs Chosen as "Your Top One" for AB (Simple) Chosen as "Most Important"

(1) AB: Helps to Enjoy the Beauty of Family and Friends

Base (Ss choosing the AB as Most Important)	16
CI chosen as Your Top One	
I wanted to capture the beauty of family and friends in my pictures.	12
I took photos just for the fun of it.	3
I was worried that a special event (for example, birthday, ceremony or get-together), would be lost if I didn't record it.	1

Original CI: I wanted to capture the beauty of family and friends in my pictures.

(2) AB: Saves Life's Experiences

Base (Ss choosing the AB as Most Important) =	15
CI chosen as Your Top One	
I wanted to save some of my life's experiences photographically.	7
I wanted to capture the beauty of family members and friends in my pictures.	2
I wanted to document my vacation experiences.	2
I needed photos to record my work/hobby.	1
My photos were a statement of who I am.	1
I wanted to photograph the beauty I saw in the world.	1
I was worried that a special event would be lost if I didn't record it.	1

Original CI: I wanted to save some of my life's experiences photographically.

(3) AB: Captures the Beauty of Everything

Base (Ss choosing the AB as Most Important) =	13
CI chosen as Your Top One	
I wanted to photograph the beauty I saw in the world.	5
I took photos just for the fun of it.	3
I wanted to save some of my life's experiences photographically.	3
I needed photos to record my work/hobby.	1
I wanted to experiment with different photographic effects.	1

Original CI: I wanted to photograph the beauty I saw in the world.

the motivational model discussed earlier (e.g., Fennell 1980), reflecting some difficulty in regard to approaching the marketplace to acquire a camera. As prospects do not buy an offering just to avoid an undesirable product feature, AB items responsive to complex DCC presuppose the presence of CIs in one or more of the simple DCCs that direct prospects to approach the marketplace in the first place. In Table 14.2, the AB items are responsive to a CI in a simple DCC (i.e., classes 1 through 5).

Considering responses shown in Table 14.1, in no instance did these respondents' Most Important product AB echo their top CI. Responding to the AB question, they gave top place to the perceived impediments, that is, fearing that the photographic outcome would be disappointing, irritation at the camera's technical complexity, and dislike of carrying around a weighty camera. Faced with eighteen camera claims, respondents whose data are shown in Table 14.1 considered an offered solution to such concerns to be the most important camera feature. However, a producer also needs to know the considerations prompting prospects to take photos in the first place, and such information is available in the CI items as reported in Table 14.1. The model already makes the point that claimed ABs will promise either presence of a positive or absence of a negative feature. When information on absence of a negative feature is all that is available, the analyst is left without access to the prospect's affirmative reason for using the product. The research outcome suggests asking the following: When asked to choose among AB items, why do these respondents rate addressing a feared product feature as Most Important even though faced with a question about their concerns and interests when last taking photographs, they did not report giving priority to a feared outcome, but instead gave priority to the considerations they were originally addressing by taking the photographs? Perhaps in the case of these respondents, the answer is all too obvious. The context for the activity question focused their attention on what they would miss if they didn't take photographs; the product feature question focused their attention on reassurance that product features would not intrude undesirably. Plainly, such an explanation doesn't hold for all respondents in our sample, as is evident from the data shown in Table 14.2.

Turning now to Table 14.2, respondents' product feature responses echoed to some degree their responses for their latest photographing occasion—in three-fourths of instances with regard to AB item 1; half in regard to AB item 2, and just under half in regard to AB item 3. The relatively high level of congruence for "capture/enjoy beauty of family and friends" suggests there is a subgroup of photographers who see the activity primarily as a feature of family life. For the others, the pattern seems to be that, when faced with a product focus, they chose features of broad applicability, for example, saves life's experiences or captures the beauty of everything. Faced with an activity focus, the actual, specific consideration prompting the activity comes to the fore.

In sum, plainly there are two distinct approaches to addressing marketing's core responsibility of helping the firm to identify and respond to user wants.

Minimally, our findings serve as a warning that attempting to understand wants via respondents' reactions to descriptions of product attributes and benefits provides information that may be less than complete but, more important, is silent or fraught with ambiguity as to the actual considerations that pertain in the context for engaging in the focal activity.

Discussion

Having recourse to a model of action draws attention to the diverse conditions that allocate behavioral resources to engaging in action, whether in the pursuit of a concern or an interest. A model of action contributes the insight that features of the upstream context for action provide information on the conditions that pertain when prospects engage in the focal activity and choose goods and services relevant to the task or interest they are pursuing. Significantly, information on the kinds of condition for which producers may tailor their offerings provides managerial guidance that may not be available from traditional decision-making research.

Components of the present model of action (Figures 14.2 and 14.3) include a motivational model of seven conditions that create behavioral demand, five simple and two complex. The conditions are stated in such a way that they can be applied to any activity and specifically, for example, to each of the 1,500 or so activities for which producers offer goods and services (see Figure 14.1 for examples). Accordingly, when conducting qualitative research to generate items for subsequent quantification, marketing researchers are guided to obtain information for the range of diverse condition in which their prospects engage in the focal activity or use the focal product category. Moreover, responses to those same items are available as managers seek to understand how prospects who experience such diverse conditions view present and candidate attributes and benefits that manufacturing—their own and competitive—can build into offerings. Such research and analysis is then available to guide managers as they select the kind(s) of condition (1) for which they will equip their offering to compete in the focal product category and (2) they will depict in promotional messages to engage the attention of their targets (i.e., the prospects for whose conditions they have tailored their offering) in the audiences of media vehicles where prospects are disproportionately present.

Research that is guided by a general model of action and its applied version as a model of brand choice (see Figure 14.3) clarifies for management that there are two systematically distinct ways of representing the "wants" to which goods and services seek to be responsive. The first is via descriptions of the upstream conditions in which prospects engage in the focal activity. The second, and more traditional, is via descriptions of the attributes of offerings that management makes available in hopes of satisfying the wants that arise from the upstream conditions.

Without a systematic way to conceive of the upstream conditions, managers can rely on only the second approach to assessing consumer wants, that is, by seeking reactions to attributes and benefits of present and candidate offerings. The approach is unsatisfactory in the absence of information on the actual upstream conditions that respondents in fact experience and have in mind as they indicate preferences among descriptions of candidate offerings. Moreover, as we saw earlier, research shows that attributes and benefits of offerings are motivationally ambiguous. Because of the ambiguity of language, respondents may construe brand features as applicable to the conditions they experience, when in fact the manufacturer's execution of the product attribute may be responsive to some other condition. Consider, for example, the attribute of a shampoo or conditioner, "makes your hair manageable," which could be checked as desirable by respondents with frizzy, limp, thin, or coarse hair. Yet the manufacturer's formulation may be appropriate for only one type of unmanageable hair. A relevant finding is available from a variety of product categories: The researchers identified a set of concerns and interests present in the context for engaging in the focal activity and then wrote responsive attributes for a responsive good or service. Across respondents the frequency rank ordering of descriptions of the conditions in which respondents engage in the focal activity shows zero correlation with respondents' preference ordering of attributes of offerings designed to be responsive to the upstream conditions. If only one measure were to be available, managerial decision makers are well advised to consider descriptions of the upstream conditions, rather than the potentially ambiguous attributes of marketplace offerings.

It could be argued that product attribute/benefit information is adequate for advertising purposes, while obtaining information on concerns and interests in the upstream context for the focal activity is appropriate for product development (e.g., new/modified brand formulation). The former suggestion may be motivated by the thought that ambiguity in advertising is good in that it may make the offering seem suitable for a wider range of conditions than is, in fact, the case. Consider "unmanageable hair" being interpreted by women with each of the difficult hair conditions, while the true state of affairs is that the offering is suitable for only limp hair, for example. Unwilling to allow their brand get a bad name for any reason, advertisers will not want to risk incurring the disappointment of sufferers of the other three conditions who, minimally, have spent their money in vain and may even find that the brand exacerbates the problem for which they sought help. Accordingly, while researchers who gather information for product development purposes will always seek to get as close as possible to the conditions that the prospect is experiencing, thus clearly favoring the upstream information for product development, it should not be forgotten that the upstream context is useful in advertising as a means of locating targets in media vehicle audiences by portraying the upstream conditions that they experience, for which the brand's formulation has been tailored. For the brand's true targets, portraying the upstream conditions to which they will immediately resonate is likely far more effective than, for example, more general claims, such as most popular or best or purest ingredients, which fail to take the opportunity to avail of targets' resonating to a well-experienced event or condition.

While the concept of a relevant universe is largely overlooked in marketing textbooks, its presence here along with some suggested parameters is valuable in sensitizing researchers in decision theory to the range of incidence of activities in a population. As incidence declines from 100 percent, noise is introduced into research, making the findings indeterminate unless the researchers show findings separately for respondents who do and do not engage in the focal activity. The managerial guidance here is to exclude from the relevant universe individuals in the population who do not currently engage in the focal activity. Plainly, such individuals are unlikely to be sufficiently informed to provide useable information as to their likely wants if they were to engage in the focal activity. In any case, they are unlikely to process advertising messages for activities in which they do not engage or have no interest or, as noncategory users, act on the messages.

Fennell's work in psychology and consumer behavior, on which I have been drawing here, has had as its purpose finding or developing behavioral models appropriate to structural features of marketing's task as a managerial function. I took as starting point long-standing practices within marketing-sophisticated firms that have yet to find resonance in the pages of principles of marketing and similar introductory textbooks. Regrettably, authors of such textbooks have not seen fit to inform themselves, or appreciate the significance, of intuitively grounded practice that is the outcome of tacit understanding among marketers charged with the responsibility of guiding managerial decisions to secure satisfactory ROI and, ultimately, stay in business in a competitive environment.

Most regrettable, in this connection, has been authors' failure to appreciate the nature of the two-step process that is required for a producer faced with a naturally occurring population to identify and respond to user wants and to communicate the existence of the offering to the targets for whom it has been fashioned. The two-step process at issue is first defining a market of prospects within a population, and then identifying diverse segments of demand within that market and selecting some to target, that is, choosing a market target. It is followed by a similar two-step process to communicate to market targets that an offering tailored to their conditions is available—management selects media vehicles that contain prospects disproportionately in which to place ad messages that engage market targets' attention by portraying the conditions for which the offering is tailored.

Nevertheless, without rational analysis or empirical data in support, the concept of a *market target* was replaced, it seems by fiat, with the ubiquitous oxymoron, *target market* (Fennell, Saegert, and Hoover 1999). True, in addition to or instead of advertising to a general market of prospects (defined as category users, or people who engage in the focal activity), producers may devise campaigns for special markets with which they believe an affinity exists, for example, blacks, sports enthusiasts of various kinds, or youth, but management is still responding to a subset of conditions within such markets, that is, to prospects within the special market for whose conditions it has fashioned the brand (i.e., special-market targets). There is no "black" washing machine, just as there is no "white" washing machine, where the notion is immediately seen to be risible. People within such objectively defined, preexisting groups are not clones of one another when it comes to their wants within specific activities. Moreover, their environmental conditions are likely diverse. Routinely, the demographic analysis in the appendix of industry marketing research reports attests to absence of relation with the within-activity findings of the subject project. Objectively defined variables (e.g., a priori groups such as demographic categories) show modest relation with engaging in the focal activity or product use and, typically, independence with subjectively experienced conditions *within* the activity, which is largely where marketers compete with each other.

Similarly, the systematically meaningful terms "market segment" and "market segmentation research," which originally referred unequivocally to segments of demand (e.g., Smith 1956) within markets/activity domains/ product categories, have been replaced, again it seems by fiat, with the asystematic "segmentation variables." As presented in textbook pages, the term comprises mainly a priori group variables that segment a population but bear no relation to want segments within markets. By such sleight of hand, marketing textbooks put on a front of addressing authentic marketing issues but, in fact, serve only to inculcate in generations of future marketers, whether practitioner or academic, what is at best nonsense and at worst outright disinformation.

Elsewhere, Fennell (1988b) has discussed possible reasons why a behavioral science tailored to the actuality of marketers' tasks has not emerged. One key fact, doubtless, has been that marketing's task—to identify and guide management to respond to user wants—is one that neither of the two longer established disciplines deemed relevant has had to address. Economics and psychology have each obtained great mileage out of a key construct—utility, in the case of economics, and reinforcement, in the case of psychology. But neither has had to identify in concrete terms, what provides utility or what is reinforcing, which, fundamentally, is the task that falls to marketers to deliver—for all the major activities of daily living and for all the diversity within activity that is there to be uncovered across the relevant universes. Drawing on Fennell's models of action, motivation, and the relevant universe, I have presented constructs and models custom-tailored to marketing's assignment as a managerial function. The behavioral scope of a business venture is no greater than that of one or a few activities and their corresponding product category, and the relevant unit of analysis is a single occasion for the focal activity. However, the relevant universe is broad and complex, comprising as it does all occasions for the focal activity in a region of geographic space (e.g., within national borders) and over a period of time (e.g., day, season, year). Within such a universe, countless instances of intersecting personal and environmental systems tap into and direct prospects' behavioral resources to consider engaging in action, as they pursue the tasks and interests that maintain life and QOL, and specifically the particular activity that is in focus for management's venture. Constructs and models appropriate to bringing order to the domain assigned to the marketing discipline are not to be found readymade in psychology or economics. Regrettably, there seems to have been an unexamined assumption among marketing scientists that appropriate models and constructs existed in psychology and economics, where, as noted, the disciplinary assignment has not reached to the specificity found in marketing: Make what the customer wants to buy. Returning to the hypothetical mid-twentieth-century meeting between marketers and behavioral scientists with which I started this chapter, the wisdom of hindsight suggests that a first step preparatory to importing constructs and models from other disciplines should have been to analyze the nature of the behavioral phenomena that it falls to marketers to address.

Managerial Guidelines

In conclusion, models of action, motivation, and the relevant universe provide managerial guidance in a variety of ways. They serve the usual purposes of models, for example, mapping a domain of interest, identifying relevant components and issues, and do so in a manner that is close to operations currently in place in marketing-sophisticated firms. They present a formal system that finds resonance with current practice via concepts and models appropriate to that practice. Specifically, management will find Fennell's (1978, 1980) seven classes of the motivational component useful for:

(a) Checking that qualitative research preparatory to the quantitative phase of market segmentation research has covered all the bases, and then reviewing the items generated for comprehensiveness and redundancy.

(b) Mapping in a preliminary way the motivating conditions to which their own brands and those of the competition appear to be responding, based on the claims being made in their respective marketing communications. Such an exercise conducted prior to market segmentation research provides preliminary ideas about conditions currently being ignored, on the one hand, or vigorously served on the other hand, with a view to generating some candidate conditions for management's brand to target, which can be investigated in the upcoming research.

(c) Considering how to allocate resources to studying the nature of prospects' wants, specifically the extent to which their research should focus on (1) identifying the concerns / interests (CI) prospects experience as they engage in the focal activity, or (2) prospects' reactions to the attributes/benefits (AB) that, given the firm's strengths and weaknesses, management can build into its brand and claim to offer, bearing in mind the systematic distinction between ABs responsive to CI classes 1 through 5, and those responsive to classes 6 and 7.

In essence, all of the above are direct beneficial outcomes of resorting to a model of action that specifically addresses the fact that action has to do with people seeking to improve their state of being by effecting environmental impacts. Accordingly, a model of action includes representations of the upstream conditions that tap into and direct peoples' behavioral resources to effecting adjustments via attempted action downstream. Most fundamentally, perhaps, its benefit is to provide a systematic analysis of the nature of hitherto unexplored terrain upstream from objects of choice.

Note

This is the range of incidence the authors found in twenty-seven papers comprising forty-eight studies of ad effects in four major journals over a three-year span.

References

Fennell, G. 1978. "Consumers' Perceptions of the Product-Use Situation." *Journal of Marketing* 42: 38–47.

———. 1980. "The Situation." *Motivation & Emotion* 4: 299–322.

———. 1985. "Persuasion: Marketing as Behavioral Science in Business and Non-Business Contexts." In *Advances in Nonprofit Marketing,* ed. R. Belk. Greenwich, CT: JAI.

———. 1987. "Reculer pour Mieux Sauter, or, Why Consumer Psychologists Need a General Model of Action." In *Proceedings, Division 23, 94th Annual Convention of the American Psychological Association*, ed. J. Saegert. Washington DC: APA.

———. 1988a. "Action as Counterchange: Identifying Antecedents of the Domain and Goal of Action." In *Proceedings, Division 23, 95th Annual Convention of the American Psychological Association*, ed. L. Alwitt. Washington DC: APA.

———. 1988b. "Reclaiming form Utility for Marketing: The Human Side of the Person-Technology Interface." In *Marketing: Return to the Broader Dimensions*, ed. S. Shapiro. Chicago: American Marketing Association.

———. 1991. "Context for Action = Context for Brand Use = Source of Valued Brand Attributes." In *Proceedings, Division 23, 98th Annual Convention of the American Psychological Association*, ed. K. Haugtvedt. Washington DC: APA.

———. 1997. "Value and Values: Relevance to Advertising." In *Values, Lifestyles, and Psychographics*, ed. L. Kahle and L. Chiagouris. Hillsdale, NJ: Lawrence Erlbaum.

Fennell, G. and J. Saegert. 1999. "Marketing Communications: Building on Existing Motivation to Process Ads." In *Marketing Communications and Consumer Behavior*, ed. W.D. Hoyer and A. Strazzieri, 218–39. Aix-en-Provence, France: Institut d'Administration des Entreprises.

———. 2004. "Diversity: Population v. Market." In *Diversity in Advertising*, ed. J.D. Williams, W.-N. Lee, and C. Haugtvedt. Hillsdale, NJ: Lawrence Erlbaum.

———. 2010a. "An Alternative View of 'Globalization.'" Unpublished manuscript.

———. 2010b. "Purposive Communicating for ROI: What? and to Whom? *Proceedings, Division 23 Convention, Society for Consumer Psychology, American Psychological Association*. Washington DC: APA.

Fennell, G., Saegert, J., and T. Gilbride. 2002. "Responding to Wants: Do Ad Effects Studies Measure the Right People?" In *Proceedings of Division 23, Society for Consumer Psychology, American Psychological Association*, ed. J. Edell and R.C. Goodstein, 142–54. Washington DC: APA.

Fennell, G., Saegert, J., and R. Hoover. 1997. "Investigating What the Customer Wants: Problems and Promises." In *Proceedings of Division 23, the Society for Consumer Psychology*, ed. C. Pechmann and S. Ratneshwar, 40–51. Washington DC: American Psychological Association.

———. 1999. "Target Market in the Textbooks: Oxymoron Unexamined." In *Proceedings of the International Trade and Finance Association*, ed. K. Fatemi, and S. Nichols, 471–92. Casablanca, Morocco: ITFA.

Lewin, K. 1936. *Principles of Topological Psychology.* New York: McGraw-Hill.

Saegert, J., and R. Hoover. 2005. *Motivational Conditions as a Basis for Segmenting the International Tourist Market.* Istanbul: International Trade and Finance Association.

Smith, W.R. 1956. "Product Differentiation and Market Segmentation as Alternative Marketing Strategies." *Journal of Marketing* 20: 3–8.

Yang, S, G.M. Allenby, and G. Fennell. 2002. "Modeling Variation in Brand Preference: The Roles of Objective Environment and Motivating Conditions." *Marketing Science* 21: 14–31.

Name Index

Subject Index

Italic page references indicate tables and figures.

About the Editor and Contributors

Editor

Steven S. Posavac (BA, Knox College; MS, PhD, University of Utah) is the E. Bronson Ingram Professor of Marketing at Vanderbilt University's Owen Graduate School of Management. Posavac is an expert in consumer and managerial decision making, and is a widely cited author of over forty journal articles and book chapters. He is an area editor for the *Journal of Consumer Psychology*, and serves on the editorial review boards of the *Journal of Consumer Research* and the *Journal of Economic Psychology*. Posavac is past president of the Society for Consumer Psychology, and does consulting work in the area of brand development.

Contributors

Yeqing Bao is associate professor of marketing at the University of Alabama in Huntsville.

Kyra Blower is a doctoral candidate in marketing at the University of Washington.

David M. Boush is the Gerald B. Bashaw professor of business and associate dean for administration at the University of Oregon.

J. Joško Brakus is a lecturer in marketing at Brunel University.

Anne M. Brumbaugh is president of Anne Brumbaugh Marketing.

Raquel Castaño is professor of marketing at EGADE Business School, Tecnologico de Monterrey.

Maria L. Cronley is associate professor of marketing at Miami University.

Hélène Deval is assistant professor of marketing at Dalhousie University.

Jennifer Edson Escalas is associate professor of marketing at Vanderbilt University.

Geraldine Fennell is visiting research professor at the University of Texas at San Antonio.

Michal Herzenstein is assistant professor of marketing at the University of Delaware.

Steve Hoeffler is associate professor of marketing at Vanderbilt University.

Meng-Hua Hsieh is a doctoral candidate in marketing at the University of Washington.

Shailendra Pratap Jain is the James D. Currie CPA endowed professor of marketing and associate professor of marketing at the University of Washington.

Frank R. Kardes is the Donald E. Weston professor of marketing at the University of Cincinnati.

Ohyoon Kwon is a doctoral candidate in advertising at the University of Texas.

Xingbo Li is a doctoral candidate in marketing at the University of Washington.

Susan Powell Mantel is associate professor of marketing at Ball State University.

Israel Martinez is a doctoral candidate at EGADE Business School, Tecnologico de Monterrey.

Keiko I. Powers is senior manager of corporate research at J.D. Power and Associates.

Claudia Quintanilla is professor of marketing at EGADE Business School, Tecnologico de Monterrey.

Martin Reimann is a fellow of consumer psychology at the University of Southern California.

David M. Sanbonmatsu is a professor in the department of psychology, University of Utah.

Bernd Schmitt is the Robert D. Calkins professor of international business at Columbia University.

James T. Simpson is distinguished professor of marketing at the University of Alabama in Huntsville.

Yongjun Sung is assistant professor of advertising at the University of Texas.

Guang-Xin Xie is assistant professor of marketing at the University of Massachusetts, Boston.

Lia Zarantonello is a post-doctoral research fellow at Bocconi University.

Shi Zhang is associate professor of marketing at the University of California–Los Angeles.